Adolescent Substance Abuse

Issue in Children's and Families' Lives

Series Editors:
Thomas P. Gullota, *Child and Family Agency of Southeastern Connecticut, New London, Connecticut*
Herbert J. Walberg, *University of Illinois at Chicago, Chicago, Illinois*
Roger P. Weissberg, *Univeristy of Illinois at Chicago, Chicago, Illinois*

For other titles in this series, go to
www.springer.com/series/6110

A Continuation Order Plan is available for this series. A continuation order will bring delivery of each new volume immediately upon publication. Volumes are billed only upon actual shipment. For further information please contact the publisher.

Carl G. Leukefeld • Thomas P. Gullotta
Michele Staton-Tindall
Editors

Jessica M. Ramos
Research Assistant

Adolescent Substance Abuse

Evidence-Based Approaches to Prevention and Treatment

 Springer

Editors
Carl G. Leukefeld
Department Behavioral Science Center
   on Drug & Alcohol Research
University of Kentucky
Lexington, KY
USA

Thomas P. Gullotta
Child & Family Agency of Southeastern
   Connecticut, Inc.,
New London, CT
USA

Michele Staton-Tindall
College of Medicine
Department Behavioral Sciences
University of Kentucky
Lexington, KY
USA

A Sponsored Publication of the Child and Family Agency
of Southeastern Connecticut, Inc.

ISSN: 1572-1981
ISBN: 978-0-387-09730-5   e-ISBN: 978-0-387-09732-9
DOI: 10.1007/978-0-387-09732-9

Library of Congress Control Number: 2008939391

springer.com

Preface

This is a book about how some young people use substances to intensify or alter perceptions, feelings, and understandings. On one level, the purpose of this volume is straightforward. Identify and share those practices that appear to be most efficacious. To this end, we asked the respected and talented teams of scholars that worked on this project to identify evidence-based treatment and prevention practices that worked, might work, or did not work. These practices are found clearly in written papers that introduce the reader to the subject area before delving into the details of those treatment and prevention techniques. On another level, the editors of this volume want the reader to appreciate the need to be persistent in youth-focused substance misuse prevention and treatment activities as well as being mindful of changing adolescent needs.

To that end, this volume opens with two foundational chapters that ground the uninitiated reader in the complexity of associated issues. In the first chapter, Gullotta makes it clear that the desire of humankind has always been to intensify or alter perceptions, feelings, and understandings to achieve some futile understanding of the unpredictable events surrounding them. With time these transporting means to other worlds lost their imagined foretelling, religious, or medicinal powers and entered the realm of personal recreational use. Every substance discussed in this book has at one time been legally used and at another time been prohibited from use – including coffee!

For example, King Charles II of England banned coffee houses in 1675 as did several other European monarchies. Those who ignored the royal decrees were beaten (Emboden, 1979). The kick in coffee is provided by caffeine that is commonly added to over the counter drinks in some beverages in outrageous amounts. Some of these substances like tobacco, alcohol, and coffee have reentered society with differing degrees of regulation.

Presently, US drug policy is to deny legitimate access to tobacco and alcohol until youth reach the legal age when use is permitted. Other substances, some legal and others not, are more rigidly administered (prescription drugs) or prohibited (cocaine, for example). The difficulty becomes, as Kandel and her associates established decades ago (1975), that tobacco and alcohol can be the entry-level substances to other illegal drugs. The availability of these entry-level substances in most households in the Americas and the marketing of these substances by those who profit from their sale is a guarantee that this book will not lose its usefulness anytime soon.

In Chapter 2, Kelly and his colleagues expand on this point by providing the reader with a biological explanation for the power of caffeine, nicotine (tobacco), and alcohol on the individual. Their review clearly establishes the rewarding, calming, or numbing aspects these chemicals exert on the brain.

With this knowledge as a backdrop, the reader is introduced by Dennis and his associates in Chapter 3 to those individual characteristics that appear to increase the susceptibility of some individuals to misuse substances. The availability of addictive drugs in society is not a guarantee that addiction will occur. Rather, there is a dynamic constant interplay between the specific chemical, the individual's genetic constitution, personality characteristics (locus of control, for example), and the larger environment and the stresses it exerts on the person.

In Chapter 4, Winters et al. review the substance abuse treatment literature by identifying promising psychosocial and pharmacological interventions. Using a meta-analysis of the literature on substance use disorder treatment among adolescents, the authors examine research studies that focus on adolescents as the primary target of an intervention or treatment, includes drug use as an outcome, and incorporates a structured evaluation. From this review, recommendations are made.

Continuing this effort, in Chapter 5, Dembo and Muck discuss the current state of knowledge about adolescent outpatient drug abuse treatment and describe promising interventions. Using the Treatment Episode Data Set (TEDS), the authors also examine the number of adolescents who received outpatient treatment in recent years, the primary substances of abuse leading to the treatment episode (alcohol and marijuana), the problem of co-occurring mental health issues among treated adolescent drug abusers, and the gap between those needing outpatient treatment and those youth actually receiving services.

Calix and Fine follow this discussion with an examination of the differing degrees of success family-based treatment has in treating adolescent substance abuse and dependence. The authors provide detailed descriptions of family-based therapeutic interventions, guiding theoretical frameworks, components of the therapy, and research evidence in support of multisystemic therapy, multidimensional family therapy, and functional family therapy. The authors describe a promising family treatment approach that integrates cognitive-behavioral therapy with functional family therapy. An overview of brief strategic family therapy is provided with attention to the therapeutic process, components of treatment, and supporting research evidence. Family-based interventions that have not been supported by research literature are also described.

Plant and Panzarella discuss adolescent residential evidence-based treatment approaches in Chapter 7. The authors point out that significant knowledge gaps exist in determining those interventions in residential treatment that matter. They highlight inconsistencies raised in the literature on the general effectiveness of residential treatment as a therapeutic milieu and limitations in the research on residential treatment outcomes which include low participation rates, low follow-up rates, and limited quality assurance. Despite these limitations, the emergence of some promising, evidence-based approaches for adolescent residential treatment in recent years including the Minnesota Model (12-steps), The Multidisciplinary Professional Model, The Seven Challenges, and the Therapeutic Community are discussed. In addition, evidence-based models that have demonstrated success in community and home settings such as cognitive-behavioral therapy, motivational enhancement therapy, and some family models are described for their potential application in residential settings.

The next four chapters are concerned with prevention and health promotion approaches to substance use in childhood and adolescence. That is, how do we develop the capacity (promotion) of young people to resist the lure of drug misuse and how do we prevent that misuse. Bloom begins this discussion by providing the reader with an understanding of the concept and examples of how primary prevention and health promotion work. He describes five technologies as essential components of any *effective* prevention effort. These are education, promotion of self-competency, natural caregiving, impacting change at the community organization and systems level, and redesigning the social environment.

An area with ties to competency enhancement and natural caregiving is spirituality discussed by Hill, Burdette, Weiss, and Chitwood in Chapter 9. Research suggests that religious involvement is associated with lower levels of alcohol consumption, tobacco smoking and illicit drug use, and more favorable substance use treatment outcomes. Hill et al. provide an overview of the theoretical and empirical explanations for the association between religious involvement and substance use which include religious factors (specific moral directives and general religious principles), social factors (social control, social learning, and social support), and psychological factors (positive self-concept, control beliefs, and psychological well-being).

In Chapter 10 Sloboda emphasizes the importance of school prevention intervention programs for adolescent substance abuse. He states the need for these efforts by noting that the possession of tobacco and alcohol by persons under the age of 18 is illegal, and that research indicates that the use of tobacco and alcohol increases the risk for later, more extensive drug use. Sloboda reviews the historical context for the development of school-based prevention programs, the developing body of research on their effectiveness, and the impact of these approaches on adolescent use of tobacco, alcohol, and illicit substances.

In Chapter 11 the prevention and health promotion approaches shift to a broader community focus. Namely, what larger community organization/system interventions might alter the availability of these to commonly available substances. D'Amico, Chinman, Stern, and Wandersman provide the reader with valuable insights on ways to intervene in the system to achieve effective change.

This volume concludes with the lessons we learned as editors in this process and as practitioners and scholars in this field for several decades. This volume contains both good and sobering news. The good news is that progress has been made to improve the likelihood that young people can be treated successfully. This book documents that fact and can be used by practitioners and program developers at local, county, and state levels to implement those practices. The good news is also that substance misuse can be prevented, and this book clearly demonstrates that fact. The prevention and health promotion examples provided and similar efforts should be copied and implemented elsewhere.

The sobering news is that if we are correct and that humankind has forever sought the means to transport itself to altered states of consciousness then problems associated with substance misuse will remain. If we are correct in believing that tobacco and alcohol can be stepping-stone drugs to more serious drug misuse for some, then our society must continually reseed itself with new generations of evidence-based treatment and prevention interventions. This means that we cannot ignore promising treatment, health promotion, or prevention activities as they are developing. Drug misuse at any age by any group is a problem that if ignored will grow worse. It calls for a reconceptualization of the tactics to *manage* drug misuse and associated problems. The first step is to heed the advice of the talented scholars in this volume. The second step is returning the phrases "harm risk reduction" and "distribution of consumption" to our lexicon and expanding on the evidence-based interventions discussed in this book.

References

Emboden, W. (1979). *Narcotic plants: Hallucinogens, stimulants, inebriants, and hypnotics, their origins and uses*. NY: Macmillan.
Kandel, D. B., & Faust, R. (1975). Sequence and stages in patterns of adolescent drug use. *Archives of General Psychiatry, 32*, 923–932.

Contents

Chapter 1
A Selected Social History
of the Stepping-Stone Drugs

Thomas P. Gullotta

In the mid 1970s, Denise Kandel and her colleagues (Kandel & Foust, 1975; Kandel, Kessler, & Margulies, 1978; Kandel, 1981; Kandel, Yamaguchi & Chen, 1992) published a series of papers establishing a sequence in the pattern of use of substances by adolescents and debunking the prevalent belief that marijuana was THE stepping-stone drug to heroin use. While this information has never been refuted, it has been ignored by generations of policymakers and their appointees to federal and state departments responsible for the prevention of substance abuse. In a volume dedicated to examining evidence-based approaches to the prevention and treatment of adolescent substance misuse, it is useful to trip down memory lane and revisit Kandel and her associates' findings and further to place three of these stepping-stone drugs into a broader social historical perspective. By so doing the reader of this volume hopefully will appreciate the challenges that confront society as it attempts to reduce the misuse of substances by its youth.

The Sequence of Adolescent Drug Use

American colonists whether English or Dutch loved their drink, preferably intoxicating. Struyvesant reported that "Almost one full fourth of the town of New Amsterdam [New York]" was occupied by "houses for the sale of brandy, tobacco, and beer" (Struyvesant cited in Child, 1896, p. 17). Whether smoking a pipe and downing a pint in a tavern to the stories of headless horsemen or attending the ordination of the new minister in a New England village, alcohol quenched the thirst of those in attendance. Consider this invoice for the community gathering accompanying an ordination in 1785:

> 30 Bowles of Punch before the People went to meeting.
> 10 Bottles of wine before they went to meeting.
> 44 Bowles of Punch while at dinner.
> 18 Bottles of wine.
> 8 Bowles of Brandy.
> Cherry Rum and Cider [quantity not mentioned].
> (Child, 1896 pp. 55–56)

C.G. Leukefeld et al. (eds.) *Adolescent Substance Abuse,*
DOI: 10.1007/978-0-387-09732-9_1, © Springer Science+Business Media LLC 2009

Given this long infatuation with intoxicating beverages, it is not surprising that Americans in their condemnation of drug abuse overlook the connection between those substances and alcohol.

The work of Denise Kandel and her associates (e.g., Kandel & Faust, 1975) was the first to establish a well-defined pathway to illicit drug use. Using representative samples of New York State high school students, these researchers established that the overwhelming majority of youth who used marijuana (98%) began with beer and wine. "Drug use begins specifically with beer and wine … These are the 'entry drugs' into the continuum of drug use" (Kandel & Faust, 1975, p. 931).

The second step toward illicit drugs in their model was either the use of stronger alcoholic beverages followed by cigarette smoking or cigarette smoking followed by stronger alcoholic beverages. In either instance this could then lead to the third stage of marijuana use and then to the fourth stage of other illicit drug use.

The authors caution, "while the data show a very clear-cut sequence in the use of various drugs, they do not prove that the use of a particular drug infallibly leads to the use of other drugs higher up in the sequence" (Kandel & Faust, 1975, p. 931). At each stage individuals choose to stop and not use the next drug in the sequence.

Having identified the stepping-stones into illicit drug misuse as beer and wine, tobacco, and marijuana, what we know about beer, tobacco, and marijuana from a social historical context is discussed next.

Beer: The Staff of Life

Lager Beer: A friendly drink,
A healthy drink, A family drink, A national drink.
(Late 19th-century poster, in Burnham, 1993)

Recently, at an eatery that brewed its own beers I sampled bread made from the grain left over from the beer-making process. That act of consumption completed a circle albeit in reverse that has gone on for thousands of years. Beer or "liquid bread" was likely discovered as the by-product of bread making by our ancient Neolithic ancestors (Tannahill, 1973 p. 63). Through a process of trial and error our distant relatives found that raw grain was made digestible by allowing it to sprout in water, then dried and ground into meal. Incidentally, this wet mixture was porridge. Left in an old earthen vessel filled with nooks and crannies harboring bacteria, this porridge would start to ferment after several days as the bacteria (yeast) consumed the sugars released by crushing the grain. The by-products released by the bacteria happened to be CO_2 and alcohol, producing a porridge that was both filling and mildly intoxicating.

Draw off the liquid from this mixture and the resulting product is nutritious beer. Tannahill (1973) informs us that the ancient Sumerians allotted 40 oz of this brew to a worker daily. That's a tad more than a half-gallon a day. Beer mattered as much for the Egyptians whose Goddess, Hathor, was the deity responsible for its presence on earth. Not only was it a food and a beverage but also a medicine appearing as an ingredient in 118 of the 600 prescriptions found in the ancient Egyptian medical text, Papyrus Ebers (Brown, 2003).

Beer as nourishment continued to recent times. For example, before pasteurizing milk became popular its consumption by children and others could be deadly. This was especially true of the milk provided to large cities like New York and Chicago where the cows that provided milk to these cities were often confined in unsanitary disease-ridden warehouses where tubercular animals quickly spread the infection to all. Thus, statements like, "You can depend on the beer, but you can't tell about the milk you get down here," speak to reasons why parents gave beer to their children to drink (Burnham, 1993, p. 60).

Despite America's propensity for alcoholic beverages and the growth in popularity of beer with the influx of immigrant groups like the Germans who brought their taste for it from the Old World to the New, concern for its harm to individuals and families grew. The minority of voices gathered strength as Saloons multiplied and more potent distilled alcoholic beverages appeared. One need only compare Hogarth's etching of a society consuming beer with the plate of that same society downing gin to understand the growing worry.[1]

In the United States, this concern reached a crescendo in 1916 with enough antidrinking candidates elected to Congress to pass a national prohibition amendment. By 1919, the necessary majority of states had ratified the 18th amendment that it became law. Interestingly, Burnham (1993) contends that due to wartime restrictions in 1916 on grain for food rather than alcohol, prohibition was essentially in place by 1918. The notorious Saloons in which most drinking occurred had virtually disappeared and the country appeared ready to accept prohibition.

More interesting still is that prohibition did not totally prohibit alcohol consumption! The Volstead Act that defined the 18th amendment "explicitly permitted religious groups to use wine, physicians to prescribe alcohol, and private citizens to own and drink it even to make small quantities of wine and beer for home use" (Burnham, 1993, p. 27). Thus, those with wealth stocked their cellars with distilled spirits. The immigrants brewed their own beer or as my Italian grandmother did crushed her own grapes in a wine press I still own, deposited the sweet liquid into oak barrels for bacteria to feed upon and transform into wine. The losers in this were the cash-rich distillers and the poor who had frequented the now closed Saloons. As we know, this experiment was not to last long. Change occurred and prohibition was repealed not because of the rise in the criminal element and the "Speak Easy" but because of the loss of tax revenue and the effective lobbying of cash-rich disgruntled distillers (Burnham, 1993).

Sobered by their recent experience, the distillers and their distributors launched a media campaign to redefine the role of beer and other alcoholic beverages in American life. Using magazines, sporting events, and even toys, beer was taken out

---

[1] During the 13th century, the process of distillation became known in Europe. Distilled beverages were treated as medicines called aqua vitae (water of life). By the 1500's, aqua vitae was associated with criminal activity in England. In the mid 1600's, gin was developed in Holland by distilling grain with juniper berries.

of the Saloon and the back room where men were grudgingly permitted to retire after supper for a smoke and a drink to the dining room table where it was consumed in front of the family. In time, mom was seen toasting her smiling husband with a foaming glass herself. Billboards spoke to the allegiance of a beer to a ball team, and I was known to stuff the ballot box in favor of my favorite Reingold Beer Beauty as a child of 9 as I played with my toy Budweiser Wagon piled high with kegs pulled by several handsome plastic white horses. The keg temporarily disappeared to be replaced by bottles and cans in a six-pack that has been replaced over time by the 12- and now 24-can case.

With the end of prohibition, consumption of beer and other alcoholic beverages gradually grew and with it returned the problem of men, women, and, shortly, youth unable to manage their drinking. Prior to prohibition, this problem was identified with the substance and its dispensing location – the Saloon. The distillers and their distributors were not to make this same mistake again. Home, the family picnic, and other G-rated celebrations would be the venues for consumption. Alcoholism was gradually redefined not as a societal issue but as an individual problem. Rather than consider distribution of consumption approaches that would limit the availability of alcohol, the focus was now on genes and the psychological fallings of that man, woman, or youth (Burnham, 1993).

In place of setting a limit on the alcoholic beverages to be consumed, the public was told to designate a driver. Appealing to individual responsibility that rings so true in a society that worships rugged individualism shifted responsibility from the makers of conveniently packaged cases with carrying handles containing cans or bottles with pop top or twist off caps and newly formulated "fortified" alcoholic beverages to the flawed soul unable to exercise control over the command to "Pick a pair of six packs – Buy Bud." Any attempt to refocus the discussion toward limiting alcohol consumption was dealt with harshly by this cash-rich powerful beer and alcohol lobby. For example, in 1995, the long brewing resentment of the beer industry against the Center for Substance Abuse Prevention found expression in its successful efforts to significantly reduce the agency's drug prevention effort in a newly elected Republican Congress. As Kuntz (1995, p. A12) reported in the *Wall Street Journal*, "Soon after the House passed its last major spending bill this month, Coors Brewing Co. sent two cases of beer to the office of the subcommittee that wrote the measure. The alcohol beverage industry has good reason to be grateful. The bill would gut the Center for Substance Abuse Prevention, an agency the industry says promotes an antidrinking message threatening to its bottom line."

Presently, the message to the public is to drink in moderation but to purchase in bulk. The effects of this mixed message on youthful drinkers can be measured in one sense by data that indicate 41% of 8th graders, 62% of 10th graders, and 73% of 12th graders reported trying alcohol in 2006 (Johnston, O'Malley, Bachman, & Schulenberg, 2007, p. 26). The source of this information is the *Monitoring the Future* survey that has been undertaken with graduating seniors since 1975 and extended to other students in the 1990s. Now, 73% of 12th graders tasting alcohol is nothing to be particularly proud of considering that the drinking age is 21 except that the parents of those youths who graduated in the class of 1979 reported that

93% of them had tried alcohol. Of course, those parents will likely share that the legal drinking age was 18 in most states in 1979. Thus, compared to their parents the graduating student in 2006 is less likely to have ever tried alcohol, but as the child who drank beer in place of milk would be quick to share – circumstances color the picture significantly.

Tobacco

> The most sovereign and precious weed that
> ever the earth tendered to the use of man.
> (Ben Johnson, 1598, cited in Shoemaker, 1898, p. xi)

While the Old World introduced small pox to the New World, "Montazuma's revenge" might better be considered syphilis and tobacco to the Europeans. The first is believed to have been returned to Europe by a less than virtuous Columbus and his crew, and the second is briefly mentioned in his log as "a few dried leaves which must be something of importance to these people" (Burns, 2006, p. 16). While syphilis spread quickly across Europe and reached epidemic proportions within a few years of its arrival, the use of those "few dried leaves" was considerably slower. Its introduction to England is credited to Sir John Hawkins, English sea captain and slave trader, who is said to have seized the crop in a raid along the Florida coast noting that:

> The Floridians when they travel have a kinde of herbe dried, who with a cane and an earthen cap in the end, with fire, and the dried berbe put together, doe sucke thorow the cane the smoke thereof, which smoke satisfieth their hunger, and therwith they live foure or five days without meat or drink. (Burns, 2006, p. 22)

It was not Hawkins, however, but Sir Walter Raleigh whose friendship with Queen Elizabeth I popularized the use of tobacco in England and earned him the distinction of a brand of cigarettes to be named after him centuries later.

Like nearly every newly discovered New World plant, tobacco was touted for its medicinal qualities. In the Old World, tobacco smoke, paste, or parts of the plant would be applied to every imaginable orifice or laid on to relieve pain, cure emotional distress, or treat sickness. Similarly, in England from 1573 to 1625 it was believed to be a helpful treatment for heart pains, snake bites, fever, exhaustion, and the Black Plague. None other than the great diarist Samuel Pepy recorded:

> This day ... I see in Drury Lane houses marked with a red cross [denoting the presence of the Plague]...which was a sad sight to me ... It put me into an ill conception of myself and of my smell, so I was forced to buy some roll tobacco to smell an chaw, which took away the apprenhension.(Burns, 2006, p. 27)

As with every great discovery, it would not be the medicinal benefits (sic) but the entertainment aspects of tobacco that would endear this plant to society. In taverns and coffee houses across Old and New Worlds the active ingredient in tobacco would work its magic of calming its consumer and subduing his hunger.

That ingredient, nicotine or more properly nicotiana, was named after the Frenchman Jean Nicot who first described the medicinal properties of the substance in 1559 (Austin, 1979). The addictive characteristics of nicotine, being as it is commonly inhaled into the lungs thus enabling its rapid passage to the brain, led the then Surgeon General C. Everett Koop in 1988 to caution that "the pharmacologic and behavioral processes that determine tobacco addiction are similar to those that determine addiction to drugs such as heroin and cocaine" (Byrne, 1988, p. 1143).

But concern about this noxious weed was evident centuries earlier. It was prohibited in the Massachusetts Bay Colony in 1632 and several years later in Connecticut. In the mid 1600s, The Roman Catholic Church concerned with the growing use of tobacco by its clergy and parishioners and the calming effects resultant from its use sought to refocus its following on more salient issues like death, damnation, and the like. Thus, papal bills prohibiting the use of tobacco under penalty of expulsion from the church were enacted. This ban remained in effect for roughly 100 years (Goodman, 1994).

In Russia, tobacco was called "the devil's plant" in the 1600s. The Russian Czar, no slouch at having his word taken seriously, saw thousands put to death who ignored his decree prohibiting its use (Goodman, 1994).

Even the English monarch James I who followed Queen Elizabeth I to the throne saw no good in this plant and tried by means of taxation to eliminate its presence on English soil. In 1604, the year after his coronation, he had published anonymously *A Counter-Blaste to Tobacco*. In it, he concluded tobacco was:

a custome lothsome to the eye, hateful to the nose,
harmefull to the braine, dangerous to the lungs, and
the blacke stinking fume thereof, neerest resembling
the horrible stygian smoke of the pit that is bottomless.
(James, 1604/1932, pp. 34–35)

Actually, what may have been driving James I mad was the reality that the tobacco England was consuming was coming from the Spanish settlements of the New World. In the sense of balance of trade payments, tobacco was costing the England what oil is costing the United States today.

Enter into this scenario the American Colonies and, in particular, Virginia. In the 1500s, the Virginia colony was a small destitute community with a history of repeated financial failure behind it. There is evidence that James I was growing tired of the financial drain Virginia was having upon the Mother Country, but this disappointment and simultaneous concern over tobacco's noxious harm vanished with the development in Virginia of a tobacco similar in quality to that being imported from Spain. Soon the revenues from the sale of Virginia tobacco erased any concern of either quelling tobacco's use or possibly disposing of this previously nonproducing asset (Virginia).

Tobacco was consumed in the colonies and in the early years of the republic by crushing the dried leaves and igniting them in a pipe, rolling the leaves and igniting them (a cigar), compacting the leaves into a tight mass and biting off a small portion which was then chewed (a chew or chaw), or, as was popular in Europe, pulverizing the leaf into a very fine powder and inhaling it through the nostrils (snuff).

The development of the cigarette must be credited to Spain. The story of its invention was that discarded cigars were gathered by the poor and the waste tobacco deposited onto paper which was then rolled, crimped, and smoked. The advantage of the cigarette over the cigar or pipe was time. A good pipe or cigar was a leisurely affair spent in contemplation of writing the next verse, savoring the aroma of a fine brandy, or attending to the learned argument of a fellow coffee house philosopher. The popularity of the cigarette was made on the battlefield. First, in the ill-fated British experience in the Crimean War and later by its export from England to the United States in the Civil War (Goodman, 1994; Wagner, 1971).

Recall that the active ingredient in tobacco is nicotine, a substance which when inhaled into the lungs travels quickly to the brain and produces a sense of calm and relaxation by interacting with brain neurotransmitters like serotonin and dopamine. Imagine being Steven Crane's (1895/2001) young protagonist, Henry Fleming, in the *Red Badge of Courage* marching forward with friends and neighbors as the unit's leader rushes before them waving his sword above his head attracting to his motions soft masses of humming lead like yellow jackets to a fall picnic. These stinging insects of death flatten on contact tearing into a face or punching a hole into flesh that cries out as it writhes on the dampened crimson ground. Still, the line of which you are a part advances slowly worming its way across the battlefield turned cemetery. The cigarette was the perfect fortifier for such a suicidal venture. Alcohol would impair motor control, cloud vision, and numb rather than stir the body to action. Better the quickly consumed cigarette to impart just enough calm before the butchery. With the close of conflict between the states, the cigarette found a home off the battlefield and in the rapidly industrializing United States. In a world where time is money, its advantages of quickly induced calm and quenched hunger favored its use over the pipe or cigar and it was cleaner than the chaw whose residue could be found nearly everywhere as this visiting Englishman observed:

> We discussed these important questions until my companions paired
> themselves off into their respective beds. I selected the cleanest corner
> of the that had been least spat upon – and lay down on the floor with my carpet-
> bag for a pillow. (Anonymous, 1863, p. 499)

Indeed, the novelist Charles Dickens (Burns, 2006) could not help but record on his first visit to the United States that on one occasion a guest chewing tobacco in his hotel room and not seeing a spittoon let loose with well-directed copious stream of juice out the window. Problem was the window was closed. There trickling down the window pane, Dickens observed, the spittal resided without its depositor taking further notice.

Like its fraternal twin – alcohol, the years after 1865 saw a rise in activity to curb the spreading use of tobacco, particularly cigarettes whose popularity had grown such that by 1885 one billion were being manufactured yearly. Indeed, a total of 14 states early in the 20th century had passed such laws but these efforts were to disappear with the advent of World War I.

The slaughter of human life had changed little since the Civil War. Frontal assaults continued to be a popular military strategy but the machine gun replaced the cannon's grape shot as the weapon of preference that segmented the line of troops worming across the open pockmarked fields of France. Between these doomed excursions, troops burrowed into the ground to hide from the death above. Again, alcohol that could numb the solider from the death encircling him was rejected in favor of the cigarette with none other than General Black Jack Pershing (Burns, 2006, p. 158) stating, "You ask me what we need to win this war? I answer tobacco as much as bullets." Indeed, he was to back these words with a demand for "tens of thousands of tons of cigarettes" from the home front which was complied with (Burns, 2006, p. 158). His endorsement of the cigarette was echoed by others on his staff, "a cigarette may make the difference between a hero and a shrinker," and even President Woodrow Wilson (a smoker himself) got into the act by endorsing the New York Sun's "Smokes for Soldier's Fund" (Burns, 2006, p.158).

The result of these demands was the demise of antismoking measures in the United States. Well-meaning groups like the YMCA, the Salvation Army, and the Red Cross responded to these requests to support the troops overseas. With the conclusion of the war to end all wars, tobacco and the cigarette especially were an inexorable part of the American landscape. For the next 40 years, a movie could not be watched without the haze of tobacco smoke on the screen; magazine and newspapers ads touted the flavor, taste, or masculinity of tobacco products; and the new medium of radio and later television brought entertainment compliments of the tobacco companies. This advertising effort was successful with yearly production of cigarettes exceeding 80 billion in the 1920s to hundreds of billions by the 1960s.

With the return of world hostilities in 1941, it was not surprising that tobacco's importance as a necessary war item was again embraced. Replacing General Black Jack Pershing was General Douglas MacArthur (corn cob pipe smoker) who encouraged one group to use the funds it had raised to spend, "the entire amount ... to buy American cigarettes," for the troops (Burns, 2006, p. 198). Franklin Roosevelt (a cigarette smoker) saw the importance of tobacco to the war effort to the extent that he instructed draft boards to provide deferments to tobacco farmers, thus ensuring an adequate supply of this once noxious weed.

It would seem that tobacco's place in American society was secured except that occasional reports would appear in the scientific literature describing the harmful effects of inhaling tobacco smoke. The first of these appeared in England in 1924 when the respected English Chemist Ernest Kennaway described a substance he called "tar" and linked this sticky substance to cancer. His study's findings were replicated over the next two decades with the findings remaining unchanged (Burns, 2006).

In 1952, a Christian Herald report of the work of the American Cancer Society was reprinted in the widely subscribed to *Reader's Digest* and the American public was made aware of the growing evidence linking tobacco to harmful health outcomes. In 1957, the UK, and in 1964, the US Government Health Services adopted formal positions linking tobacco to cancer and other diseases. Still, more than three decades would pass in the United States and it would not be until potentially bankrupting lawsuits against the makers of tobacco products were awarded that significant steps were taken to curtail tobacco use by the general public and especially youth (Burns, 2006).

Examining the data gathered from the Monitoring the Future (Johnston et al., 2007, p. 105) study indicates that 24.6% of 8th graders, 36.1% of 10th graders, and 47.1% of 12th graders in 2006 reported trying cigarettes at least once. This compared to 74% of the graduating class of 1979. If Kandel and her associates (Kandel, 1981; Kandel & Foust, 1975; Kandel et al., 1978, 1992) are correct then the decline reported by the youth of 2006 in their lifetime use of cigarettes and alcohol in comparison to their parents' lifetime use in 1979 should be evident in how many decided to try marijuana compared to their parents reported lifetime use.

Marijuana

> When I was in England I experimented with marijuana a time or two, and I
> Didn't like it. I didn't inhale.
> (Candidate, Bill Clinton in Ifill, 1992, of the *New York Times*)
> One reason why we appreciated pot, as y'all call it now, was the warmth
> it always brought forth from the other person – especially the ones that lit
> up a good stick of that shuzzit or gage.
> (Louie Armstrong cited in Sloman 1979, p. 133)[2]

For 450 years and more another weed in the New World went relatively unnoticed. It may be that the greater calm and sense of well-being it conferred over tobacco interfered with the work to be done or that Alice B. Tokilas' recipe for brownies suffered by association with Gertrude Stein's often indecipherable writing. In any case, the evilness of marijuana as the entry drug into the wasteland of drug abuse dates from the late 1930s.

Marijuana or hemp had been known to civilization for thousands of years before that date. Like other substances in this chapter, it too was used as a medicinal substance for a variety of health problems. Among those uses, the Chinese mixed it with wine and administered it as an analgesic before surgery (Grinspoon & Bakalar, 1993). Others believed it to be helpful in treating malaria and venereal disease, and Robert Burton (1621/1851) in his compendium *The Anatomy of Melancholy* reported its use to treat depression.

Marijuana was raised as a cash crop in the English colonies. The fibers of the hemp plant were a valuable commodity and were and continue today to be turned into a variety of products including cloth and rope. Indeed, George Washington cultivated

---

[2] It was difficult to choose a single quote to open this section so I chose two. Joining Bill and Louie in acknowledging their use are Arnold Schwarzenegger, John Kerry, Bing Crosby (his son revealed his use), Newt Gingrich, Margaret Mead, Michael Bloomberg, Carl Sagan, and Donna Shalala to name but a few (www.alternet.org/dugreporter/18941).

the plant. Hemp production in the United States continued until about the time of the Civil War when other nations replaced the United States as its major producer. Its use as a medicinal substance declined in the late 1800s for two principal reasons.

The first was the uncertain effect of its psychoactive ingredient, THC (delta-9-tetra-hydrocannabinol), compared to other substances like opium and coca and their derivatives (morphine and cocaine). The second was the increased use of the hypodermic syringe after 1860 enabling soluble drugs to be injected and speed relief to the patient. In this second respect, marijuana was not soluble in water (Grinspoon & Bakalar, 1993).

Recent histories of marijuana suggest that the events that moved marijuana from being considered a relatively harmless plant to the status of "killer weed" originated in the southwest during the 1930s. Prior to that time, the substance was essentially ignored. For example, it was not regulated by the Harrison Narcotics Act of 1914. Indeed, in 1920 the US Department of Agriculture published a booklet encouraging its production as a cash crop. The circumstances surrounding marijuana's decline from relative obscurity to infamy involved the migration of Mexicans into the United States during the Great Depression and the scarcity of work.

Other than Alice and Gertrude, it appears that in the late 1920s and early 1930s the largest group of users of marijuana for recreational purposes was Mexican Americans. Recall the treatment of the Joad family in its migration from Oklahoma to California in search of work in Steinbeck's epic novel *The Grapes of Wrath* and the tensions are evident. Add to those tensions of high unemployment and ethnic prejudice and the conditions are ripe for harmful actions to be taken (Austin, 1979; Grinspoon, 1971; Sloman, 1979).

Interestingly, while legislative delegations from the southwest lobbied the federal government for action, those requests were initially ignored by Harry Anslinger then heading the Federal Bureau of Narcotics. However, neither the requests nor the depression disappeared and by 1937 Congress had enacted the Marijuana Tax Act. With marijuana now a substance of concern, legal authorities in the southwest acted quickly by deporting individuals found in possession of marijuana. In their zealousness – perhaps prejudice is the better word – against those with a South American ancestry, individuals deported included native-born Americans with family histories extending back generations in the United States to a nation that was foreign to them – Mexico.

Since the 1930s, marijuana has been understood at various times in North American society to offer "one moment of bliss and a lifetime of regret" or to provide "a mildly intoxicating, sensory altering, view of the cosmos." Some have suggested the substance possesses no legitimate medicinal uses. Others believe marijuana has medicinal value in reducing side effects experienced in the treatment of cancer, for example. In recent years, state legislatures, notably Oregon, have passed laws allowing individuals with a variety of medical issues to possess and use marijuana for medical purposes.

The data from Johnston et al. (2007) indicate that 15.7% of 8th graders, 31.8% of 10th graders, and 42.3% of seniors in 2006 admitted to having tried marijuana at least once. This compared to 60.4% of the graduating class of 1979. In my admittedly unscientific approach, the question posed in the last section would be answered thusly. Graduating seniors of the Class of 2006 acknowledged having ever tried cigarettes and alcohol less than the graduating Class of 1979. Not surprisingly for those who subscribe to Kandel's and her associates work and, hopefully, by know you do, their lifetime use of marijuana is less than the Class of 1979.

Closing Thoughts

From this excursion down history's pathways what inferences can be drawn?

Whether they calmed nerves, lessened hunger, offered new insights into the cosmos, or cured illness, the initial use of each substance was regulated by the shaman or community leaders. The rules governing use enabled the community to seemingly function successfully. Difficulties arose when these substances were taken out of their original context and placed into another. That is, from medicine or religious use to recreational use and from special circumstance or ceremonial use to continual use by those who would misuse them. With the growth of knowledge, these ancient substances lost their magical ability to answer questions, cure illness, and satisfy hunger. No longer did they open doors to insight and new information valuable to the group. Instead their usefulness became personal pleasure, and it is in this context that we find ourselves today.

As a species we seem to have evolved little from our cousins who discovered that grain or fruits left in vessels fermented into an often unpleasant tasting beverage with pleasant and sought-after mood-altering characteristics or that some plants had similar qualities. It's a pity that this world does not contain enough wonderment to satisfy our needs for exploration and seeking contentment. But clearly the use of these and other substances suggest it does not. For those who would disagree with me, consider the trouble Venezuela natives go to make the native beer – Chicha. Corn would be raised, gathered, and the women of the village would chew the corn kernels. These they would then spit into a community bowl. The process of chewing the corn splits the kernels, which mixed with the saliva in their mouths and transformed the starch found in the corn to sugar. Yeast feeds on the sugar, releasing alcohol and CO_2. Viola, the end result is Chicha – alledgedly a "tasty beer" (Emboden, 1979, p. 154)! Lastly, the reality that alcohol and tobacco are permitted for use suggests that these stepping-stone drugs to marijuana will not turn to sand anytime soon.

Thus, we find ourselves in a quandary that is reflected in the circumstances described in the chapters to follow. We lament the number of youth who have traveled this well-worn path to other addictive drugs and the harm brought on them as a result, the expense to society for their addictive behavior, and the less than stellar success rate of their rehabilitation. Society speaks much of prevention but really means by that word "please wait your time and then don't overindulge."

Perhaps, if society did not then immerse youth in a world of temptation far more enticing than Eden's one lone apple tree they might wait but that is not the case. In our society tempting apple trees are abundant, and their luscious fruit are ever ripe for the tasting. As the reader is soon to learn, prevention approaches aimed at strengthening the will power of our young Adams and Eves (using prevention's tools of education, social competency promotion, and natural caregiving) to resist those apples are increasingly being paired with approaches that build fences around those trees like ID carding and arresting adults who serve or purchase alcohol and tobacco for minors (using the prevention tools of community organization and systems intervention). Encouragingly, this multifaceted approach has shown positive results. Discouragingly, this fencing approach has not focused attention on the manufacturing or distribution element of the equation, for example, reducing the alcoholic content of beverages or the chemical composition of cigarettes. These are "harm risk reduction" approaches. A phrase dropped from the lexicon of substance abuse prevention that deserves reinstatement if we are to be serious in our efforts to limit the use of stepping-stone substances by underage Adams and Eves.

References

Anonymous. (1863). A run through the southern states. *Cornhill Magazine, 7*(4), 495–515.

Austin, G. A. (1979). *Research issues 24: Perspectives on the history of psychoactive substance use*. Washington, DC: US Government Printing Office.

Brown, P. (2003). *Man walks into a pub: A sociable history of beer*. London, UK: Macmillan.

Burnham, J. C. (1993). *Bad habits: Drinking, smoking, taking drugs, gambling, sexual misbehavior, and swearing in American history*. New York: New York University Press.

Burns, E. (2006). *The smoke of the gods: A social history of tobacco*. New York: Temple University Press.

Burton, R. (1621/1851). *The anatomy of melancholy* (4th ed.). Philadelphia, PA: J. W. Moore.

Byrne, G. (1988). Nicotine likened to cocaine, heroin. *Science, 240*, 1143.

Child, F. S. (1896). *The colonial parson of New England*. New York: Baker & Taylor.

Crane, S. (1895/2001). *The red badge of courage*. New York: Barnes and Noble.

Emboden, W. (1979). *Narcotic plants: Hallucinogens, stimulants, inebriants, and hypnotics, their origins and uses*. New York: Macmillan.

Goodman, J. (1994). *Tobacco in history: The cultures of dependence*. New York: George Routledge.

Grinspoon, L. (1971). *Marijuana reconsidered*. Cambridge, MA: Harvard University Press.

Grinspoon, L., & Bakalar, J. B. (1993). *Marijuana forbidden medicine*. New Haven, CT: Yale University Press.

Ifill, G. (1992, March 30). *The 1992 campaign: New York; Clinton admits experiment with marijuana in 1960's. The New York Times*, March 30, 1992, A15.

Johnston, L. D., O'Malley, P. M., Bachman, J. G., & Schulenberg, J. E. (2007). *Monitoring the future: National survey results on drug use, 1975–2006*. Bethesda, MD: National Institute on Drug Abuse.

Kandel, D. B. (1981). Drug use by youth: An overview. In D. J. Lettieri & J. P. Lundford (Eds.), *Drug abuse and the American adolescent* (NIDA Research Monograph No. 38, # ADM 81-1166, pp. 1–24). Washington, DC: U.S. Government Printing Office.

Kandel, D. B., & Faust, R. (1975). Sequence and stages in patterns of adolescent drug use. *Archives of General Psychiatry, 32*, 923–932.

Kandel, D. B., Kessler, R., & Margulies, R. (1978). Adolescent initiation into stages of drug use: A developmental analysis. In D. B. Kandel (Ed.), *Longitudinal research on drug use: Empirical findings and methodological issues* (pp. 225–252), Washington, DC: Hemisphere-Wiley.

Kandel, D. B., Yamaguchi, K., & Chen, K. (1992). Stages of progression in drug involvement from adolescence to adulthood: Further evidence for the gateway theory. *Journal of Studies on Alcohol, 53*, 447–457.

James, I. (1604/1932). *A counter-blaste to tobacco*. Yellow Springs, OH: Antioch Press.

Kuntz, P. (1995). *Alcohol beverage industry lobbies for bill to gut substance abuse agency see as threat, Monday, August 14, A. 12*, New York: Wall Street Journal.

Tannahill, R. (1973). *Food in history*. New York: Stein & Day.

Shoemaker, W. L. (1898). *La santa yerba*. Boston, MA: Copeland and Day.

Sloman, L. (1979). *The history of marijuana in America: Reefer madness*. New York: Bobbs-Merrill.

Wagner, S. (1971). *Cigarette country: Tobacco in American history and politics*. New York: Praeger.

Chapter 2
A Biological/Genetic Perspective: The Addicted Brain

Thomas H. Kelly, Alessandra N. Kazura, Karen M. Lommel, Shanna Babalonis, and Catherine A. Martin

Introduction

Exposure to medications, chemicals, infectious disease, or environmental agents (i.e., potential teratogens) presents a significant health risk during human development, particularly during critical periods of organ and system development. Risk of exposure during the critical periods of embryonic and fetal development has been well documented, but recent evidence suggests that critical periods of organ development, especially brain development, extend into childhood and adolescence. Given the extended period of brain development, risks associated with exposure to teratogens having direct effects on the brain (i.e., psychoactive drugs) may also extend into childhood and adolescence. This chapter will examine the health risks associated with developmental exposure to psychoactive drugs of abuse.

Exposure to psychoactive drugs can impact normal biological development in ways that are similar to other teratogens. However, psychoactive drugs can also influence brain and behavioral functions through direct pharmacological modulation of neuronal function and structure. As such, the developmental risk related to exposure to psychoactive drugs is exacerbated by the potential for adverse consequences related to the neuropharmacological effects of the drugs occurring during critical periods of development. Concerns are further heightened if one considers frequency of exposure. Some psychoactive drugs function as reinforcers and engender repeated drug-taking behavior. Repeated episodes of drug-taking behavior during development exacerbate risk by increasing the frequency of neuropharmacological exposure.

Risk of prenatal exposure to psychoactive drugs of abuse is substantial, given that rates of drug use in the general population are highest among individuals of reproductive age and that significant drug use is reported among pregnant women (i.e., in some populations, up to 27% of pregnant women report occasional drug use during pregnancy, Rayburn & Bogenschutz, 2004). Exposure to psychoactive drugs of abuse can occur postnatally through passive exposure from environmental sources (e.g., tobacco smoke, methamphetamine production). Developmental exposure to drugs of abuse among children and adolescents has escalated in the past decades as drugs have become increasingly available to younger age groups and experimentation has increased. Furthermore, genetic, developmental, and other neurobiological factors influence individual sensitivity to the reinforcing and other neuropharmacological

C.G. Leukefeld et al. (eds.) *Adolescent Substance Abuse,*
DOI: 10.1007/978-0-387-09732-9_2, © Springer Science + Business Media LLC 2009

effects of psychoactive drugs (Chambers, Taylor, & Potenza, 2003). In combination with cultural, peer, and family influences, enhanced sensitivity to the reinforcing and other pharmacological effects of drugs place some children and adolescents at increased vulnerability for repeated drug use (e.g., Kelly et al., 2006; Stoops et al., 2007) and for the development of heavy use, abuse, and dependence (Chaloupka & Johnston, 2007). Individual differences in sensitivity to the neuropharmacological effects of drugs can increase the risk of adverse health consequences associated with drug use, including engaging in other risky behaviors (e.g., sexual behavior, driving behavior, self-injurious behavior, and gambling), as well as adverse short- and long-term social (education, peer and family relations), medical (mental and physical health), and legal consequences. Finally, evidence links exposure to psychoactive drugs of abuse during critical periods of development to enhanced sensitivity to the reinforcing and other neuropharmacological effects of drugs, which, in turn, leads to enhanced likelihood of repeating drug use, followed by further enhancement of sensitivity (e.g., Glantz & Chambers, 2006; Krasnegor, Gray, & Thompson, 1986).

Neurodevelopment

Substantial neuronal growth occurs during prenatal embryonic development. However, critical periods of neurogenesis and synaptic remodeling also occur in response to environmental experiences and continue after birth and throughout childhood and adolescence (e.g., Crews, He, & Hodge, 2007). For example, maturation of the mesolimbic reward pathway continues during childhood and early adolescence. In contrast, the inhibitory functions of the orbitofrontal cortex, a brain region shown to be involved in self-control, continue to develop into the early twenties (e.g., Galvan et al., 2006). High levels of impulsiveness and risk-taking behavior among adolescents have been linked to asynchronous development of reward and inhibitory functions, with the alerting and motivating functions of the dopaminergic reward pathway emerging during early adolescence, while the inhibitory processes of the frontal cortex that hold these functions in check may not become fully mature until early adulthood (Crews et al., 2007). Risk associated with psychoactive drug exposure during critical periods of pre- and postnatal human brain development has been well recognized. However, since periods of critical development continue throughout childhood and adolescence, it is important to recognize that risks to optimal brain development associated with psychoactive drug exposure extend well beyond this period of embryonic growth (Crews et al., 2007).

Pharmacology

Drugs enter the body through several routes: parenteral (intravenous, intramuscular, and subcutaneous), enteral (oral, sublingual, and rectal), inhalation, intranasal, intrathecal, transdermal, and topical. Research has established that a rapid rise in plasma levels, quick entry into the brain, and relatively short-acting behavioral effects increase the reinforcing effects and abuse liability of a compound (Feldman, Meyer, & Quenzer, 1997). Drugs enter the bloodstream and reach the brain most rapidly when administered intravenously or via inhalation (i.e., smoking).

Drugs also leave the body through various pathways in drug metabolism and excretion. Body mass, total body water, amount of body fat, and maturity of liver enzymes involved in drug metabolism influence the rate at which a drug is metabolized and eliminated. Each of these factors varies as a function of stage of development. For example, children and adolescents are more vulnerable to some drug effects because they do not have the ability to metabolize certain drugs in as efficient a manner as adults (Goodman, Hardman, Limbird, & Gilman, 2001). The implications of a slower metabolic transformation are that the active drug or active metabolite remains in the bloodstream for a longer period of time and often increases the duration of the drug's effects. Blood level engendered by a dose of drug is also an important determinant of the effect of a drug (e.g., blood alcohol levels and performance impairment). Body mass is an important determinant of blood levels engendered by a dose of a drug such that blood concentration is proportional to body mass. Because children and adolescents are typically smaller than the average adult, drug doses typically used by adults will engender relatively higher blood concentrations in children and adolescents than in adults. For example, when a 200 lb (or 90.72 kg) man consumes 100 mg of caffeine, he consumes a dose of 1.10 mg/kg of his body weight. If a 90 lb (or 40.82 kg) adolescent boy consumes the same beverage containing 100 mg of caffeine, he consumes a dose of 2.45 mg/kg, over two times the relative dose consumed by the adult man.

Relative drug dose determined by body mass is relevant when examining the effects of drugs in the fetus and infant. Drugs pass from mother to fetus through the vasculature of the placenta and to the newborn through breast milk. Many compounds that the mother consumes during pregnancy cross the placenta and enter the bloodstream of the fetus (Myllynen, Pasanen, & Pelkonen, 2005). The total dose of the drug that reaches the fetus is dependent on the dose of the drug ingested by the mother, the manner in which the drug is excreted, and the metabolic rate and pathway of the drug (Ostrea, Mantaring, & Silvestre, 2004). Several reviews detail the effects and risks associated with placental transfer of a wide range of licit and illicit drugs (Briggs, Freeman, & Yaffe, 1998; Garland, 1998; Ostrea et al., 2004). Mothers can also expose infants to drugs through breast milk. The total dose that reaches the infant depends on the dose the mother ingested, the duration of the drug regimen (occasional vs. consistent use), the route of administration (drugs that enter the mother's system parenterally are typically less concentrated in the breast milk than those administered orally), the pharmacokinetics of the drug (drugs with longer half-lives have greater potential to collect in significant amounts in milk), and the infant's ability to absorb, metabolize, and excrete the drug, with older infants being able to process most drugs more efficiently than premature or younger infants (Ostrea et al., 2004).

Neuropharmacology

Neuronal communication in the brain occurs through an electrochemical process, with electrical impulses in a neuron modulating the release of chemicals [i.e., neurotransmitters, such as dopamine, serotonin, endogenous opiates, N-methyl-D-aspartate (NMDA), gamma-aminobutyric acid (GABA), and acetylcholine], and released chemicals diffusing across small spaces (i.e., synapse) between adjacent neurons and binding with proteins (i.e., receptors) on the membranes of the adjacent neurons to modulate electrical signals and other activities in the adjacent neurons. Neurotransmitters are then deactivated through metabolism or reabsorbed by neurons for reuse. Psychoactive drugs capitalize on this system, modulating action at the receptor level and altering the manner in which neurons regulate neurotransmitters. Homeostatic functions keep a regular balance of neurotransmitter release and inhibition, so when drugs act on this tightly-regulated system, effects may occur in hormonal action, learning, memory, mood, reward, and behavior.

Most drugs of abuse have direct or indirect effects on neurons utilizing dopamine as the neurotransmitter signal, particularly those in the dopamine-rich mesolimbocortical system (e.g., caudate/putamen, nucleus accumbens, tuberculum olfactorium, and prefrontal and frontal cortex), sometimes referred to as the dopamine reward pathway. Increased activation of dopamine release (i.e., potentiation) in this pathway is a common neuropharmacological mechanism of action of the drugs that function as reinforcers (i.e., drugs with abuse liability). The mesolimbocortical system is still undergoing development in childhood and adolescence, and it has been argued that enhanced stimulation of this pathway during development, as would occur during exposure to drugs of abuse, can cause permanent changes in the sensitivity of these regions (e.g., Andersen & Navalta, 2004).

Summary

The prenatal fetal stage, continuing through birth, childhood, and adolescence, is a time of rapid neurodevelopment with synaptic connections continually forming and brain structures constantly developing. Exposure to drugs and other teratogens during these critical periods of development has both short- and long-term health consequences. Psychoactive drugs are of particular concern, given that these compounds have direct effects on brain function and engender both short- and long-term effects on the brain and behavior, with risk of exposure elevated among psychoactive drugs of abuse.

Caffeine

Caffeine is the most widely consumed psychoactive drug, with 80% of the world's population consuming caffeine daily (Barone & Roberts, 1996; James, 1991). It is estimated that 96% of adults (Hughes & Oliveto, 1997) and 98% of children

(Morgan, Stults, & Zabik, 1982) consume caffeine on a weekly basis. Despite the seeming ubiquity of caffeine exposure, the health and behavioral implications of caffeine exposure have received minimal attention, particularly prenatal and post-natal exposure.

Mechanisms of Action

Caffeine (1,3,7-trimethylxanthine) is a purine alkaloid found in the beans, leaves, and fruits of over 60 plants (Weinberg & Bealer, 2001). Effects in the central nerv-ous system (CNS) occur primarily through binding with and blocking the mem-brane proteins (i.e., receptors) that are activated by the endogenous neurotransmitter adenosine (Daly & Fredholm, 1998; Fredholm, Bättig, Holmén, Nehlig, & Zvartau, 1999). Adenosine is an inhibitory neuromodulator that increases sedation and acts as an anticonvulsant. In addition, adenosine decreases blood pressure, respiration, gastric secretions, diuresis, and lipolysis (Daly & Fredholm, 1998; Garrett & Griffiths, 1996). By blocking adenosine receptors, caffeine antagonizes the typical effects of adenosine, such as sedation, which results in the stimulant-like effects of the drug.

Caffeine has indirect agonist effects on dopamine activity which is related to its adenosine receptor blockade. Heavy concentrations of adenosine receptors are found in the dopamine reward pathway (Daly & Fredholm, 1998; Ferre, Fuxe, von Euler, Johansson, & Fredholm, 1992; Ferre, von Euler, Johansson, Fredholm, & Fuxe, 1991). Adenosine receptors regulate dopamine release as well as GABA neuron activation; GABA serves an inhibitory role in the dopamine reward path-way. By antagonizing adenosine, caffeine indirectly enhances dopamine release and diminishes the inhibitory functions of the GABA system (Daly & Fredholm, 1998; Ferre et al., 1992; Garrett & Griffiths, 1996).

Epidemiology and Health Consequences of Prenatal, Early Childhood, and Adolescent Caffeine Exposure

On average, a mug of drip-brewed coffee contains ~100 mg of caffeine. A similar size serving of tea contains 80 mg, and a 12-oz serving of a caffeinated soda con-tains ~40 mg. The average daily amount of caffeine consumption for adults is ~230 mg/day (3.3 mg/kg/day), with 30% of adults consuming more than 500 mg/day (7.1 mg/kg/day; DSM-IV). Caffeine is the psychotropic drug most commonly consumed by pregnant and nursing women, with 60–68% of this population con-suming moderate amounts (100–200 mg) of caffeine daily (Frary, Johnson, & Wang, 2005; Pirie, Lando, Curry, McBride, & Grothaus, 2000). While mean daily caffeine consumption for children and adolescents has been estimated to range from 37 mg/day to 63 mg/day (Morgan, Stults, & Zabik, 1982; Valek, Laslavi , &

Laslavić, 2004), 20–25% of this population consume over 100 mg/day, with occasional reports of consumption of 290–500 mg/day or more (Leviton, 1992; Rapoport, Berg, Ismond, Zahn, & Neims, 1984). Caffeine consumption does not vary as a function of gender, but differences have been reported among racially classified groups (Arbeit et al., 1988; Leviton, 1992). It is important to point out that soft drink consumption, which is the major source of caffeine in school-aged children, has more than tripled since 1970 (Story & Neumark-Sztainer, 1998; Valek, Laslavić, & Laslavić, 2004). Sales of caffeinated "energy" drinks, which contain 2–3 times the amount of caffeine per given volume compared to conventional caffeinated soft drinks, are increasing among adolescents and young adults (Malinauskas, Aeby, Overton, Carpenter-Aeby, & Barber-Heidal, 2007).

In the third trimester of pregnancy, caffeine's half-life (amount of time required to eliminate 50% of the drug concentration) increases from 2–6 h to 10–20 h (Brazier, Ritter, Berland, Khenfer, & Faucon, 1983; Knutti, Rothweiler, & Schlatter, 1982). In utero, caffeine is passed from mother to child through the placenta, readily entering the fetal bloodstream, such that ~75% of babies are born with detectable levels of caffeine in their blood (Brazier & Salle, 1981; Dumas et al., 1982). After birth, it is also passed via breast milk to nursing infants (Benowitz, 1990; Julien, 2001). From prenatal stages to at least 3 months of age, the hepatic enzymes necessary to metabolize the drug are absent or immature, causing the drug's half-life to be anywhere from 32 h to 149 h (Parsons & Neims, 1981). As such, blood levels of caffeine may be elevated in the neonate and newborn in relation to that seen in adolescents and adults. After the metabolic enzymes develop, metabolic rates approximate that of adults (James, 1991).

The degree to which caffeine exposure affects the health and well-being of a fetus, neonate, newborn, or infant remains unclear. The research literature on this topic is vast and equivocal, with reports ranging from virtually no adverse health consequences (Giannelli, Doyle, Roman, Pelerin, & Hermon, 2003; Leviton & Cowan, 2002; Savitz, Chan, Herring, Howards, & Hartmann, 2008) to early term birth and increased risk of miscarriage (Bech, Nohr, Vaeth, Henriksen, & Olsen, 2005; George, Granath, Johansson, Olander, & Cnattingius, 2006; Rasch, 2003). There have also been reports of a neonatal abstinence syndrome (Leviton, 1992), but it has not been thoroughly investigated. More research is needed to clarify the effects of caffeine exposure in utero and in the early stages of infancy.

A variety of studies have examined the effects of caffeine in children and adolescents. In normal children and adolescents, low doses of caffeine (3 mg/kg) have been reported to improve attention and performance of vigilance tasks, reduce reaction time, improve manual dexterity, improve memory, reduce errors of omission on continuous performance tests, and increase speech production (Castellanos & Rapoport, 2002; Elkins et al., 1981; Hughes & Hale, 1998; Leon, 2000; Leviton, 1992; Stein, Krasowski, Leventhal, Phillips, & Bender, 1996; Rapoport, Elkins, Neims, Zahn, & Berg, 1981), particularly when performance is less than optimal due to boredom or fatigue. Higher doses of caffeine (>3 mg/kg) can be associated with difficulty sleeping and feeling tired in the morning, inattentiveness, restlessness, nausea, stomachache, and dysphoria – including nervousness, jitteriness, and anxiety (Hughes & Hale,

1998; Orbeta, Overpeck, Ramcharran, Kogan, & Ledsky, 2006; Pollak & Bright, 2003). Symptoms of caffeine withdrawal (Bernstein et al., 1998; Hughes & Hale, 1998) and caffeinism (Castellanos & Rapoport, 2002) have been noted in children and adolescents. In general, these effects are similar to those reported in adults.

There is evidence that heavy caffeine use is associated with drug use and other problem behaviors in children and adolescents (Tennant & Detels, 1976). High levels of caffeine consumption in early- and mid-adolescents are associated with cigarette use and aggressive behavior, conduct problems, social problems, attention problems, and attention deficit/hyperactivity disorder (ADHD) problems, as reported by adolescents and their parents (Martin, personal communication). It is not known whether behavioral problems in children and adolescents who consume large amounts of caffeine are due to caffeine, or whether children and adolescents with these problems consume large amounts of caffeine in order to self-medicate their symptoms (Leviton, 1992).

Caffeine may interact with and enhance the effects of other drugs of abuse. For example, caffeine has been found to enhance the reinforcing and stimulant subjective effects of nicotine in adult cigarette smokers (Jones & Griffiths, 2003). It is not known if this interaction occurs among children and adolescents, and further research is required to examine whether caffeine use increases sensitivity to the pharmacological effects of other drugs of abuse during development.

Implications

Levels of caffeine exposure during human development are higher than any other psychoactive drug. Caffeine levels during prenatal development and for the first several months after birth are elevated due to the absence of enzymes required for efficient caffeine metabolism. Caffeine intake in sodas and energy drinks is increasing among children and adolescents, and heavy intake has been linked to drug use and other problem behaviors. Despite the somewhat ubiquitous nature of its exposure during development, with detectable levels of caffeine even appearing in drinking water (Soliman et al., 2007), there is no consensus regarding the health consequences of caffeine exposure, and additional research is warranted.

Tobacco

Tobacco is one of the most common and harmful substances used by humans. Health-related problems associated with tobacco use contribute to 400,000 premature deaths annually (Centers for Disease Control and Prevention, CDCP, 2005). Based on the current rates of daily smoking among high school seniors – 12.2% in 2006, down from a 10-year high of 24.6% in 1997 (Johnston, O'Malley, Bachman, & Schulenbert, 2007) – it is estimated that over 2 million people currently under the age of 18 will die prematurely from tobacco (e.g., CDCP, 1997).

Mechanisms of Action

Nicotine binds with membrane proteins (i.e., receptors) widely distributed throughout the brain that bind with the endogenous neurotransmitter acetylcholine. These "nicotinic acetylcholine" receptors are made up of alpha and beta protein subunits. Nicotinic acetylcholine receptors exert a variety of effects in the CNS, including modulation of dopamine function. As with other drugs of abuse, nicotine modulation of the dopamine reward pathway is considered a primary mechanism for its abuse liability (Picciotto & Corrigall, 2002). The alpha-4, beta-2 nicotinic acetylcholine receptor type is most closely linked with dopamine modulation and nicotine dependence (Tapper et al., 2004). Nicotine enhancement of dopamine neurotransmission is believed to be responsible for tolerance to nicotine and for the development of conditioning to environmental cues associated with smoking behavior (Liu et al., 2003; Maskos et al., 2005; Picciotto, Zoli, & Changeux, 1999; Pidoplichko et al., 2004; Salminen et al., 2004; Tapper et al., 2004).

Epidemiology and Health Consequences of Prenatal, Early Childhood, and Adolescent Nicotine Exposure

Approximately 23% of pregnant women report smoking during the 3 months prior to pregnancy, with 13% continuing to smoke throughout pregnancy (CDCP, 2002). This frequency is likely to be an underestimate of true rates since it is based on survey data. Rates of smoking identified with surveys are generally lower than those identified when quantitative measures of smoking (e.g., salivary cotinine) are used to determine smoking rates (Walsh, Redman, & Adamson, 1996).

In utero exposure to nicotine has important implications for brain development. Nicotine receptors appear by the end of the first month of human fetal life and are thought to be critical for brain growth and neuronal connectivity, including modulation of nerve growth and formation of new synapse connections among neurons in the brain (Hellstrom-Lindahl, Seiger, Kjaeldgaard, & Nordberg, 2001). Animal studies have found that pre- and postnatal nicotine exposure has been associated with alterations of a variety of endogenous neurotransmitter systems, including dopamine, norepinephrine, and serotonin (Muneoka et al., 2001; Richardson & Tizabi, 1994; Slotkin, Pinkerton, Auman, Qiaio, & Seidler, 2002; Xu, Seidler, Ali, Slikker, & Slotkin, 2001). A recent study suggests that the thickness of regions in the cortex (orbitofrontal, middle frontal, and parahippocampal) associated with cognition and social control is reduced in adolescents exposed to maternal smoking (Toro et al., 2008).

In utero exposure to nicotine has important implications for behavioral development. Prenatal nicotine exposure is associated with the development of altered patterns of behavior during early postnatal life (Law et al., 2003). For example, toddlers exposed in utero are more likely to be impulsive, hyperactive, and oppositional and to have lower language skills than their unexposed peers (Day, Richardson, Goldschmidt, & Cornelius, 2000; Faden & Graubard, 2000; Fried & Watkinson,

1990; Wakschlag, Leventhal, Pine, Pickett, & Carter., 2006). Multiple studies suggest that these effects continue to be expressed during adolescence. Furthermore, in utero exposure increases the risk of developing both internalizing and externalizing disorders (e.g., mood disorders, conduct disorder) known to be risk factors for the emergence of adolescent experimental and persistent smoking (Fried & Watkinson, 2001; Upadhyaya, Deas, Brady, & Kruesi, 2002). Postnatal environmental tobacco smoke exposure may also have an impact on child and adolescent brain and behavioral development (Okoli, Kelly, & Hahn, 2007), although disentangling postnatal and prenatal associations is methodologically difficult (Eskenazi & Castorina, 1999).

By the age of 10, nicotine-exposed offspring are more likely to have tried smoking, and smoking rates among the prenatally exposed remain higher during adolescence (Cornelius, Leech, Goldschmidt, & Day, 2000; Nichter, Nichter, Thompson, Shiffman, & Moscicki, 2002). Adult women exposed to tobacco in utero are 4 times more likely to be smokers than those who were not exposed (Kandel, Wu & Davies, 1994). It is clear that there are multiple environmental, biological, and genetic factors that contribute to tobacco use, and many of these factors may contribute to multigenerational tobacco use.

Lifetime tobacco use, from one-time experimentation through heavy daily smoking, has been decreasing from a 10-year peak of 65.4% in 1997 to 47.1% in 2006, although the downward trend has begun to level off in recent years (Johnston et al., 2007). The majority of adult smokers initiate tobacco use before age 18, and the earlier the age of smoking initiation, the greater the likelihood of lifetime use (Kopstein, 2001).

Nicotine has been described as one of the most addicting substances of abuse based on observations that close to 32% of individuals who "ever" smoke go on to develop nicotine dependence (Anthony, Warner, & Kessler, 1994). The next closest drug is heroin, with 23% of ever users developing dependence, followed by cocaine at 17% and alcohol at 15%. Rates of nicotine dependence among adolescents have been difficult to determine, in part, because the criteria used to establish dependence among adults may not be as effective in assessing dependence among adolescents (Colby, Tiffany, Shiffman, & Niaura, 2000). Adolescents endorse more symptoms of dependence than do adults smoking the same number of cigarettes per day, suggesting that adolescents may be more sensitive to the effects of nicotine (Kandel & Chen, 2000). Kandel and colleagues (2005) found that various measures of nicotine dependence yielded different rates of dependence between adolescents and adults, especially at low levels of smoking. However, dependence rates became more consistent between adolescents and adults as the smoking rate approached one pack per day. In cross-sectional studies, withdrawal symptoms have been reported earlier in the course of tobacco use among adolescents than among adults, and may precede regular or daily use among adolescent smokers (DiFranza et al., 2007; O'Loughlin et al., 2003). It is possible that the reinforcing effects of nicotine are enhanced among adolescents, and that young smokers may develop tolerance and physical dependence more rapidly upon initiation of tobacco smoking than do adults. Based on when smoking is initiated and the associated adverse lifetime health consequences of tobacco use, nicotine addiction has been labeled a disease of adolescence (Kessler et al., 1997).

For at least some neurotransmitter systems (e.g., serotonin and acetylcholine), the CNS responses to nicotine during adolescence appear to be similar to those observed during other stages of life (Trauth, McCook, Seidler, & Slotkin, 2000a; Xu, Seidler, Ali, Slikker, & Slotkin, 2001). However, some unique nicotine effects occur during adolescence (i.e., effects that are different than those observed during either in utero or adult nicotine exposure [Slotkin, 2002]). Laboratory experiments demonstrate differences between adolescent and adult behavioral responses to nicotine. Trauth, Seidler, and Slotkin (2000b), for example, gave nicotine to adolescent rats in a manner designed to mimic the effects of smoking over a period of days, then observed them in a novel environment and while performing a passive avoidance task. Contrary to effects seen in adult rats, nicotine decreased grooming behavior in the novel environment by adolescent females and enhanced passive avoidance behavior 24 h posttraining. Kota and Martin (2007), in a series of behavioral experiments with mice, found that adolescent mice exhibited nicotine-induced changes in receptor sensitivity and fewer withdrawal signs than did adult mice. A series of experiments by Faraday, Elliot, Phillips, and Grunberg (2003) demonstrated that behavioral sensitivity to nicotine in adult rats was increased by prior exposure to nicotine during adolescence. Timing of initial exposure also impacted rates of nicotine self-administration during adulthood, with adolescent-exposed rats self-administering more nicotine than did adult-exposed rats (Adriani et al., 2003; Levin, Rezvani, Montoya, Rose, & Swartzwelder, 2003).

Implications

There is considerable evidence indicating that risk for development of nicotine dependence is increased by nicotine exposure during development (Ginzel et al., 2007). Prenatal nicotine exposure engenders adverse behavioral outcomes that, in turn, are associated with increased risk of adolescent smoking. Growing evidence supports the importance of adolescence as a critical time period during which nicotine exposure may permanently restructure brain form and function and increase lifetime risk of smoking. Environmental factors interacting with this biological vulnerability may set the stage for adult nicotine dependence and other psychopathology. Consequently, strategies and policies designed to limit exposure to nicotine during adolescence have the potential for prevention of significant adult morbidity and mortality.

Alcohol

In the year 2000, it was estimated that 85,000 deaths in the United States (3.5% of all deaths) were attributed to alcohol consumption, among behavioral risk factors, the third-leading cause of death behind tobacco use and poor diet and exercise (Mokdad, Marks, Stroup, & Gerberding, 2004). Alcohol-associated motor vehicle accidents alone are responsible for 5,000 adolescent deaths annually (National

Highway Traffic Safety Administration, NHTSA, 2003). In addition to physical injuries, adverse consequences related to excessive alcohol consumption include development of chronic diseases, including psychiatric disorders, neurologic impairment, cardiovascular disease, malignant neoplasms, and fetal alcohol spectrum disorders (Cargiulo, 2007). Adverse social and cultural consequences of alcohol use are also apparent (National Institute on Alcohol Abuse and Alcoholism, NIAAA, 2004–2005). Fetal and infantile alcohol exposure is predictive of subsequent alcohol use during adolescence, and alcohol use during adolescence is associated with excessive alcohol use later in life (Spear, 2002; Spear & Molina, 2005). Alcohol use during adolescence is associated with elevated risks for liver disease and adverse endocrine and metabolic effects (NIAAA, 2004–2005). As with tobacco, it has become apparent that alcohol is a problem of adolescence.

Mechanisms of Action

Alcohol engenders multiple neurochemical effects and has a potent adverse impact on the developing brain. Changes in the integrity of the neuronal cell membrane occur during intoxication (Deitrich, Dunwiddie, Harris, & Erwin, 1989). Alcohol acts on multiple neurotransmitter systems, including NMDA, GABA, serotonin, and the endogenous opiate systems, with variability in the form and function of these neurotransmitter systems having a likely role in interindividual sensitivity to alcohol's effects (Charness, Hu, Edwards, & Querimit, 1993; Lesch, 2005; Wafford, Burnett, Harris, & Whiting, 1993). The NMDA and GABA systems modulate dopamine function, and alcohol modulates the dopamine reward pathway via its effects on NMDA and GABA receptors (Grobin, Mattews, Devaud, & Morrow, 1998; Verheul, van den Brink, & Geerlings, 1999; Zhang, Maldve, & Morrisett, 2006). The neurotoxic effects of acute and chronic alcohol exposure are also mediated via these mechanisms. Abstinence following heavy alcohol exposure (e.g., alcohol withdrawal) has adverse effects on brain neurotransmitter systems and neuronal cell function (Grobin et al., 1998; Tsai et al., 1998).

Epidemiology and Health Consequences of Prenatal, Early Childhood, and Adolescent Alcohol Exposure

As with nicotine, in utero alcohol exposure can have a profound impact on brain development, placing exposed adolescents at greater risk of developing adverse behavioral health outcomes. In utero rates of alcohol exposure are estimated at 13% of all pregnancies with 3% of pregnant women reporting frequent (seven or more drinks per week) or binge drinking (five or more drinks in one setting) (Bertrand et al., 2004). In the United States, about 1,000–6,000 babies are born with fetal alcohol syndrome every year, and an estimated 3,000–18,000 infants/year are born with fetal alcohol effects (CDCP, 2004). Even very low levels of in utero exposure have been associated with adverse cognitive and other behavioral health effects, including inattention, reduced memory, hyperactivity, impulsivity, and aggression; these effects may persist into adolescence (Sokol, Delaney-Black, & Nordstrom, 2003; Sood et al., 2001).

Lifetime alcohol use reported by high school seniors surpasses tobacco and marijuana use (Johnston et al., 2007). During the last 10 years, lifetime use (which includes one time use through heavy use) peaked at 81.7% in 1997 and decreased to 72.7% in 2006 (Johnston et al., 2007). Binge drinking (defined as consumption of five or more drinks in a row in the 2 weeks preceding the survey) peaked at 31.5% in 1997 and was down to 25.4% in 2006. In contrast to lifetime use, daily use of alcohol among high school seniors is lower than that of tobacco and marijuana, ranging from 3.9% in 1997 to about 3% in recent years.

Among alcohol-abusing adults, onset of alcohol use typically occurs before age 21, with increases in consumption occurring across early- and mid-adolescence (Wagner & Anthony, 2002). Similar to patterns seen with tobacco, earlier onset of alcohol use is associated with higher rates of alcohol dependence, and close to half of those who initiate alcohol use prior to age 14 subsequently develop alcohol dependence (Fergusson, Lynskey, & Horwood, 1994; Grant & Dawson, 1997).

The creation of new brain cells during adolescence (and other times) is important for the development of optimal learning and memory capacity. Crews, Mdzinarishvili, Kim, He, and Nixon (2006) demonstrated that acute alcohol interfered with the formation of new neuronal cells in adolescent rats, a process that may disrupt optimal cognitive development at a critical time. Structural changes have also been identified in adolescents and adults as a function of heavy alcohol consumption over many years. DeBellis and colleagues (2005) found reduced prefrontal cortex volume in adolescents with early onset alcohol use and comorbid mental health conditions, although the study design was not able to differentiate acquired from preexisting volume decrements. Another study by DeBellis and colleagues (2000) found reduced hippocampal volumes in individuals with early onset alcohol-use disorders, and age of onset was inversely associated with total volume, suggesting that hippocampal development and associated memory processes may be particularly vulnerable to the impairing effects of alcohol during adolescence.

Evidence of differences in sensitivity to alcohol as a function of age is mixed in rodent models. Compared to adults, adolescent rats are less sensitive to sedation and motor impairment but more sensitive to social facilitation (Spear, 2004). Sensitivity differences have been associated with alcohol effects on NMDA receptor activity (Swartzwelder, Wilson, & Tayyeb, 1995). In humans, tolerance to the effects of alcohol has been shown to be greater in males with a family history of alcohol dependence and fetal alcohol exposure (Schuckit & Smith, 2004; Spear, 2002).

Adolescents using alcohol are at risk for cognitive impairments thought to be associated with the toxic effects of the alcohol on brain development. Brown and Tapert (2004) found visuospatial deficits and information retrieval deficits 3 weeks after adolescents detoxified from heavy drinking patterns. Among adolescents, the presence of an alcohol-use disorder has been associated with changes in working memory task performance in a functional neuroimaging study (Sher, 2006).

Changes such as these may contribute to a dynamic negatively spiraling interaction between biological and environmental risk factors. For example, students with low school connectedness are at increased risk of problematic use of alcohol, and if cognitive impairments develop with use, then the likelihood of a negative trajectory of poor academic achievement and further disconnection with school is more likely, intensifying the risk for continued heavy alcohol use and dependence.

Environmental and biological factors may interact to shape neuroadaptation. Exposure to traumatic experiences, such as violence, is a well-known risk factor for adolescent alcohol use (Vermeiren, Schwab-Stone, Deboutte, Leckman, & Ruchkin, 2003). Less dramatic, but not less important as a risk factor, the experience of stress in social interactions increases the risk for alcohol use and progression to dependence (Kreek & Koob, 1998). Animal models suggest age-differentiated responses to alcohol-associated learning under stress and nonstress conditions. For example, Song and colleagues (2007) found that adolescent mice were more sensitive than adult mice to the effects of stress during an alcohol-conditioned place preference paradigm. After exposure to chronic stress, adolescent mice demonstrated greater preference for an alcohol-paired environment (compared to the saline paired), whereas for adult mice, the stress exposure did not change place preference.

In addition to affecting the development of dependence, the age of initial alcohol use may have an impact on response to treatment. Odansetron decreases alcohol craving by reducing serotonin receptor activity. Subjects with onset of alcohol dependence before the age of 25 years were found to have a more robust therapeutic response to odansetron than did those exhibiting alcohol-related problems at a later age (Johnson et al., 2000).

Implications

Consistent with findings for nicotine and other drugs, there is a considerable body of evidence that the brain of the developing organism is at increased vulnerability to the adverse effects of alcohol from conception through adolescence and that exposure to alcohol during this period of development may cause long-lasting or permanent neuroadaptation that may be associated with deficits in cognitive, emotional, and behavioral function during later life. These findings underscore the critical importance of early prevention and treatment of alcohol problems among children and adolescents.

Therapeutic Stimulants

Stimulants are the most frequently prescribed and thoroughly investigated medications for the management of ADHD (e.g., Barkley, 1991; Swanson et al., 2002a; Zito et al., 1999), which is most commonly diagnosed and treated during childhood.

Medical use of stimulants has steadily increased in the past 20 years, and use in the United States is much greater than in other countries (Scheffler, Hinshaw, Modrek, & Levine, 2007; Zuvekas, Vitiello, & Norquist, 2006). Associated with the rise in therapeutic stimulant use, there is increasing concern about the misuse of stimulants by students and the diversion of prescription stimulants both in college student and patient populations (Johnston, O'Malley, & Bachman, 2003; McCabe, Teter, & Boyd, 2004b, 2006a, 2006b; McCabe, Teter, Boyd, & Guthrie, 2004a; Upadhyaya et al., 2005b; Wilens, Gignac, Swezey, Monuteaux, & Biederman, 2006).

Mechanisms of Action

Most therapeutic stimulants have two overlapping neuropharmacological effects: they inhibit monoamine reuptake and they enhance monoamine neurotransmitter release. Both these actions increase the extracellular concentrations of dopamine and norepinephrine, although magnitude of effect is greater at dopamine sites, particularly those in the dopamine reward pathway (e.g., Solanto, 1998; Volkow et al., 2001). The specific mechanisms by which these effects are produced vary among the different stimulant medications (e.g., Ritalin, Adderall, and Dexedrine). Increased extracellular dopamine and norepinephrine is associated with enhanced wakefulness, alertness, mood, initiative, confidence, concentration, motor activity, and task performance and decreased fatigue (Goodman, Hardman, Limbird, & Gilman, 2001).

Epidemiology and Health Consequences of Prenatal, Early Childhood, and Adolescent

While it had long been thought that abuse of prescription stimulant medication was low, recent evidence suggests that prescription stimulant misuse may be a growing problem. In healthy adults, stimulant medications function as potent reinforcers and have a well-established abuse liability (e.g., Henningfield, Johnson, Jasinski, & Bozarth, 1987; Jasinski, Johnson, & Henningfield, 1984; Martin, Sloan, Sapira, & Jasinski, 1971). Nonmedical prescription stimulant use (i.e., diversion of prescription medication) appears to be on the rise. Significant numbers of college-aged individuals who have received prescriptions for stimulant medication report misusing their own or other prescription medication (Arria et al., 2008; Upadhyaya et al., 2005b). Many of those who misuse prescription medication meet the criteria for conduct disorder and substance use disorder (Wilens et al., 2006). Diversion of prescription stimulant medication in college-aged students who initiated treatment in grade school is no greater than that of the general population, but diversion escalates among college-aged students who were first prescribed stimulant medication after completing grade school (McCabe et al., 2006a). Nonmedical stimulant use is also increasing among high-school aged adolescents, particularly among those with lower grade point averages. Poulin (2007) reported that about 26% of junior and senior high school students who were receiving prescribed stimulants had given or sold their medication to others. Illicit stimulant medication use among high school students has been linked with the use of other drugs, including tobacco cigarette smoking, heavy episodic drinking, marijuana and cocaine use, as well as peer drug use (McCabe et al., 2004a; Poulin, 2007).

It is important to balance the risk of prescription stimulant misuse with the potential clinical benefits of the medication. It is somewhat ironic, for example, that while there is risk for the misuse of prescription stimulants, these medications may also be protective for other forms of drug abuse, with the possible exception of tobacco. The interval of time between initial use of a drug and the development of abuse or dependence is significantly shorter for adolescents with ADHD than for age-matched normals (Biederman et al., 1997), even when controlling for comorbid conditions, such as conduct disorder (Wilens, Biederman, Mick, Faraone, & Spencer, 1997). However, rates of drug abuse and dependence are actually lower in ADHD adolescents who are treated effectively with stimulants as compared to ADHD adolescents who are not treated (Biederman, Wilens, Mick, Spencer, & Faraone, 1999; Wilens, Faraone, Biederman, & Gunawardene, 2003).

It is possible, however, that stimulant medication may actually exacerbate the risk of tobacco use. ADHD is a risk factor for early initiation of tobacco use (Milberger, Biederman, Faraone, Chen, & Jones, 1997). Stimulant medications increase tobacco-smoking behavior in healthy adults (e.g., Henningfield & Griffiths, 1981; Kelly, Foltin, & Fischman, 1991; Rush et al., 2005). Among ADHD patients who are treated effectively with stimulants, tobacco-smoking rates are higher than among those who are not taking prescription stimulants (Lambert & Hartsough, 1998). It is possible that the severity of ADHD symptoms was higher among those receiving stimulant medications in this study, so additional research is required to determine whether stimulant medication use alters the risk of tobacco smoking among individuals with ADHD.

While the rates of stimulant medication use among pregnant women are not known, it is likely that as the rates of prescription stimulant medication use increase, the numbers of females of child-bearing age who become pregnant while taking prescription stimulant medications will also increase (note: stimulant medications can interfere with the efficacy of oral birth control medication). Preclinical studies indicate that exposure to drugs during early brain development can cause lasting effects at the cellular level. For example, daily prenatal exposure to dl-amphetamine (0.5 mg/kg/day) induced changes in the biochemistry of the central catecholaminergic system of the adult rat (Nasello, Astrada, & Ramirez, 1974; Nasello & Ramirez, 1978a, 1978b; Ramirez & Carrer 1983; Ramirez, Carrer, & Nasello, 1979). Nasif, Cuadra, and Ramirez (1999) did not observe any gross teratogenic effects of prenatal exposure to d-amphetamine, but they did observe decreased firing rate of norepinephrine neurons in the locus ceruleus in adult rats that had received prenatal exposure to the drug. As such, there is some evidence that prenatal exposure to stimulant drugs can produce long-term changes in neuronal cellular function.

The Food and Drug Administration (FDA) has placed therapeutic stimulants in Category C (i.e., animal reproduction studies have shown an adverse effect on the fetus, or there are no adequate and well-controlled studies in humans, and/or the benefits from the use of the drug in pregnant women may be acceptable despite its potential risks), and as such, these medications should be prescribed to pregnant women only if the benefit justifies the potential risk to the fetus (Berkowitz, Coustan, & Mochizuki, 1998). Despite escalating use of stimulant medications, few clinical studies have examined their potential teratogenic effects. Several studies examining the potential teratogenic effects of nonmedical stimulant use (cocaine and methamphetamine) have been conducted and found growth restrictive effects on the fetus (Bada et al., 2002; Smith et al., 2006).

Preclinical studies suggest that exposure to stimulant medication during early childhood may have the potential to disrupt the normal sequence of gene expression in the developing brain, resulting in altered neurochemistry and behavior, and that these effects can endure into adulthood (Chase, Carrey, Brown, & Wilkinson, 2005a). Moll, Hause, Ruether, Rothenberger, and Huether (2001), for example, found that methylphenidate exposure in young rats caused a 25% decrease in the density of striatal dopamine transporters which persisted into adulthood, even after discontinuation of the medication in the prepubertal rat. In a three-part study using adolescent gerbils, Grund and colleagues (2007) demonstrated that (1) early exposure to methamphetamine resulted in a 30% decrease in dopamine fiber innervations in the prefrontal cortex and amygdala complex; (2) these abnormalities were prevented by methylphenidate administration during adolescence; and (3) methylphenidate alone did not alter dopamine innervation. Researchers have documented other effects of stimulant medications on gene expression, but the clinical implications remain to be explored (Chase, Carrey, Brown, & Wilkinson, 2005b; Chase, Carrey, Soo, & Wilkinson, 2007; Hawken, Brown, Carrey, & Wilkinson, 2004).

Sensitization (progressively augmented behavioral response following repetitive administration of a drug) and cross-sensitization associated with repeated or chronic stimulant administration have been commonly reported in preclinical studies (Brandon, Marinelli, Baker, & Whiteet, 2001; Gaytan, Yang, Swann, & Dafny, 2000; Guerriero, Hayes, Dhaliwal, Ren, & Kosofsky, 2006; Kuczenski & Segal, 2001, 2002; Torres-Reveron & Dow-Edwards, 2005; Yang, Swann, & Dafny, 2003). Valvassori et al. (2007) demonstrated that early exposure to methylphenidate in adolescent rats resulted in augmented locomotor response after amphetamine challenge as compared to the control group, suggesting pretreatment with methylphenidate during adolescence elicited cross-sensitization (the behavioral augmentation that occurs when pretreatment leads to a greater sensitivity to another substance) to subsequent amphetamine administration in adulthood (Aizenstein, Segal, & Kuczenski, 1990).

Among children, the most common side effects of therapeutic stimulant use are insomnia, decreased appetite and weight loss, headache, fatigue, abdominal cramps, jitteriness, increase in heart rate and blood pressure, and emotional liability including depression, irritability, and increased frequency of crying. Delirium, psychotic symptoms with vivid hallucinations and paranoia, can be seen with higher doses. Stimulants have peripheral adrenergic effects and increase systolic and diastolic blood pressure and heart rate (Efron, Jarman, & Barker et al., 1998; Goodman, Hardman, Limbird, & Gilman, 2001; Wolraich & Doffing, 2004). Amphetamine abuse is associated with increased risk of hemorrhagic stroke in young adults (Westover, McBride, & Haley, 2007). (Note: an FDA committee recently decided to require a warning label on stimulant drugs used to treat ADHD. The warning is required because stimulants cause a rise in blood pressure and heart rate and may increase the risk of heart attack, stroke, or sudden death [Charatan, 2006]). As mentioned earlier, stimulant medications have a well-documented abuse liability among healthy adults. Evidence suggesting that stimulant medications may have abuse liability in children and adolescents has been reported. In 1937, Bradley demonstrated that hospitalized children reported positive subjective effects, such as euphoria, following the administration of Benzedrine. Martin, Guenther, Bingcang, Rayens, and Kelly (2007) recently examined the behavioral effects of methylphenidate (0, 0.25 mg/kg) under randomized, double-blind conditions in 24 children with ADHD between the ages of 11 and 15 years. Methylphenidate increased measures of abuse liability adopted for use in children with ADHD (e.g., modified MBG scale of the Addiction Research Center Inventory). In a pilot study, Fredericks and Kollins (2005) observed that three of the five children and adolescents with ADHD reliably chose methylphenidate over placebo under controlled double-blind conditions, suggesting that the drug functions as a reinforcer, at least under some conditions. In an earlier study, they found that young adults with ADHD chose methylphenidate significantly more frequently than placebo or no capsule (Fredericks & Kollins, 2004). The subjects who chose methylphenidate more reliably exhibited greater methylphenidate-induced reductions in ADHD symptoms, suggesting that the reinforcing effects of the drug may have been influenced by the drug's therapeutic effect. These results suggest that stimulant medications may have abuse liability in children comparable to that in adults. However, it is important to note that even given these concerns, if used as prescribed and as indicated, stimulants have a high margin of safety and have been used effectively for decades in treating ADHD (Barkley, 1991; Klein-Schwartz, 2002; Swanson et al., 2002b; Zito et al., 1999).

Implications

It is essential that stimulants should be prescribed only for well-documented disorders. For example, if an adolescent presents for the first time with symptoms of ADHD, the diagnosis must be made rigorously with input from the adolescent, as well as confirmation from parents and educators. Standardized and structured testing including the Conners Rating Scale assist in validation of the diagnosis (Conners, Sitarenios, Parker & Epstein, 1998). The Achenbach, Connors, Quay behavior (ACQ) check list for parents, teachers, and youth is useful for confirming the diagnosis of ADHD and can be used to evaluate comorbidities such as conduct disorder (Achenbach, 1991). Self-report measures and urine drug screening may be helpful in assessing whether or not the patient has a comorbid substance use disorder.

In the clinic setting the decision to use stimulants to treat ADHD may be especially challenging for parents when their adolescents are at the age when risk for experimentation with drugs is increasing. Parents are often concerned about whether the medical use of stimulants could increase the risk of future drug use in their children. The medical and scientific community has also raised concerns about ongoing psychostimulant treatment based on compelling preclinical evidence for the development of behavioral sensitization following repeated exposure to psychostimulants, particularly among adolescent animals (Caster, Walker, & Kuhn, 2007; Kalivas, Sorg, & Hooks, 1993; Schenk & Izenwasser, 2002; Torres-Reveron & Dow-Edwards, 2005), as well as growing numbers of reports of misuse and diversion of prescription stimulants (Johnston et al., 2003; Poulin, 2007; Upadhyaya, Deas, & Brady, 2005a; Wilens et al., 2006). Clinicians who prescribe stimulants (pediatricians, child psychiatrists, family physicians, and neurologists) should inform their patients of the risk of medication diversion. Patients and if appropriate their parents should be informed of potential pressures to share or sell stimulant medication. Prescription-monitoring programs should be considered (Sussman, Pentz, Spruijt-Metz, & Miller, 2006), and random urine drug screening could aid in early identification and prevention of prescription misuse and diversion. Likewise, adolescents who are not being treated for ADHD should be warned about the risks of nonmedical use of prescription medication.

Prescription stimulant misuse and diversion is more likely among individuals with ADHD who are not diagnosed or treated until entering high school. Late treatment and undertreatment of ADHD is associated with the emergence of a constellation of high-risk behaviors; drug diversion may be an element of this constellation. It is equally possible that ADHD is not easily diagnosed in some individuals until supplemental symptom clusters or associated comorbidities, such as sensation seeking or conduct disorder, emerge during the developmental process (Martin et al., 2004). It may be that this subgroup of ADHD adolescents who are engaged in a range of problem behaviors, including other drug use and poor school performance, are at increased risk for misuse and diversion of prescription stimulants (McCabe et al., 2004a, 2004b). While stimulants are the first-line treatment for early-onset ADHD, it remains to be seen whether they should be used for late-onset ADHD patients with high-risk behavior comorbidities. Interestingly, Klein and colleagues (1997) demonstrated that high-dose stimulants enhanced outcome of ADHD with comorbid conduct disorder, and Biederman and colleagues (1999) observed that drug use did not escalate when ADHD adolescents and young adults with substance abuse disorders were treated with stimulants.

Conclusions

This chapter examined the neurobiological implications of exposure to nicotine, alcohol, caffeine, and therapeutic stimulants, the drugs of abuse that are most frequently encountered during human development. Each of these drugs

produces potent neuropharmacological effects on brain function. While it
remains difficult to isolate direct causal influences and disentangle the direct
effects of drug exposure from indirect effects associated with environmental,
social, and cultural influences that are often closely associated with drug exposure, particularly in clinical studies, this chapter provides compelling evidence
that developmental exposure to drugs of abuse can have both subtle and dramatic effects with important behavioral and societal consequences. Levels of
exposure are substantial during all phases of development (i.e., prenatal, postnatal, childhood, and adolescence), and evidence indicates that exposure to
these drugs during critical phases of development have both short- and long-
term consequences. Of critical importance, exposure to psychoactive drugs of
abuse during critical periods of development can engender increased sensitivity
to the neuropharmacological effects of drugs, which, in turn, lead to increased
frequencies of drug use and further changes in sensitivity (e.g., Glantz &
Chambers, 2006; Krasnegor et al., 1986).

References

Achenbach, T. M. (1991). *Integrative guide for the 1991 CBCL 14–18, YSR, and TRF profiles.*
  Burlington, VT: University of Vermont Department of Psychiatry.
Adriani, W., Spijker, S., Deroche-Gamonet, V., Laviola, G., Le Moal, M., Smit, A. B., et al.
  (2003). Evidence for enhanced neurobehavioral vulnerability to nicotine during periadoles-
  cence in rats. *Journal of Neuroscience, 23*(11), 4712–4716.
Aizenstein, M. L., Segal, D. S., & Kuczenski, R. (1990). Repeated amphetamine and fencamfam-
  ine: Sensitization and reciprocal cross-sensitization. *Neuropsychopharmacology, 3*, 283–290.
Andersen, S. L., & Navalta, C. P. (2004). Altering the course of neurodevelopment: A framework
  for understanding the enduring effects of psychotropic drugs. *International Journal of
  Developmental Neuroscience, 22*, 423–440.
Anthony, J. C., Warner, L. A., & Kessler, R. C. (1994). Comparative epidemiology of dependence
  on tobacco, alcohol, controlled substances, and inhalants: Basic findings from the National
  Comorbidity Survey. *Experimental and Clinical Psychopharmacology, 2*, 244–268.
Arbeit, M. L., Nicklas, T. A., Frank, G. C., Webber, L. S., Miner, M. H., & Berenson, G. S. (1988).
  Caffeine intakes of children from a biracial population: The Bogalusa Heart Study. *Journal of
  the American Dietetic Association, 88*(4), 466–471.
Arria, A. M., Caldeira, K. M., O'Grady, K. E., Vincent, K. B., Johnson, E. P., & Wish, E. D.
  (2008). Nonmedical use of prescription stimulants among college students: Associations with
  attention-deficit-hyperactivity disorder and polydrug use. *Pharmacotherapy, 28*(2), 156–169.
Bada, H. S., Das, A., Bauer, C. R., Shankaran, S., Lester, B., Wright, L. L., et al. (2002).
  Gestational cocaine exposure and intrauterine growth: Maternal lifestyle study. *Obstetrics and
  Gynecology, 100*(5 Pt. 1), 916–924.
Barkley, R. A. (1991). The ecological validity of laboratory and analogue assessment methods of
  ADHD symptoms. *Journal of Abnormal Child Psychology, 19*(2), 149–178.
Barone, J. J., & Roberts, H. R. (1996). Caffeine consumption. *Food and Chemical Toxicology,
  34*(1), 119–129.
Bech, B. H., Nohr, E. A., Vaeth, M., Henriksen, T. B., & Olsen, J. (2005). Coffee and fetal death:
  A cohort study with prospective data. *American Journal of Epidemiology, 162*(10), 983–990.
Benowitz, N. L. (1990). Clinical pharmacology of caffeine. *Annual Review of Medicine, 41*,
  277–288.

Berkowitz, R. L., Coustan, D. R., & Mochizuki, T. K. (1998). *Handbook for prescribing medication during pregnancy*. Philadelphia, PA: Lippincott-Raven.

Bernstein, G. A., Carroll, M. E., Dean, N. W., Crosby, R. D., Perwien, A. R., & Benowitz, N. L. (1998). Caffeine withdrawal in normal school-age children. *Journal of the American Academy of Child and Adolescent Psychiatry, 37*, 858–865.

Bertrand, J., Floyd, R. L., Weber, M. K., O'Connor, M. J., Riley, E., Johnson, K. A., et al. (2004). *National Task Force on fetal alcohol syndrome/fetal alcohol effects. Fetal Alcohol Syndrome: Guidelines for Referral and Diagnosis. Screening and Brief Intervention*. Atlanta, GA: Centers for Disease Control and Prevention.

Biederman, J., Wilens, T., Mick, E., Faraone, S. V., Weber, W., Curtis, S., et al. (1997). Is ADHD a risk factor for psychoactive substance use disorders? Findings from a four-year prospective follow-up study. *Journal of the American Academy Child Adolescent Psychiatry, 36*(1), 21–29.

Biederman, J., Wilens, T., Mick, E., Spencer, T., & Faraone, S. V. (1999). Pharmacotherapy of Attention-Deficit/Hyperactivity Disorder reduces risk for substance use disorder. *Pediatrics, 104*(2), e20.

Bradley, C. (1937). The behavior of children receiving benzedrine. *American Journal of Psychiatry, 94*, 577–585.

Brandon, C. L., Marinelli, M., Baker, L. K., & White, F. J. (2001). Enhanced reactivity and vulnerability to cocaine following methylphenidate treatment in adolescent rats. *Neuropsychopharmacology, 25*, 651–661.

Brazier, J. L. & Salle, B. (1981). Conversion of theophylline to caffeine by the human fetus. *Seminars in Perinatology, 5*, 315–320.

Brazier, J. L., Ritter, J., Berland, M., Khenfer, D., & Faucon, G. (1983). Pharmacokinetics of caffeine during and after pregnancy. *Developmental Pharmacology and Therapeutics, 6*(5), 315–322.

Briggs, G. G., Freeman, R. K., & Yaffe, S. J. (1998). *Drugs in Pregnancy and Lactation*. 4th ed. Baltimore, MD: Wilkins & Wilkins.

Brown, S. A., & Tapert, S. F. (2004). Adolescence and the trajectory of alcohol use: Basic to clinical studies. *Annals of the New York Academy of Sciences, 1021*, 234–244.

Cargiulo, T. (2007). Understanding the health impact of alcohol dependence. *American Journal of Health-System Pharmacy, 64*(5 Suppl. 3), S5–S11.

Castellanos, F. X., & Rapoport, J. L. (2002). Effects of caffeine on development and behavior in infancy and childhood: A review of the published literature. *Food and Chemical Toxicology, 40*(9), 1235–1242.

Caster, J. M., Walker, Q. D., & Kuhn, C. M. (2007). A single high dose of cocaine induces differential sensitization to specific behaviors across adolescence. *Psychopharmacology, 193*(2), 247–260.

Centers for Disease Control and Prevention (CDCP). (1997). Perspectives in disease prevention and health promotion, smoking-attributable mortality and years of potential life lost-United States, 1984. (Morbidity and mortality Weekly Report [serial online] *46*, 441–451). Retrieved January 15, 2008, from http://www.cdc.gov/mmwr/preview/mmwrhtml/00047690.htm.

Centers for Disease Control and Prevention (CDCP). (2002). PRAMS Surveillance Report. Retrieved December 11, 2007, from http://www.cdc.gov/prams/2002PRAMSSurvReport/.

Centers for Disease Control and Prevention (CDCP). (2004). Frequently asked questions: Fetal alcohol syndrome. Retrieved December 11, 2007, from http://www.cdc.gov/NCBDDD/fas/faqs.htm.

Centers for Disease Control and Prevention (CDCP). (2005). Annual smoking-attirbutable mortality, years of potential life lost, and productivity losses – United States, 1997–2001. (Morbidity and Mortality Weekly Report [serial online] *54*(25), 625–628). Retrieved December 11, 2007, from http://www.cdc.gov/mmwr/preview/mmwrhtml/mm5425a1.htm.

Chaloupka, F. J., & Johnston, L. D. (2007). Bridging the gap: Research informing practice and policy for healthy youth behavior. *American Journal of Preventive Medicine, 33*(Suppl. 4), S147–S161.

Chambers, R. A., Taylor, J. R., & Potenza, M. N. (2003). Developmental neurocircuitry of motivation in adolescence: A critical period of addiction vulnerability. *American Journal of Psychiatry, 160*(6), 1041–1052.

Charatan, F. (2006). FDA committee votes for warning labels on stimulant drugs. *British Medical Journal, 332*(7538), 380.

Charness, M. E., Hu, G., Edwards, R. H., & Querimit, L. A. (1993). Ethanol increases delta-opioid receptor gene expression in neuronal cell lines. *Molecular Pharmacology, 44*(6), 1119–1127.

Chase, T. D., Carrey, N., Brown, R. E., & Wilkinson, M. (2005a). Methylphenidate regulates c-fos and fosB expression in multiple regions of the immature rat brain. *Brain Research, Developmental Brain Research, 156*(1), 1–12.

Chase, T. D., Carrey, N., Brown, R. E., & Wilkinson, M. (2005b). Methylphenidate differentially regulates c-fos and fosB expression in the developing rat striatum. *Brain Research, Developmental Brain Research, 157*(2), 181–191.

Chase, T., Carrey, N., Soo, E., & Wilkinson, M. (2007). Methylphenidate regulates activity regulated cytoskeletal associated but not brain-derived neurotrophic factor gene expression in the developing rat striatum. *Neuroscience, 144*(3), 969–984.

Colby, S. M., Tiffany, S. T., Shiffman, S., & Niaura, R. S. (2000). Are adolescent smokers dependent on nicotine? A review of the evidence. *Drug and Alcohol Dependence, 59*(Suppl. 1), S83–S95.

Conners, C. K., Sitarenios, G., Parker, J. D., & Epstein, J. N. (1998). The revised Conners' Parent Rating Scale (CPRS-R): Factor structure, reliability, and criterion validity. *Journal of Abnormal Child Psychology, 26*(4), 257–268.

Cornelius, M. D., Leech, S. L., Goldschmidt, L., & Day, N. L. (2000). Prenatal tobacco exposure: Is it a risk factor for early tobacco experimentation? *Nicotine and Tobacco Research, 2*(1), 45–52.

Crews, F., He, J., & Hodge, C. (2007). Adolescent cortical development: A critical period of vulnerability for addiction. *Pharmacology Biochemistry and Behavior, 86*(2), 189–199.

Crews, F. T., Mdzinarishvili, A., Kim, D., He, J., & Nixon, R. (2006). Neurogenesis in adolescent brain is potently inhibited by ethanol. *Neuroscience, 137*(2), 437–445.

Daly, J. W., & Fredholm, B. B. (1998). Caffeine – an atypical drug of dependence. *Drug and Alcohol Dependence, 51*(1–2), 199–206.

Day, N. L., Richardson, G. A., Goldschmidt, L., & Cornelius, M. D. (2000). Effects of prenatal tobacco exposure on preschoolers' behavior. *Journal of Developmental and Behavioral Pediatrics, 21*(3), 180–188.

DeBellis, M. D., Clark, D. B., Beers, S. R., Soloff, P. H., Boring, A. M., Hall, J., et al. (2000). Hippocampal volume in adolescent-onset alcohol use disorders. *American Journal of Psychiatry, 158*(5), 820–821.

DeBellis, M. D., Narasimhan, A., Thatcher, D. L., Keshaven, M. S., Soloff, P., & Clark, D. B. (2005). Prefrontal cortex, thalamus, and cerebellar volumes in adolescents and young adults with adolescent-onset alcohol use disorders and comorbid mental disorders. *Alcoholism, Clinical and Experimental Research, 29*(9), 1590–1600.

Deitrich, R. A., Dunwiddie, T. V., Harris, R. A., & Erwin, V. G. (1989). Mechanism of action of ethanol: Initial central nervous system actions. *Pharmacological Reviews, 41*, 489–537.

DiFranza, J. R., Savageau, J. A., Fletcher, K., O'Loughlin, J., Pbert, L., Ockene, J., et al. (2007). Symptoms of tobacco dependence after brief intermittent use: The development and assessment of nicotine dependence in youth-2 study. *Archives of Pediatric and Adolescent Medicine, 161*, 704–710.

Dumas, M., Gouyon, J. B., Tenenbaum, D., Michiels, Y., Escousse, A., & Alison, M. (1982). Systematic determination of caffeine plasma concentrations at birth in preterm and full term infants. *Developmental Pharmacology and Therapeutics, 4*(Suppl.), 182–186.

Efron, D., Jarman, F. C., & Barker, M. J. (1998). Child and parent perceptions of stimulant medication treatment in attention deficit hyperactivity disorder. *Journal of Paediatrics and Child Health, 34*(3), 288–292.

Elkins, R. N., Rapoport, J. L., Zahn, T. P., Buchsbaum, M. S., Weingartner, H., Kopin, I. J., et al. (1981). Acute effects of caffeine in normal prepubertal boys. *American Journal of Psychiatry*, *138*, 178–183.

Eskenazi, B. & Castorina, R. (1999). Association of prenatal maternal or postnatal environmental tobacco smoke exposure and neurodevelopmental and behavioral problems in children. *Environmental Health Perspectives*, *107*, 991–1000.

Faden, V.B., & Graubard, B.I. (2000). Maternal substance use during pregnancy and developmental outcome at age three. *Journal of Substance Abuse*, *12*(4), 329–340.

Faraday, M. M., Elliott, B. M., Phillips, J. M., & Grunberg, N. E. (2003). Adolescent and adult male rats differ in sensitivity to nicotine's activity effects. *Pharmacology, Biochemistry, and Behavior*, *74*(4), 917–931.

Feldman, R. S., Meyer, J. S., & Quenzer, L. F. (1997). *Principles of neuropsychopharmacology*. Sutherland, MA: Sinauer Associates, Inc.

Fergusson, D. M., Lynskey, M. T., & Horwood, L. J. (1994). Childhood exposure to alcohol and adolescent drinking patterns. *Addiction*, *89*(8), 1007–1016.

Ferre, S., Fuxe, K., von Euler, G., Johansson, B., & Fredholm, B. B. (1992). Adenosine-dopamine interactions in the brain. *Neuroscience*, *51*(3), 501–512.

Ferre, S., von Euler, G., Johansson, B., Fredholm, B. B., & Fuxe, K. (1991). Stimulation of high-affinity adenosine A2 receptors decreases the affinity of dopamine D2 receptors in rat striatal membranes. *Proceedings of the National Academy of Sciences of the United States of America*, *88*(16), 7238–7241.

Frary, C. D., Johnson, R. K., & Wang, M. Q. (2005). Food sources and intakes of caffeine in the diets of persons in the United States. *Journal of the American Dietetic Association*, *105*(1), 110–113.

Fredericks, E. M., & Kollins, S. H. (2004). Assessing methylphenidate preference in ADHD patients using a choice procedure. *Psychopharmacology*, *175*, 391–398.

Fredericks, E. M., & Kollins, S. H. (2005). A pilot study of methylphenidate preference assessment in children diagnosed with ADHD. *Journal of Child and Adolescent Psychopharmacology*, *15*(5), 729–741.

Fredholm, B. B., Bättig, K., Holmén, J., Nehlig, A., & Zvartau, E. E. (1999). Actions of caffeine in the brain with special reference to factors that contribute to its widespread use. *Pharmacological Reviews*, *51*(1), 83–133.

Fried, P. A., & Watkinson, B. (1990). 36- and 48-month neurobehavioral follow-up of children prenatally exposed to marijuana, cigarettes, and alcohol. *Journal of Developmental and Behavioral Pediatrics*, *11*(2), 49–58.

Fried, P. A., & Watkinson, B. (2001). Differential effects on facets of attention in adolescents prenatally exposed to cigarettes and marijuana. *Neurotoxicology and Teratology*, *23*(5), 421–430.

Galvan, A., Hare, T. A., Parra, C. E., Penn, J., Voss, H., Glover, G., et al. (2006). Earlier development of the accumbens relative to orbitofrontal cortex might underlie risk-taking behavior in adolescents. *Journal of Neuroscience*, *26*(25), 6885–6892.

Garland, M. (1998). Pharmacology of drug transfer across the placenta: Substance use in pregnancy. *Obstetrics and Gynecology Clinics of North America*, *25*(1), 21–42.

Garrett, B. E., & Griffiths, R. R. (1996). The role of dopamine in the behavioral effects of caffeine in animals and humans. *Pharmacology, Biochemistry and Behavior*, *57*(3), 533–541.

Gaytan, O., Yang, P., Swann, A., & Dafny, N. (2000). Diurnal differences in sensitization to methylphenidate. *Brain Research*, *846*, 24–39.

George, L., Granath, F., Johansson, A. L., Olander, B., & Cnattingius, S. (2006). Risks of repeated miscarriage. *Paediatric and Perinatal Epidemiology*, *20*(2), 119–126.

Giannelli, M., Doyle, P., Roman, E., Pelerin, M., & Hermon, C. (2003). The effect of caffeine consumption and nausea on the risk of miscarriage. *Paediatric and Perinatal Epidemiology*, *17*(4), 316–323.

Ginzel, K. H., Maritz, G. S., Marks, D. F., Neuberger, M., Pauly, J. R., Polito, J. R., et al. (2007). Critical review: Nicotine for the fetus, the infant and the adolescent? *Journal of Health Psychology*, *12*(2), 215–224.

Glantz, M. D., & Chambers, J. C. (2006). Prenatal drug exposure effects on subsequent vulnerability to drug abuse. *Development & Psychopathology, 18*(3), 893–922.

Goodman, L. S., Hardman, J. G., Limbird, L. E., & Gilman, A. G. (2001). *Goodman & Gilman's The Pharmacological Basis of Therapeutics.* 10th ed. New York: McGraw-Hill.

Grant, B. F., & Dawson, D. F. (1997). Age of onset and alcohol use and its association with DSM-IV alcohol abuse and dependence: Results of the National Longitudinal Alcohol Epidemiological Survey. *Journal of Substance Abuse, 9,* 103–110.

Grobin, A. C., Matthews, D. B., Devaud, L. L., & Morrow, A. L. (1998). The role of $GABA_A$ receptors in the acute and chronic effects of ethanol. *Psychopharmacology, 139,* 2–19.

Grund, T., Teuchert-Noodt, G., Busche, A., Neddens, J., Brummelte, S., Moll, G. H., et al. (2007). Administration of oral methylphenidate during adolescence prevents suppressive development of dopamine projections into prefrontal cortex and amygdala after an early pharmacological challenge in gerbils. *Brain Research, 1176,* 124–132.

Guerriero, R. M., Hayes, M. M., Dhaliwal, S. K., Ren, J. Q., & Kosofsky, B. E. (2006). Preadolescent methylphenidate versus cocaine treatment differ in the expression of cocaine-induced locomotor sensitization during adolescence and adulthood. *Biological Psychiatry, 60,* 1171–1180.

Hawken, C. M., Brown, R. E., Carrey, N., & Wilkinson, M. (2004). Long-term methylphenidate treatment down-regulates c-fos in the striatum of male CD-1 mice. *Neuroreport, 15*(6), 1045–1048.

Hellstrom-Lindahl, E., Seiger, A., Kjaeldgaard, A., & Nordberg, A. (2001). Nicotine-induced alterations in the expression of receptors in primary culture from human prenatal brain. *Neuroscience, 105*(3), 527–534.

Henningfield, J. E., & Griffiths, R. R. (1981). Cigarette smoking and subjective response: Effects of d-amphetamine. *Clinical Pharmacology and Therapeutics, 30,* 497–505.

Henningfield, J. E., Johnson, R. E., Jasinski, D. R., & Bozarth, M. A. (1987). *Clinical procedures for the assessment of abuse potential.* In M. A. Bozarth (Ed.), Methods of assessing the reinforcing properties of abused drugs (pp. 573–590). New York: Springer-Verlag.

Hughes, J. R., & Hale, K. L. (1998). Behavioral effects of caffeine and other methylxanthines on children. *Experimental and Clinical Psychopharmacology, 6,* 87–95.

Hughes, J. R., & Oliveto, A. H. (1997). A systematic survey of caffeine intake in Vermont. *Experimental and Clinical Psychopharmacology, 5*(4), 393–398.

James, J. E. (1991). *Caffeine and Health.* San Diego, CA: Academic Press, Ltd.

Jasinski, D. R., Johnson, R. E., & Henningfield, J. E. (1984). Abuse liability assessment in human subjects. *Trends in Pharmacological Sciences, 5,* 196–200.

Johnson, B. A., Roache, J. D., Javors, M. A., DiClemente, C. C., Cloninger, C. R., Prihoda, T. J., et al. (2000). Ondansetron for reduction of drinking among biologically predisposed alcoholic patients: A randomized controlled trial. *Journal of the American Medical Association, 284*(8), 963–971.

Johnston, L. D., O'Malley, P. M., & Bachman, J. G. (2003). Monitoring the future national survey results on drug use, 1975–2002. *National Institute on Drug Abuse, 1,* 386–391.

Johnston, L. D., O'Malley, P. M., Bachman, J. G., & Schulenbert, J. E. (2007). The Monitoring the Future Study. Retrieved December 15, 2007, from http://www.monitoringthefuturestudy.org/data.

Jones, H. E., & Griffiths, R. R. (2003). Oral caffeine maintenance potentiates the reinforcing and stimulant subjective effects of intravenous nicotine in cigarette smokers. *Psychopharmacology, 165,* 280–290.

Julien, R. M. (2001). *A primer of drug action,* 9th ed. New York: Worth Publishers.

Kalivas, P. W., Sorg, B. A., & Hooks, M. S. (1993). The pharmacology and neural circuitry of sensitization to psychostimulants. *Behavioral Pharmacology, 4,* 315–334.

Kandel, D. B., & Chen, K. (2000). Extent of smoking and nicotine dependence in the United States: 1991–1993. *Nicotine and Tobacco Research, 2*(3), 263–274.

Kandel, D. B., Schaffran, C., Griesler, P., Samuolis, J., Davies, M., & Galanti, R. (2005). On the measurement of nicotine dependence in adolescence: Comparisons of the mFTQ and a DSM-IV-based scale. *Journal of Pediatric Psychology, 30*(4), 319–332.

38 T.H. Kelly et al.

Kandel, D. B., Wu, P., & Davies, M. (1994). Maternal smoking during pregnancy and smoking by adolescent daughters. *American Journal of Public Health, 84*(9), 1407–1413.

Kelly, T. H., Foltin, R. W., & Fischman, M. W. (1991). Effects of repeated amphetamine exposure on multiple measures of human behavior. *Pharmacology Biochemistry and Behavior, 38*, 417–426.

Kelly, T. H., Robbins, G., Martin, C. A., Fillmore, M. T., Lane, S. D., Harrington, N. G., et al. (2006). Individual differences in drug abuse vulnerability: d-amphetamine and sensation-seeking status. *Psychopharmacology, 189*(1), 17–25.

Kessler, D. A., Natanblut, S. L., Wilkenfeld, J. P., Lorraine, C. C., Mayl, S. L., Bernstien, I. B. G., et al. (1997). Nicotine addiction: A pediatric disease. *Journal of Pediatrics, 130*(4), 518–524.

Klein, R. G., Abikoff, H., Klass, E., Ganeles, D., Seese, L. M., & Pollack, S. (1997). Clinical efficacy of methylphenidate in conduct disorder with and without attention deficit hyperactivity disorder. *Archives of General Psychiatry, 54*(12), 1073–1080.

Klein-Schwartz, W. (2002). Abuse and toxicity of methylphenidate. *Current Opinion in Pediatrics, 14*, 219–223.

Knutti, R., Rothweiler, H., & Schlatter, C. (1982). The effect of pregnancy on the pharmacokinetics of caffeine. *Archives of Toxicology Supplement, 5*, 187–192.

Kopstein, A. (2001). *Tobacco use in America: Findings from the 1999 National Household Survey on drug abuse. (Analytic series: A-15, DHHS Publication N. SMA 02-3622).* Rockville, MD: Substance Abuse and Mental Health Services Administration, Office of Applied Studies.

Kota, D., & Martin, B. R. (2007). Nicotine dependence and reward differ between adolescent and adult male mice. *The Journal of Pharmacology and Experimental Therapeutics, 322*(1), 399–401.

Krasnegor, N. A., Gray, D. B., & Thompson, T. (1986). *Advances in behavioral pharmacology, Vol. 5: Developmental behavioral pharmacology.* Hillsdale, NJ: Lawrence Erlbaum Associates.

Kreek, M. J., & Koob, G. F. (1998). Drug dependence: Stress and dysregulation of reward pathways. *Drug and Alcohol Dependence, 51*, 23–47.

Kuczenski, R., & Segal, D. S. (2001). Locomotor effects of acute and repeated threshold doses of amphetamine and methylphenidate: Relative roles of dopamine and norepinephrine. *The Journal of Pharmacology and Experimental Therapeutics, 296*, 876–883.

Kuczenski, R., & Segal, D. S. (2002). Exposure of adolescent rats to oral methylphenidate: Preferential effects on extracellular norepinephrine and absence of sensitization and cross-sensitization to methamphetamine. *Journal of Neuroscience, 22*(16), 7264–7271.

Lambert, N. M., & Hartsough, C. S. (1998). Prospective study of tobacco smoking and substance dependencies among samples of ADHD and non-ADHD participants. *Journal of Learning Disabilities, 31*(6), 533–544.

Law, K. L., Stroud, L. R., LaGasse, L. L., Niaura, R., Liu, J., & Lester, B. M. (2003). Smoking during pregnancy and newborn neurobehavior. *Pediatrics, 111*(6 Pt. 1), 1318–1323.

Leon, M. R. (2000). Effects of caffeine on cognitive, psychomotor, and affective performance of children with attention-deficit/hyperactivity disorder. *Journal of Attention Disorders, 4*, 27–47.

Lesch, K. P. (2005). Alcohol dependence and gene x environment interaction in emotion regulation: Is serotonin the link? *European Journal of Pharmacology, 526*(1–3), 113–124.

Levin, E. D., Rezvani, A. H., Montoya, D., Rose, J. E., & Swartzwelder, H. S. (2003). Adolescent-onset nicotine self-administration modeled in female rats. *Psychopharmacology, 169*(2), 141–149.

Leviton, A. (1992). Behavioral correlates of caffeine consumption by children. *Clinical Pediatrics, 31*(12), 742–750.

Leviton, A., & Cowan, L. (2002). A review of the literature relating caffeine consumption by women to their risk of reproductive hazards. *Food and Chemical Toxicology, 40*(9), 1271–1310.

Liu, X., Koren, A. O., Yee, S. K., Pechnick, R. N., Poland, R. E., & London, E. D. (2003). Self-administration of 5-iodo-A-85380, a beta-2 selective nicotinic receptor ligand by operantly trained rats. *Neuroreports, 14*, 1503–1505.

Malinauskas, B. M., Aeby, V. G., Overton, R. F., Carpenter-Aeby, T., & Barber-Heidal, K. (2007). A survey of energy drink consumption patterns among college students. *Nutrition Journal, 6,* 35.

Martin, C. A., Guenther, G., Bingcang, C., Rayens, M. K., & Kelly, T. H. (2007). Measurement of the subjective effects of methylphenidate in 11-to-15 year old children with the attention-deficit/hyperactivity disorder. *Journal of Child and Adolescent Psychopharmacology, 17*(1), 63–73.

Martin, C. A., Kelly, T. H., Rayens, M. K., Brogli, B., Himelreich, K., Brenzel, A., et al. (2004). Sensation seeking and symptoms of disruptive disorder: Association with nicotine, alcohol and marijuana use in early-and mid-adolescents. *Psychological Reports, 94*(3 Pt. 1), 75–82.

Martin, W. R., Sloan, J. W., Sapira, J. D., & Jasinski, D. R. (1971). Physiologic, subjective, and behavioral effects of amphetamine, methamphetamine, ephedrine, phenmetrazine, and methylphenidate in man. *Clinical Pharmacology and Therapeutics, 12,* 245–258.

Maskos, U., Molles, B. E., Pons, S., Besson, M., Guiard, B. P., Guilloux, J. P., et al. (2005). Nicotine reinforcement and cognition restored by targeted expression of nicotinic receptors. *Nature, 436,* 103–107.

McCabe, S. E., Teter, C. J., & Boyd, C. J. (2004a). The use, misuse and diversion of prescription stimulants among middle and high school students. *Substance Use & Misuse, 39*(7), 1095–1116.

McCabe, S. E., Teter, C. J., & Boyd, C. J. (2006a). Medical use, illicit use and diversion of prescription stimulant medication. *Journal of Psychoactive Drugs, 38*(1), 43–56.

McCabe, S. E., Teter, C. J., & Boyd, C. J. (2006b). Medical use, illicit use and diversion of abusable prescription drugs. *Journal of American College Health, 54*(5), 269–278.

McCabe, S. E., Teter, C. J., Boyd, C. J., & Guthrie, S. K. (2004b). Prevalence and correlates of illicit methylphenidate use among 8th, 10th, and 12th grade students in the United States, 2001. *Journal of Adolescent Health, 35*(6), 501–504.

Milberger, S., Biederman, J., Faraone, S. V., Chen, L., & Jones, J. (1997). ADHD is associated with early initiation of cigarette smoking in children and adolescents. *Journal of the American Academy of Child and Adolescent Psychiatry, 36*(1), 37–44.

Mokdad, A. H., Marks, J. S., Stroup, D. F., & Gerberding, J. L. (2004). Actual causes of death in the United States, 2000. *The Journal of the American Medical Association, 291*(10), 1238–1245.

Moll, G. H., Hause, S., Ruether, E., Rothenberger, A., & Huether, G. (2001). Early methylphenidate administration to young rats causes a persistent reduction in the density of striatal dopamine transporters. *Journal of Child and Adolescent Psychopharmacology, 11*(1), 15–24.

Morgan, K. J., Stults, V. J., & Zabik, M. E. (1982). Amount and dietary sources of caffeine and saccharin intake by individuals ages 5 to 18 years. *Regulatory Toxicology and Pharmacology, 2*(4), 296–307.

Muneoka, K., Ogawa, T., Kamei, K., Mimura, Y., Kato, H., & Takigawa, M. (2001). Nicotine exposure during pregnancy is a factor which influences serotonin transporter density in the rat brain. *European Journal of Pharmacology, 411*(3), 279–282.

Myllynen, P., Pasanen, M., & Pelkonen, O. (2005). Human placenta: A human organ for developmental toxicology research and biomonitoring. *Placenta, 26*(5), 361–371.

Nasello, A. G., & Ramirez, O. A. (1978a). Open field and Lashley III maze behavior of the offspring of amphetamine treated rats. *Psychopharmacology, 58,* 171–173.

Nasello, A. G., & Ramirez, O. A. (1978b). Brain catecholamines metabolism in the offspring of amphetamine treated rats. *Pharmacology, Biochemistry and Behavior, 9,* 17–20.

Nasello, A. G., Astrada, A. C., & Ramirez, O. A. (1974). Effects on the acquisition of conditioned avoidance responses and seizure threshold in the offspring of amphetamine treated gravid rats. *Psychopharmacology, 40,* 25–31.

Nasif, F. J., Cuadra, G. R., & Ramirez, O. A. (1999). Permanent alteration of central noradrenergic system by prenatally administered amphetamine. *Developmental Brain Research, 112,* 181–188.

National Highway Traffic Safety Administration (NHTSA). (2003). Traffic Safety Facts 2002: Alcohol (DOT Publication No. HS-809–606). Washington, DC: NHTSA, National Center for Statistics & Analysis. Retrieved March 27, 2008, from http://www-nrd.nhtsa.dot.gov/pdf/ nrd-30/NCSA/TSF2002/2002alcfacts.pdf.

National Institute on Alcohol Abuse and Alcoholism (NIAAA) (2004–2005). Alcohol and development in youth – A multidisciplinary overview. *Alcohol Research & Health, 28*(3).

Nichter, M., Nichter, M., Thompson, P. J., Shiffman, S., & Moscicki, A. B. (2002). Using qualitative research to inform survey development on nicotine dependence among adolescents. *Drug and Alcohol Dependence, 68*(Suppl. 1), S41–S56.

Okoli, C. T. C., Kelly, T. H., & Hahn, E. L. (2007). Secondhand smoke and nicotine exposure: A brief review. *Addictive Behaviors, 32*, 1977–1988.

O'Loughlin, J., DiFranza, J., Tyndale, R. F., Meshefedjian, G., McMillan-Davey, E., Clarke, P. B. et al. (2003). Nicotine-dependence symptoms are associated with smoking frequency in adolescents. *American Journal of Preventive Medicine, 25*(3), 219–225.

Orbeta, R. L., Overpeck, M. D., Ramcharran, D., Kogan, M. D., & Ledsky, R. (2006). High caffeine intake in adolescents: Associations with difficulty sleeping and feeling tired in the morning. *Journal of Adolescent Health, 38*, 451–453.

Ostrea, E. M., Mantaring, J. B., III, & Silvestre, M. A. (2004). Drugs that affect the fetus and newborn infant via the placenta or breast milk. *Pediatric Clinics of North America, 51*, 539–579.

Parsons, W. D., & Neims, A. H. (1981). Prolonged half-life of caffeine in healthy term newborn infants. *Journal of Pediatrics, 98*(4), 640–641.

Picciotto, M. R., & Corrigall, W. A. (2002). Neuronal systems underlying behaviors related to nicotine addiction: Neural circuits and molecular genetics. *Journal of Neuroscience, 22*(9), 3338–3341.

Picciotto, M. R., Zoli, M., & Changeux, J. P. (1999). Use of knock-out mice to determine the molecular basics for the actions of nicotine. *Nicotine and Tobacco Research, 1*(Suppl. 2), S121–S125.

Pidoplichko, V. I., Noguchi, J., Areola, O. O., Liang, Y., Peterson, J., Zhang, T., et al. (2004). Nicotinic cholinergic synaptic mechanisms in the ventral tegmental area contribute to nicotine addiction. *Learning and Memory, 11*(1), 60–69.

Pirie, P. L., Lando, H., Curry, S. J., McBride, C., & Grothaus, L. C. (2000). Tobacco, alcohol, and caffeine use and cessation in early pregnancy. *American Journal of Preventive Medicine, 18*(1), 54–61

Pollak, C. P., & Bright, D. (2003). Caffeine consumption and weekly sleep patterns in US seventh-, eighth-, and ninth-graders. *Pediatrics, 111*, 42–46.

Poulin, C. (2007). From attention-deficit/hyperactivity disorder to medical stimulant use to diversion of prescribed stimulants to non-medical stimulant use: Connecting the dots. *Addiction, 102*, 740–752.

Ramirez, O. A., & Carrer, H. F. (1983). Noradrenergic modulation of neural transmission in the offspring of amphetamine treated rats. *Canadian Journal of Physiology and Pharmacology, 2*, 766–769.

Ramirez, O. A., Carrer, H. F., & Nasello, A. G. (1979). Prenatal amphetamine exposure: Ovulation, sexual behavior and hypothalamic monoamine. *Pharmacology, Biochemistry and Behavior, 11*, 605–609.

Rapoport, J. L., Berg, C. J., Ismond, D. R., Zahn, T. P., & Neims, A. (1984). Behavioral effects of caffeine in children. Relationship between dietary choice and effects of caffeine challenge. *Archives of General Psychiatry, 41*, 1073–1079.

Rapoport, J. L., Elkins, R., Neims, A., Zahn, T., & Berg, C. J. (1981). Behavioral and autonomic effects of caffeine in normal boys. *Developmental Pharmacology and Therapeutics, 3*, 74–82.

Rasch, V. (2003). Cigarette, alcohol, and caffeine consumption: Risk factors for spontaneous abortion. *Acta Obstetricia et Gynecologica Scandinavica, 82*(2), 182–188.

Rayburn, W. F., & Bogenschutz, M. P. (2004). Pharmacotherapy for pregnant women with addictions. *American Journal of Obstetrics and Gynecology, 191*(6), 1885–1897.

Richardson, S. A., & Tizabi, Y. (1994). Hyperactivity in the offspring of nicotine-treated rats: Role of the mesolimbic and nigrostriatal pathways. *Pharmacology, Biochemistry and Behavior*, *47*(2), 331–337.

Rush, C. R., Higgins, S. T., Vansickel, A. R., Stoops, W. W., Lile, J. A., & Glaser, P. E. (2005). Methylphenidate increases cigarette smoking. *Psychopharmacology*, *181*(4), 781–789.

Salminen, O., Murphy, K. L., McIntosh, J. M., Drago, J., Marks, M. J., Collins, A. X., et al. (2004). Subunit composition and pharmacology of two classes of striatal presynaptic nicotinic acetylcholine receptors mediating dopamine release in mice. *Molecular Pharmacology*, *65*, 1526–1535.

Savitz, D. A., Chan, R. L., Herring, A. H., Howards, P. P., & Hartmann, K. E. (2008). Caffeine and miscarriage risk. *Epidemiology*, *19*(1), 55–62.

Scheffler, R. M., Hinshaw, S. P., Modrek, S., & Levine, P. (2007). The global market for ADHD medications. *Health Affairs*, *26*(2), 450–457.

Schenk, S. & Izenwasser, S. (2002). Pretreatment with methylphenidate sensitizes rats to the reinforcing effects of cocaine. *Pharmacology, Biochemistry and Behavior*, *72*(3), 651–657.

Schuckit, M. A. & Smith, T. L. (2004). Changes over time in the self-reported level of response to alcohol. *Alcohol and Alcoholism*, *39*(5), 433–438.

Sher, L. (2006). Functional magnetic resonance imaging studies of neurocognitve effects of alcohol use on adolescents and young adults. *International Journal of Adolescent Medicine and Health*, *18*(1), 3–7.

Slotkin, T. A. (2002). Nicotine and the adolescent brain: Insights from an animal model. *Neurotoxicology and Teratology*, *24*(3), 369–384.

Slotkin, T. A., Pinkerton, K. E., Auman, J. T., Qiaio, D., & Seidler, F. J. (2002). Perinatal exposure to environmental tobacco smoke upregulates nicotinic cholinergic receptors in monkey brain. *Brain Research, Developmental Brain Research*, *133*(2), 175–179.

Smith, L. M., LaGasse, L. L., Derauf, C., Grant, P., Shah, R., Arria, A., et al. (2006). The infant development, environment, and lifestyle study: Effects of prenatal methamphetamine exposure, polydrug exposure, and poverty on intrauterine growth. *Pediatrics*, *118*(3), 1149–1156.

Sokol, R. J., Delaney-Black, V., Nordstrom, B. (2003). Fetal alcohol syndrome disorder. *Journal of the American Medical Association*, *290*(22), 2996–2999.

Solanto, M. V. (1998). Neuropsychopharmacology mechanisms of stimulant drug action in attention-deficit hyperactivity disorder: A review and integration. *Behavioural Brain Research*, *94*, 127–152.

Soliman, M. A., Pedersen, J. A., Park, H., Castaneda-Jimenez, A., Stenstrom, M. K., & Suffet, I. H. (2007). Human pharmaceuticals, antioxidants, and plasticizers in wastewater treatment plant and water reclamation plant effluents. *Water Environment Research*, *79*(2), 156–167.

Song, M., Wang, X. Y., Zhao, M., Wang, X. Y., Zhai, H. F., & Lu, L. (2007). Role of stress in acquisition of alcohol-conditioned place preference in adolescent and adult mice. *Alcoholism, Clinical and Experimental Research*, *31*(12), 2001–2005.

Sood, B., Delaney-Black, V., Covington, C., Nordstrom-Klee, B., Ager, J., Templin, T., et al. (2001). Prenatal alcohol exposure and childhood behavior at age 6 and 7. *Pediatrics*, *108*(2), e34.

Spear, L. P. (2002). The adolescent brain and the college drinker: Biological basis of propensity to use and misuse alcohol. *Journal of Studies on Alcohol*, (Suppl. 14), 71–81.

Spear, L. P. (2004). Adolescence and the trajectory of alcohol use: Introduction to part VI. *Annals of the New York Academy of Sciences*, *1021*, 202–205.

Spear, N. E., & Molina, J. C. (2005). Fetal or infantile exposure to ethanol promotes ethanol ingestion in adolescence and adulthood: A theoretical review. *Alcoholism, Clinical and Experimental Research*, *29*(6), 909–929.

Stein, M. A., Krasowski, M., Leventhal, B. L., Phillips, W., & Bender, B. G. (1996). Behavioral and cognitive effects of methylxanthines. A meta-analysis of theophylline and caffeine. *Archives of Pediatric and Adolescent Medicine*, *150*, 284–288.

Stoops, W. W., Lile, J. A., Robbins, C. G., Martin, C. A., Rush, C. R., & Kelly, T. H. (2007). The reinforcing, subject-rated, performance, and cardiovascular effects of d-amphetamine: Influence of sensation-seeking status. *Addictive Behaviors*, *32*(6), 1177–1188.

Story, M., & Neumark-Sztainer, D. (1998). Diet and adolescent behavior: Is there a relationship. *Adolescent Medicine, 9,* 283–298.

Sussman, S., Pentz, M.A., Spruijt-Metz, D., & Miller, T. (2006). Misuse of "study drugs": Prevalence, consequences, and implications for policy. *Substance Abuse Treatment, Prevention and Policy, 1,* 15.

Swanson, J. M., Gupta, S., Williams, L., Agler, D., Lerner, M., & Wigal, S. (2002a). Efficacy of a new pattern of methylphenidate for the treatment of ADHD: Effects on activity level in the classroom and on the playground. *Journal of the American Academy of Child and Adolescent Psychiatry, 41*(11), 1306–1314.

Swanson, J. M., Lerner, M., Wigal, T., Steinhoff, K., Greenhill, L., Posner, K., et al. (2002b). The use of a laboratory school protocol to evaluate concepts about efficacy and side effects of new formulations of stimulant medications. *Journal of Attention Disorders, 6*(Suppl. 1), S73–S88.

Swartzwelder, H. S., Wilson, W. A., & Tayyeb, M. I. (1995). Age-dependent inhibition of long-term potentiation by ethanol in immature versus mature hippocampus. *Alcoholism, Clinical and Experimental Research, 19*(6), 1480–1485.

Tapper, A. E., McKinney, S. L., Nashmi, R., Schwarz, J., Deshpande, P., Labarca, C., et al. (2004). Nicotine activation of alpha4* receptors: Sufficient for reward, tolerance, and sensitization. *Science, 306,* 1029–1032.

Tennant, F. S., & Detels, R. (1976). Relationship of alcohol, cigarette, and drug abuse in adulthood with alcohol, cigarette and coffee consumption in childhood. *Preventive Medicine, 5,* 70–77.

Toro, R., Leonard, G., Lerner, J. V., Lerner, R. M., Perron, M., Pike, G. B., et al. (2008). Prenatal exposure to maternal cigarette smoking and the adolescent cerebral cortex. *Neuropsychopharmacology, 33*(5), 1019–1027.

Torres-Reveron, A. & Dow-Edwards, D. L. (2005). Repeated administration of methylphenidate in young, adolescent and mature rat affects the response to cocaine later in adulthood. *Psychopharmacology, 181*(1), 38–47.

Trauth, J. A., McCook, E. C., Seidler, F. J., & Slotkin, T. A. (2000a). Modeling adolescent nicotine exposure: Effects on cholinergic systems in rat brain regions. *Brain Research, 873,* 18–25.

Trauth, J. A., Seidler, F. J., & Slotkin, T. A. (2000b). Persistent and delayed behavioral changes after nicotine treatment in adolescent rats. *Brain Research, 880*(1–2), 167–172.

Tsai, G. E., Ragan, P., Chang, R., Chen, S., Linnoila, M. I., & Coyle, J. T. (1998). Increased glutamatergic neurotransmission and oxidative stress after alcohol withdrawal. *American Journal of Psychiatry, 155*(6), 726–732.

Upadhyaya, H. P., Deas, D., & Brady, K. (2005a). A practical clinic approach to the treatment of nicotine dependence in adolescents. *Clinical Perspectives, 44*(9), 942–946.

Upadhyaya, H. P., Deas, D., Brady, K. T., & Kruesi, M. (2002). Cigarette smoking and psychiatric comorbidity in children and adolescents. *Journal of the American Academy of Child and Adolescent Psychiatry, 41*(11), 1294–1305.

Upadhyaya, H. P., Rose, K., Wang, W., O'Rourke, K., Sullivan, B., Deas, D., et al. (2005b). Attention-deficit/hyperactivity disorder, medication treatment, and substance use patterns among adolescents and young adults. *Journal of Child and Adolescent Psychopharmacology, 15*(5), 799–809.

Valek, M., Laslavić, B., & Laslavić, Z. (2004). Daily caffeine intake among Osijek high school students: Questionnaire study. *Croatian Medical Journal, 45,* 72–75.

Valvassori, S. S., Frey, B. N., Martins, M. R., Reus, G. Z., Schimidtz, F., Inacio, C. G., et al. (2007). Sensitization and cross-sensitization after chronic treatment with methylphenidate in adolescent Wistar rats. *Behavioural Pharmacology, 18,* 205–212.

Verheul, R., van den Brink, W., & Geerlings, P. (1999). A three-pathway psychobiological model of craving for alcohol. *Alcohol and Alcoholism, 34*(2), 197–222.

Vermeiren, R., Schwab-Stone, M., Deboutte, D., Leckman, P. E., & Ruchkin, V. (2003). Violence exposure and substance use in adolescents: Findings from three countries. *Pediatrics, 111,* 535–540.

Volkow, N. D., Wang, G., Fowler, J. S., Logan, J., Gerasimov, M., Maynard, L., et al. (2001). Therapeutic doses of oral methylphenidate significantly increase extracellular dopamine in the human brain. *The Journal of Neuroscience, 21*(RC121), 1–5.

Wafford, K. A., Burnett, D., Harris, R. A., & Whiting, P. J. (1993). GABA$_A$ receptor subunit expression and sensitivity to ethanol. *Alcohol and Alcoholism*, (Suppl. 2), 327–330.

Wagner, F. A. & Anthony, J. C. (2002). From first drug use to drug dependence: Developmental periods of risk for dependence upon marijuana, cocaine, and alcohol. *Neuropsychopharmacology*, *26*(4), 479–488.

Wakschlag, L. S., Leventhal, B. L., Pine, D. S., Pickett, K. E., & Carter, A. S. (2006). Elucidating early mechanisms of developmental psychopathology: The case of prenatal smoking and disruptive behavior. *Child Development*, *77*(4), 893–906.

Walsh, R. A., Redman, S., & Adamson, L. (1996). The accuracy of self-report of smoking status in pregnant women. *Addictive Behaviors*, *21*(5), 675–679.

Weinberg, B. A. & Bealer, B. K. (2001). *The world of caffeine*. New York: Routledge.

Westover, A. N., McBride, S., & Haley, R. W. (2007). Stroke in young adults who abuse amphetamines or cocaine. *Archives of General Psychiatry*, *64*(4), 495–502.

Wilens, T. E., Biederman, J., Mick, E., Faraone, S. V., & Spencer, T. (1997). Attention deficit hyperactivity disorder (ADHD) is associated with early onset substance use disorders. *Journal of Nervous and Mental Disease*, *185*(8), 475–482.

Wilens, T. E., Faraone, S. V., Biederman, J., & Gunawardene, S. (2003). Does stimulant therapy of attention-deficit hyperactivity disorder beget later substance abuse? A meta-analytic review of literature. *Pediatrics*, *111*(1), 179–185.

Wilens, T. E., Gignac, M., Swezey, A., Monuteaux, M. C., & Biederman, J. (2006). Characteristics of adolescents and young adults with ADHD who divert or misuses their prescribed medications. *Journal of the American Academy of Child and Adolescent Psychiatry*, *45*(4), 408–414.

Wolraich, M. L., & Doffing, M. A. (2004). Pharmacokinetic considerations in the treatment of attention-deficit hyperactivity disorder with methylphenidate. *CNS Drugs*, *18*(4), 243–250.

Xu, Z., Seidler, F. J., Ali, S. F., Slikker, W., & Slotkin, T. A. (2001). Fetal and adolescent nicotine administration: Effects on CNS serotonergic systems. *Brain Research*, *914*, 166–178.

Yang, P.B., Swann, A.C., & Dafny, N. (2003). Chronic pretreatment with methylphenidate induces cross-sensitization with amphetamine. *Life Sciences*, *73*(22), 2899–2891.

Zhang, T. A., Maldve, R. E., & Morrisett, R. A. (2006). Coincident signaling in mesolimbic structures underlying alcohol reinforcement. *Biochemical Pharmacology*, *72*(8), 919–927.

Zito, J. M., Safer, D. J., dosReis, S., Magder, L. S., Gardner, J. F., & Zarin, D. A. (1999). Psychotherapeutic medication patterns for youths with attention-deficit hyperactivity disorder. *Archives of Pediatric and Adolescent Medicine*, *153*(12), 1257–1263.

Zuvekas, S. H., Vitiello, B., & Norquist, G. S. (2006). Recent trends in stimulant medication use among U.S. children. *The American Journal of Psychiatry*, *163*(4), 579–585.

Chapter 3
Individual Characteristics and Needs Associated with Substance Misuse of Adolescents and Young Adults in Addiction Treatment

Michael L. Dennis, Michelle K. White, and Melissa L. Ives

This chapter examines the characteristics and needs of substance misusing adolescents (ages 12–17) and young adults (ages 18–25), as well as implications for improving practice. The chapter begins with a review of the literature on the prevalence, course, and correlates of adolescent substance misuse. It then uses a large treatment data set to provide a detailed description of the different demographic, substance use, and comorbidity characteristics of adolescents presenting to substance abuse treatment and explores how they vary by three demographic groups, systems where they could be recruited from, and levels of addiction treatment. The chapter then focuses on using more detailed data on 14,776 adolescents from 113 Substance Abuse and Mental Health Services Administration (SAMHSA) Center for Substance Abuse Treatment (CSAT) grantee treatment programs in the United States who were interviewed with a standardized biopsychosocial assessment called the Global Appraisal of Individual Needs (GAIN; Dennis, Titus, White, Unsicker, & Hodgkins, 2003). The chapter concludes with implications for early intervention (EI) and treatment.

Background on the Prevalence, Course, and Correlates of Adolescent Substance Misuse

Prevalence

Using a life course perspective, the prevalence of substance use, abuse, and dependence rises through the teen years, peaking at around 20% between ages 18 and 20, then declines gradually over the next four decades (Dennis & Scott, 2007). Of the ~24.3 million adolescents (ages 12–17) in the US, ~16.6% have used alcohol in the past month (10.3% to the point of intoxication), 9.8% have used illicit drugs (6.7% marijuana), and 8.0% self-report criteria for substance abuse or dependence in the past year (SAMHSA, 2007a). Of the ~32.4 million young adults (ages 18–25) in the US, ~61.9% have used alcohol in the past month (42.2% to the point of intoxication), 19.8% have used illicit drugs (16.3% marijuana), and 21.3% self-report criteria for substance abuse or dependence in the past year (SAMHSA, 2007a). Yet it is estimated that less than 1 in 6 adolescents (1.4% of the population) and 1 in 12 young adults with abuse or dependence (1.7% of the population) received any kind of addiction treatment in the past year (SAMHSA, 2007a). It has been further noted that over 90% of those who develop substance dependence in their lifetime started using under the age of 18 and half started using under the age of 15 (Dennis, Babor, Roebuck, & Donaldson, 2002). *Thus, substance misuse is primarily an adolescent-onset disorder.*

Long-Term Course and Demographic Correlates

The age of onset is related to the long-term course of addiction. Those who initiate substance use prior to the age of 15 are significantly more likely than those who start over the age of 18 to have symptoms of dependence as an adult an average of 20 years later (Dennis, Babor, Roebuck, & Donaldson, 2002). In a study of adults in treatment (Dennis, Scott, Funk, & Foss, 2005), the median time from first use to at least a year of abstinence was significantly longer for people who started using before the age of 15 (median of 29 years of use before a year of abstinence) than those who started between the ages of 15 and 20 (26 years of use) or who started at the age of 21 or older (18 years of use). Conversely, even after controlling for age of onset, the median duration of use was significantly shorter for those treated in the first 9 years of use (15 years of use) than for those first treated after 10–19 years of use (23 years of use) or after 20 or more years of use (over 35 years of use). Multiple investigations have suggested that in addition to the age of onset, gender and race are related to the rates of initiation, prevalence, and remission from substance use and substance use disorders (Dennis, Foss, & Scott, 2007; Grant & Dawson, 1998; Rounds-Bryant & Staab, 2001; Van Etten & Anthony, 1999). While they have similar rates of abuse and dependence as boys in the community (SAMHSA, 2007a), on average girls represent only about one-third of the people who receive publicly funded treatment (SAMHSA, 2008). *Thus, intervention during adolescence and young adulthood is an important strategy for reducing long-term use but it is important to explore gender differences.*

Need for Screening and Intervention in Multiple Systems

Relative to adolescents who are abstinent, those who report the use of marijuana (and typically alcohol as well) weekly or more often are 4–47 times more likely to have a wide range of past-year problems including symptoms of cannabis dependence (0% vs 77%), alcohol dependence (0% vs 67%), clinically severe symptoms of attention deficit, hyperactivity, or conduct disorder (CD; 13% vs 57%), getting into physical fights (11% vs 47%), dropping out of school (6% vs 25%), emergency room admissions (17% vs 33%), any illegal activity (17% vs 69%), and any arrest (1% vs 23%) (Dennis & McGeary, 1999). In fact, substance use is increasingly recognized as the leading malleable cause of death in the US (Mokdad, Marks, Stroup, & Gerberding, 2004). As a person develops from ages 6–11 to ages 12–17 to ages 18–20, there are dramatic increases in the rate of emergency departments admissions with problems related to illicit drug use (2.4 to 197.9 to 517.5 per 100,000 population) with higher rates for males at all ages than females (SAMHSA, 2007b). While interventions at this point can be effective (e.g., Spirito et al., 2004), from a public health perspective it makes more sense to intervene within other systems of care before problems become life threatening.

Some of the other major systems that provide opportunities for screening and early interventions with adolescent substance users include schools, the workplace, child welfare systems, and the justice system. In schools, among 12th graders, 48.2% have used illicit drugs at some point in their lives (21.5% in the past month) and 56.4% have been drunk in their lifetime (30.0% in the past month) (Johnston, O'Malley, Bachman, & Schulenberg, 2007). Among adolescents in the workplace, 23.3% reported lifetime illicit drug use (19.1% in the past month), 17.5% have been drunk in the past month, and 4.4% self-report criteria for substance abuse or dependence in the past year; among young adults in the workplace, 76.7% report lifetime illicit drug use (24.7% in the past month), 82.5% have been drunk in the past month, and 6.2% self-report criteria for substance abuse or dependence in the past year (SAMHSA, 2007a). Clearly, there is a need for screening and intervention in school and workplace settings.

The child welfare system also has a need for screening and intervention: research suggests that 50–90% of child welfare cases involve one or more family members with a substance use disorder (Marsh, Ryan, Choi, & Testa, 2006; McAlpine, Marshall, & Doran, 2001) and 60–87% of adolescents in substance abuse treatment self-report having been victimized (Shane, Diamond, Mensinger, Shera, & Wintersteen, 2006; Titus, Dennis, White, Scott, & Funk, 2003). Within the system, tremendous racial disparities exist – for African-Americans in particular – including higher likelihood of cases being opened, more case dispositions resulting in out-of-home placement, longer foster care stays, reduced likelihood of family reunification, and longer time to reunification (Government Accountability Office [GAO], 2007; Green, Rockhill, & Furrer, 2007; Lu et al., 2004). Further, African-American families in the child welfare system are less likely to have received addiction treatment and other services than Caucasian and Latino families and experience overall poorer case outcomes (Courtney et al., 1996).

Of the adolescents and young adults who reported lifetime arrests, 81.9% had used illicit drugs (61.1% in the past month), 56.1% had been drunk in the past month, and 11.5% self-report criteria for substance abuse or dependence in the past year (SAMHSA, 2007a). From 1992 to 2006 the number of adolescents referred to publicly funded treatment from the juvenile or criminal justice systems increased from 35,369 to 67,437 (39.0% to 50.6% of all public treatment admissions); in the same time period the number of young adults referred to publicly funded treatment from the justice system increased from 105,560 to 163,179 (43.3% to 50.2%) of all public treatment admissions (SAMHSA, 2008). Across ages, referral to treatment by the juvenile or criminal justice system was much more likely for males than for females (56.6% vs 36.9%) and for African-American and mixed-race adolescents than for Caucasian youth (60.0% and 51.1% vs 47.8%) (SAMHSA, 2008). *Thus, there are multiple promising systems for identifying and intervening with more adolescents and young adult substance users, and doing so systematically has the potential to reduce current health disparities.*

Variations by Level of Care

While policymakers and researchers have often attempted to compare outpatient (OP) and inpatient treatment, these programs have historically served different adolescents in terms of the severity of substance use disorders and other co-occurring problems (Dennis, Dawud-Noursi, Muck, & McDermeit (Ives), 2003; Gerstein & Johnson, 1999; Hser et al., 2001; Hubbard, Cavanaugh, Craddock, & Rachal, 1985; Rounds-Bryant, Kristiansen, & Hubbard, 1999; Sells & Simpson, 1979; Simpson, Savage, & Sells, 1978). These differences grew in the 1990s with the increasing use of more explicit patient placement criteria, such as those recommended by the American Society of Addiction Medicine (ASAM, 1996, 2001), the use of which has been mandated in several states. The guidelines recommend (and studies have increasingly also found) that the severity of substance use disorders and co-occurring problems increase with the intensity of services (i.e., EI, OP, intensive outpatient (IOP), residential). One of the major shifts that has been noted in the past decade is a significant drop in the number of short-term residential (STR) programs for low-severity youth. The short-term programs remaining today are typically more likely to target dual diagnosis and high-severity youth (at least in terms of medical and psychiatric needs) than are long-term programs (Dennis, Dawud-Noursi, Muck, & McDermeit (Ives), 2003). *Thus, it is important to recognize the heterogeneity of who is served in different types of treatment programs.*

Methods

Data Source

The rest of this chapter will explore the needs and correlates of adolescents presenting to treatment in more depth, and how they vary by the systems they are involved in and by their demographics. The data for the rest of this chapter are from 14,776 adolescents interviewed from 1998 to 2007 as part of 113 SAMHSA/CSAT adolescent and young adult treatment grants across the United States. These studies were

conducted across a variety of addiction treatment levels of care (e.g., early intervention, regular and intensive outpatient, short-, moderate-, and long-term residential)
and institutional settings (e.g., addiction agencies, student assistance programs,
child protective service agencies, justice agencies). All data were collected as part
of general clinical practice or specific research studies under their respective voluntary consent procedures and have been pooled for secondary analysis here under the
terms of data sharing agreements and the supervision of Chestnut's Institutional
Review Board.

Measures

The participant characteristics, substance use, and comorbidity profiles were
based on participant self-report to in-person interviews with the Global
Appraisal of Individual Needs (GAIN; Dennis, Titus, White, Unsicker, &
Hodgkins, 2003). GAIN is a standardized biopsychosocial assessment that integrates
clinical and research measures into one comprehensive structured interview
with eight main sections: background, substance use, physical health, risk
behaviors, mental health, environment risk, legal involvement, and vocational
correlates. GAIN has been used primarily to assess problems in order to support
clinical decision making related to diagnosis, placement, and treatment planning,
to measure change, and to document service utilization. GAIN incorporates
DSM-IV-TR (American Psychiatric Association [APA], 2000) symptoms for
common disorders, the American Society of Addiction Medicine's (ASAM,
2001) patient-placement criteria for the treatment of substance-related disorders, the Joint Commission on Accreditation of Healthcare Organization's
standards (JCAHO, 1995), epidemiological questions from the National
Household Survey on Drug Abuse (NHSDA; SAMHSA, 1996), and items
which have been economically valued for benefit–cost analysis with adults and
adolescents by Dr. Michael French (1994, 2003) and colleagues.

The GAIN's main scales have demonstrated excellent to good internal consistency (alpha over .90 on main scales, .70 on subscales), and test-retest reliability
(Rho over .70 on problem counts, Kappa over .60 on categorical measures) (Dennis,
Chan, & Funk, 2006; Dennis, Dawud-Noursi, Muck, & McDermeit (Ives), 2003;
Dennis, Ives, White, & Muck, 2008; Dennis, Scott, & Funk, 2003; Dennis et al.,
2004). GAIN measures have been validated with time line follow-back methods,
urine tests, collateral reports, treatment records, blind psychiatric diagnosis, Rasch
measurement models, confirmatory factor analysis, structural equation models, and
via construct or predictive validation (Dennis, Chan, & Funk, 2006; Dennis, Scott,
& Funk, 2003; Dennis et al., 2002, 2004; Godley, Godley, Dennis, Funk, & Passetti,
2002; Godley, Godley, Dennis, Funk, & Passetti, 2007; Lennox, Dennis, Ives, &
White, 2006; Lennox, Dennis, Scott, & Funk, 2006; Riley, Conrad, Bezruczko, &
Dennis, 2007; Shane, Jasiukaitis, & Green, 2003; White, 2005; White, Funk,
White, & Dennis, 2004). GAIN has also been demonstrated to be sensitive to

changes in clinical diagnosis and needs by age (Chan, Dennis, & Funk, 2008; Dennis, Chan, & Funk, 2006). A more detailed list of studies, copies of the actual GAIN instruments and items, and the syntax for creating the scales and diagnostic group variables are publicly available at www.chestnut.org/li/gain.

Participant Characteristics

The youth in this sample (n = 14,776) were interviewed across multiple levels of care including 7% early intervention, 62% outpatient, 7% IOP, 2% short-term (under 30 day) residential, 8% moderate-term (30–90 days) residential, 7% long-term (more than 90 days) residential, 2% correctional, and 5% outpatient continuing care (OPCC). In terms of current systems involvement, 88% were in school, 31% employed, 31% involved in the child welfare system, and 70% involved in the justice system (including 16% with 14 or more days in detention/jail of the 90 days before intake). Note that information on the degree of child welfare system involvement was available only for a subset of 5,934 clients (40% of the total). Clients involved in child welfare systems represented 31% of this subset or 1,815. Demographically, the youth in this sample were 73% male and 27% female; 16% African-American, 44% Caucasian, 21% Hispanic, 14% Mixed, and 6% other; 19% under the age of 15, 74% between the ages of 15 and 17, and 8% between the ages of 18 and 25 (range 9–25; mean age = 15.8, SD. = 1.5).

Analyses

Descriptive data is presented in the tables and sections below overall and then by level of care, system involvement, gender, race, and age. The differences were tested with chi-square analysis for the mutually exclusive groups (level of care, gender, race, and age). Clients were often involved in more than one system, thus chi-square analyses were done comparing those involved in the system versus those who were not. For space purposes the latter is not shown. Chi-square analyses were not done when a variable was part of the definition of a group (e.g., race by race). The results are organized in terms of the overall characteristics of adolescents in the data set, with comments on how they vary by each of the subgroups. Because the large sample sizes make even small differences statistically significant, the latter focuses on differences that are statistically significant at $p < .05$ and at least 25% different from the overall average (e.g., 1% if average is 4%; 10% if average is 40%) or more than a 9 percentage point difference (e.g., 65% vs 75%).

Characteristics and Correlates of Adolescents in Treatment

Overall Findings

Demographic and Environmental Characteristics

As noted earlier and shown in the first column of Table 3.1, the adolescent and young adult clients in this sample were predominately male, nonwhite, and between the ages of 15 and 17. Overall 49% of the clients were in the custody of a single parent, 27% reported weekly alcohol use in the home, 13% reported weekly drug use in the home, and 31% reported having been homeless or runaway. Clients reported high levels of social peer drug use (72%), vocational peer (at work/school) drug use (64%), and social peer weekly alcohol use (53%), with only slightly fewer reporting weekly alcohol use among vocational peers (48%). *Thus, many clients had one more major environmental risk factor associated with continued use or relapse.*

Most (88%) of the clients had been in school in the past 90 days (88%), and 31% had worked in the same time period. About 31% reported some kind of involvement in the child welfare system, either for themselves or their own children. Most (70%) were currently involved in juvenile or criminal justice system. *Thus, there was clearly overlap with the populations seen by other systems of care.*

Substance Use Characteristics

As shown in the first column of Table 3.2, the average age of first use was 12.6 years of age (range 1–20, SD. = 2.2), with 73% beginning use between the ages of 10 and 14. Clients reported an average of 3.2 years of substance use prior to intake (range 0–19, SD. = 2.3), with 23% reporting more than 5 years of use. Most (56%) self-reported criteria for lifetime substance dependence, with an additional 31% self-report criteria of lifetime abuse, and 12% self-reporting use with no abuse or dependence symptoms and 1% reporting no use or symptoms. In the 90 days before intake, 56% reported using substances weekly or more often, with the most common substances being marijuana (44%), alcohol (15%), cocaine (3%), heroin (2%), or other drugs (6%; includes amphetamines, tranquilizers, inhalants, PCP, etc.). In addition, 52% reported using tobacco weekly or more often. It should be noted that these rates were somewhat suppressed because 38% had been in a controlled environment (e.g., incarceration, residential/inpatient treatment) during the 90 days prior to intake (including 25% for 13 or more of 90 days). Many (42%) reported lifetime withdrawal symptoms, with 27% reporting withdrawal in the past week and 6% reporting a high number (11 or more) of withdrawal symptoms in the past week. Only 33% had been in treatment before, but almost half of those (14%) had

Table 3.1 Participant demographics by level of care, system involvement, gender, race group, and age group

	Total	Early Intervention (EI)	Outpatient (OP)	Intensive OP (IOP)	Short-Term Resid. (STR)	Mod.-Term Resid. (MTR)	Long-Term Resid. (LTR)	Corrections	OP Cont. Care (OPCC)	In School	In Workforce	In Child Welfare	In Justice System	Male	Female	African-American	White	Hispanic	Mixed	Other	Under 15	Age 15–17	Age 18–25
	14,776	991	9,156	1,095	361	1,219	998	275	681	12,993	4,522	1,815	10,352	10,745	4,024	2,399	6,412	3,032	2,032	865	2,739	10,886	1,149
Total%	100%	7%	62%	7%	2%	8%	7%	2%	5%	88%	31%	31%	70%	73%	27%	16%	43%	21%	14%	6%	19%	74%	8%
Demographics[a]																							
Female	27%	**18%**	28%	28%	33%	28%	27%	21%	28%	28%	23%	**38%**	24%	-	100%	**18%**	31%	22%	33%	33%	34%	26%	22%
African-American/Black	16%	20%	15%	**23%**	18%	17%	15%	**30%**	16%	16%	**10%**	16%	17%	18%	**11%**	100%	-	-	-	-	17%	16%	20%
Caucasian/White	44%	**24%**	50%	39%	37%	**27%**	25%	37%	49%	44%	**58%**	41%	41%	41%	49%	-	100%	-	-	-	36%	45%	47%
Hispanic	21%	**38%**	19%	25%	23%	18%	17%	16%	**14%**	20%	**15%**	**13%**	23%	22%	16%	-	-	100%	-	-	25%	20%	16%
Mixed	14%	16%	12%	12%	14%	11%	**33%**	16%	15%	14%	12%	**22%**	14%	**13%**	17%	-	-	-	100%	-	15%	14%	**10%**
Other (NA, Asian, Other)	6%	**2%**	**4%**	2%	9%	**27%**	9%	**1%**	6%	5%	5%	8%	5%	5%	7%	-	-	-	-	100%	7%	6%	6%
Age < 15-years	19%	19%	20%	18%	**11%**	22%	**12%**	19%	6%	20%	**7%**	18%	16%	17%	23%	19%	15%	22%	21%	21%	100%	-	-
15–17-years	74%	74%	72%	80%	**85%**	72%	81%	81%	67%	74%	81%	80%	76%	75%	71%	71%	76%	71%	73%	70%	-	100%	-
18–25-years	8%	7%	8%	**2%**	**4%**	6%	7%	**0%**	**27%**	6%	12%	**1%**	8%	8%	6%	9%	8%	6%	**6%**	8%	-	-	100%
Family/living																							
Single parent family	49%	57%	47%	57%	58%	48%	46%	**62%**	47%	49%	43%	**39%**	51%	48%	50%	**62%**	43%	52%	50%	43%	53%	48%	**7%**
Weekly alcohol use in home	27%	**18%**	26%	26%	49%	29%	28%	**19%**	**16%**	27%	31%	23%	26%	26%	30%	17%	33%	21%	29%	24%	26%	23%	28%
Weekly dug use in home	13%	10%	10%	**16%**	31%	22%	23%	11%	10%	12%	13%	16%	12%	11%	**17%**	12%	13%	11%	15%	14%	12%	20%	17%
Ever homeless/runaway	31%	36%	24%	37%	44%	40%	51%	44%	**48%**	30%	27%	**53%**	32%	26%	**43%**	24%	29%	31%	**44%**	32%	29%	31%	31%
Social peers																							
Regular peer alcohol use at Work/school[a]	48%	41%	45%	54%	65%	59%	55%	43%	**38%**	49%	53%	48%	48%	48%	47%	**31%**	52%	49%	49%	54%	40%	50%	40%
Regular peer drug use[a]	53%	52%	49%	53%	79%	72%	68%	45%	50%	53%	53%	56%	55%	53%	54%	**41%**	57%	53%	54%	60%	**43%**	57%	49%
Regular peer drug use at Work/school[b]	64%	**54%**	66%	65%	78%	67%	64%	61%	**41%**	67%	70%	57%	62%	64%	63%	**50%**	71%	61%	64%	62%	62%	66%	**46%**
Regular peer drug use[b]	72%	66%	70%	72%	**90%**	82%	81%	69%	**53%**	71%	76%	69%	71%	72%	72%	**62%**	78%	66%	72%	69%	66%	74%	**60%**

Environment

In school[c]	88%	85%	91%	88%	**75%**	**76%**	84%	83%	89%	**100%**	86%	88%	87%	88%	90%	88%	90%	88%	90%	**79%**	95%	89%
Employed[e]	31%	**22%**	35%	28%	32%	24%	24%	**10%**	**22%**	30%	**100%**	**21%**	30%	32%	26%	**19%**	**41%**	**22%**	23%	25%	**11%**	34%
Any child welfare involvement[d]	31%	**45%**	**22%**	38%	**17%**	30%	**81%**	**97%**	**85%**	30%	**21%**	**100%**	32%	27%	**39%**	32%	25%	29%	**47%**	33%	32%	30%

66%	48%	73%

Note: Differences that are statistically significant at *p*<.05 and 25% (or more than 9 points) higher than average are in bold; those lower than average by this much are **bold and under-lined**. Child welfare based on *n* = 5934.

[a] Spent time in the past year with on or more people at work/school or socially who got drunk weekly.

[b] Spent time in the past year with one or more people at work/school or socially who used drugs quarterly.

[c] During the past 90 days.

[d] Reports days in foster care or a group home, referred to treatment by social worker or DCFS/welfare, has child in foster care, group or institution.

Table 3.2 Participant substance use history at intake by level of care, system involvement, gender, race group, and age group

	Total	Early Intervention (EI)	Outpatient (OP)	Intensive OP (IOP)	Short-Term Resid (STR)	Mod-Term Resid. (MIT)	Long Term Resid. (LTR)	Corrections	OP Cont. Care (OPCC)	In School	In Workforce	In Child Welfare	In Justice System	Male	Female	African-American	White	Hispanic	Mixed	Other	Under 15	Age 15-17	Age 18-25
	14,776	991	9,156	1,095	361	1,219	998	275	681	12,993	4,522	1,815	10,352	10,745	4,024	2,399	6,412	3,032	2,032	865	2,739	10,886	1,149
Total %	100%	7%	62%	7%	2%	8%	7%	2%	5%	88%	31%	31%	70%	73%	27%	16%	43%	21%	14%	6%	19%	74%	8%
Age of first use																							
Under 10	9%	8%	**6%**	7%	**20%**	**13%**	**13%**	**11%**	**13%**	8%	8%	**13%**	9%	10%	**7%**	**7%**	8%	9%	**12%**	**15%**	11%	9%	7%
Age 10-14	73%	73%	72%	76%	73%	77%	78%	79%	75%	74%	65%	77%	74%	72%	76%	73%	71%	78%	74%	72%	**89%**	72%	**54%**
Age 15+	18%	19%	22%	**10%**	**8%**	**8%**	**9%**	**10%**	**12%**	18%	27%	**11%**	17%	18%	17%	21%	21%	**13%**	14%	14%	**0%**	20%	39%
Lifetime substance severity																							
No Use	1%	2%	2%	**1%**	**0%**	**1%**	**1%**	**0%**	**0%**	2%	**0%**	2%	**1%**	1%	2%	4%	**1%**	**1%**	**1%**	3%	5%	**1%**	**0%**
Use	12%	12%	16%	**6%**	**1%**	**2%**	**5%**	9%	**2%**	12%	11%	**8%**	11%	11%	12%	**16%**	11%	12%	11%	**8%**	16%	11%	**9%**
Abuse	31%	26%	37%	29%	**9%**	**17%**	**16%**	29%	**9%**	31%	32%	24%	31%	33%	24%	**39%**	30%	30%	25%	23%	35%	30%	24%
Dependence	56%	60%	**45%**	64%	**91%**	**81%**	**78%**	62%	**89%**	55%	57%	**66%**	57%	54%	61%	**41%**	58%	57%	63%	67%	44%	58%	67%
Drug Use past 90 days:																							
Weekly User of anything[a]	56%	**43%**	53%	62%	**89%**	**81%**	**72%**	54%	**20%**	55%	60%	49%	55%	57%	53%	56%	57%	57%	54%	55%	50%	58%	49%
Weekly Alcohol Use[a]	15%	12%	12%	15%	**37%**	**31%**	**26%**	**11%**	**6%**	14%	18%	14%	15%	15%	16%	**10%**	16%	16%	17%	**19%**	**11%**	16%	19%
Weekly Tobacco Use[a]	52%	**38%**	51%	55%	**81%**	55%	**64%**	51%	56%	51%	59%	59%	52%	50%	57%	45%	**62%**	**37%**	54%	**37%**	**40%**	54%	61%
Weekly Marijuana User[a]	44%	**33%**	41%	48%	**72%**	**65%**	**56%**	44%	**15%**	43%	47%	36%	43%	46%	37%	49%	44%	44%	41%	40%	40%	46%	33%
Weekly Crack/Cocaine Use[a]	3%	**2%**	**1%**	4%	**15%**	11%	6%	**4%**	**2%**	3%	4%	3%	3%	3%	4%	**1%**	3%	6%	3%	2%	1%	2%	5%
Weekly Heroin/Opioid User[a]	2%	**2%**	**1%**	2%	**8%**	6%	5%	1%	**1%**	2%	3%	2%	2%	3%	3%	**1%**	3%	2%	**2%**	2%	1%	6%	5%
Weekly Other Drug Use[a]	6%	**2%**	**3%**	6%	**20%**	14%	20%	4%	**1%**	5%	7%	7%	6%	**4%**	10%	**1%**	6%	6%	8%	7%	4%	6%	4%
13+ Days controlled environment[a]	25%	**44%**	**12%**	36%	42%	35%	53%	69%	76%	24%	**16%**	56%	32%	26%	24%	30%	19%	27%	**34%**	33%	18%	26%	34%

Withdrawal severity

Any lifetime	42%	37%	36%	49%	**60%**	**65%**	**58%**	34%	**55%**	41%	43%	50%	41%	40%	49%	<u>**29%**</u>	42%	45%	47%	54%	38%	43%	45%
Any past week	27%	<u>**18%**</u>	26%	28%	34%	43%	**39%**	<u>**16%**</u>	**8%**	27%	29%	28%	26%	27%	28%	**22%**	26%	29%	30%	33%	27%	27%	25%
High (11+) past week symptoms	6%	<u>**3%**</u>	<u>**4%**</u>	8%	**18%**	**18%**	**13%**	<u>**1%**</u>	**1%**	5%	7%	6%	5%	5%	8%	<u>**3%**</u>	6%	6%	5%	14%	5%	6%	6%

Prior SA treatment episodes

Any	33%	28%	<u>**22%**</u>	43%	**54%**	**54%**	**53%**	45%	**85%**	31%	33%	47%	35%	32%	33%	**24%**	33%	32%	38%	43%	19%	34%	48%
Two or more	14%	<u>**8%**</u>	<u>**7%**</u>	22%	**24%**	**24%**	**28%**	17%	**51%**	13%	14%	26%	16%	13%	15%	<u>**8%**</u>	15%	13%	**17%**	19%	6%	15%	24%

Perception

Perceives AOD as a problem[c]	27%	26%	<u>**18%**</u>	31%	**64%**	**48%**	**50%**	25%	**45%**	25%	28%	35%	27%	25%	32%	<u>**16%**</u>	30%	24%	31%	**34%**	**17%**	28%	**36%**
Perceives need for treatment	69%	70%	<u>**61%**</u>	83%	**95%**	**89%**	**90%**	64%	**94%**	68%	67%	76%	69%	68%	70%	67%	70%	67%	71%	71%	64%	70%	76%

Note: Differences that are statistically significant at $p < 05$ and 25% (or more than 9 points) higher than average are in **bold**, those lower than average by this much are **bold and underlined**. Child welfare based on $n = 5934$.

[a] During the past 90 days.

[b] Hospitals, treatment, detention, or Jail (where not free to come and go as you please).

[c] Do you currently have any problems related to alcohol or drug use?

been in treatment two or more times before. While only 27% believed they had a problem related to alcohol or other drugs (AOD), 69% recognized that they needed treatment to deal with some substance-related problem. *While certainly in need of treatment, this profile also suggests that the adolescents and young adults present- ing to treatment are largely being seen earlier (i.e., first 10 years) in the course of their addiction.*

Co-occurring Psychiatric, Victimization, HIV Risk, Crime Problems

As shown in the first column of Table 3.3, 67% of the clients self-reported criteria for one or more major psychiatric problems, including externalizing disorders (59%) such as CD (50%) or attention-deficit hyperactivity disorder (ADHD, 43%), and internalizing disorders (42%), such as depression (major depressive disorder, MDD, 35%), traumatic distress disorders (TDD, 24%), suicidal thoughts or actions (22%), or generalized anxiety disorders (GAD, 14%). This includes over half (52% of those with any, 35% of total) self-reporting criteria for both internalizing and externalizing disorders. However, only 40% reported having received prior mental health treatment. *Thus, co-occurring psychiatric problems are the norm and often have not been treated.*

Most (63%) of the clients reported being victimized (physically, sexually, or emo- tionally) in their lifetime, with almost half (45%) reporting high levels of victimiza- tion (i.e., multiple types of victimization, multiple times or people involved, people they trusted involved, physical harm, fear of death, no one believed them when they sought help, ongoing concerns about it happening again) and 20% reporting recent victimization in the 90 days prior to their intake assessment. In the 90 days prior to intake, the most common HIV-risk behaviors were having sex (65%), having sex with multiple sexual partners (30%), and having unprotected sex (25%); though present, needle use was relatively rare (2% in the past 90 days). In the year prior to intake, 80% self-reported violence toward others (68%) and/or illegal activity (64%), with the latter including property crimes (48%), violent crimes (43%), and drug-related/ other crimes (45%; not including just use). Figure 3.1 shows the number of past-year problems endorsed in 12 areas: alcohol disorder (abuse or dependence), marijuana disorder, other substance disorder, depression, anxiety, suicide, traumatic distress, CD, ADHD, victimization, physical violence, and illegal activities. Most (94%) reported at least one problem, with the majority reporting multiple problems, 84% reporting two or more problems, 72% reporting three or more problems, 58% report- ing four or more problems, and 45% reporting five or more problems. *Thus, multiple co-occurring problems are the norm of people entering treatment.*

The following three sections summarize the characteristics of clients by the ini- tial study treatment level of care, by four measures of system involvement (school, work, child welfare, justice), and by key demographics (gender, race group, and age group) using breakouts found to the right of the total in these three tables and the figure. The rest of the chapter highlights only differences of 25% or more from the overall average characteristics described above.

Table 3.3 Co-occuring problems by level of care, system involvement, gender, race group and age group

Variable	Total	Early Intervention (EI)	Outpatient (OP)	Intensive OP (IOP)	Short-Term Resid. (MTR)	Mod-Term Resid. (LTR)	Long-Term Resid. (LTR)	Corrections	OP Cont. Care (OPCC)	In School	In Workforce	In Child Welfare	In Justice System	Male	Female	African-American	White	Hispanic	Mixed	Other	Under 15	Age 15–17	Age 18–25
Total N	14,776	991	9,156	1,095	361	1,219	998	275	681	12,993	4,522	1,815	10,352	10,745	4,024	2,399	6,412	3,032	2,032	865	2,739	10,886	1,149
Total %	100%	7%	62%	7%	2%	8%	7%	2%	5%	88%	31%	12%	70%	73%	27%	16%	43%	21%	14%	6%	19%	74%	8%
Any past year psychiatric problems	67%	66%	60%	73%	93%	81%	83%	78%	73%	67%	65%	78%	66%	62%	78%	_54%_	69%	66%	74%	68%	69%	67%	**_57%_**
Past year internalizing problems																							
Any past year internal disorder	42%	39%	36%	49%	**73%**	**60%**	**61%**	44%	**55%**	42%	41%	**55%**	41%	35%	**62%**	**_30%_**	43%	42%	**52%**	48%	39%	43%	44%
Major Depression disorder	35%	31%	29%	42%	**58%**	**49%**	**52%**	36%	**47%**	34%	33%	**47%**	33%	28%	**54%**	**_22%_**	36%	35%	**44%**	39%	33%	35%	36%
Generalized Anxiety disorder	14%	12%	_10%_	18%	**42%**	**28%**	**27%**	**11%**	**18%**	14%	15%	**18%**	14%	11%	**23%**	**8%**	15%	14%	**17%**	**22%**	**_11%_**	15%	**19%**
Suicidal thoughts or actions	22%	18%	19%	28%	**43%**	**33%**	**33%**	23%	**32%**	22%	22%	**30%**	21%	20%	**29%**	18%	23%	21%	26%	28%	23%	22%	22%
Traumatic distress disorder[a]	24%	22%	19%	**31%**	**49%**	**33%**	**41%**	26%	**37%**	23%	24%	**33%**	23%	18%	**40%**	**_17%_**	24%	23%	**30%**	28%	22%	24%	26%
Past year externalizing problems																							
Any past year external disorder	59%	57%	54%	66%	**87%**	**72%**	**76%**	**75%**	62%	60%	58%	**70%**	59%	56%	67%	**_46%_**	63%	58%	65%	58%	63%	60%	**_45%_**
Conduct disorder	50%	48%	43%	59%	**82%**	**68%**	**72%**	**69%**	50%	50%	49%	**61%**	51%	48%	56%	**_40%_**	52%	50%	56%	50%	53%	52%	**_33%_**
Attention Deficit-Hyperactivity disorder	43%	38%	38%	48%	**68%**	**52%**	**58%**	**53%**	48%	43%	42%	**53%**	42%	39%	**53%**	**_29%_**	48%	39%	50%	40%	46%	43%	34%
Pattern of psychiatric problems																							
Neither	33%	34%	40%	27%	**7%**	**19%**	**17%**	**22%**	27%	33%	35%	**22%**	34%	38%	**22%**	**46%**	31%	34%	26%	32%	31%	33%	**43%**
Internalizing only	7%	8%	7%	7%	**5%**	8%	7%	**3%**	**10%**	7%	7%	8%	6%	8%	**10%**	8%	5%	5%	8%	**10%**	5%	7%	**12%**
Externalizing only	24%	27%	25%	24%	20%	21%	23%	**34%**	**17%**	25%	24%	23%	25%	27%	**_15%_**	24%	25%	24%	22%	20%	29%	24%	**_13%_**
Both internalizing and externalizing	35%	30%	29%	42%	**68%**	**52%**	**54%**	41%	**45%**	35%	34%	**47%**	34%	29%	**52%**	**_22%_**	38%	34%	44%	39%	34%	36%	32%
Any prior mental health treatment	40%	32%	37%	43%	48%	45%	46%	**52%**	**50%**	39%	40%	**58%**	38%	36%	**50%**	**_26%_**	**50%**	**_25%_**	47%	35%	37%	40%	42%
Physical, sexual, or Emotional Victimization																							
Any history of victim or current worries	65%	68%	60%	72%	**84%**	**76%**	**79%**	59%	**77%**	64%	66%	**75%**	66%	64%	69%	59%	65%	65%	73%	70%	60%	66%	70%
Lifetime history of victimization	63%	67%	57%	69%	**83%**	**74%**	**77%**	58%	**78%**	61%	63%	**73%**	64%	61%	67%	55%	62%	63%	**72%**	67%	57%	64%	69%
High levels of victimization[b]	45%	49%	38%	53%	**70%**	**59%**	**64%**	41%	**63%**	44%	45%	**58%**	46%	41%	**55%**	36%	44%	45%	**56%**	**54%**	41%	46%	50%
Past year	37%	40%	32%	45%	**59%**	**52%**	**51%**	31%	36%	37%	36%	41%	38%	36%	41%	30%	36%	38%	44%	39%	44%	38%	**_27%_**
Past 90 days	20%	16%	18%	24%	**34%**	**29%**	**25%**	15%	**_10%_**	20%	21%	20%	20%	18%	**24%**	17%	20%	20%	23%	18%	23%	20%	**_13%_**
Current worry about victimization	18%	17%	16%	22%	**39%**	**25%**	**24%**	**_9%_**	20%	18%	17%	22%	18%	16%	**25%**	16%	16%	20%	22%	27%	21%	18%	16%

(continued)

Table 3.3 (continued)

Variable	Total	Early Intervention(EI)	Outpatient (OP)	Intensive OP (IOP)	Short-Term Resid. (MTR)	Mod-Term Resid. (LTR)	Long-Term Resid. (LTR)	Corrections	OP Cont. Care (OPCC)	In School	In Workforce	In Child Welfare	In Justice System	Male	Female	African-American	White	Hispanic	Mixed	Other	Under 15	Age 15–17	Age 18–25
	14,776	991	9,156	1,095	361	1,219	998	275	681	12,993	4,522	1,815	10,352	10,745	4,024	2,399	6,412	3,032	2,032	865	2,739	10,886	1,149
Total %	100%	7%	62%	7%	2%	8%	7%	2%	5%	88%	31%	31%	70%	73%	27%	16%	43%	21%	14%	6%	19%	74%	8%
HIV Risks																							
Any past 90 days needle use	2%	**1%**	**1%**	**1%**	**7%**	**5%**	**10%**	**1%**	**1%**	2%	2%	**3%**	2%	2%	**3%**	**1%**	2%	**3%**	**1%**	3%	**1%**	2%	4%
Any past 90 days sexual experience	65%	56%	62%	66%	**82%**	**75%**	**79%**	60%	72%	63%	72%	65%	67%	65%	63%	**74%**	62%	65%	66%	57%	**46%**	68%	73%
Any past 90 day unprotected sex	25%	22%	22%	26%	**45%**	**33%**	**40%**	20%	29%	24%	30%	26%	27%	23%	31%	23%	25%	28%	28%	**18%**	**15%**	27%	36%
Multiple sexual partners in past 90 days	30%	25%	27%	33%	**52%**	**38%**	**39%**	34%	**21%**	29%	32%	30%	31%	32%	23%	**44%**	25%	31%	29%	**22%**	22%	31%	30%
Violence and Illegal activity (other than possession use)																							
Any violence or Illegal activity	80%	**85%**	76%	**85%**	**94%**	**89%**	**91%**	**91%**	76%	80%	79%	83%	84%	81%	77%	80%	78%	81%	83%	81%	80%	81%	**70%**
Acts of physical Violence[c]	68%	**74%**	63%	**73%**	**84%**	**76%**	**80%**	**80%**	68%	67%	64%	74%	71%	69%	66%	70%	63%	72%	75%	68%	72%	68%	**57%**
Any Illegal Activity	64%	**73%**	57%	**72%**	**87%**	**79%**	**78%**	**78%**	57%	63%	65%	65%	71%	67%	55%	61%	63%	66%	66%	66%	61%	66%	**49%**
Property Crimes[d]	48%	**55%**	40%	**56%**	**78%**	**65%**	**70%**	**63%**	49%	48%	47%	54%	52%	50%	41%	42%	47%	50%	53%	51%	48%	50%	**32%**
Violent Crimes[e]	43%	**54%**	36%	**53%**	**67%**	**54%**	**55%**	**55%**	42%	43%	41%	48%	48%	46%	35%	44%	39%	48%	49%	43%	45%	44%	**29%**
Other drug related crimes[f]	45%	**53%**	37%	**55%**	**79%**	**62%**	**67%**	**56%**	44%	44%	50%	47%	51%	49%	**34%**	41%	44%	49%	47%	47%	37%	48%	38%

Note: Differences that are statistically significant at p<.05 and 25% (or more than 9 points) higher than average are in **bold** those lower by this much are in **bold and underlined**. Child welfare based on 5934

[a] Post traumatic distress, acute traumatic distress disorders of extreme stress not otherwise specified.

[b] Reporting 4 or more of the following types of victimization, traumagenic factors (e.g., multiple people, someone they trusted, fearing for life, sexual penetration, people didn't believe them or continuing fear it will reoccur.

[c] Physical assault of another person within the past year.

[d] Self report of or arrests related to vandalism, forgery, bad checks shoplifting theft, robbery, auto theft.

[e] Self report of or arrests related to assault aggravated assault with a weapon, rape, murder, and arson.

[f] Self report of or arrests related to driving under the influence, manufacture or distribution, prostitution, gang involvement.

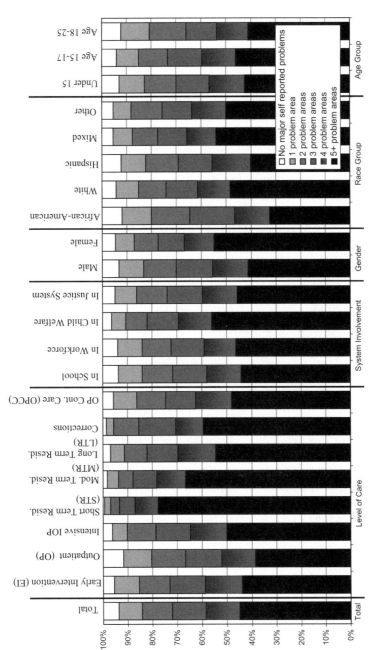

*Count of the number of problems endorsed in any the following areas during the past year: alcohol disorder, marijuana disorder, other substance disorder, internalizing problems, externalizing problems, victimization, physical violence, illegal activities. While level of care, gender, race and age group show all levels or group, the four system involvement items present data only for those involved in the given system (as compared to those not involved with that system). All comparisons are significant with the exception of working compared to those not working.

Fig. 3.1 Number of major clinical problem areas*

Variation by Level of Care

Early Intervention (*n* = 991)

As shown in Table 3.1, EI clients were more likely than average to be Hispanic (38%) and to be involved with child welfare (45%), but were less likely than average to be female (18%), Caucasian (24%), to have weekly alcohol use in the home (18%), to report regular drug use among vocational peers (54%), or to be employed (22%). Table 3.2 shows that EI clients had the lowest rates of weekly tobacco use (38%) and lower than average weekly use of any substance (43%), including marijuana (33%), cocaine (2%), and other drugs (2%). They were more likely than average to have been in a controlled environment in the past 90 days (44%). They were less likely than average to report withdrawal in each time period. They reported slightly lower levels of prior treatment (28%) and were much less likely to report multiple episodes of treatment (8%). Table 3.3 shows that EI clients reported the lowest rates of suicidal thoughts (18%). As would be expected from their higher than average justice system involvement, this group had higher than average illegal activity (73%) and involvement in violent crime (54%). In Figure 3.1, the total number of problems reported by EI clients is equal to or higher than for clients in OP. *Thus, rather than reaching lower severity people, EI is more characterized by reaching people who are appropriate but not yet reaching outpatient treatment (whether due to motivation, barrier, or opportunity).*

Outpatient (*n* = 9,156)

As shown in Table 3.1 OP clients were the largest group. They were less likely to have child welfare system involvement (22%), but on other measures, this group was close to average. Table 3.2 shows that OP clients had the lowest proportion of those who started using under the age of 10 (6%) and the lowest percentage with lifetime dependence (45%), perceiving the need for treatment (61%) and of perceiving AOD use as a problem (18%). They were also the least likely to have had any prior treatment (22%) and to have 2⁺ prior episodes (7%). Their rates of weekly use were average for most substances. Table 3.3 shows that OP clients reported the lowest or among the lowest rates of internalizing problems (36% any) and externalizing problems (54% any). In Fig. 3.1, OP clients were most likely to report no problems (8%) and the least likely to report five or more problems (39%).

Intensive Outpatient (*n* = 1,095)

As shown in Table 3.1, IOP clients were more likely than average to be African-American (23%) and less likely to be aged 18–25 (2%). Table 3.2 shows that IOP clients were more likely to have started using under the age of 10 (13%) and less likely to have started over the age of 15 (10%). They were more likely than EI or OP clients to have had prior treatment (43%). Table 3.3 shows that IOP clients had higher than average rates of TDD (31%), violent crime (53%), and drug crimes (55%). In Fig. 3.1, this group was more severe that EI or OP, but less severe than STR.

Short-Term Residential (*n* = 361)

As shown in Table 3.1, STR clients were the most likely to report weekly alcohol (49%) or drug (31%) use in the home, weekly alcohol or drug use among social (79% and 90%, respectively) or vocational (65% and 78%, respectively) peers. STR clients were more likely than average to have ever been homeless or runaway (44%), but were least likely to be involved with the child welfare system (17%). Those in STR had the highest percentage who started using under the age of 10 (20%) and had the highest percentage of clients with lifetime dependence (91%), as well as the highest with weekly use of each substance (89% of any substance, 81% tobacco, 72% marijuana, 37% alcohol, 15% cocaine, 8% opioids, and 20% other) and more than average for 13^+ days in a controlled environment (42%). Clients in STR were most likely to perceive a need for any treatment (95%) and AOD use as a problem (64%). They were also among the highest in reporting withdrawal (60% lifetime, 34% past week, 18% acute past week) and prior treatment (54%), including two or more prior treatment episodes (24%). Table 3.3 shows that STR clients reported the highest rates of most co-occurring problems. The exceptions, where STR clients were among the lowest, were having "only" internalizing problems (5%) and "only" externalizing (20%), as opposed to both (STR was highest at 68%) or neither (STR was lowest at 7%). While higher than average, these clients were not the most likely to have received prior mental health treatment (48%). Past 90-day needle use was higher than average for STR (7%). In Fig. 3.1, STR clients were the most likely to report problems in five or more areas (78%), and least likely to report no problems (1%). *Thus, STR clients are actually a subset of the most severe clients who have often gotten the farthest into trouble, often very quickly.*

Moderate-Term Residential (*n* = 1,219)

As shown in Table 3.1, moderate-term residential (MTR) clients were the second largest group and the most likely to be under 15 years of age (22%), of other race groups (27%, including Native American, Alaskan, Hawaiian, Pacific Islander, Asian, Other). Similar to STR, those in MTR were more likely to report weekly drug use in the home (22%), ever being homeless or runaway (40%), and regular peer drug (82%) and alcohol use (72% social peers; 59% vocational peers). Table 3.2 shows that MTR had the highest withdrawal severity rates across time periods.

They were higher than average in starting use under the age of 10 (15%), reporting lifetime dependence (81%), in weekly use of each substance (81% of any substance), having 13+ days in a controlled environment (35%), having prior treatment (54%; including 2+ episodes (24%), perceiving a need for any treatment (89%), and for perceiving AOD as a problem (48%). Table 3.3 shows that MTR clients had a similar pattern of high comorbidity as those in STR, but with slightly lower rates than that group. In Fig. 3.1, this group was more severe than EI or OP, but less severe than STR.

Long-Term Residential (*n=998*)

As shown in Table 3.1, LTR clients were the most likely to be of mixed race (33%), to have been homeless or runaway (51%), to report weekly drug use in the home (23%), and weekly alcohol use among social peers (68%). LTR clients were also more likely than average to have regular peer drug users (81%) and be involved in the child welfare system (81%) and/or justice system (83%). Table 3.2 shows that LTR clients were quite similar to MTR clients, but weekly tobacco use was higher among LTR (64%) than among MTR (55%) clients, and LTR clients were more likely to have 13+ days in a controlled environment (53%). Table 3.3 shows that LTR clients were the most likely to report needle use in the past 90 days (10%); otherwise their rates generally fell between the high rates of STR clients and the lower rates for MTR clients. Of the three groups of residential clients, they were the least likely to report anxiety (27%) and recent victimization (25%) and the most likely to report externalizing problems only (23%). In Fig. 3.1, this group was more severe than EI or OP, but less severe than STR. *Thus, LTR (and to a lesser extent MTR) serve clients who are characterized by high levels of involvement in welfare and justice systems and higher than average psychiatric severity (but not the highest).*

Corrections (*n* = 275)

As shown in Table 3.1, corrections settings were the smallest group and were most likely to be African-American (30%), from a single parent family (62%), and involved in the child welfare system (97%). None in this sample were over the age of 18. By definition they were 100% involved in the justice system. They were less likely than average to report weekly alcohol use in the home (19%) and were least likely to be employed (10%). Table 3.2 shows that correctional setting clients had the highest percentage starting use between the ages of 10 and 14 (79%). While similar to average or slightly lower for weekly use of most substance, this group had high rates of 13+ days in a controlled environment (69%), second only to OPCC (76%). Withdrawal was lowest for those in corrections (34% lifetime, 1% acute past week) and they were more likely than average to report prior treatment (45%). Table 3.3 shows that corrections clients reported average rates of internalizing problems (44%), but higher than average rates of externalizing problems (75%), including both CD (69%) and ADHD (53%). They were the most likely to have received prior mental health treatment (52%) and the least likely to report current worries about victimization (9%). As expected, they were among the most likely to report acts of physical violence (any 80%), any illegal activity (78%), property crime (63%), violent crime (55%), and drug-related crime (56%). In Fig. 3.1, this group was more severe than EI, OP, or LTR, but less severe than STR or MTR. *Having nearly twice the average number of African-Americans as the overall average suggests the need to better understand and address health disparities in the justice system.*

Outpatient Continuing Care (*n* = 681)

As shown in Table 3.1, OPCC clients are unique in having been in a controlled environment (residential treatment or correctional) for some period of time prior to their current treatment. They were the most likely to be of ages 18–25 (27%), more likely than average to be Caucasian (49%), and the least likely to be Hispanic (14%). OPCC clients were more likely to have been homeless or runaway (48%) and to be involved with the child welfare system (85%). They were the least likely of all groups to be under 18 (67% 15–17 and 6% under 15), to report weekly alcohol use in the home (16%), or regular drug use among social (53%) or vocational (41%) peers. This group was also less likely than average to be employed (22%) or to have current justice system involvement (66%). With the exception of weekly tobacco use (56%), OPCC clients reported close to or the lowest rate of any weekly substance use (20%) and each specific substance (presumably related to being in a controlled environment). As expected, OPCC had the highest rates of prior treatment (85%) and two or more episodes of prior treatment (51%). They were the most likely to have been 13+ days in a controlled environment (76%), and had higher than average rates of lifetime dependence (89%) and lifetime withdrawal (55%). Past-week withdrawal, however, was lower than average for OPCC (8% past week, 1% acute past week). OPCC clients were the more likely to perceive a need for treatment (94%), and that their AOD use was a problem (45%). Table 3.3 shows that OPCC clients were the most likely to report "only" internalizing problems (10%) and the least likely to report "only" externalizing problems (17%). They were more likely than average to report both internalizing and externalizing problems (45%) and lifetime victimization (78%). However, they were the least likely to report recent victimization (10%). They were also the least likely to report needle use (<1%) and multiple sex partners (21%). OPCC clients with OP clients were the least likely to report any violence or illegal activities (76%). In Fig. 3.1, this group was more severe than EI or OP, but less severe than STR or MTR. *Thus, while they have high severity in the past year, OPCC serves clients characterized by high levels of service and recent reductions in problems.*

Variation by System Involvement

In School (*n* =12,993)

Since 88% of the clients were in school, the characteristic of those in school was within 2 percentage points of the total for most of Tables 3.1–3.3 and Fig. 3.1 (see overview above). The exception is that those in school were less likely to be of ages 18–25 (6%) compared to those who were not in school.

In the Workforce (*n* = 4,522)

In Table 3.1, clients in the workforce were more likely to be white (58%) and of ages 18–25 (12%); they were less likely to be African-American (10%), Hispanic (15%), under the age of 15 (7%), or involved in the welfare system (21%). Table 3.2 shows that clients in the workforce were more likely to have started use over the age of 15 (27%) and to report weekly use of opiates (3%). Clients in the workforce reported average rates of mental health, HIV risk, and crime-related problems (Table 3.3) and number of other problems (Fig. 3.1).

Child Welfare (*n* = 1,815 of 5,934)

In Table 3.1, clients involved in the child welfare system (themselves or via their children) were more likely to be female (38%), of mixed race (22%) or other race (8%), to have weekly drug use in the home (16%), or to have a history of running away or being homeless (53%). They were less likely to be Hispanic (13%), of ages 18–25 (1%), from a single parent family (39%), or employed (21%). Table 3.2 shows that they were more likely to have started using before the age of 10 (13%), self-report criteria for dependence (66%), to have spent 13 or more of the 90 days before intake in a controlled environment (56%), to report prior treatment (47%; 26% multiple episodes of treatment), to perceive AOD use as a problem (35%), and/or to perceive the need for treatment (76%). Table 3.3 shows that they were more likely to report having any psychiatric problem (78%) overall and for each type of disorder listed. They were also more likely to report having both internalizing and externalizing disorders (47%) and a history of mental health treatment (58%). They were more likely to report both lifetime victimization (73%), high levels of victimization (58%), and needle use (3%). In Fig. 3.1, they were more likely to report having problems in five or more areas (56%). *Thus, clients in the welfare system are more severe than average and a particularly high risk of long-term substance misuse.*

Justice System (*n* = 10,352)

Since 70% of the clients were involved in the justice system, the characteristic of those involved in the justice system was generally within a few percentage points of the total for most of Tables 3.1–3.3 and Fig. 3.1 (see overview above). Not surprisingly, the exception is that those involved in the justice system were more likely to have spent 13 or more days prior to intake in a controlled environment (32%).

Variation by Demographic Groups

Gender (*n* = 10,745 males and 4,024 females)

In Table 3.1, females are more likely than males to have weekly drug use in their home (17% vs. 11%), a history of running away or being homeless (43% vs 26%), and be involved in the child welfare system (39% vs 27%); they are less likely to be African-American (11% vs 18%) and involved in the juvenile justice system (61% vs 74%). Table 3.2 shows that females are more likely than males to report weekly use of cocaine (4% vs 3%), opioids (3% vs 2%), and other drugs (10% vs 4%), and to report a high number of withdrawal symptoms in the past week (8% vs 5%); they were less likely to have started using under the age of 10 (7% vs 10%). Table 3.3 shows that females are more likely than males to report each mental health problem and to have higher rates of any psychological problem (78% vs 62%), including higher self-reported rates of any internalizing disorder (62% vs 35%), any externalizing disorder (67% vs 56%), having both internalizing and externalizing disorders (52% vs 29%), and having a history of prior mental health treatment (50% vs 36%). Females were also more likely than males to report high levels of victimization (55% vs 41%) and report needle use in the past 90 days (3% vs 2%); they were less likely to report having multiple sexual partners in the past 90 days (23% vs 32%), any illegal activity (55% vs 67%), and each type of crime. In Fig. 3.1, females are more likely than males to report five or more major problems (55% vs 41%). *Thus, female clients tend to be more severe on average, but have different issues (more mental health, less illegal activity) than do male clients.*

Race (*n* = 2,399 African-American; 6,412 White; 3,032 Hispanic; 2,032 Mixed; and 865 Other)

In Table 3.1, African-American clients were less likely than average to be female (18%), and the least likely of all race groups to report weekly alcohol use in their home (17%), regular peer alcohol use (31% vocational, 41% social) or drug use (50% vocational, 62% social), and to be employed (19%), and the most likely of any race to be of ages 18–25 (9%) or from a single parent family (62%). White clients were more likely to be employed (41%) while Hispanic clients were less likely to be employed (22%). Mixed race clients were more likely to report a history of running away or being homeless (44%) and being involved in the child welfare system (47%); they were less likely to be of ages 18–25 (6%). Table 3.2 shows that African-Americans were less likely to report starting under the age of 10 (7%), dependence (41%), weekly use of alcohol (10%), cocaine (1%), opioids (1%), other drugs (1%), and withdrawal symptoms (29% lifetime, 22% past week, 3% high number of symptoms in the past week), prior treatment (24% any, 8% more than once), and to perceive that their alcohol or drug use is a problem (16%). White clients were most likely to report weekly use of opioids (3%) or tobacco (62%). Hispanic clients were more likely to report weekly cocaine use (6%) and less likely to report first use over the age of 15 (13%) and weekly tobacco use (37%). Mixed race clients were more likely to report first use under the age of 10 (12%), weekly use of other drugs (8%), being in a controlled environment for 13 or more of the past 90 days (34%), and having been in treatment two or more times (17%). Other race clients were the most likely to have started using under the age of 10 (15%) and to report weekly alcohol use (19%), lifetime dependence (67%), prior treatment (43% any, 19% two or more times), and to perceive their alcohol or drug use as a problem (34%). They were more likely to report being in a controlled environment 13 or more of the past 90 days (33%) and withdrawal symptoms (54% lifetime, 33% past week, and 14% a high number in the past week), and with Hispanics, the least likely to report weekly tobacco use (37%). Table 3.3 shows that African-American clients report the lowest rates for any race group of each psychological disorder including any disorder (54%), internalizing disorders (30%), externalizing disorders (46%), and both internalizing and externalizing disorders (22%), as well as prior mental health treatment (26%). Although both were relatively average in their rates of mental disorders, White clients had higher than average rates of prior mental health treatments (50%), while Hispanic clients had lower than average rates of prior treatment (25%). Mixed race clients were the most likely to report any internalizing disorder (52%), particularly symptoms suggestive of depression (44%), traumatic stress disorders (30%), and victimization (72% lifetime; 56% high levels). Other race clients were more likely to report symptoms suggestive of anxiety disorders (22%) and concerns about future violence (27%) and were the most likely to report only internalizing disorders (10%). Past-year needle use was higher than average for Hispanics (3%) and other race clients (3%) and lower than average for African-Americans (1%) and mixed race clients (1%). In the past 90 days, African-Americans were the most likely to report any sexual experience (74%) and multiple sexual partners (44%) while other race clients were less likely to report unprotected sex (18%) or multiple sexual partners (22%). In Fig. 3.1, African-American clients had lower than average problem counts while those of mixed and other race had the highest. *This demonstrates the importance of adapting materials to target the different perspectives and risks associated with clients who are mixed and other races.*

Variation by Age Group (*n* = 2,739 under the age of 15; 10,886 age 15–17; 1,149 age 18–25)

Since three-quarters of all clients were of ages 15–17, this group was generally within a few percentage points of the total for most of Tables 3.1–3.3 and Fig. 3.1.

However, differences were evident for younger and older clients. In Table 3.1, clients under the age of 15 were less likely to report regular peer alcohol use (43%), to be employed (11%), and to be involved in the justice system (61%). Clients of ages 18–25 were more likely to report weekly drug use in their home (17%), to be employed (48%), and to be involved in the child welfare system (73%); they were less likely than average to report being of mixed race (10%), from a single parent or from a single parent family (7%), regular peer drug use at work (46%) or socially (60%), and being in school (66%). Table 3.2 shows that clients under the age of 15 were more likely to report first use between the ages of 10 and 14 (89%) and less likely than average to report criteria for dependence (44%), weekly use of alcohol (11%), tobacco (40%), cocaine (2%), opioids (1%), and other drugs (4%), being in a controlled environment for 13 or more of the past 90 days (18%), prior addiction treatment (19% any, 6% multiple), and to perceive their alcohol or drug use as a problem (17%). Clients of the ages 18–25 were more likely to report first use over the age of 15 (39%), dependence (67%), weekly use of alcohol (19%), tobacco (61%), cocaine (5%), and opioids (5%), being in a controlled environment for 13 or more of the past 90 days (34%), prior addiction treatment (48% any, 24% multiple), and to perceive their alcohol or drug use as a problem (36%). They were less likely than average to report weekly marijuana use (33%). Table 3.3 shows that clients under the age of 15 report slightly lower rates of internalizing disorders, slightly higher rates of externalizing disorders, and lower rates of HIV risk behaviors. Clients of ages 18–25 conversely report higher rates of internalizing disorders, lower rates of externalizing disorders, and higher rates of HIV risk behaviors; they were less likely to report any past-year violence or illegal activity (70%). These trends cancel each other out and produce little difference in Fig. 3.1. *Thus, severity and mix of focal clinical conditions shift with the client's age.*

Discussion

Implications for Improving Practice

The background literature and data presented here demonstrate that adolescents and young adults are at high risk of substance misuse, that this misuse is associated with a wide range of problems, and that the consequences of misuse (particularly early onset) may last for decades. While intervention during the first decade of use is associated with a reduced duration of problems (Dennis, Scott, Funk, & Foss, 2005), relapse is also common after adolescent treatment (Dennis et al., 2004; Godley et al., 2007). Given that 73% of the youth presenting to treatment had 3 or more (45% 5 or more) of the 12 co-occurring risk factors in the following areas – substance use, mental health, victimization, physical violence, and illegal activity problems – it is likely that in addition to addressing substance use, it is important to address other co-occurring problems to reduce the likelihood of relapse.

Consistent with the treatment literature reviewed earlier, it is important to recognize that different levels of care are targeting clients with different needs and that these needs are sometimes different than commonly expected. For instance, the severity of clients in early intervention in school settings was very similar to those in regular outpatient settings. Rather than reaching a lower severity client, these programs appear to be more assertive in reaching adolescents where they are. Consistent with trends for short-term programs to be increasingly focused on dual diagnosis, the STR programs were serving the most severe clients. Clients in moderate- and long-term programs were still more severe than average, but were as or more defined by environmental risks and their involvement in the welfare and justice systems.

The literature and data presented here demonstrate that a large number of youth with substance misuse are involved in school, workplace, welfare, and justice systems. These systems represent an important opportunity for screening and earlier intervention to reduce substance misuse. They also have implications for practice. Most youth in treatment were involved in school, suggesting the importance of making treatment more convenient (e.g., via schedule, location) so that these youth can continue with their schooling and providing opportunities to continue with school while in residential treatment. After treatment, the high rates of substance misuse in schools suggest that they are also potentially risky recovery environments and suggest the need to provide youth with formal programs and support to re-enter school or to consider providing special programs like recovery schools (e.g., http://www.recoveryschools.org/). While becoming vocationally engaged is a positive outcome in its own right, data on use in the workplace suggests that this is by no means a substitute for treatment and that clients need help in negotiating it as a recovery environment as well. Clients in the child welfare system are at particularly high risk of relapse and continued use given their higher rates of early onset and co-occurring problems. While it is understandable that these systems focus first on the safety of the child and the public, the data presented here suggest that substance abuse and other behavioral health treatment is likely to be vital to their long-term course of recovery as individuals and as families. Targeting these systems with increased screening and referral protocols and enhanced multiple-system interaction has the potential to reduce some of the health disparities that have been previously noted in the literature (e.g., lower rates of girls in treatment than expected, higher rates of African-Americans in welfare).

While there is often much discussion about making treatment more gender, culturally, or age appropriate in abstract terms, the data presented here suggest that there are also some explicit implications for treatment. Girls are more likely to need psychiatric services while boys need more services related to controlling anger, violence, and illegal activities. African-Americans are at lower overall risk of problems on average while Hispanic, mixed, and other race youth are at much higher risk and each group has different problems. This suggests the importance of adapting materials to include issues relevant to the subgroup. This said, clients in each subgroup experienced each type of problem, hence the need for comprehensive screening. Age was associated less with a change in the overall severity than in a shift of the problem mix. As age increased the severity of system involvement, substance use disorders, internalizing disorder problems, and HIV risk behaviors increased while the rates of externalizing disorders, crime, and violence decreased.

Adolescents and young adults have high rates of substance misuse. The heterogeneity and number of different clinical problems suggest the need for comprehensive screening and intervention. Given the high rates of youth involved in other systems and their rates of use/problems, these systems represent an important potential venue for further screening and intervention. The fact that most clients had multiple problems points to the need to develop better approaches for cross-system collaboration. Given the high rates of use in those environments, treatment providers need to develop protocols to support youth trying to negotiate these environments during their recovery.

Acknowledgment The development of this chapter was supported by the Center for Substance Abuse Treatment (CSAT), Substance Abuse and Mental Health Services Administration (SAMHSA) contract 270-07-0191 using data provided by the following grants and contracts from CSAT (TI11317, TI11321, TI11323, TI11324, TI11422, TI11423, TI11424, TI11432, TI11433, TI11871, TI11874, TI11888, TI11892, TI11894, TI13190, TI13305, TI13308, TI13309, TI13313, TI13322, TI13323, TI13340, TI13344, TI3345, TI13354, TI13356, TI13601, TI14090, TI14188, TI14189, TI14196, TI14214, TI14252, TI14254, TI14261, TI14267, TI14271, TI14272, TI14283, TI14311, TI14315, TI14355, TI14376, TI15348, TI15413, TI15415, TI15421, TI15433, TI15446, TI15447, TI15458, TI15461, TI15466, TI15467, TI15469, TI15475, TI15478, TI15479, TI15481, TI15483, TI15485, TI15486, TI15489, TI15511, TI15514, TI15524, TI15527, TI15545, TI15562, TI15577, TI15586, TI15670, TI15671, TI15672, TI15674, TI15677, TI15678, TI15682, TI15686, TI16386, TI16400, TI16414, TI16904, TI16928, TI16939, TI16984, TI16992, TI17046, TI17055, TI17070, TI17071, TI17433, TI17434, TI17446, TI17476, TI17484, TI17490, TI17523, TI17604, TI17605, TI17638, TI17728, TI17761, TI17763, TI17765, TI17769, TI17779, TI17786, TI17788, TI17812, TI17825, TI17830, TI18406, Contract 207-98-7047, Contract 277-00-6500, Contract 270-2003-00006). The opinions are those of the author and do not reflect official positions of the contributing project directors or government.

References

American Psychiatric Association. (2000). *Diagnostic and statistical manual of mental disorders version 4 text revised (DSM-IV-TR)*. Washington, DC: American Psychiatric Association.

American Society of Addiction Medicine (ASAM). (1996). *Patient placement criteria for the treatment of psychoactive substance disorders* (2nd ed.). Chevy Chase, MD: American Society of Addiction Medicine.

American Society of Addiction Medicine (ASAM). (2001). *Patient placement criteria for the treatment of substance-related disorders* (2nd ed.). Chevy Chase, MD: American Society of Addiction Medicine.

Chan, Y. F., Dennis, M. L., & Funk, R. R. (2008). Prevalence and comorbidity co-occurrence of major internalizing and externalizing disorders among adolescents and adults presenting to substance abuse treatment. *Journal of Substance Abuse Treatment, 34*, 14–24.

Courtney, M. E., Barth, R. P., Berrick, J. D., Brooks, D., Needell, B., & Park, L. (1996). Race and child welfare service: Past research and future direction. *Child Welfare, 75*, 99–138.

Dennis, M. L., Babor, T., Roebuck, M. C., & Donaldson, J. (2002). Changing the focus: The case for recognizing and treating marijuana use disorders. *Addiction, 97*(Suppl. 1), S4–S15.

Dennis, M. L., Chan, Y. -F., & Funk, R. (2006). Development and validation of the GAIN Short Screener (GSS) for internalizing, externalizing, and substance use disorders and crime/violence problems among adolescents and adults. *American Journal on Addictions, 15*, 80–91.

Dennis, M. L., Dawud-Noursi, S., Muck, R. D., & McDermeit (Ives), M. (2003). The need for developing and evaluating adolescent treatment models. In S. J. Stevens & A. R. Morral (Eds.), *Adolescent substance abuse treatment in the United States: Exemplary models from a National Evaluation Study* (pp. 3–34). Binghamton, NY: Haworth Press.

Dennis, M. L., Foss, M. A., & Scott, C. K (2007). Correlates of long-term recovery after treatment. *Evaluation Review, 31*(6), 585–612.

Dennis, M. L., Godley, S. H., Diamond, G., Tims, F. M., Babor, T., Donaldson, J. (2004). The Cannabis Youth Treatment (CYT) Study: Main findings from two randomized trials. *Journal of Substance Abuse Treatment, 27*(3), 197–213.

Dennis, M. L., Ives, M. L., White, M. K., & Muck, R. D. (2008). The Strengthening Communities For Youth (SCY) initiative: A cluster analysis of the services received, their correlates and how they are associated with outcomes. *Journal of Psychoactive Drugs, 40*(1), 3–16.

Dennis, M. L., & McGeary, K. A. (1999, fall). Adolescent alcohol and marijuana treatment: Kids need it now. *TIE Communique*, 10–12. (Retrieved from http://www.chestnut.org/li/trends/Adolescent%20Problems/youth_need_treat.html on May 7, 2008.)

Dennis, M. L. & Scott, C. K (2007). Managing addiction as a chronic condition. *Addiction Science & Clinical Practice, 4*(1), 45–55.

Dennis, M. L., Scott, C. K, & Funk, R. (2003). An experimental evaluation of recovery management checkups (RMC) for people with chronic substance use disorders. *Evaluation and Program Planning, 26*(3), 339–352.

Dennis, M. L., Scott, C. K, Funk, R., & Foss, M. A. (2005). The duration and correlates of addiction and treatment careers. *Journal of Substance Abuse Treatment, 28*(Supplement 1), S51–S62.

Dennis, M. L., Titus, J. C., Diamond, G., Donaldson, J., Godley, S.H., Tims, F. (2002). The Cannabis Youth Treatment (CYT) experiment: Rationale, study design, and analysis plans. *Addiction, 97*(Suppl. 1), S16–S34.

Dennis, M. L., Titus, J. C., White, M., Unsicker, J., & Hodgkins, D. (2003). *Global Appraisal of Individual Needs (GAIN): Administration guide for the GAIN and related measures.* (Version 5). Bloomington, IL: Chestnut Health Systems. Retrieved from http://www.chestnut.org/LI/gain/index.html on May 7, 2008.

French, M. T., Bradley, C. J., Calingaert, B., Dennis, M. L., & Karuntzos, G. T. (1994). Cost analysis of training and employment services in methadone treatment. *Evaluation and Program Planning, 17*(2), 107–120.

French, M. T., Roebuck, M. C., Dennis, M. L., Diamond, G., Godley, S. H., Liddle, H. A., & Tims, F. M. (2003). Outpatient marijuana treatment for adolescents: Economic evaluation of a multi-site field experiment. *Evaluation Review, 27*(4), 421–459.

Gerstein, D. R., & Johnson, R. A. (1999). *Adolescents and young adults in the National Treatment Improvement Evaluation Study* (National Evaluation Data Services Report). Rockville, MD: Center for Substance Abuse Treatment.

Godley, M. D., Godley, S. H., Dennis, M. L., Funk, R., & Passetti, L. (2002). Preliminary outcomes from the assertive continuing care experiment for adolescents discharged from residential treatment. *Journal of Substance Abuse Treatment, 23*(1), 21–32.

Godley, M. D., Godley, S. H., Dennis, M. L., Funk, R. R., & Passetti, L. L. (2007). The effect of Assertive Continuing Care (ACC) on continuing care linkage, adherence and abstinence following residential treatment for adolescents. *Psychology of Addictive Behaviors, 102*, 81–93.

Government Accountability Office (GAO). (2007). *African American children in foster care.* Washington, DC: Author.

Grant, B. F., & Dawson, D. A. (1998). Age of onset of drug use and its association with DSM-IV drug abuse and dependence. *Journal of Substance Abuse, 10*, 163–173.

Green, B. L., Rockhill, A., & Furrer, C. (2007). Does substance abuse treatment make a difference for child welfare case outcomes?: A statewide longitudinal study. *Children and Youth Services Review, 29*(4), 460–473.

Hser, Y. I., Grella, C. E., Hubbard, R. L., Hsieh, S. C., Fletcher, B.W., Brown, B. S., & Anglin, M. D. (2001). An evaluation of drug treatments for adolescents in four U.S. cities. *Archives of General Psychiatry, 58*, 689–695.

Hubbard, R. L., Cavanaugh, E. R., Craddock, S. G., & Rachal, J.V. (1985). Characteristics, behaviors, and outcomes for youth in the TOPS: Treatment services for adolescent substance abusers. In A. S. Friedman & G. M. Beschner (Eds.), *Treatment services for adolescent substance abusers* (pp. 49–65). Rockville, MD: National Institute on Drug Abuse.

Joint Commission on Accreditation of Healthcare Organization (JCAHO). (1995). *Accreditation manual for mental health, chemical dependency, and mental retardation/developmental disabilities services: Standards.* Oakbrook Terrace, IL: Author.

Johnston, L. D., O'Malley, P. M., Bachman, J. G., & Schulenberg, J.E. (2007). *Monitoring the Future national results on adolescent drug use: Overview of key findings, 2006.* (NIH Publication No. 07-6202). Bethesda, MD: National Institute on Drug Abuse. Retrieved from http://eric.ed.gov/ERICDocs/data/ericdocs2sql/content_storage_01/0000019b/80/2a/75/88.pdf on April 5, 2008.

Lennox, R., Dennis, M. L., Ives, M., & White, M. K. (2006). The construct and predictive validity of different approaches to combining urine and self-reported drug use measures among older adolescents after substance abuse treatment. *American Journal on Addictions, 15,* 92–101.

Lennox, R. D., Dennis, M. L., Scott, C. K, & Funk, R. R. (2006). Combining psychometric and biometric measures of substance use. *Drug and Alcohol Dependence, 83*, 95–103.

Lu, Y. E., Landsverk, J., Ellis-Macleod, E., Newton, R., Ganger, W., & Johnson, I. (2004). Race, ethnicity, and case outcomes in child protective services. *Children and Youth Services Review. 26,* 447–461.

Marsh, J. C., Ryan, J. P., Choi, S., & Testa, M. F. (2006). Integrated services for families with multiple problems: Obstacles to family reunification. *Children and Youth Services Review, 28*, 1074–1087.

McAlpine, C., Marshall, C. C., & Doran, N. H. (2001). Combining child welfare and substance abuse services: A blended model of intervention. *Child Welfare, 80*(2), 129–149.

Mokdad, A. H., Marks, J. S., Stroup, D. F., & Gerberding, J. L. (2004). Actual causes of death in the United States, 2000. *Journal of the American Medical Association, 291*(10), 1238–1245.

Riley, B. B., Conrad, K. J., Bezruczko, N., & Dennis, M. L. (2007). Relative precision, efficiency and construct validity of different starting and stopping rules for a computerized adaptive test: The GAIN substance problem scale. *Journal of Applied Measurement, 8*(1), 48–64.

Rounds-Bryant, J. L., Kristiansen, P. L., & Hubbard, R. L. (1999). Drug Abuse Treatment Outcome Study of Adolescents: A comparison of client characteristics and pretreatment behaviors in three treatment modalities. *American Journal of Drug and Alcohol Abuse, 25*(4), 573–591.

Rounds-Bryant, J. L., & Staab, J. (2001). Patient characteristics and treatment outcomes for African American, Hispanic, and White adolescents in DATOS-A. *Journal of Adolescent Research, 16*(6), 624–641.

Sells, S. B., & Simpson, D. D. (1979). Evaluation of treatment outcome for youths in the Drug Abuse Reporting Program (DARP): A follow-up study. In G. M. Beschner & A. S. Friedman (Eds.), *Youth drug abuse: Problems, issues, and treatment* (pp. 571–628). Lexington, MA: DC Heath.

Shane, P., Diamond, G. S., Mensinger, J. L., Shera, D., & Wintersteen, M. B. (2006). Impact of victimization on substance abuse treatment outcomes for adolescents in outpatient and residential substance abuse treatment. *American Journal on Addictions, 15*(Suppl 1), 34–42.

Shane, P., Jasiukaitis, P., & Green, R. S. (2003). Treatment outcomes among adolescents with substance abuse problems: The relationship between comorbidities and post-treatment substance involvement. *Evaluation and Program Planning, 26*(4), 393–402.

Simpson, D. D., Savage, L. J., & Sells, S. B. (1978). *Data book on drug treatment outcomes. Follow-up study of the 1969–1977 admissions to the Drug Abuse Reporting Program (IRB Report No. 78-10).* Fort Worth, TX: Texas Christian University.

Spirito, A., Monti, P. M., Barnett, N. P., Colby, S. M., Sindelar, H., Rohsenow, D. J., Lewander, W., & Myers, M. (2004). A randomized clinical trial of a brief motivational intervention for alcohol-positive adolescents treated in an emergency department. *The Journal of Pediatrics, 145*(3), 396–402.

Substance Abuse and Mental Health Services Administration (SAMHSA), (1996). *Preliminary estimates from the 1995 National Household Survey on Drug Abuse* (Advance Report No. 18). Rockville, MD: Office of Applied Studies.

Substance Abuse and Mental Health Services Administration (SAMHSA), (2007a). *Results from the 2006 National Survey on Drug Use and Health: National Findings* (Office of Applied Studies, NSDUH Series H-32, DHHS Publication No. SMA 07-4293). Rockville, MD: Office of Applied Studies. Retrieved from http://www.oas.samhsa.gov/nsduh/2k6nsduh/2k6Results.pdf and http://www.icpsr.umich.edu/SAMHDA/ on April 5, 2008.

Substance Abuse and Mental Health Services Administration (SAMHSA), (2007b). *Drug Abuse Warning Network, 2005: National Estimates of Drug-Related Emergency Department Visits.* DAWN Series D-29, DHHS Publication No. (SMA) 07-4256, Rockville, MD: Office of Applied Studies. Retrived from http://dawninfo.samhsa.gov/files/DAWN-ED-2005-Web.pdf and http://www.icpsr.umich.edu/SAMHDA/ on April 5, 2008.

Substance Abuse and Mental Health Services Administration (SAMHSA), (2008). Treatment Episode Data Set (TEDS). Highlights – 2006. National Admissions to Substance Abuse Treatment Services, DASIS Series: S-40, DHHS Publication No. (SMA) 08-4313. Rockville, MD: Office of Applied Studies. Retrieved from http://www.oas.samhsa.gov/teds2k6highlights/teds2k6highWeb.pdf and http://www.icpsr.umich.edu/SAMHDA/ on April 5, 2008.

Titus, J. C., Dennis, M. L., White, W. L., Scott, C. K, & Funk, R.R. (2003). Gender differences in victimization severity and outcomes among adolescents treated for substance abuse. *Journal of Child Maltreatment, 8*(1), 19–35.

U.S. Department of Health and Human Services, Administration on Children, Youth and Families. (ACYF) (2006). *Child maltreatment 2004.* Washington, DC: U.S. Government Printing Office.

Van Etten, M. L., & Anthony, J. C. (1999). Comparative epidemiology of initial drug opportunities and transitions to first use: marijuana, cocaine, hallucinogens and heroin. *Drug and Alcohol Dependence, 54,* 117–125.

White, M. (2005). Predicting violence in juvenile offenders: The interaction of individual, social, and environmental influences. *Offender Substance Abuse Report,* 83–84, 89–90.

White, M. K., Funk, R. R., White, W. L., & Dennis, M. L. (2004). Predicting violent behavior in adolescent cannabis users: The GAIN-CVI. In K. Knight & D. Farabee (Eds.), *Treating addicted offenders: A continuum of effective practices* (pp. 3-1–3-7). Kingston, NJ: Civic Research Institute.

Chapter 4
Adolescent Substance Abuse Treatment: A Review of Evidence-Based Research

Ken C. Winters, Andria M. Botzet, Tamara Fahnhorst, Randy Stinchfield, and Rachel Koskey

Introduction

The public health significance of adolescent drug[1] abuse is highlighted by the fact that early initiation of drug use is associated with an increased risk for a constellation of problem behaviors (Weinberg, Rahdert, Colliver, & Glantz, 1998) and increased risk for later development of a substance use disorder (SUD) (e.g., Chen, O'Brien, & Anthony, 2005). Whereas most adolescents who use drugs do not escalate into abuse or dependence (Newcomb, 1995), it is estimated that about 11% of teenagers meet criteria for an SUD (Winters, Leitten, Wagner, & O'Leary Tevyaw, 2007). Thus, the prevalence of adolescent SUDs and related health consequences reinforces the need for evidence-based treatments for this population.

This chapter summarizes the research literature regarding the treatment of adolescents with an SUD. We limited our literature search to controlled evaluations of drug abuse treatment approaches for adolescent clients since 1990, owing to the principle that drug treatment for adolescents prior to that time may not be comparable to more contemporary standards. The criteria for study inclusion were as follows: (1) adolescents had to be the primary target of the intervention or treatment; (2) drug use outcomes had to be measured; and (3) the study consisted of essential components of a controlled evaluation, including favorable sample sizes, comparison group (i.e., control group, waiting list control, or contrasting treatment group), use of standardized assessment instruments, treatment interventions that are well-described, and outcome evaluation ratings by individuals who did not conduct the therapy.

Treatment outcome studies were identified from a computerized literature search of standard journal databases (e.g., MEDLINE, PsychINFO, Social Sciences Abstracts), as well as from drug treatment websites and the sites of well-known treatment research organizations. Close reviews of the reference sections of relevant books, identified studies, and the handful of literature summaries and reviews were also conducted. We benefited from two recent reviews of the literature (Deas & Thomas, 2001; Vaughn & Howard, 2004). By applying our study selection criteria to all of the citations that were located, and removing duplicate citations, we

---

[1] We use the term *drug* in this chapter to refer to alcohol and other drugs.

C.G. Leukefeld et al. (eds.) Adolescent Substance Abuse,
DOI: 10.1007/978-0-387-09732-9_4, © Springer Science + Business Media LLC 2009

identified 21 investigations published between 1990 and 2007 that constituted the final study sample. The review is organized around these approaches: 12-step based therapy, therapeutic community (TC), family-based interventions, behavioral therapy, cognitive behavioral therapy (CBT), motivational-based therapy (motivational enhancement and motivational interviewing), pharmacotherapy, and mixed or other approaches. Please note that an integration of multiple approaches is commonly utilized in clinical interventions, and thus, some overlap of approaches exists within the review presented here. We also discuss the outcome literature in terms of predictors of relapse.

Treatment Outcome Literature

12-Step-Based Treatment

Organized around the basic tenets of Alcoholics Anonymous (AA), it is generally accepted in the field that this treatment approach is the most commonly applied strategy to youth with an SUD. The first 5 steps of the 12 steps are typically addressed with adolescents during the primary treatment experience. These five steps are the following: (1) admitting that you are powerless over the addictive substance and that it has made life unmanageable, (2) believing that a power greater than yourself could restore you to health, (3) making a decision to turn your will over to a higher power as you interpret it to be, (4) taking moral inventory of yourself, and (5) admitting to yourself and to others the nature of your wrongs. One typically embarks upon the remaining seven steps during aftercare.

Applicability of the 12-step method for youth has been questioned due to limitations in developmentally appropriate content. Adolescence is a time of identifying a personal identity and independence from authority figures, developmental milestones that can be inconsistent with the main tenants of AA of acceptance and surrender. In addition, 12-step-based aftercare programs (e.g., AA, NA) are mainly composed of adults. It is estimated that only 2% of participants in self-help groups are under the age of 21 (Alcoholics Anonymous Membership Survey, 2001), which creates barriers for adolescents as they may struggle to relate to older group members (Kelly, Myers, & Brown, 2005). Thus, efforts to adapt 12-step treatment for adolescents are important. Current adaptations of this approach include the Minnesota Model treatment approach for adolescents (Anderson, McGovern, & DuPont, 1999) and Jaffe's (1990) developmentally appropriate modifications of the first five steps of a 12-step program.

Controlled evaluations of this approach with youth have not been conducted. However, an approach that incorporates the 12-step method, the Minnesota Model, has been researched. The Minnesota Model includes a range of therapeutic elements (e.g., group and family therapy) in conjunction with the 12-step method (Winters,

Stinchfield, Opland, Weller, & Latimer, 2000). We located one evaluation in the literature that met our review inclusion criteria. Winters and colleagues followed a group of 179 adolescents who participated in either an outpatient or inpatient Minnesota Model treatment and a group of 66 adolescents who were on a treatment waiting-list (primarily due to insurance coverage limitations or no insurance). Results indicated that among the 179 youth, those who finished the treatment program reported superior outcomes in contrast to those who left the program prior to completion and to a waiting-list group (Winters et al., 2000). At the 12-month follow-up, categorical data revealed that 53% of the treatment completers reported abstinence or minor relapse (used once or twice) compared to 15% for the treatment incompleters and to 27% for the waiting-list group. Continuous variable data revealed similar results. Interestingly, more favorable outcomes anticipated for those in an inpatient setting were not observed compared to adolescents who attended an outpatient program. A long-term follow-up study of the same youth (Winters, Stinchfield, Latimer, & Lee, 2007) showed a similar pattern of outcome, although the major predictor of favorable outcomes was involvement in aftercare. Whereas these studies showed that favorable outcome is associated with treatment engagement, the study designs did not permit opportunity to evaluate the specific contribution of 12-step elements.

Therapeutic Community

Like the 12-step Minnesota Model, TC is typically classified as a community-based therapy which is rooted in self-help principles and experiential knowledge of the recovery community (Morral, McCaffrey, & Ridgeway, 2004). The TC approach to drug abuse is holistic in nature, viewing the community as the key agent of change and emphasizing mutual self-help, behavioral consequences, and shared values for a healthy lifestyle (Jainchill, 1997). Among the adult population, a TC may be organized as a day treatment, a series of outpatient sessions, or a medium- to long-term residential treatment. Adolescent TCs, however, tend to be long-term residential treatment programs, and often implement a wide variety of therapeutic techniques, including (but not limited to) individual counseling sessions, family therapy, 12-step method, life-skills, and recreational techniques.

We located one study on TC that met our review inclusion criteria. Morral and colleagues (2004) examined the TC approach using a rigorous evaluation design that compared nearly 450 adolescents in a 9- to 12- month residential TC program (Phoenix Academy) with adolescents in a comparison group of "treatment as usual" probation dispositions. Their results indicated that participation in Phoenix Academy was associated with significantly reduced drug use and improved psychological functioning outcomes compared to the comparison group at 12-month post-treatment. These improvements were observed on all three of the substance use measures and across mental health and delinquency variables.

Family-Based Therapy

The family therapy approach seeks to reduce an adolescent's use of drugs and correct the problem behaviors that often accompany drug use by addressing the mediating family risk factors such as poor family communication, cohesiveness, and problem solving. This approach is based on the therapeutic premise that the family carries the most profound and long-lasting influence on child and adolescent development (Szapocznik & Coatsworth, 1999). Family therapy typically includes the adolescent and at least one other parent or guardian. Ideally, siblings and other adult household members are included. Other approaches and theoretical positions are commonly integrated into family-based treatment, such as CBT and developmental and attachment theories. In addition, social, neighborhood, community, and cultural factors are also considered within the treatment plan (Ozechowski & Liddle, 2002).

This approach has attracted enough attention in the field that it was the focus of a recent review by Austin and colleagues (Austin, Macgowan, & Wagner, 2005). These authors identified and reviewed five family-based treatment approaches, all of which involved random assignment and other rigorous design features: (1) Brief strategic family therapy (BSFT; Santisteban et al., 2003); (2) Family behavior therapy (FBT; also referenced in the *Behavioral* section of this chapter) (Azrin, Donohue, Besalel, Kogan, & Acierno, 1994)]; (3) Functional family therapy (FFT; Waldron, Slesnick, Brody, Turner, & Peterson, 2001); (4) Multidimensional family therapy (MDFT; also referenced in the *Cannabis Youth Treatment*, CYT, section of this chapter) (Liddle et al., 2001); and (5) Multisystemic treatment (MST; Henggeler, Clingempeel, Brondino, & Pickrel, 2002; Henggeler, Pickrel, & Brondino, 1999).

Of these five, MDFT demonstrated both clinically and statistically significant favorable drug use outcomes at the conclusion of treatment and at the 1-year posttreatment assessment. Whereas the other four approaches (BSFT, MST, FFT, and FBT) showed greater improvement compared to the control group at the completion of treatment, posttreatment follow-up assessments did not reveal group differences for MST and FFT, and there are no posttreatment outcomes reported for the BSFT and FBT studies (Austin et al., 2005).

We located additional studies not included in Austin review. Smith and colleagues (Smith, Hall, Williams, An, & Gotman, 2006) compared an outpatient family intervention (Strengths oriented family therapy, SOFT; Smith & Hall, 2008), with a group therapy approach (The Seven Challenges®; Schwebel, 2004) The SOFT intervention incorporated a pretreatment motivational family session, multi-family skills training, and case management. The comparison group (Seven Challenges) utilized interactive journaling, skills training, and motivational interviewing. Results at 6-month posttreatment revealed that the two interventions were comparable in terms of achieving abstinence (39% for SOFT and 31% for Seven Challenges), being symptom free (61% and 60%, respectively), and extent of reduction of drug use frequency and affiliated problems (Smith et al., 2006).

Latimer and colleagues (Latimer, Winters, D'Zurilla, & Nichols, 2003) compared an integrated family and CBT (IFCBT) intervention against a drugs harm psychoeducational curriculum (DHPE). Results at the 6-month posttreatment period indicated that the DHPE group used alcohol and marijuana significantly more days each month than did the IFCBT group (average = 6.06 days vs 2.03 days for alcohol; 13.83 vs 5.67 days for marijuana, respectively). Urinalysis results also indicated a significant group difference in use rates for marijuana at the 6-month assessment; 85.7% of participants tested positive for marijuana in the DHPE group compared to 42.9% in the IFCBT group.

Dembo and colleagues (2000) compared a family empowerment intervention (FEI) against an extended services intervention (ESI). The FEI program included personal in-home visits with a trained paraprofessional, whose goals included improving family boundaries, enhancing parenting skills, improving communication, and restoring family hierarchy. The ESI program, used in this study as a comparison condition, involved monthly phone contacts by project research assistants. Results revealed statistically significant reductions in self-reported marijuana use at the 1-year follow-up for the FEI group in comparison with the ESI group (Dembo et al., 2000).

Behavioral therapy

Therapeutic techniques based on behavioral psychology theories are another approach to treating adolescent substance abuse. Behavioral strategies, which target actions and behaviors presumed to be influenced by one's environment, include modeling, rehearsal, self-recording, stimulus control, urge control, and written assignments. In current practice, behaviorism is most often coupled with techniques that modify cognitions, referred to as CBT (which we review in the next section). We identified one behavioral study that met our review inclusion criteria. Azrin and colleagues randomly assigned drug-abusing youth to either a supportive counseling group (n = 11) or a behavioral treatment group (n = 15) for ~6 months of treatment (Azrin et al., 1994). The results indicated that drug use significantly decreased over the course of the treatment for the behavioral treatment group, with 73% reporting abstinence during the last month of treatment, compared to only 9% of the comparison group. Other drug use outcome measures were also significantly improved for the behavioral group.

Cognitive Behavioral Therapy

CBT is based in the belief that thoughts cause behaviors, and these thoughts determine the way in which people perceive, interpret, and assign meaning to the environment (Beck & Weishaar, 2005). Thus, by changing our thought processes, maladaptive behaviors can be changed even if our environment does not change. When used within the context of adolescent substance use, CBT encourages adolescents to develop self-regulation and coping skills. Techniques commonly used include the identification of stimulus cues preceding drug use, the use of strategies to avoid situations that may trigger the urge to use, and skill development for refusal techniques, communication, and problem solving (Waldron et al., 2001). CBT is a frequently used therapeutic approach, but it is commonly integrated into other approaches (Beck & Weishaar, 2005), especially family systems therapy and motivational enhancement/brief interventions (BIs). For this reason, some CBT methods are also mentioned in other sections of this chapter as an integral part of another therapeutic approach.

One CBT study, investigated as a stand-alone approach, met our inclusion criteria. Kaminer, Burleson, and Goldberger (2002) examined a sample of 51 adolescents who were randomly assigned to a CBT intervention in comparison to 37 adolescents who received psychoeducational treatment. A greater reduction in substance use was found for older adolescents and for males in the CBT group at a 3-month follow-up, as compared to the pscyhoeducational group, but at 9-month follow-up the two groups did not differ on drug use outcome.

Motivational Enhancement Therapy (MET)/Brief Intervention

MET techniques have recently come to the forefront of therapeutic approaches for addiction, and even more so recently for adolescents. MET (also referred to as motivational interviewing) utilizes a person-centered, nonconfrontational approach to assist the youth to explore the different facets of their use patterns. Clients are encouraged to examine the pros and cons of their use and to create goals to help them achieve a healthier lifestyle. The therapist provides personalized feedback and respects the youth's freedom of choice regarding his/her own behavior. Although the relationship between the therapist and client is more of a partnership than an expert/recipient role, the therapist is directive in assisting the individual to examine and resolve ambivalence and to encourage the client's responsibility for selecting and working on healthy changes in behavior (Rollnick & Miller, 1995).

MET is frequently incorporated into a BI format, in which a therapist meets with the client for only a brief period, anywhere from a single 10-min session to multiple 1-h sessions. BIs are becoming an attractive therapeutic approach due to cost-containment policies of managed care. They may be particularly attractive to youth because of the brief number of therapeutic contacts, and the approach is developmentally fitting given that many drug-abusing youth are not "career" drug abusers and young people are likely to be more receptive to self-guided behavior change strategies, a cornerstone of MET (Miller & Sanchez, 1994; Winters, Leitten, et al., 2007).

Our review located several MET/BI investigations with youth, and most of them were conducted in school settings. Schools can be an ideal site in which to conduct BIs, given their natural fit within a school-based chemical health or student assistance program. McCambridge and Strang (2004) examined 200 16- to 20-year-olds in London who had current usage of cannabis or stimulants, and were randomly allocated to a single 1-h session of MET/BI or to a control sample that was considered "education-as-usual." Results from this study indicate that participants receiving the MET/BI significantly reduced their usage of cigarettes, alcohol, and cannabis as compared to the control group. In addition, the effect sizes for reductions in substance use were greater among youth who are usually considered vulnerable or high-risk, indicating that high-risk youth derived the greatest benefit.

Positive results were also found in a school-based BI study in Thailand (Srisurapanont, Sombatmai, & Boripuntakul, 2007), where researchers focused on methamphetamine use among students aged 14–19 years. Forty-eight participants were randomly placed into either a BI group, which met twice weekly for 2 weeks (20-min sessions), or a psychoeducational group, in which students received a 15-min session of education on methamphetamine and its effects. At 2-month postintervention, the BI group had significantly decreased its frequency of methamphetamine use as compared to the psychoeducational group. However, the two groups did not significantly differ in terms of the number of tablets ingested (per day when used) and the number of positive urine tests for methamphetamine. Thus, the additional harm reduction benefits of the BI only slightly outperformed the benefits from the control condition.

The final school-based BI study we located investigated two variants of a BI on a group of students, aged 14–17 years, who met criteria for mild-to-moderate drug abuse (Winters & Leitten, 2007). Students/parents ($n = 79$) were randomly assigned to receive a two-session adolescent only (BI-A), two-session adolescent and additional parent session (BI-AP), or assessment-only control condition. Follow-up assessments at 6-month postintervention on 78 subjects showed that the adolescents in the BI-A and BI-AP conditions generally showed superior outcome on the drug use behaviors compared to the control group. Also, those receiving the BI-AP had better outcomes compared to adolescent receiving BI-A on most outcome variables. However, the 6-month abstinence rates did not differ across groups.

A controlled evaluation of BI for homeless youth was conducted by Peterson and colleagues (Peterson, Baer, Wells, Ginzler, & Garrett, 2006). They recruited homeless adolescents from the streets or from homeless shelters in the Seattle, Washington area. Participants ($n = 212$) were randomly assigned to either a BI group that received two 1-h sessions, an assessment-only control group, or an assessment-only at follow-up control group. The results showed limited intervention effect: the BI group reported reduced illicit drug use at 1-month follow-up compared to the two control groups, but there were no group differences in terms of alcohol use and marijuana use.

Other settings, such as juvenile detention centers, mental health centers, and health care settings, may also be valuable venues in which to administer BIs. Promising examples of such application have been studied by Monti and colleagues; they have shown substance use-related benefits of applying a single session MET/BI to youth in emergency rooms following an alcohol-related accident (Monti et al., 1999) and to previously-incarcerated teenagers (Stein et al., 2006).

Pharmacotherapy

Recent advances in the neurochemistry and neuroanatomy of addiction have fostered increased investigation of various medications. Three medications are currently approved by the Food and Drug Administration that target alcohol dependence. Disulfiram (Antabus) is a type of aversive therapy that causes severe nausea, vomiting, and flushing (via the blockage of an enzyme involved in the metabolism of alcohol) when a person consumes alcohol. Although disulfiram appears to be most effective with older individuals who are motivated to make changes (Fuller et al., 1986), we did locate one adolescent study. Austrian researchers, Niederhofer and Staffen (2003a), conducted a placebo-controlled study on disulfiram and reported that the 13 adolescents receiving medication had more days of abstinence during the 90-day trial than did the 13 adolescents on placebo. However, the results may be biased given that 23 patients did not complete the study and were not included in the follow-up assessment.

Naltrexone (ReVia) has shown effectiveness in improving recovery with adults with alcohol dependence (e.g., Morris, Hopwood, Whelan, Gardiner, & Drummond, 2001), and its efficacy may be enhanced when used in conjunction with CBT psychotherapy (e.g., Anton et al., 2001). Although no studies on naltrexone with youth met our review criteria, it is important to note that a small open-label trial with adolescents has been reported. Deas and colleagues (2005) found reductions in both craving and alcohol consumption, and that naltrexone was well-tolerated and safe when dosage levels were reduced (Deas, May, Randall, Johnson, & Anton, 2005).

Acamprosate (Campral) has been used in Europe for nearly 20 years for treating alcohol dependence (e.g., Mann, Lehert, & Morgan, 2004). A number of European controlled studies found acamprosate to reduce drinking relapse and increase days of abstinence for alcohol-dependent adults (e.g., Mason & Ownby, 2000), yet recent studies with adolescents are mixed. Beneficial results were not found in two studies (e.g., Anton et al., 2006; Morley et al., 2006), whereas one study did report positive findings. In this study, acamprosate and placebo groups were compared in a very small sample ($n = 13$). This 90-day trial revealed significantly increased rates of abstinence in the acamprosate group compared to the placebo group (Niederhofer & Staffen, 2003b).

Mixed/Other Approaches

The Cannabis Youth Treatment Study

A major effort to advance contemporary research on treatment effectiveness for drug-abusing adolescents is the CYT cooperative agreement. Initiated by the Center for Substance Abuse Treatment, this project was designed to compare the clinical efficacy and cost-effectiveness of multiple short-term (less than 3 months) interventions for adolescents who have a cannabis use problem (Dennis et al., 2004). Researchers from four sites [University of Connecticut Health Center (UCHC), Operation PAR, Inc. (PAR), Chestnut Health Systems (CHS), and Children's Hospital of Philadelphia (CHOP)], along with other community stakeholders, formed a 35-member steering committee and selected five short-term, manual-driven interventions to investigate. Feasibility limitations guided the study to be divided into two trials. Trial 1, implemented at UCHC and PAR, compared three interventions (see Table 4.1): (1) MET

Table 4.1 Summary of cannabis youth treatment (CYT) interventions

Title/citation	Approach / No. of sessions	Goals	Total potential contacts
Motivational enhancement therapy/ cognitive behavioral therapy (MET/ CBT 5)	2 MET sessions	MET	5
Sampl and Kadden (2001)	3 group CBT sessions	1. Increase knowledge of problem with cannabis 2. Increase motivation to stop using cannabis CBT 1. Develop drug-use refusal skills 2. Establish recovery-oriented social support network 3. Increase opportunities and engagement in pleasurable nondrug use activities 4. Increase general coping and problem-solving skills 5. Increase skills for recovering from relapse (if applicable)	
MET/CBT 12 Webb et al. (2002)	2 MET sessions 10 group CBT sessions	MET 1. Increase knowledge of problem with cannabis 2. Increase motivation to stop using cannabis CBT 1. Develop drug-use refusal skills 2. Establish recovery-oriented social support network 3. Increase opportunities and engagement in pleasurable nondrug use activities 4. Increase general coping and problem-solving skills 5. Increase skills for recovering from relapse (if applicable) 6. Increase coping skills for: a. interpersonal problems b. down mood c. cannabis use triggers	12

(continued)

Table 4.1 (continued)

Title/citation	Approach / No. of sessions	Goals	Total potential contacts
		d. psychological dependence	
Family Support Network (FSN)	2 MET sessions	MET	22+
Bunch et al. (1998)	10 group CBT sessions	1. Increase knowledge of problem with cannabis	
	6 Parent education group meetings	2. Increase motivation to stop using cannabis	
	4 Therapeutic home visits	CBT	
	Referral to self-help support groups	1. Develop drug-use refusal skills	
	Case management	2. Establish recovery-oriented social support network	
		3. Increase opportunities and engagement in pleasurable nondrug use activities	
		4. Increase general coping and problem-solving skills	
		5. Increase skills for recovering from relapse (if applicable)	
		6. Coping skills for: a. interpersonal problems b. down mood c. cannabis use triggers d. psychological dependence	
		Parental outreach services	
		1. Increase parent and family functioning	
		2. Improve parent knowledge	
		3. Promote adolescent/parent engagement in treatment	
Adolescent community reinforcement approach (ACRA)	10 Individual adolescent sessions	Adolescent sessions	14+
Godley, S.H., et al. (2001)	2 Caregiver sessions	1. Promote drug use abstinence	
	2 Family sessions	2. Recognition of antecedents of use	
	Some case management	3. Recognition of consequences of use	
		4. Identification of prosocial behaviors incompatible with use	
		5. Increase positive relationships	

(continued)

Table 4.1 (continued)

Title/citation	Approach / No. of sessions	Goals	Total potential contacts
		6. Increase skills in relapse prevention, communication, and problem solving	
		Parent/Family Sessions	
		1. Increase positive family communication	
		2. Increase family problem solving	
		3. Increase parent education/parent practices	
Multidimensional family therapy(MDFT)	6 Individual adolescent sessions	Adolescent sessions	15+
Liddle (2002)	3 Parent sessions	1. Enhance competency	
	6 Family sessions	2. Decrease involvement with deviant peers	
	Some case management	3. Increase coping skills for:	
		a. regulation of mood	
		b. problem solving	
		Parent sessions	
		1. Improve support network	
		2. Increase parent practices	
		3. Reduce:	
		a. psychiatric distress	
		b. drug use	
		c. financial stress	
		Family sessions	
		1. Increase parent–child attachment	
		2. Enhance family organization warmth and emotional investment	

and five sessions of CBT; (2) MET and 12 sessions of CBT; and (3) Family Support Network (FSN). Trial 2, conducted at CHS and CHOP, also compared three interventions: (1) MET and five sessions of CBT; (2) Adolescent community reinforcement approach (ACRA); and (3) MDFT. Participants were randomly assigned to the various interventions per site and qualified for this study if they were 12–18 years old, reported one or more cannabis abuse or dependence symptom(s) (*DSM-IV*; American Psychiatric Association, 1994), and qualified for outpatient treatment (American Society of Addiction Medicine, 1996). Additional information about participant qualifications and other methodological specifications of this study are reported elsewhere (Dennis et al., 2004; Diamond et al., 2002).

Favorable treatment effects for each of the five interventions implemented via the CYT were found. Outcomes pertaining to increased days of abstinence during the 12 months following treatment and percentage of adolescents in recovery at the end of the study were found to be stable across initiatives (Dennis et al., 2004). Highly similar clinical outcomes were also observed across sites and conditions. Significant differences in the cost of implementation among programs was apparent, although they were all roughly within the parameters currently spent on adolescent outpatient treatment (French et al., 2002). Examination of cost-effectiveness indicated that FSN in Trial 1 and MDFT in Trial 2 were the least cost-effective. Additional findings from the CYT initiative revealed that increased dosage did not necessarily evoke differential effects on substance use and associated problems. Furthermore, concern for possible iatrogenic effects with group therapy sessions did not materialize. Examination of the results revealed that the CYT interventions were relatively effective as initial interventions, although 50% of the adolescents went in and out of recovery and relapse one or more times following intervention, and at the 12-month follow-up, two-thirds were still reporting substance use or related problems. Dennis and his colleagues (2004) concluded that a focus on increasing awareness that drug problems are a chronic condition (Kazdin, 1987) and incorporating continued care following the initial intervention are essential to longer-lasting treatment efficacy.

Predictors of Relapse

Despite the therapeutic modality, one underlying goal of adolescent treatment for drug abuse involves the prevention of relapse. The definition of relapse varies, but in most instances it refers to a return to drug use. Some definitions of relapse include categories for the level of problems resulting from the return to drug use or for the levels of drug use frequency. Among youth receiving treatment for an SUD, it can be expected that from one-third to one-half are likely to return to some drug use at least once within 12 months following treatment (Grella, Joshi, & Hser, 2004; Williams, Chang, & Addiction Centre Adolescent Research Group, 2000). In this section we review the research on factors that are associated with relapse among adolescents.

Client Variables

Demographic Variables

There are a small number of studies that have identified an association of demographic characteristics and treatment outcome. In regards to gender, girls have been shown to use drugs less than do boys after discharge from treatment (Catalano, Hawkins, Wells, Miller, & Brewer, 1991; Latimer, Winters, Stinchfield, & Traver, 2000), though most studies do not find (or report) this gender effect (see Williams et al., 2000; Winters, 1999). Regarding other demographic variables, we did not find any studies that showed the impact of ethnicity and social and economic status on outcome, and we found only one study that showed an age effect. Anderson and colleagues (Anderson, Ramo, Schulte, Cummins, & Brown, 2007) found that younger teens were more likely to be minor relapsers (used less than three consecutive days and did not return to intake level of use), whereas older teens tended to be major relapsers (reverted to pretreatment levels of use or an episode of use that lasted longer than 3 days).

Psychiatric Comorbidity

The general consensus in this literature is that the risk of relapse is greatly increased when the adolescent with an SUD also has a coexisting mental or behavioral disorder. Several studies have shown the prognostic significance of cooccurring conduct disorder and related externalizing disorders (e.g., oppositional defiant disorder and ADHD) for substance abusing youth (Brown, Gleghorn, Schuckit, Myers, & Mott, 1996; Crowley, Mikulich, MacDonald, Young, & Zerbe, 1998; Myers, Brown, & Mott, 1995; Winters, Stinchfield, Latimer, & Stone, 2008). Thus, youth with externalizing disorders have reliably revealed poorer outcomes, including poorer treatment retention and greater drug use and drug disorder symptoms at each follow-up point. For adolescents with externalizing disorders, their extant problems of poor affiliation with parents, schools, and prosocial institutions may be contributing to poorer treatment outcome. One study (Rowe, Liddle, Greenbaum, & Henderson, 2004) found that adolescents with both internalizing and externalizing disorders returned to intake levels of drug use at 1-year posttreatment, whereas adolescents without comorbid disorders showed significantly reduced levels of use at 6- and 12-month posttreatment.

Drug Use Severity at Intake

Relapse has been linked to intake level of drug use severity. Anderson and colleagues (2007) found that the number of dependence symptoms reported at intake was predictive of the number of dependence symptoms at a 1-year follow-up. Other studies have also indicated that drug use severity at intake is a significant predictor in treatment retention, which often is associated with relapse (see *Discharge Status* section below; Battjes, Gordon, O'Grady, & Kinlock, 2004; Godley, Godley, Funk, Dennis, & Loveland, 2001).

Family Variables

Despite some exceptions (e.g., Anderson et al., 2007; Whitney, Kelly, Myers, & Brown, 2002), it is not surprising that a family environment that encourages or supports the use of drugs or alcohol increases an adolescent's risk for relapse (i.e. Dakof, Tejeda & Liddle, 2001; Grella et al., 2004). Also, the extent of family helpfulness and family attendance at aftercare meetings has been found to be a significant predictor of posttreatment drug use. For example, adolescents who rated their family as more helpful in the recovery process had significantly more days of abstinence during the 3- and 6-month follow-up periods (Whitney et al., 2002).

Peer Variables

The influence of peers as a risk factor for initiating and maintaining drug use has been well-researched. We located two studies in which this variable exerted an influence on treatment outcome. In both studies (Anderson et al., 2007; Winters, Lee, Stinchfield, & Latimer, 2008), having social support network that favors abstinence increased an adolescent's likelihood of improved outcome Peer interaction has also been found to influence time spent in outpatient treatment (Battjes et al., 2004).

Traumatic Experiences

Traumagenic factors (i.e., victimization before age 12, victimized by more than 1 person, current worry of victimization, not believed by the people they told) may play a significant role in treatment outcome for youth (Hawke, Jainchill, & DeLeon, 2000). One study found that adolescents who did not reduce their level of alcohol and marijuana use at treatment discharge had significantly more pre-treatment traumagenic factors than did those who did reduce use (Funk, McDermeit, Godley, & Adams, 2003). In regard to posttreatment trauma, Hawke, Jainchill, and DeLeon (2003) conducted 5-year follow-ups on adolescents who had participated in a TC program for substance abuse. Their results show that post-treatment victimization was strongly associated with drug trafficking and drug involvement. The directionality of the two sets of variables in this study cannot be determined, but the persistence of trauma during the posttreatment period can be a barrier to recovery.

Treatment Variables

Here we discuss components or elements of treatment (as opposed to theoretical approaches) that are associated with outcome.

Discharge Status

The completion of a treatment program is frequently utilized as an outcome measure, given its link to treatment intensity. Indeed, treatment completion has been linked to improved posttreatment outcome (Godley, M.D., et al., 2001; Winters et al., 2000). An extension of this research is the examination of variables that predict discharge status. Research has identified several pretreatment characteristics, such as greater severity of use at intake (Friedman, Terras, & Ali, 1998), lack of family and social support, and presence of coexisting psychiatric disorders (Tims, Fletcher, & Hubbard, 1991).

Counselor Rapport

One of the most powerful predictors of treatment outcome in the general addiction field is the quality of the therapeutic alliance between therapist and client. Several studies have highlighted the importance of this variable for treating adolescents with an SUD. For example, the CYT research group found that a higher patient-rated alliance with the therapist predicted fewer days of cannabis use at 3- and 6-month posttreatment (Diamond et al., 2006). The family study research team at the University of Miami examined therapeutic alliance between adolescent and therapist and between parent and therapist; therapeutic alliance within the first two sessions predicted dropout rates (Robbins et al., 2006). Similarly, Battjes and colleagues (2004) reported that the length of time spent in outpatient treatment was significantly influenced by the perception of the counselor's skills; the more highly-skilled the counselor, the more likely the youth were to stay in treatment.

Aftercare Variables

Aftercare Involvement

Continuity of care, or aftercare, for adolescents has been repeatedly shown to reduce the risk of relapse and enhance the maintenance of treatment gains (e.g., Williams et al., 2000; Whitney et al., 2002). Yet getting youth to adhere to aftercare services is challenging. There are some indications that aftercare participation by young people increases when the aftercare group contains a sizeable number of young people (Brown & Ramo, 2006). Research has shown that participants who receive a more intensive, yet convenient aftercare program that included a home-visiting case manager for 90 days following treatment were significantly more likely to continue with their aftercare, as well as abstain from marijuana use (Godley, Godley, Dennis, Funk, & Passetti, 2007). The long-term study of youth who received a Minnesota Model treatment approach (Winters, Stinchfield, et al., 2007) showed that youth with more favorable outcome patterns over a 5.5-year period had a significantly higher rate of moderate or regular aftercare attendance (84%) compared to those with a poor outcome pattern (16%).

Recovery Schools

Another type of aftercare option lies within the academic setting. Since the late 1970s, several high schools and colleges across the United States have incorporated recovery-based academic programs. These services were created with the intention of providing confidential and emotionally healthy environments for students experiencing drug use recovery issues, and to offer social support necessary to sustain sobriety while students continue their education (McSharry, 2007). Currently, there are 19 recovery high schools reporting membership with the Association for Recovery Schools (http://www.recoveryschools.org/schools_highschool.html), as well as 14 Recovery College programs. The existence of recovery schools for nearly three decades has contributed to an interest in evaluating them. The authors know of an in-progress NIH study that is systematically describing existing programs; and there is one descriptive study of a recovery college program and it reported that the large majority of students in that program were maintaining sobriety (Botzet, Winters, & Fahnhorst, 2007).

Electronic Aftercare

A new tactic to the aftercare approach involves the use of electronic resources, such as the computer and telephone. Electronic mediums have the advantage of being a less expensive alternative to clinician-administered assessments, as well as the potential for increasing client participation in therapeutic activities, and streamlining client input and data. Current use of electronic-assisted therapy includes Internet "treatment programs" that employ various elements, such as psychoeducation, social support through chat rooms, monitoring of symptoms and progress, and feedback (Taylor & Luce, 2003). Online consultation is also available, in which individuals can chat online with therapists who have verified credentials (e.g., the International Society for Mental Health Online, www.ismpo.org). As an aftercare approach, Kaminer and colleagues (Kaminer, Litt, Burke, & Burleson, 2006) had youth in recovery use an interactive voice response (IVR) system to report on their daily use of alcohol following treatment. Youth were asked to call into the IVR system every evening for 14 days following treatment and report on their drug usage for that day. The authors found a high rate of compliance by youth, suggesting that it may be a feasible method to monitor aftercare substance use.

Summary

Overall, great advances have been made since 1990 in the development and evaluation of treatments for adolescent drug abuse. This body of research reflects a greater focus on varying interventions using different theory-related psychotherapies, and we can now say with relative certainty that several modalities and approaches meet standards of evidence-based treatments. The field is revealing its maturity in several ways: the use of assessment tools developed and validated on adolescent populations is the norm; many treatment approaches target multiple drugs, reflecting the fact that most clinical populations of teenagers abuse multiple substances; treatment manuals and specific protocols that permit treatment replication are available; and an increased rigor in evaluating the effectiveness of these approaches.

It is our assessment of the treatment outcome studies that the field is still dominated by psychosocial-based modalities, and that family systems-based treatments and MET/BI approaches have received the most empirical support compared to other modalities. Two approaches that have been applied to drug-abusing youth over time and still retain a core position among treatment options – the 12-step approach and TCs – have received very little investigation with clinical trials. Also, few pharmacological treatments of adolescents with an SUD have been published; their role as an effective adjunct to psychosocial-based approaches merits more research.

Future Directions

It is important for the reader to put into perspective the need for more research in the adolescent drug abuse treatment field compared to related treatment literatures. It is estimated that there are more than 300 controlled evaluations of alcohol dependence treatments in the adult literature (Miller & Wilbourne, 2002), and there are also numerous controlled evaluations of drug dependence treatments for adults. By comparison, there is a very modest number of controlled evaluations of adolescent drug abuse treatments. Thus, despite recent advances in research, we still know much less about the nature and extent of effective treatments for drug-abusing youth compared to adults who seek treatment for addiction. A related research need includes a more standardized measurement of outcome. Outcomes for the studies mentioned in this chapter include abstinence rates, number of symptoms, reduction of drug use, effect size, etc. A more uniform measurement practice across studies would facilitate comparisons across studies.

Additional investigations are needed to explore the mediating and moderating effects of outcome. Whether effectiveness of treatment is for reasons related to the assumed mechanisms of action, or whether treatment affects recovery. The literature has begun to identify some promising candidates of specific elements: aftercare involvement, coexisting disorders, coping skills, peer drug use, parental support, and motivational factors. A related question is whether "aggressive" confrontational approaches, which have a long-standing tradition in many forms of addiction treatment for all ages (White & Miller, 2007), are effective with young people, or if variants of confrontational strategies are more effective with adolescents (e.g., attempts to raise a person's problem recognition).

Table 4.2 Summary of evidence-based therapeutic approaches for adolescents by typology

Primary intervention	Comparison	Study authors	No.	Comments
12-step	Waiting list	Winters et al. (2000, 2007)	245	
Therapeutic community	Treatment as usual	Morral et al. (2004)	449	
Family-based	Extended services	Dembo et al. (2000)	163	Juvenile offender population
	Pscyhoeducation	Latimer et al. (2003)	43	Cognitive behavioral therapy (CBT) and family-based combined approach
	Group therapy and psychoeducation	Liddle et al. (2001)	182	
	Group therapy	Santisteban et al. (2003)	126	Hispanic-only population
	Group therapy	Smith et al. (2006)	98	
	Usual community service	Henggeler et al. (1999)	118	
	Usual community service	Henggeler et al. (2002)	80	
	Family therapy and group therapy	Waldron et al. (2001)	114	
Behavioral	Supportive counseling	Azrin et al. (1994)	26	
Cognitive-behavioral	Psychoeducation	Kaminer et al. (2002)	51	
Psychopharmaceutical	Placebo	Niederhofer and Staffen (2003a)	26	High drop-out rate
	Placebo	Niederhofer and Staffen (2003b)	26	
Motivational interviewing/brief intervention	Education as usual	McCambridge and Strang (2004)	200	
	Assessment only	Peterson et al. (2006)	285	Population was homeless adolescents
	Psychoeducation	Srisurapanont et al. (2007)	48	Targeted methamphetamine abuse/dependence in Thailand only; high drop-out rate
	Standard care	Monti et al. (1999)	94	
	Behavioral (relaxation training)	Stein et al. (2006)	105	

Table 4.2 (continued)

Primary intervention	Comparison	Study authors	No.	Comments
	Assessment only	Winters and Leitten (2007)	79	
Mixed therapeutic approaches	Compared against multiple therapeutic approaches	Dennis et al. (2004)	600	

Future research should also explore in more depth factors affecting long-term recovery. The field has identified general principles of recovery, but little is known about the recovery process for subgroups of youth (e.g., those with an externalizing disorder versus those with an internalizing disorder; those returning to a family with active drug abuse versus those with a nondrug using family). Also, the emerging interest in the use of electronic-based aftercare services seems to be a promising approach, given the ease of administrating this approach, the comfort level by youth with e-communication, and the applicability regardless of the location of the client.

Finally, there is still a need for greater understanding of common practices and standards in community-based programs. We still know very little as to what extent community programs provide essential clinical elements or characteristics of effective treatment, such as use of standardized adolescent assessment measures and developmentally-adjusted strategies for treatment engagement. Two studies that have attempted to look at this topic suggest that many programs fall short of providing most of the essential elements of treatment (as identified by experts) (Brannigan, Schackman, Falco, & Millman, 2004; Mark et al., 2006) (Table 4.2).

References

Alcoholics Anonymous 2001 Membership Survey. (2001). New York: AA Grapevine Inc.

American Psychiatric Association. (1994). *Diagnostic and statistical manual of mental disorders* (4th ed.). Washington, DC: Author.

American Society of Addiction Medicine. (1996). *Patient placement criteria for the treatment of psychoactive substance disorders* (2nd ed.). Chevy Chase, MD: Author.

Anderson, D. J., McGovern, J. P., & DuPont, R. L. (1999). The origins of the Minnesota Model of addiction treatment: A first person account. *Journal of Addictive Diseases, 18*, 107–114.

Anderson, K. G., Ramo, D. E., Schulte, M. T., Cummins, K., & Brown, S. A. (2007). Substance use treatment outcomes for youth: Integrating personal and environmental predictors. *Drug and Alcohol Dependence, 88*, 42–28.

Anton, R. F., Moak, D. H., Latham, P. K., Wald, L. R., Malcolm, R. J., Dias, J. K. et al. (2001). Posttreatment results of combining naltrexone with cognitive behavior therapy for the treatment of outpatient alcoholism. *Journal of Clinical Psychopharmacology, 21*, 72–77.

Anton, R. F., O'Malley, S. S., Ciraulo, D. A., Cisler, R. A., Couper, D., Donovan, D. M., et al. (2006). Combined pharmacotherapies and behavioral interventions for alcohol dependence: The COMBINE study: A randomized controlled trial. Journal of American Medical Association, 29, 2003–2017.

Austin, A. M., Macgowan, M. J., & Wagner, E. F. (2005). Effective family-based interventions for adolescents with substance use problems: A systemic review. *Research on Social Work Practice, 15,* 67–83.

Azrin, N. H., Donohue, B., Besalel, V. A., Kogan, E. S., & Acierno, R. (1994). Youth drug abuse treatment: A controlled outcome study. *Journal of Child and Adolescent Substance Abuse, 3,* 1–16.

Battjes, R. J., Gordon, M. S., O'Grady, K. E., & Kinlock, T. W. (2004). Predicting retention of adolescents in substance abuse treatment. *Addictive Behaviors, 29,* 1021–1027.

Beck, A., & Weishaar, M. (2005). Cognitive therapy. In R. J. Corsini & D. Wedding (Eds.), *Current Psychotherapies* (7th ed., pp. 238–268). Belmont, CA: Thomson Brooks/Cole Publishing.

Botzet, A. M., Winters, K. C., & Fahnhorst, T. (2007). An exploratory assessment of a college substance abuse recovery program: Augsburg College's StepUP program. *Journal of Groups in Addiction and Recovery, 2,* 257–270.

Brannigan, R., Schackman, B. R., Falco, M., & Millman, R. B. (2004). The quality of highly regarded adolescent substance abuse treatment programs: Results of an in-depth national survey. *Archives of Pediatrics and Adolescent Medicine, 158,* 904–909.

Brown, S. A., Gleghorn, A., Schuckit, M. A., Myers, M. G., & Mott, M. A. (1996). Conduct disorder among adolescent alcohol and drug abusers. Journal of Studies on Alcohol, 57, 314–324.

Brown, S. A., & Ramo, D. E. (2006). Clinical course of youth following treatment for alcohol and drug problems. In H. Liddle, & C. Rowe (Eds.), *Adolescent substance abuse: Research and clinical advances* (pp. 79–103). New York, NY: Cambridge University Press.

Bunch, L., Hamilton, N., Tims, F., Angelovich, N., & McDougall, B. (1998). *CYT: A multi-site study of the effectiveness of treatment for cannabis dependant youth, Family Support Network.* St. Petersburg, FL: Operation PAR, Inc.

Catalano, R. F., Hawkins, J. D., Wells, E. A., Miller, J. L., & Brewer, D. (1991). Evaluation of the effectiveness of adolescent drug abuse treatment, assessment of risks for relapse, and promising approaches for relapse prevention. *International Journal of the Addictions, 25,* 1085–1140.

Chen, C., O'Brien, M. S., & Anthony, J. C. (2005). Who becomes cannabis dependent soon after onset of use? Epidemiological evidence from the United States: 2000–2001. *Drug and Alcohol Dependence, 79,* 11–22.

Crowley, T. J., Mikulich, S. K., MacDonald, M., Young, S. E., & Zerbe, G. O. (1998). Substance-dependent, conduct-disordered adolescent males: Severity of diagnosis predicts 2-year outcome. Drug and Alcohol Dependence, 49, 225–237.

Dakof, G. A., Tejeda, M., & Liddle, H. A. (2001). Predictors of engagement in adolescent drug abuse treatment. Journal of the American Academy of Child & Adolescent Psychiatry, 40, 274–281.

Deas, D., May, K., Randall, C., Johnson, N., & Anton, R. (2005). Naltrexone treatment of adolescent alcoholics: An open-label pilot study. *Journal of Child and Adolescent Psychopharmacology, 15,* 723–728.

Deas, D., & Thomas, S. E. (2001). An overview of controlled studies of adolescent substance abuse treatment. *The American Journal on Addictions, 10,* 178–189.

Dembo, R., Shemwell, M., Pacheco, K., Seeberger, W., Rollie, M., Schmeidler, J., et al. (2000). A longitudinal study of the impact of a Family Empowerment Intervention on juvenile offender psychosocial functioning: An expanded assessment. *Journal of Child & Adolescent Substance Abuse, 10,* 1–7.

Dennis, M., Godley, S. H., Diamond, G., Tims, F. M., Babor, T., Donaldson, J., et al. (2004). The Cannabis Youth Treatment (CYT) study: Main findings from two randomized trials. *Journal of Substance Abuse Treatment, 27,* 197–213.

Diamond, G. S., Godley, S. H., Liddle, H. A., Sampl, S., Webb, C., Tims, F. M., et al. (2002). Five outpatient treatment models for adolescent marijuana use: A description of the Cannabis Youth Treatment Interventions. *Addiction, 97,* S70–S83.

Diamond, G. S., Liddle, H. A., Wintersteen, M. B., Dennis, M. L., Godley, S. H., & Tims, F. (2006). Early Therapeutic Alliance as a Predictor of Treatment Outcome for Adolescent Cannabis Users in Outpatient Treatment. *The American Journal on Addictions*, 15(Suppl. 1), 26–33.

French, M. T., Roebuck, M. C., Dennis, M., Diamond, G., Godley, S., Tims, F., et al. (2002). The economic cost of outpatient marijuana treatment for adolescents: Findings from a mulitsite experiment. *Addiction*, 97, S84–S97.

Friedman, A. S., Terras, A., & Ali, A. (1998). Differences in characteristics of adolescent drug abuse clients that predict to improvement: For impatient treatment versus outpatient treatment. Journal of Child & Adolescent Substance Abuse, 7, 97–119.

Fuller, R. K., Branchey, L., Brightwell, D. R., Derman, R. M., Emrick, C. D., Iber, F. L., et al. (1986). Disulfiram treatment of alcoholism. *Journal of the American Medical Association*, 256, 1449–1455.

Funk, R. R., McDermeit, M., Godley, S. H., & Adams, L. (2003). Maltreatment issues by level of adolescent substance abuse treatment: The extent of the problem at intake and relationship to early outcomes. *Child Maltreatment*, 8, 36–45.

Godley, M. D., Godley, S. H., Dennis, M. L., Funk, R. R., & Passetti, L. L. (2007). The effect of assertive continuing care on continuing care linkage, adherence and abstinence following residential treatment for adolescents with substance use disorders. *Addiction*, 102, 81–93.

Godley, M. D., Godley, S. H., Funk, R. R., Dennis, M. L., & Loveland, D. (2001). Discharge status as a performance indicator: Can it predict adolescent substance abuse treatment outcome? *Journal of Child and Adolescent Substance Abuse*, 11, 91–109.

Godley, S. H., Meyers, R. J., Smith, J. E., Godley, M. D., Titus, J. M., Karvinen, T., et al. (2001). *The Adolescent Community Reinforcement Approach (ACRA) for adolescent cannabis users.* Rockville, MD: Center for Substance Abuse Treatment.

Grella, C. E., Joshi, V., & Hser, Y. I. (2004). Effects of comorbidity on treatment processes and outcomes among adolescents in drug treatment programs. *Journal of Child and Adolescent Substance Abuse*, 13, 13–31.

Hawke, J. M., Jainchill, N., & DeLeon, G. (2000). The prevalence of sexual abuse and its impact on the onset of drug use among adolescents in therapeutic community drug treatment. *Journal of Child and Adolescent Substance Abuse*, 9, 35–49.

Hawke, J. M., Jainchill, N., & DeLeon, G. (2003). Posttreatment victimization and violence among adolescents following residential drug treatment. *Child Maltreatment*, 8, 58–71.

Henggeler, S. W., Clingempeel, W. G., Brondino, M. J., & Pickrel, S. G. (2002). Four year follow-up of Multisystemic Therapy with substance-abusing and substance-dependent juvenile offenders. *Journal of the American Academy of Child & Adolescent Psychiatry*, 41, 868–874.

Henggeler, S. W., Pickrel, S. G., & Brondino, M. J. (1999). Multisystemic treatment of substance abusing and dependent delinquents: Outcomes, treatment fidelity, and transportability. *Mental Health Services Research*, 1, 171–184.

Jaffe, S. (1990). *Step workbook for adolescent chemical dependence recovery.* Washington, DC: American Academy of Child and Adolescent Psychiatry.

Jainchill, N. (1997). Therapeutic communities for adolescents: The same and not the same. In G. DeLeon (Ed.), *Community as method: Therapeutic communities for special populations and special settings* (pp. 161–178). Westport, CT: Praeger.

Kaminer, Y., Burleson, J. A., & Goldberger, R. (2002). Cognitive-behavioral coping skills and psychoeducation therapies for adolescent substance abuse. *The Journal of Nervous and Mental Disease*, 190, 737–745.

Kaminer, Y., Litt, M. D., Burke, R. H., & Burleson, J. A. (2006). An interactive voice response (IVR) system for adolescents with alcohol use disorders: A pilot study. *The American Journal on Addictions*, 15, 122–125.

Kazdin, A. E. (1987). Treatment of antisocial behavior in children: Current status and future directions. *Psychological Bulletin*, 102, 187–202.

Kelly, J. F., Myers, M. G., & Brown, S. A. (2005). The effects of age composition of 12-Step groups on adolescent 12-Step participation and substance use outcome. *Journal of Child and Adolescent Substance Abuse, 15*, 63–72.

Latimer, W. W., Winters, K. C., D'Zurilla, T., & Nichols, M. (2003). Integrated family and Cognitive-Behavior Therapy for adolescent substance abusers: A stage I efficacy study. *Drug and Alcohol Dependence, 71*, 303–317.

Latimer, W. W., Winters, K. C., Stinchfield, R., & Traver, R. E. (2000). Demographic, individual, and interpersonal predictors of adolescent alcohol and marijuana use following treatment. Psychology of Addictive Behaviors, 14, 162–173.

Liddle, H. A. (2002). *Multidimensional Family Therapy (MDFT) for adolescent cannabis users.* Rockville, MD: Center for Substance Abuse Treatment, Substance Abuse and Mental Health Services Administration.

Liddle, H. A., Dakof, G. A., Parker, K., Diamond, G. S., Barrett, K., & Tejeda, M. (2001). Multidimensional family therapy for adolescent drug abuse: Results of a randomized clinical trial. *The American Journal of Drug and Alcohol Abuse, 27*, 651–688.

Mann, K., Lehert, P., & Morgan, M. Y. (2004). The efficacy of acomprosate in the maintenance of abstinence on alcohol-dependent individuals: Results of a meta-analysis. *Alcohol Clinical and Experimental Research, 28*, 51–63.

Mark, T. L., Song, X., Vandivort, R., Duffy, S., Butler, J., Coffey, R., et al. (2006). Characterizing substance abuse programs that treat adolescents. Journal of Substance Abuse Treatment, 31, 59–65.

Mason, B., & Ownby, R. (2000). Acamprosate for the treatment of alcohol dependence: A review of double-blind, placebo-controlled trials. *CNS Sprectrums, 5*, 58–69.

McCambridge, J., & Strang, J. (2004). The efficacy of a single-session motivational interviewing in reducing drug consumption and perceptions of drug-related risk and harm among young people: Results from a muli-site cluster randomized trial. *Addiction, 99*, 39–52.

McSharry, K. (2007, February). *Issues of chemical dependency.* Brown University. Retrieved February 6, 2007, from http://www.brown.edu/Administration/Dean_of_the_College/resources/?id=256

Miller, W. R., & Sanchez, V. C. (1994). Motivating young adults for treatment and lifestyle change. In: G.S. Howard and P.E. Nathan (Eds.), *Alcohol use and misuse by young adults* (pp. 55–81). Notre Dame, IN: University of Notre Dame Press.

Miller, W. R., & Wilbourne, P. L. (2002). Mesa Grande: A methodological analysis of clinical trials of treatment for alcohol use disorders. Addiction, 97, 265–277.

Monti, P. M., Colby, S. M., Barnett, N. P., Spirito, A., Rohsenow, D. J., Myers, M. et al. (1999). Brief intervention for harm reduction with alcohol-positive older adolescents in a hospital emergency department. *Journal of Consulting and Clinical Psychology, 67*, 989–994.

Morley, K. C., Teesson, M., Reid, S. C., Sannibale, C., Thomson, C., Phung, N., et al. (2006). Naltroxene versus acamprosate in the treatment of alcohol dependence: A multi-centre, randomized, double-blind, placebo-controlled trial. *Addiction, 101*, 1451–1462.

Morral, A. R., McCaffrey, D. F., & Ridgeway, G. (2004). Effectiveness of community-based treatment for substance-abusing adolescents: 12-month outcomes of youth entering Phoenix Academy or Alternative Probation Dispositions. *Psychology of Addictive Behaviors, 18*, 257–268.

Morris, P.L., Hopwood, M., Whelan, G., Gardiner, J., & Drummond, E. (2001). Naltrexone for alcohol dependence: A randomized controlled trial. *Addiction, 96*, 1565–1573.

Myers, M. G., Brown, S. A., & Mott, M. A. (1995). Preadolescent conduct disorder behaviors predict relapse and progression of addiction for adolescent alcohol and drug abusers. Alcoholism: Clinical and Experimental Research, 19, 1528–1536.

Newcomb, M. D. (1995). Identifying high risk youth: Prevalence and patterns of adolescent drug abuse. In E. Rahdert & D. Czerkowicz (Eds.), *Adolescent drug abuse: Clinical assessment and therapeutic interventions* (pp. 7–38). Rockville, MD: U.S. Department of Health and Human Services.

Niederhofer, H., & Staffen, W. (2003a). Comparison of disulfiram and placebo in treatment of alcohol dependence of adolescents. *Drug and Alcohol Review*, *22*, 295–297.

Niederhofer, H., & Staffen, W. (2003b). Acamprosate and its efficacy in treating alcohol dependent adolescents. *European Child & Adolescent Psychiatry*, *12*, 144–148.

Ozechowski, T. J., & Liddle, H. A. (2002). Family-based therapy. In C.A. Essau (Ed.), *Substance abuse and dependence in adolescence: Epidemiology, risk factors, and treatment* (pp. 203–226). East Sussex, UK: Brunner-Routledge.

Peterson, P. L., Baer, J. S., Wells, E. A., Ginzler, J. A., & Garrett, S. B. (2006). Short-term effects of a brief motivational intervention to reduce alcohol and drug risk among homeless adolescents. *Psychology of Addictive Behaviors*, *20*, 254–264.

Robbins, M. S., Liddle, H. A., Turner, C. W., Dakof, G. A., Alexander, J. F., & Kogan, S. M. (2006). Adolescent and parent therapeutic alliances as predictors of dropout in multidimensional family therapy. *Journal of Family Psychology*, *20*, 108–116.

Rollnick, S., & Miller, W. R. (1995). What is motivational interviewing? *Behavioural and Cognitive Psychotherapy*, *23*, 325–334.

Rowe, C. L., Liddle, H. A., Greenbaum, P. E., & Henderson, C. E. (2004). Impact of psychiatric comorbidity on treatment of adolescent drug abusers. *Journal of Substance Abuse Treatment*, *26*, 129–140.

Sampl, S., & Kadden, R. (2001). *Motivational Enhancement Therapy and Cognitive Behavioral Therapy (MET-CBT-5) for adolescent cannabis users*. Rockville, MD: Center for Substance Abuse Treatment, Substance Abuse and Mental Health Services Administration.

Santisteban, D. A., Coatsworth, J. D., Perez-Vidal, A., Kurtines, W. M., Schwartz, S. J., LaPerriere, A., et al. (2003). Efficacy of brief strategic family therapy in modifying Hispanic adolescent behavior problems and substance use. Journal of Family Psychology, 17, 121–133.

Schwebel, R. (2004). *The seven challenges manual*. Tucson, AZ: Viva Press.

Smith, D. C., & Hall, J. A. (2008). Strengths oriented family therapy for adolescents with substance abuse problems. *Social Work. 53*, 185–188.

Smith, D. C., Hall, J. A., Williams, J. K., An, H., & Gotman, N. (2006). Comparative efficacy of family and group treatment for adolescent substance abuse. *The American Journal on Addictions*, *15*(Suppl. 1), 131–136.

Srisurapanont, M., Sombatmai, S., & Boripuntakul, T. (2007). Brief intervention for students with methamphetamine use disorders: A randomized controlled trial. *The American Journal on Addictions*, *16*, 111–116.

Stein, L. A., Colby, S. M., Barnett, N. P., Monti, P. M., Golembeske, C., & Lebeau-Craven, R. (2006). Effects of motivational interviewing for incarcerated adolescents on driving under the influence after release. *The American Journal on Addictions*, *15*, 50–57.

Szapocznik, J., & Coatsworth, D. (1999). An ecodevelopmental framework for organizing the influences on drug abuse: A developmental model of risk and protection. In M.D. Glantz (Ed.), *Drug abuse: Origins and interventions* (pp. 331–366). Washington, DC: American Psychological Association.

Taylor, C. B., & Luce, K. H. (2003). Computer and internet-based psychotherapy interventions. *Current Directions in Psychological Science*, *12*(1), 18–22.

Tims, F. M., Fletcher, B. W., & Hubbard, R. L. (1991). Treatment outcomes for drug abuse clients. *NIDA Research Monograph*, *106*, 93–113.

Vaughn, M. G., & Howard, M. O. (2004). Adolescent substance abuse treatment: A synthesis of controlled evaluations. *Research on Social Work Practice*, *14*, 325–335.

Waldron, H. B., Slesnick, N., Brody, J. L., Turner, C. W., & Peterson, T. R. (2001). Treatment outcomes for adolescent substance abuse at 4- and 7-month assessments. *Journal of Consulting and Clinical Psychology*, *69*, 802–813.

Webb, C., Scudder, M., Kaminer, Y., Kadden, R., & Tawfik, Z. (2002). *The MET/CBT 5 Supplement: 7 Sessions of Cognitive Behavioral Therapy (CBT 7) for adolescent cannabis users*. Rockville, MD: Center for Substance Abuse Treatment.

Weinberg, N. Z., Rahdert, E., Colliver, J. D., & Glantz, M. D. (1998). Adolescent substance abuse: A review of the past 10 years. *Journal of the American Academy of Child and Adolescent Psychiatry, 37*, 252–261.

White, W. L., & Miller, W. R. (2007). The use of confrontation in addiction treatment: History, science, and time for change. *Counselor, 8*, 12–30.

Whitney, S. D., Kelly, J. F., Myers, M. G., & Brown, S. A. (2002). Parental substance use, family support and outcome following treatment for adolescent psychoactive substance use disorders. *Journal of Child &* Adolescent *Substance Abuse, 11*, 67–81.

Williams, R. J., Chang, S. Y., & Addiction Centre Adolescent Research Group. (2000). A comprehensive and comparative review of adolescent substance abuse treatment outcome. *Clinical Psychology: Science and Practice, 7*, 138–166.

Winters, K. C. (1999). Treating adolescents with substance use disorders: An overview of practice issues and treatment outcomes. *Substance Abuse, 20*, 203–225.

Winters, K. C., Lee, S., Stinchfield, R. D., & Latimer, W. W. (2008). Interplay of psychosocial factors and the long-term course of adolescents with a substance are disorder. *Substance Abuse, 29*, 107–119.

Winters, K. C., & Leitten, W. (2007). Brief interventions for moderate drug abusing adolescents. *Psychology of Addictive Behaviors, 21*, 151–156.

Winters, K. C., Leitten, W., Wagner, E., & O'Leary Tevyaw, T. (2007). Use of brief interventions in a middle and high school setting. *Journal of School Health, 77*, 196–206.

Winters, K. C., Stinchfield, R. D., Latimer, W. W., & Lee, S. (2007). Long-term outcome of substance dependent youth following 12-Step treatment. *Journal of Substance Abuse Treatment, 33*, 61–69.

Winters, K. C., Stinchfield, R. D., Latimer, W. W., & Stone, A. (2008). Internalizing and externalizing behaviors and their association to the treatment of adolescents with a substance use disorder. *Journal of Substance Abuse Treatment, 35*, 269–278.

Winters, K. C., Stinchfield, R. D., Opland, E., Weller, C., & Latimer, W. W. (2000). The effectiveness of the Minnesota Model approach in the treatment of adolescent drug abusers. *Addiction, 95*, 601–612.

Chapter 5
Adolescent Outpatient Treatment

Richard Dembo and Randolph D. Muck

Introduction

Recent decades have seen an increase in research on adolescent drug abuse treatment. As Dennis and Kaminer (2006) point out, in 1997 there were less than 25 published studies of adolescent treatment and no published intervention manuals. In great part due to increased federal funding, and state and federal interest in evidence-based practices, the past decade has seen a significant increase in the number of published adolescent treatment studies. Currently, there are over 200 adolescent treatment studies and over 20 published adolescent treatment manuals. Further, some large-scale clinical trials have been completed [such as the Cannabis Youth Treatment (CYT) study] (Dennis et al., 2004) or are now being conducted (such as the Two Reentry Strategies project) (Jainchill, Dembo, Turner, Fong, & Farkas, 2007) that promise to increase our developing knowledge about adolescent treatment needs and their responses to care. Knowledge has also increased in regard to residential drug abuse treatment, particularly that occurring in the context of modified therapeutic community treatment for adolescents.

There is an equally important need to increase our knowledge of adolescent outpatient treatment, for several reasons. First, most adolescent drug abusers are treated in outpatient programs. Second, the number of outpatient treatment services has increased in the past 15 years. Third, a serious ongoing effort is in place to identify a number of evidence-based outpatient interventions. Fourth, economic impact studies indicate outpatient treatment, especially for marijuana use (the primary drug of choice among adolescents), can significantly reduce societal costs (e.g., inpatient hospital stays and days of schooling or training missed), with positive economic benefits equaling or exceeding the cost of treatment (French et al., 2003).

This chapter takes stock of our current state of knowledge about adolescent outpatient drug abuse treatment. We provide estimates of the number of adolescents receiving outpatient treatment in recent years, the specific drugs for which they received treatment, the co-occurrence of mental health issues among treated adolescent drug abusers, and the gap between adolescent treatment need and treatment received. Next, we review key principles that inform effective treatment

C.G. Leukefeld et al. (eds.) *Adolescent Substance Abuse,*
DOI: 10.1007/978-0-387-09732-9_5, © Springer Science+Business Media LLC 2009

programs, and, then, drawing on descriptions of evidence-based practices identified by various states, discuss effective approaches to adolescent outpatient treatment. We, then, discuss promising interventions and interventions that do not seem to work. We end with recommendations for new or additional adolescent outpatient treatment services to expand the range of treatment options for drug abusing adolescents.

There is a sizable literature on the efficacy of family interventions for drug use and other antisocial behavior. The reader should consult this literature for information on these interventions, such as multisystemic therapy (Curtis, Ronan, & Borduin, 2004; Henggeler, Melton, Smith, Schoenwald, & Hanley, 1993; Henggeler, Schoenwald, Borduin, Rowland, & Cunningham, 1998), functional family therapy (Alexander & Parsons, 1982), brief strategic family therapy (Robbins & Szapocznik, 2000; Szapocznik & Kurtines, 1989), and multidimensional family therapy (Liddle & Rowe, 2002; Liddle, in press). In this chapter, we limit our discussion to nonfamily, outpatient interventions for drug-abusing adolescents.

The Number of Adolescents in Treatment

Information on treatment admissions was drawn from online analyses of the Treatment Episode Data Set (TEDS), an administrative data set supported and maintained by the Substance Abuse and Mental Health Services Administration, Office of Applied Studies. TEDS provides nationwide, descriptive information on admissions to specialty providers of alcohol and/or substance abuse treatment who receive public funds. Data on treatment admissions are collected from the 50 states, the District of Columbia, and Puerto Rico.

Since TEDS includes information on treatment admissions, clients with multiple admissions are represented in the data set. Data on admissions to privately funded treatment programs are not included in TEDS. The number of TEDS admissions does not represent the total national demand for substance abuse treatment, or the prevalence of drug abuse in the US general population (Department of Health and Human Services, DHHS, 2006). At the same time, the admission coverage of TEDS is very large. For example, in 1997, TEDS was estimated to include 83% of TEDS-eligible admissions and 67% of all known admissions" (DHHS, 2004).

Information in TEDS indicates that there were 11,188,388 admissions to drug abuse treatment between 2000 and 2005. Eight percent, or 908,498, of these admissions were for adolescents (i.e., youths between 12 years and 17 years of age), with no significant change in this ratio for the 6-year period. For each year between 2000 and 2005, more males (70%) than females (30%) were admitted to drug abuse treatment, again with no significant change over this period (Table 5.1).

Table 5.1 Number and percentage of all adolescent (12–17 years) treatment episodes: 2000–2005

Year	Total no. of treatment episodes	No. of adolescent treatment episodes	Adolescent total (%)	Adolescent male (%)	Adolescent female (%)
2000	1,797,981	140,542	7.8	70.6	29.4
2001	1,821,054	148,772	8.2	70.3	29.7
2002	1,936,711	160,750	8.3	70.2	29.8
2003	1,897,164	158,752	8.0	69.9	30.1
2004	1,885,930	157,036	8.3	69.4	30.6
2005	1,849,548	142,646	7.7	68.7	31.3

The data reported were drawn from Treatment Episode Data Sets (TEDS) sponsored and maintained by the Office of Applied Studies at the Substance Abuse and Mental Health Services Administration (SAMHSA)

Drugs of Use, Type of Treatment, and Co-occurring Problems: 2000–2005

Alcohol and marijuana are the primary substances used by adolescents admitted to treatment between 2000 and 2005. However, there are important differences in primary substances used by male and female admittees. Compared to males, females are more often admitted to treatment for the problem use of alcohol, methamphetamines, and cocaine/crack (Table 5.2).

The vast majority of male and female adolescents admitted to treatment received ambulatory, outpatient services. Ambulatory, nonintensive outpatient treatment was the most frequent type of treatment service provided (about two-thirds of cases), followed by ambulatory, intensive treatment (for 13–15% of male and female adolescents) (Tables 5.3 and 5.4).

Many adolescents admitted to drug abuse treatment experience co-occurring mental health problems. Without effective intervention, mental health problems can result in premature termination from treatment and relapse (Chan, Dennis, & Funk, in press). Analysis of TEDS data identified sizable rates of mental health problems among adolescents admitted to drug abuse treatment. Male and female adolescents differed in regard to the co-occurring mental health problems they were experiencing. Compared to male admittees, females had higher rates of psychiatric problems (Table 5.5). Females admitted to treatment had higher rates of depressive disorders than did their male counterparts.

The Gap Between Adolescent Treatment Need and Treatment Received

A recent study involving 43,000 US adults 18 years of age or older found that most drug abusers do not receive intervention or treatment services. Specifically, 8% of individuals identified as drug abusers, and less than 40% of individuals diagnosed

Table 5.2 Primary substance problem for male and female adolescents (12–17 years) admitted to treatment: 2000–2005

	Primary substance abuse problem			
	Alcohol (%)	Marijuana (%)	Methamphetamines (%)	Cocaine/crack (%)
2000				
Male (n = 97,642)	22.5	67.8	1.4	1.5
Female (n = 40,462)	29.6	51.0	4.6	3.0
2001				
Male (n = 102,363)	21.1	68.8	1.6	1.4
Female (n = 42,831)	28.1	51.6	5.5	2.9
2002				
Male (n = 109,365)	19.2	70.4	1.9	1.4
Female (n = 45,554)	26.2	52.9	6.0	3.2
2003				
Male (n = 107,665)	17.0	72.4	2.2	1.6
Female (n = 45,919)	25.2	53.0	7.1	3.5
2004				
Male (n = 105,979)	17.1	72.4	2.6	1.8
Female (n = 46,077)	24.6	52.4	8.1	3.8
2005				
Male (n = 96,988)	16.5	72.2	3.2	2.0
Female (n = 44,077)	23.3	51.8	10.0	3.9

The data reported were drawn from Treatment Episode Data Sets (TEDS) sponsored and maintained by the Office of Applied Studies at the Substance Abuse and Mental Health Services Administration (SAMHSA)

as drug dependent, reported receiving any treatment (Compton, Thomas, Stinson, & Grant, 2007). Similar findings have emerged from research identifying adolescent drug abuse treatment need. The National Survey on Drug Use and Health, involving persons 12 or older in the United States, included questions on symptoms of dependence on, or abuse of, alcohol or illicit drugs in the past year. Results indicate that in 2003–2004, 6% of adolescents were classified as needing treatment for alcohol abuse, and 5% were identified as needing treatment for illicit drug use. However, only 7% of youths meeting criteria for dependence on or abuse of alcohol, and only 9% of youths classified as needing treatment for illicit drug use, received specialty treatment for each respective substance (Lennings, Kenny, & Nelson, 2006). Further, males who were classified as needing alcohol use treatment were more likely to receive specialty care than were females (Substance Abuse and Mental Health Services Administration, 2006).

Implementing effective substance abuse interventions (for illicit drug use, alcohol, and tobacco use) can result in significant savings to society. It is estimated that the cost to society of illicit drug abuse alone was US $181 billion in 2002. For some outpatient programs, total savings can exceed costs by a ratio of 12:1 (National Institute on Drug Abuse, NIDA, 2006).

Table 5.3 Type of service at admission: male adolescents: 2000–2005 (in percent)[a]

Treatment setting[b]	2000 (n = 99,140)	2001 (n = 104,592)	2002 (n = 112,946)	2003 (n = 110,983)	2004 (n = 108,919)	2005 (n = 98,003)
1. Detox: 24-h hospital inpatient	0.2	0.3	0.4	0.2	0.2	0.3
2. Detox: 24-h free-standing residential	1.9	1.4	1.3	1.2	1.6	1.9
3. Rehab/residential hospital (nondetox)	0.8	0.9	0.8	0.6	0.6	0.5
4. Rehab/residential short-term (≤30 days)	6.4	6.0	5.3	5.3	5.5	6.2
5. Rehab/residential long-term (>30 days)	8.8	8.6	9.0	9.3	9.2	7.7
6. Ambulatory, intensive outpatient	13.6	13.4	12.7	13.3	13.3	15.2
7. Ambulatory, nonintensive outpatient	67.0	67.9	69.0	68.4	68.8	68.0
8. Ambulatory detoxification	1.4	1.4	1.5	1.6	0.8	0.2
	100	100	100	100	100	100

[a]The data reported were drawn from Treatment Episode Data Sets (TEDS) sponsored and maintained by the Office of Applied Studies at the Substance Abuse and Mental Health Services Administration (SAMHSA)

[b]Type of service at admission describes the type of service the client received:

1. Detoxification, 24-h service, hospital inpatient – 24-h per day medical acute care services in a hospital setting for detoxification for persons with severe medical complications associated with withdrawal

2. Detoxification, 24-h service, free-standing residential – 24-h per day services in a nonhospital setting providing for safe withdrawal and transition to ongoing treatment

3. Rehabilitation/residential, hospital (other than detoxification) – 24-h per day medical care in a hospital facility in conjunction with treatment services for alcohol and other drug abuse and dependency

4. Rehabilitation/residential, short-term (30 days or fewer) – Typically, 30 days or fewer nonacute care in a setting with treatment services for alcohol and other drug abuse and dependency

5. Rehabilitation/residential, long-term (30 days or longer) – Typically, more than 30 days of nonacute care in a setting with treatment services for alcohol and other drug abuse and dependency; this may include transitional living arrangements such as halfway houses

6. Ambulatory, intensive outpatient – As a minimum, the client must receive treatment lasting 2 h or more per day for 3 days or more per week

7. Ambulatory, nonintensive outpatient – Ambulatory treatment services including individual, family, and/or group services; these may include pharmacological therapies

8. Ambulatory, detoxification – Outpatient treatment services providing for safe withdrawal in an ambulatory setting (pharmacological or nonpharmacological)

Table 5.4 Type of service at admission: female adolescents: 2000–2005 (in percent)[a]

Treatment setting[b]	2000 (n = 41,339)	2001 (n = 44,166)	2002 (n = 47,793)	2003 (n = 47,750)	2004 (n = 48,071)	2005 (n = 44,627)
1. Detox: 24-h hospital inpatient	0.3	0.6	0.7	0.4	0.4	0.3
2. Detox: 24-h free-standing residential	2.3	1.8	1.5	1.5	2.3	2.6
3. Rehab/residential hospital (nondetox)	1.4	1.4	1.0	0.9	0.9	0.8
4. Rehab/residential short-term (≤30 days)	7.0	6.5	6.2	6.1	6.3	6.6
5. Rehab/residential long-term (>30 days)	7.3	7.8	8.2	8.5	8.0	7.1
6. Ambulatory, intensive outpatient	13.2	13.1	12.6	13.1	13.2	14.7
7. Ambulatory, non-intensive outpatient	66.8	67.1	68.0	67.7	68.2	67.7
8. Ambulatory detoxification	1.6	1.6	1.7	1.8	0.8	0.2
	100	100	100	100	100	100

[a]The data reported were drawn from Treatment Episode Data Sets (TEDS) sponsored and maintained by the Office of Applied Studies at the Substance Abuse and Mental Health Services Administration (SAMHSA)

[b]Type of service at admission describes the type of service the client received:

1. Detoxification, 24-h service, hospital inpatient – 24-h per day medical acute care services in a hospital setting for detoxification for persons with severe medical complications associated with withdrawal

2. Detoxification, 24-h service, free-standing residential – 24-h per day services in a nonhospital setting providing for safe withdrawal and transition to ongoing treatment

3. Rehabilitation/residential, hospital (other than detoxification) – 24-h per day medical care in a hospital facility in conjunction with treatment services for alcohol and other drug abuse and dependency

4. Rehabilitation/residential, short-term (30 days or fewer) – Typically, 30 days or fewer nonacute care in a setting with treatment services for alcohol and other drug abuse and dependency

5. Rehabilitation/residential, long-term (30 days or longer) – Typically, more than 30 days of nonacute care in a setting with treatment services for alcohol and other drug abuse and dependency; this may include transitional living arrangements such as halfway houses

6. Ambulatory, intensive outpatient – As a minimum, the client must receive treatment lasting 2 h or more per day for 3 days or more per week

7. Ambulatory, nonintensive outpatient – Ambulatory treatment services including individual, family, and/or group services; these may include pharmacological therapies

8. Ambulatory, detoxification – Outpatient treatment services providing for safe withdrawal in an ambulatory setting (pharmacological or nonpharmacological

Table 5.5 Psychiatric problems in addition to alcohol/other drug problems for male and female adolescents (12–17 years) admitted to treatment: 2000–2005

Year	Male	Female
2000	19.0%	26.1%
	(*n* = 65,261)	(*n* = 26,355)
2001	19.0%	25.4%
	(*n* = 70,843)	(*n* = 29,484)
2002	20.1%	26.9%
	(*n* = 78,480)	(*n* = 33,055)
2003	19.8%	27.9%
	(*n* = 75,724)	(*n* = 32, 682)
2004	19.3%	26.1%
	(*n* = 71,503)	(*n* = 31,203)
2005	20.5%	27.0%
	(*n* = 58,664)	(*n* = 26,272)

The data reported were drawn from Treatment Episode Data Sets (TEDS) sponsored and maintained by the Office of Applied Studies at the Substance Abuse and Mental Health Services Administration (SAMHSA)

Key Principles That Should Inform Effective Treatment Programs

The National Institute on Drug Abuse (NIDA) has identified 13 principles that should undergrid substance abuse treatment efforts (National Institute on Drug Abuse, NIDA, 1999). Ideally, these principles should form the basis of all treatment:

(1) No single treatment is appropriate for all individuals.
(2) Treatment should be readily available.
(3) Effective treatment needs to attend to the multiple needs of the individual, not just his/her drug abuse.
(4) An individual's treatment and service plan must be assessed often and modified to meet the person's changing needs.
(5) Remaining in treatment for an adequate period of time is critical for treatment effectiveness.
(6) Counseling and other behavior therapies are critical components of virtually all effective treatments for addiction.
(7) For certain types of disorders, medications are an important element of treatment, especially when combined with counseling and other behavioral therapies.
(8) Addicted or drug-abusing individuals with coexisting mental disorders should have both disorders treated in an integrated way.
(9) Medical management of withdrawal syndrome is only the first stage of addiction treatment and by itself does little to change long-term drug use.
(10) Treatment does not need to be voluntary to be effective.
(11) Possible drug use during treatment must be monitored continuously.

(12) Treatment programs should provide assessment for HIV/AIDS, hepatitis B and C, tuberculosis, and other infectious diseases, and should provide counseling to help patients modify or change behaviors that place themselves or others at risk of infection.

(13) As is the case with other chronic, relapsing diseases, recovery from drug addiction can be a long-term process and typically requires multiple episodes of treatment, including "booster" sessions and other forms of continuing care.

Although improvements have occurred in the quality of treatment, much remains to be accomplished, as far as adolescent substance abuse treatment programs are concerned. For example, a recent, in-depth, national survey of highly regarded adolescent programs determined that most of these programs did not adequately address key elements of effective substance abuse treatment. The need to increase program ability to engage and retain youths, provide greater attention to cultural and gender competence, use standardized assessment instruments, and invest in scientific assessment of treatment outcome were identified as critical needs (Brannigan, Schackman, Falco, & Millman, 2004).

Effective Approaches to Adolescent Treatment in Outpatient Settings

In recent years, a number of federal and state agencies, federally funded entities, as well as academic organizations have sought to identify evidence-based practices and interventions for implementation by treatment providers. Evidence-based practices are rapidly becoming standard practice and are required by funding agencies. Evidence-based practices refer to programs or practices that are proven to be successful by research methodology and have produced consistently positive patterns of results. Evidence-based practices or model programs that have shown the greatest levels of effectiveness are those that have established generalizability (replicated in different settings and with different populations over time) through research studies (Waters, 2007).

In particular, the states of Hawaii, Oregon, and Washington have devoted significant efforts to identify evidence-based practices they recommend for implementation by treatment providers in their jurisdictions. The following outpatient treatment services are recommended.

Hawaii (www.hawaii.gov/health)

Hawaii groups its evidence-based child and adolescent psychosocial interventions by level of support: Level 1 (best support), Level 2 (good support), Level 3 (moderate support), Level 4 (minimal support), and Level 5 (known risks). Following are the listed nonfamily adolescent substance use interventions:

Best support: Cognitive behavioral therapy (CBT)
Good support: Behavior therapy

Moderate support: None
Minimal support: Individual or group (supportive) therapy; interactional therapy
Known risks: Group therapy

Oregon (www.oregon.gov/DHS/mentalhealth/ebp/practices.html)

Similar to Hawaii, Oregon also ranks substance use intervention practices along a continuum. Placement on the continuum is based on several criteria: (1) transparency (the criteria and process of review are open for observation by public description), (2) research (accumulated scientific evidence based on controlled study; research published in peer-review journals), (3) standardization (the intervention can be reliably replicated elsewhere by others), (4) replication (more than one study and more than one group of researchers have found similar positive effects to result from the practice), (5) fidelity scale (a fidelity scale is used to verify that the intervention is being implemented consistent with the treatment model), and (6) meaningful outcomes (interventions are able to show that they can help consumers achieve important goals or outcomes related to impairments and/or risk factors). Following are key features of this continuum (Oregon Addictions and Mental Health Division, 2006).

Evidence-Based Practices

Level 1: Supported by scientifically sound randomized controlled studies that have shown consistent positive outcomes. Positive outcomes have been achieved in scientifically controlled and routine care settings.

Level 2: Supported by scientifically sound experimental studies that have demonstrated consistently positive outcomes. Positive outcomes have been achieved in scientifically controlled settings or routine care settings.

Level 3: Modified from Level 1 or Level 2 practice and applied in a setting or for a population that differs from the original practice. Practice may be difficult to study in a controlled setting.

Non-evidence–Based Practice Levels

Level 4: Service or practice not yet sufficiently documented and/or replicated through scientifically sound research procedures. Intended to fill a gap in the service system and supported through sound research, documentation of service procedures, and consistently measured outcomes.

Level 5: Service based solely on clinical opinion and/or noncontrolled studies without comparison groups. Practice is not currently research based or replicable.

Level 6: Service for which evidence points to demonstrable and consistently poor outcomes.

Following are level 1, 2, and 3 nonfamily, evidence-based practices/treatment for substance abusing adolescents approved by the Oregon Office of Mental Health and Addiction Services for adolescents: (1) CBT for depressed adolescents, (2) CBT (Project Match), (3) trauma-focused CBT, (4) motivational enhancement therapy (MET), (5) relapse prevention therapy (RPT), and (6) multidimensional treatment foster care (MTFC).

Washington State (adai.washington.edu/ebp)

Developed by the University of Washington, Alcohol & Drug Abuse Institute, the Washington State website contains a detailed matrix of evidence-based practices for treating substance use disorders (SUDs) for different populations experiencing different drug abuse problems. The information presented in the Washington State website is more detailed and comprehensive than that given on the Hawaii and Oregon sites. Overall, 43 practices are listed, with most meeting five criteria: (1) research, (2) meaningful outcomes, (3) standardization, (4) replication, and (5) fidelity measure, defined in the same manner as in Oregon. Ten nonfamily interventions for adolescents are identified. We group them below into drug specific and not specific to one drug interventions.

Interventions Not Specific to One Drug

(1) Behavioral therapy, (2) Brief interventions, (3) Node-link mapping: Mapping new roads to recovery: Cognitive enhancements to counseling, (4) RPT, and (5) Seeking safety: A psychotherapy for trauma/posttraumatic stress disorder and substance abuse.

Drug-Specific Interventions

(1) CYT, (2) MET and CBT for adolescent cannabis users, (3) Combined scheduled reduced smoking and CBT, (4) Matrix-intensive outpatient program for the treatment of stimulant abuse, and (5) Treating tobacco use and dependence.

Substance Abuse and Mental Health Service Administration (SAMHSA)

The Substance Abuse and Mental Health Service Administration (SAMHSA) maintains a National Registry of Evidence-Based Programs and Practices (NREPP) (www.nrepp.samhsa.gov). NREPP is an online, searchable service providing access to information on substance abuse and mental health interventions that have been reviewed and rated by independent research and readiness for dissemination reviewers. Intervention developers wishing their interventions to be listed in the NREPP submit an application and support documentation to SAMHSA, which undergoes a prereview, formal review, with a summary report being shared with the developer for final review. Approved interventions are posted on the NREPP website. Website visitors can request information on intervention programs for specific target groups by use of search terms [topics (e.g., co-occurring disorders), areas of interest (e.g., criminal/juvenile justice), age group (e.g., 13–17), race/ethnicity, gender, setting (e.g., urban), evaluation/study design (e.g., quasiexperimental), intervention history, and public/proprietary nature of the intervention materials and components (e.g., proprietary)]. The generated summary also includes descriptive information about the intervention and its targeted outcomes, its quality of research and readiness for dissemination ratings, a list of studies and materials submitted for review, and intervention developer contact information.

Summary of Most Frequently Cited Interventions That Work

We discuss here the major adolescent non-drug–specific outpatient therapies and brief interventions recommended by at least two of the states of Hawaii, Oregon, and Washington as evidence-based best practices. Detailed information on the other interventions listed above can be found on the above noted, state evidence-based practices websites.

Cognitive Behavioral Therapy

This intervention focuses on improving the patient's cognitive (i.e., attitudes and values) and behavioral skills for changing his/her problematic drug use.

CBT is based on social learning theory and views drug use as functionally related to major problems the patient is experiencing. Stress is placed on overcoming skill deficits and strengthening the patient's ability to cope with high-risk situations, including intrapersonal (e.g., anger) and interpersonal difficulties that trigger relapse (Kadden et al., 1995).

Behavioral Therapy

This is similar to CBT, but emphasizes overcoming skill deficits and strengthening the patient's ability to cope with high-risk situations.

Brief Interventions

These are short-term interventions, involving a small number of sessions, which capitalize on the readiness of individuals to change their behavior. MET is a widely used example of this type of intervention. Based on the principles of motivational psychology and designed to effect rapid and internally motivated change, MET consists of four individual treatment sessions. In sessions 1 and 2, the therapist provides structured feedback from an initial assessment, motivation for change, and future plans. In sessions 3 and 4, the therapist reinforces progress, encourages reassessment, and provides an objective viewpoint on the client's process of change (Miller, 1995; see also Miller, Zweben, DiClemente, & Rychtarik, 1995).

Node-Link Mapping: Mapping New Roads to Recovery: Cognitive Enhancements to Counseling

Node-link mapping is a technique for visually representing the range of difficulties, issues, and their potential solutions facing persons involved in drug abuse treatment.

The client and his/her counselor develop a graphic representation of the various treatment issues they are exploring. The mapping provides a reflection of the client's thoughts, activities, and feelings, as well as their consequences, and provides a basis for exploring solutions to these issues. Mapping also helps improve communication between clients and their counselors, particularly among clients who have difficulty focusing their thinking and communicating verbally (see Dansereau, Dees, Bartholomew, & Simpson, 2000; Knight, Dansereau, Joe, & Simpson, 1994; National Institute on Drug Abuse, NIDA, 1996).

Relapse Prevention Therapy

Based on the view that the maladaptive behavior patterns are a consequence of learning processes, RPT is a CBT in which individuals learn to identify and change problematic behavior. Specific techniques are used to examine the positive and negative consequences of continued drug use, to identify and monitor drug use cravings and high-risk for drug use situations, and to develop strategies to avoid these situations and the desire to use drugs. RPT can be used alone or as an adjunct to other treatment interventions (Irwin, Bowers, Dunn, & Wang, 1999; Larimer, Palmer, & Marlatt, 1999; Marlatt & Donovan, 2005).

Trauma-Focused Cognitive Behavioral Therapy

This is a CBT adapted for use among children who have been exposed to such traumatic experiences as physical abuse, loss of a loved one, domestic or community violence, motor vehicle accidents, fires, natural disasters (e.g., hurricanes and tornadoes), industrial accidents, and terrorist attacks. Such children often develop serious emotional or behavioral problems, including drug abuse, and abuse issues complicate the patient's response to treatment and moderate the effect of treatment on outcomes (Ford, Chapman, Hawke, & Albert, 2007; Grella & Joshi, 2003; Shane, Diamond, Mensinger, Shera, & Wintersteen, 2006). The treatment involves parallel sessions with the youth and her/his nonoffending parent(s), as well as child–parent sessions at latter stages of the therapy (Cohen, Mannarino, Berliner, & Deblinger, 2000).

Seeking Safety, a psychotherapy for trauma/posttraumatic stress disorder and substance abuse, is also a widely used evidence-based intervention for abused or traumatized, substance-abusing patients (Najavits, 2005).

Multidimensional Treatment Foster Care

A behavioral intervention, based on social learning theory, MTFC is a foster care program for delinquent youths and youths in need of out-of-home placement, providing them with close supervision, fair and consistent limits, clear consequences for rule breaking, a supportive association with one or more mentoring adults, and reduced exposure to delinquent peers. Originally developed for serious/violent juvenile offenders, emotionally and behaviorally disturbed children, and developmentally disabled adolescents with a history of sexually acting out, MTFC has also been recommended as an evidenced-based practice for drug-using youths (Chamberlain & Reid, 1998).

Interventions That Do Not Seem to Work

Individual or Group (Supportive) Therapy and Interactional Therapy

These interventions have, in general, been found to be ineffective. A primary factor in their ineffectiveness is the absence of developing specific behavioral skills to improve the client's ability to handle high-risk situations.

Group Therapy

Because of its lower cost and ability to serve many youths at one time, group therapy is the most widely used intervention for troubled, including drug using, youths. However, unless properly implemented, group therapy can have negative effects.

For example, some researchers have found evidence that group intervention partici- pants sometimes experience a deviant peer contagion effect. Deviant youth who are placed in a group intervention setting with other deviant youths, such as group counseling by a probation officer, guided group interaction, Scared Straight pro- grams, positive peer culture groups, or vocational training groups, often experience a strengthening or reinforcing, rather than a reduction, of their antisocial behavior (Dodge, Dishion, & Lansford, 2007; Lipsey, 2006).

On the contrary, when properly implemented, the negative effects of group ther- apy can be avoided, and the experience can, in fact, lead to positive outcomes (Burleson, Kaminer, & Dennis, 2006; Lipsey, 2006; see also Weiss et al., 2005). Burleson et al. (2006, p. 13) offer some suggestions to optimize the usefulness of group therapy: (1) the recruitment of adolescents from diverse referral sources, (2) maintaining group heterogeneity by including prosocial youth, if for no other rea- son than to replicate a real-world social environment, (3) employing competent and well-trained therapists, (4) maintaining an effective supervision apparatus, and (5) conducting manualized interventions that include clear "trouble shooting" proto- cols (e.g., how to prevent "war stories," negative and verbally offensive references to group members and leaders).

Recommendations for New Services

It is now well established that many adolescents entering substance abuse treatment are experiencing co-occurring mental health problems (including internalizing and externalizing symptoms) (Chan et al., in press; Shane et al., 2006). Unless addressed, these co-occurring problems result in poor treatment participation and outcomes (Grella, Hser, Joshi, & Rounds-Bryant, 2001). For youths experiencing these conditions, there is a need to develop interventions that simultaneously address both of them. Integrated approaches are also needed for youths who present with trauma and an SUD. More needs to be understood about which treatments are most effective for which subpopulations of youth. To date the majority of our infor- mation concerns the aggregate effect of a treatment intervention on outcomes. To deliver services that are tru ly individualized, more needs to be known about what works best and for whom.

Promising Interventions

Many promising interventions have been developed and tested in recent years. While showing promise, these interventions were tested in fewer than three clinical trials. However, the extant research on these interventions has demonstrated positive effects.

Treatment as usual for youth in early studies of adolescent treatment showed mixed or negative results. In several early large-scale national efforts to look at treatment outcomes of adolescents and adults, the outcomes for youth were mixed. Only in the past 10–15 years has treatment research focused exclusively on adolescent treatment outcomes. With this focus on developing and investigating interventions that are developmentally appropriate and exclusively focused on adolescents, treatment outcomes for many promising models have shown great potential for treatment of youth SUDs (Muck et al., 2001).

In 1997, the Center for Substance Abuse Treatment (CSAT), an agency within SAMHSA, launched the CYT study. Although the focus of this study was on youth with cannabis use disorders, youth who were admitted to the study, when compared to youth nationally receiving treatment, were at higher severity and displayed similar patterns of drug abuse as the youth in TEDS.

CYT demonstrated positive outcomes in all five of the interventions tested, produced outcomes that were better than treatment as usual, and resulted in treatment manuals for each of the interventions which are in the public domain. The five tested interventions were MET/CBT-5 sessions, CBT-7 sessions, family support network, adolescent community reinforcement approach (ACRA), and multidimensional family therapy (Dennis et al., 2004). These manuals can be found at http://www.chestnut.org/LI/BookStore/index.html.

In an effort to evaluate programs that were potentially exemplary, CSAT launched the Adolescent Treatment Models study (Dennis, Dawud-Noursi, Muck, & McDermeit, 2002). The manuals developed from this effort (which include outpatient interventions) are also available at the above-noted web link.

MET/CBT-5 is a five-session intervention that includes two individual sessions of MET and three group sessions of CBT. The MET sessions focus on facilitating change using factors that motivate the client. The CBT sessions teach skills to assist clients in dealing with their problems in ways that do not include substance use (Sampl & Kadden, 2002). There is currently a replication of this model, funded by CSAT, in 36 sites across the country (DHHS, 2003). A variety of settings and populations is included in this replication. Preliminary data show the intervention to be equally effective regardless of gender, race, ethnicity, or age of the youths. The preliminary data also suggest that the outcomes are comparable to the initial CYT study.

CBT-7 was developed to follow MET/CBT-5 to study the effect of increased dosage. It adds seven CBT sessions to focus on additional coping skills (Webb, Scudder, Kaminer, & Kadden, 2002). Likewise, family support network was developed to augment MET/CBT-5 and CBT-7 with support for families that included home visits, parent education meetings, parent support groups, as well as aftercare and case management (Hamilton, Brantley, Tims, Angelovich, & McDougall, 2002).

ACRA is composed of 12 individual sessions with the youth and additional sessions with the adolescent's parent, primary caregiver, or an adult concerned about the youth's problems. Efforts are made to influence or change environmental factors related to substance use (Godley, Godley, Dennis, Funk, & Passetti, 2002). This intervention is also being replicated through grants from CSAT (DHHS, 2006). Fifteen sites have just completed their first year, and another 17 sites began operation on September 30, 2007. The ACRA replications also include the addition of assertive continuing care (Godley, Godley, Karvinen, & Slown, 2001) following

ACRA. Continuing care is widely recommended following the formal phase of treatment, and assertive continuing care has shown promising results in maintaining the gains youth have made in treatment (Godley, Godley, Dennis, & Funk, 2007; Godley, Risbert, Adams, & Sodetz, 2002).

Dialectical behavioral therapy, which has been used to treat patients with borderline personality disorder and drug-dependence (Linehan et al., 1999), is seen by many as a promising approach for youth. In the original trial with dialectical behavioral therapy (Linehan, Armstrong, Suarez, Allmon, & Heard, 1991), parasuicidal behavior and areas of behavioral dyscontrol were decreased. It remains to be seen whether this intervention will be effective with youth; however, the foci of this intervention are intriguing in their potential for youth in need of SUD treatment.

The Chestnut Health Systems–Bloomington Adolescent Outpatient and Intensive Outpatient model was developed drawing from four theoretical approaches (Rogerian, behavioral, cognitive, and reality). The focus is on behavioral and emotional change. The individualized treatment plan includes the family as well as the adolescent (Godley, Jones, Funk, Ives, & Passetti, 2004; Godley, Risbert, et al., 2002). It was recently included in NREPP, and can be found at http://www.nrepp. samhsa.gov/programfulldetails.asp?PROGRAM_ID = 120#studies.

Trauma has been identified as a frequently occurring experience for youth in SUD treatment and has been correlated to higher rates of comorbidity and poorer outcomes (Dennis, 2004). SAMHSAs Center for Mental Health Services also recognized a number of youth entering mental health treatment who had an SUD and coexisting traumatic stress. Through the National Child Traumatic Stress Network, the Center for Mental Health Services awarded a grant to develop interventions for youth with mental health disorders, SUD, and trauma. A toolkit (National Child Traumatic Stress Network, NCTSN, 2007) has been developed for use by treatment providers, parents, and youth and is available at http://www.nctsnet.org/nccts/nav. do?pid = ctr_top_adol. This toolkit identifies a number of promising practices for youth with substance use problems and co-occurring trauma. However, to date there is no evidence-based integrated approach for this population.

Beyond high levels of trauma in the population of youth who present to publicly funded adolescent SUD treatment, other co-occurring mental health disorders are the norm for these youth (Turner, Muck, Muck, Stephens, & Sukumar, 2004). As with trauma and SUD, there are relatively few approaches or studies on integrated treatment of mental health and SUD for adolescents. One resource for shaping practice for youth with co-occurring mental health and SUD is a trainers' manual entitled *Co-occurring Substance Use and Mental Health Disorders in Adolescents: Integrating Approaches for Assessment and Treatment of the Individual Young Person*, which is available from the Northeast Addiction Technology Transfer Center at www.neattc.org.

Seven Challenges is a group treatment intervention that is based on stages of change theory. The initial focus is on assisting the youth to develop motivation for change (Schwebel, 2004). Seven Challenges has been tested in two studies and has shown promising results, particularly with youth who have co-occurring internalizing mental health disorders (Schwebel, 2004; Smith, Hall, Williams, An, & Gotman, 2006; Stevens, Ruiz, & Schwebel, 2007).

Conclusions

Substance abuse treatment for youth has progressed rapidly during the last decade. Protocols have been developed and tested with good results, manuals have been written and are readily available for replicating these approaches, and training and certification is available for most of these interventions. Many states are moving toward establishing a menu of treatment interventions which they will fund, basing their lists on the evidence base for treatment outcomes.

Integrated approaches to address mental health and SUD treatment for youth need further development and testing. As more information becomes available about other issues faced by youth who present for SUD treatment (e.g., trauma), integrated approaches that target the SUD and the conjoint clinical issue(s) need development and testing. In the future, attention will shift toward what works for the individual(s) and their clinical profile(s), rather than aggregated outcome reporting on group means.

The development of evidence-based and promising practices over the last decade has spurred increased interest in the field of adolescent SUD treatment. In a period of increasing demands on federal, state, and local government budgets, it will take a concerted effort at all levels to continue this trend and fully realize treatment interventions which are portable and sufficiently individualized to provide the best treatment possible for troubled youth.

Acknowledgment The authors express their appreciation to Ms. Kristina Childs for organizing the references for this chapter.

References

Alexander, J. F., & Parsons, B. V. (1982). *Functional family therapy: Principles and procedures.* Carmel, CA: Brooks/Cole.

Brannigan, R., Schackman, B. R., Falco, M., & Millman, R. B. (2004). The quality of highly regarded adolescent substance abuse treatment programs: Results of an in-depth national survey. *Archives of Adolescent Pediatric Medicine, 158,* 904–909.

Burleson, J. A., Kaminer, Y., & Dennis, M. (2006). Absence of iatrogenic or contagion effects in adolescent group therapy: Findings from the Cannabis Youth Treatment (CYT) study. *The American Journal of Addictions, 15,* 4–15.

Chamberlain, P., & Reid, J. B. (1998). Comparison of two community alternatives to incarceration for chronic juvenile offenders. *Journal of Consulting and Clinical Psychology, 66*(4), 624–633.

Chan, Y., Dennis, M. L., & Funk, R. R. (2008). Journal of Substance Abuse, *34*(1), 14–24. Prevalence and comorbidity of major internalizing and externalizing problems among adolescents and adults presenting to substance abuse treatment. *Journal of Substance Abuse.*

Cohen, J., Mannarino, A. P., Berliner, L., & Deblinger, E. (2000). Trauma focused cognitive behavioral therapy for children and adolescents: An empirical update. *Journal of Interpersonal Violence, 15*(11), 1202–1224.

Compton, W. M., Thomas, Y. E., Stinson, F. S., & Grant, B. F. (2007). Prevalence, correlates, disability, and comorbidity of DSM-IV drug abuse and dependence in the United States. *Archives of General Psychiatry, 64,* 566–576.

Curtis, N., Ronan, K. R., & Borduin, C. M. (2004). Multisystemic treatment: A meta-analysis of outcome studies. *Journal of Family Psychology*, *18*, 411–419.

Dansereau, D. F., Dees, S. M., Bartholomew, N. G., & Simpson, D. D. (2000). *Mapping as a cognitive intervention*, Research Summary. Fort Worth, TX: Institute of Behavioral Research at Texas Christian University, .

Dennis, M. (2004). Traumatic victimization among adolescents in substance abuse treatment: Time to stop ignoring the elephant in our counseling rooms. *Counselor: The Magazine for Addiction Professionals*, *5*(2), 36–40.

Dennis, M., Godley, S. H., Diamond, G., Tims, F. M., Babor, T., Donaldson, J., et al. . (2004). The Cannabis Youth Treatment (CYT) study: Main findings from two randomized trials. *Journal of Substance Abuse Treatment*, *27*, 197–213.

Dennis, M. L., Dawud-Noursi, S., Muck, R. D., & McDermeit, M. (2002). The need for developing and evaluating adolescent treatment models. In S.J. Stevens & A.R. Morral (Eds.), *Adolescent substance abuse treatment in the United States: Exemplary models from national evaluation study* (pp. 3–34). Binghamton, New York: The Haworth Press.

Dennis, M. L., & Kaminer, Y. (2006). Introduction to special issue on advances in the assessment and treatment of adolescent substance use disorders. *The American Journal on addictions*, *15*, 1–3.

Department of Health and Human Services (DHHS), Substance Abuse and Mental Health Administration. (2006). Family centered substance abuse treatment grants for adolescents and their families. Short title: Assertive adolescent and family treatment (Initial announcement) TI-06-007. Catalogue of Federal Domestic Assistance (CFDA) No. 93.243. Rockville, MD: DHHS.

Department of Health and Human Services (DHHS), Substance Abuse and Mental Health Administration, Center for Substance Abuse Treatment. (2003). Adopt/expand effective adolescent alcohol and drug abuse treatment. Short title: Effective adolescent treatment (request for applications (RFA) No. TI-03-007). Rockville, MD: DHHS.

Department of Health and Human Services (DHHS), Substance Abuse and Mental Health Services Administration, Office of Applied Studies. (2004). *Treatment Episode Data Set (TEDS) 2004*. Ann Arbor, MI: The Inter-University Consortium for Political and Social Research.

Dodge, K. A., Dishion, T. J., & Lansford, J. E. (2007). *Deviant peer influences in programs for youth: problems and solutions*. New York: Guilford Press.

Ford, J. D., Chapman, J. F., Hawke, J., & Albert, D. (2007, June). *Trauma among youth in the juvenile justice system: Critical issues and new directions*. Delmar, NY: National Center for Mental Health and Juvenile Justice.

French, M. T., Roebuck, M. C., Dennis, M. L., Godley, S. H., Liddle, H. A., & Tims, F. (2003). Outpatient marijuana treatment for adolescents: Economic evaluation of a multi-site field experiment. *Evaluation Review*, *27*(4), 421–459.

Godley, J. D., Godley, S. H., Dennis, M. L., Funk, R., & Passetti, L. L. (2002). Preliminary outcomes from the assertive continuing care experiment for adolescents discharged from residential treatment. *Journal of Substance Abuse Treatment*, *23*, 21–32.

Godley, M. D., Godley, S. H., Dennis, M. L., & Funk, R. R. (2007). The effect of assertive continuing care on continuing care linkage, a residential treatment for adolescents with substance use disorders. *Addiction*, *102*(1), 81–93.

Godley, S. H., Godley, M. D., Karvinen, T., & Slown, L. L. (2001). *ACC The assertive continuing care protocol: A case manager's manual for working with adolescents after residential treatment of alcohol and other substance use disorders*. National Institute on Alcohol Abuse and Alcoholism (NIAAA), U.S. Public Health Service (PHS); U.S. Department of Health and Human Services (DHHS) (Grant #AA10368).

Godley, S. H., Jones, N., Funk, R., Ives, M., & Passetti, L. L. (2004). Comparing outcomes of best-practice and research-based outpatient treatment protocols for adolescents. *Journal of Psychoactive Drugs*, *36*(1), 35–48.

Godley, S., Risbert, R., Adams, L., & Sodetz, A. (2002). *Chestnut Health Systems Treatment Manual: Bloomington's outpatient and intensive outpatient treatment model*. Bloomington, IL: Chestnut Health Systems.

Grella, C. E., Hser, Y. I., Joshi, V., & Rounds-Bryant, J. (2001). Drug treatment outcomes for adolescents with comorbid mental and substance use disorders. *Journal of Nervous and Mental Disease, 189*, 384–392.

Grella, C. E., & Joshi, V. (2003). Treatment processes and outcomes among adolescents with a history of abuse who are in drug treatment. *Child Maltreatment, 8*(1), 7–18.

Hamilton, N. L., Brantley, L. B., Tims, F. M., Angelovich, N., & McDougall, B. (2002). *Family support network for adolescent Cannabis users, Cannabis Youth Treatment (CYT) series* (Vol. 3). Rockville, MD: Center for Substance Abuse Treatment, Substance Abuse and Mental Health Services Administration, BKD386.

Henggeler, S. W., Melton, G. B., Smith, L. A., Schoenwald, S. W., & Hanley, J. H. (1993). Family preservation using multi-systemic treatment: Long term follow-up to a clinical trial with serious juvenile offenders. *Journal of Child and Family Studies, 2*, 283–293.

Henggeler, S. W., Schoenwald, S. K., Borduin, C. M., Rowland, M. D., & Cunningham, P. B. (1998). *Multisystemic treatment of antisocial behavior in children and adolescents*. New Brunswick, NJ: Guilford Press.

Irwin, J. E., Bowers, C. A., Dunn, M. E., & Wang, M. C. (1999). Efficacy of relapse prevention: A meta-analytic review. *Journal of Consulting and Clinical Psychology, 76*(4), 563–570.

Jainchill, N., Dembo, R., Turner, C., Fong, C., & Farkas, S. (2007). CJ-DATS brief report series: Comparing two reentry strategies for drug abusing juvenile offenders. New York: http://cjdats.org.

Kadden, R. M., Carroll, K. M., Donovan, D. M., Cooney, N. L., Monti, P. M., Abrams, D. B., et al. (1995). *Cognitive-behavioral coping skills therapy manual: A clinical research guide for therapists treating individuals with alcohol abuse and dependence* (NIH Publication No. 94-3724). Rockville, MD: National Institute on Alcohol Abuse and Alcoholism.

Knight, D. K., Dansereau, D. F., Joe, G. W., & Simpson, D. D. (1994). The role of node-link mapping in individual and group counseling. *American Journal of Drug and Alcohol Abuse, 20*(4), 517–527.

Larimer, M. E., Palmer, R. S., & Marlatt, G. A. (1999). Relapse prevention: An overview of Marlatt's cognitive-behavioral model. *Alcohol Research & Health, 23*, 151–160.

Lennings, C. J., Kenny, D. T., & Nelson, P. (2006). Substance use and treatment seeking in young offenders on community orders. *Journal of Substance Abuse Treatment, 31*, 425–432.

Liddle, H. A. (in press). *Multidimensional family therapy: An effective treatment for juvenile-justice involved adolescent substance abusers*. Washington, DC: OJJDP Publication Series on Science-Supported Treatments.

Liddle, H. A., & Rowe, C. L. (2002). Multidimensional family therapy for adolescent drug abuse. In D. Brook & H. Spitz (Eds.), *The group psychotherapy of substance abuse* (pp. 275–298). Washington, DC: American Psychiatric Association Press.

Linehan, M. M., Armstrong, H. E., Suarez, A., Allmon, D., & Heard, H. L. (1991). Cognitive-behavioral treatment of chronically parasuicidal borderline patients. *Archives of General Psychiatry, 48*, 1060–1064.

Linehan, M. M., Schmidt, H., Dimeff, L. A., Craft, J. C., Kanter, J., & Comtois, K. A. (1999). Dialectical behavior therapy for patients with borderline personality disorder and drug dependence. *The American Journal of Addictions, 8*, 279–292.

Lipsey, M. W. (2006). The effects of community-based group treatment for delinquency: A meta-analytic search for cross-study generalizations. In K.A. Dodge, T.J. Dishion, & J.E. Lansford (Eds.), *Deviant peer influences in programs for youth: Problems and solutions* (pp. 162–184). New York: Guilford Press.

Marlatt, G. A., & Donovan, D. M. (2005). *Relapse prevention: Maintenance strategies in the treatment of addictive behaviors* (2nd ed.). New York: Guilford Press.

Miller, W. R. (1995). *Motivational enhancement therapy with drug abusers.* Center for Alcoholism, Substance Abuse, and Addictions (CASAA). Albuquerque, NM: University of New Mexico.

Miller, W. R., Zweben, A., DiClemente, C. C., & Rychtarik, R. G. (1995). *Motivational enhancement therapy manual: A clinical research guide for therapists treating individuals with alcohol abuse and dependence.* Rockville, MD: NIH/NIAAA.

Muck, R., Zempolich, K. A., Titus, J. C., Fishman, M., Godley, M. D., & Schwebel, R. (2001). An overview of the effectiveness of adolescent substance abuse treatment models. *Youth & Society, 33*(2), 143–168.

Najavits, L. M. (2005). Theoretical perspectives on posttraumatic stress disorder and substance disorder. *Australian Psychologist, 40*(2), 118–129.

National Child Traumatic Stress Network (NCTSN). (2007). Understanding the link between adolescent trauma and substance abuse: A toolkit for providers. Retrieved October 10, 2007, from http://www.nctsnet.org/nccts/nav.do?pid = ctr_top_adol.

National Institute on Drug Abuse. (1996). Visual technique helps drug abuse treatment patients map road to recovery. *NIDA Notes, 11*(2), (Robert Mathias, Staff Writer).

National Institute on Drug Abuse. (1999). *Principles of drug abuse treatment: A research-based guide* (NIH Publication No. 00-4180). Bethesda, MD: NIDA.

National Institute on Drug Abuse. (2006). Treatment for drug abusers in the criminal justice system. *NIDA information facts.* Bethesda, MD: NIDA.

Oregon Addictions and Mental Health Division. (2006). Operational definition for evidence-based practices addictions and mental health division. Retrieved Ocotober 2, 2007, from http://www.oregon.gov/DHS/mentalhealth/ebp/practices.shtml.

Robbins, M. S., & Szapocznik, J. (2000). *Brief strategic family therapy.* Washington DC: Office of Juvenile Justice Delinquency Prevention.

Sampl, S., & Kadden, R. (2002). *Motivational enhancement therapy and cognitive behavioral therapy for adolescent cannabis users: 5 sessions, Cannabis Youth Treatment (CYT) series* (Vol. 1). Rockville, MD: Center for Substance Abuse Treatment, Substance Abuse and Mental Health Services Administration.

Schwebel, R. (2004). *The seven challenges manual.* Tucson, AZ: The Viva Press.

Shane, P., Diamond, G. S., Mensinger, J. L., Shera, D., & Wintersteen, M. B. (2006). Impact of victimization on substance abuse treatment outcomes for adolescents in outpatient and residential substance abuse treatment. *The American Journal of Addiction, 15*(1), 34–42.

Smith, D. C., Hall, J. A., Williams, J. K., An, H., & Gotman, N. (2006). Comparative efficacy of family and group treatment for adolescent substance abuse. *American Journal on Addictions, 15*(1), 131–136.

Stevens, S., Ruiz, B., & Schwebel, R. (2007). Seven challenges: An effective treatment for adolescents with co-occurring substance abuse and mental health problems. *Journal of Social Work Practice in the Addictions, 7*(3), 29–49.

Substance Abuse and Mental Health Services Administration. (2006). *Treatment episode data set (TEDS) highlights 2005.* National admissions to substance abuse treatment services, DASIS Series: S-36 (DHHS Publication No. (SMA) 07-4229). Rockville, MD.

Szapocznik, J., & Kurtines, W. M. (1989). *Breakthroughs in family therapy with drug-abusing and problem youth.* New York: Springer.

Turner, W. C., Muck, R. D., Muck, R. J., Stephens, R. L., & Sukumar, B. (2004). Co-occurring disorders in the adolescent mental health and substance abuse treatment systems. *Journal of Psychoactive Drugs: A Multidisciplinary Forum, 36*(4), 455–461.

Waters, P. (2007). *Evidence-based practices: A three part series.* Southern Coast Addiction Technology Center (SCATTC), Substance Abuse and Mental Health Services Administration. Retreived October 2, 2007, from www.scattc.org.

Webb, C., Scudder, M., Kaminer, Y., & Kadden, R. (2002). *The motivational enhancement therapy and cognitive behavioral therapy supplement: 7 sessions of cognitive behavioral therapy for adolescent cannabis users, Cannabis Youth Treatment (CYT) series* (Vol. 2). Rockville,

MD: Center for Substance Abuse Treatment, Substance Abuse and Mental Health Services Administration, BKD385.

Weiss, B., Caron, A., Ball, S., Trapp, J., Johnson, M., & Weisz, J. R. (2005). Iatrogenic effects of group treatment for antisocial youth. *Journal of Consulting and Clinical Psychology*, *73*(6), 1036–1044.

Chapter 6
Evidence-Based Family Treatment of Adolescent Substance Abuse and Dependence

Shaun I. Calix and Mark A. Fine

Introduction

Most scholars and practitioners agree that adolescence is a critical period of individual development. During adolescence, young people develop their identity and begin to recognize their role in a larger society. Substance abuse and dependence during adolescence has a detrimental influence on development, and in some ways even halts it. In addition, adolescent substance abuse and dependence influences family development and has consequences for communities and the larger society.

Family systems researchers have confirmed that not only does an individual affect his or her surrounding systems, but also that individuals and their surrounding systems mutually influence each other (Bronfenbrenner, 1988). Bronfenbrenner also proposes that the family is at the center of influence in our society, and therefore must be nurtured. In the context of adolescent drug abuse, Weidman (1987) recognized that the families of adolescent drug abusers can either help or hinder treatment, and proposed that families should be at least somewhat involved in the treatment of adolescents and preferably engaged in family therapy.

On the basis of a review of the clinical literature, Liddle (2004) concluded that family-based treatments of adolescent substance abuse have been shown to be more effective than alternative treatments in producing short-term and long-term change. To bring about lasting change, clinicians have proposed that they must not only treat the family system in which the adolescent develops but also address extrafamilial systems. Sexton and Alexander (2005) identified several approaches that fulfill those criteria: multisystemic therapy (MST), multidimensional family therapy (MDFT), functional family therapy (FFT), and structural family therapy (which has been redeveloped as brief strategic family therapy, BSFT).

C.G. Leukefeld et al. (eds.) *Adolescent Substance Abuse,*
DOI: 10.1007/978-0-387-09732-9_6, © Springer Science + Business Media LLC 2009

Prevalence of Substance Abuse and Dependence

Drug Abuse

According to the Substance Abuse and Mental Health Services Administration (2005), the national rate of current illicit drug use in adolescents (ages 12–17 years) in 2005 (9.9%) was lower than in 2002 (11.6%). Various age groups of youths used different types of illicit drugs. Of youths aged 12–13, 1.7% illegally used prescription drugs, 1.5% used inhalants, and .9% used marijuana (Substance Abuse and Mental Health Services Administration, 2005). Marijuana is the most frequently used drug among 14–15–year-olds (5.9%), followed by the illegal use of prescription drugs (2.8%) and inhalants (1.2%). Youths aged 16–17 used the widest variety of drugs, with marijuana being the most common (13.6%), followed by prescription drugs (5.4%), hallucinogens (1.7%), cocaine (1.2%), and inhalants (1.0%). In terms of comparisons between males and females, illicit drug use was similar in prevalence between boys (10.1%) and girls (9.7%). However, boys were more likely to use marijuana than were girls (7.5% vs 6.2%; Substance Abuse and Mental Health Services Administration, 2005).

In sum, drug use is more prevalent and more varied for older teenagers than for younger teenagers. Younger teenagers seem to use drugs that are easier to access, possibly in their own or their peers' households. Older teenagers appear to use drugs that are more illicit and that they may have accessed at parties.

Alcohol Abuse

The survey also found that 28.2% of people aged 12–20 reported drinking alcohol in the past month (Substance Abuse and Mental Health Services Administration, 2005). Males were more likely to drink than were females. For males and females, 28.9% versus 27.5% reported current alcohol use, 21.3% versus 16.1% reported binge drinking, and 7.6% versus 4.3% reported heavy drinking, respectively. Interestingly, though, a higher percentage of females than males aged 12–17 reported currently drinking (17.2% vs 15.9%).

Even though the use of illicit drugs has decreased in recent years, substance abuse and dependence that begins in adolescence can have long-term consequences. Adults who first used alcohol before the age of 21 were more likely to be classified as abusing or dependent on alcohol than those who had their first drink at the age of 21 or older (9.6% vs 2.1%, respectively; Substance Abuse and Mental Health Services Administration, 2005). Similar figures for illicit drug use are not available, but considering the highly addictive nature of illicit drugs, the same trend probably exists.

The Substance Abuse and Mental Health Services Administration (2005) estimates that 1.4% of all adolescents received treatment for either illicit drug use or alcohol use in 2005, compared to 1.6% in 2004. The decrease corresponds to a decrease in substance dependence between 2004 and 2005. However, the percentage of adolescents dependent on either illicit drugs or alcohol in 2005 was 4.1%, which indicates that there is a large gap between the number of adolescents who need treatment and those who actually receive it.

Evidence-Based Family Treatments

Several family-based treatments have displayed varying levels of success in treating adolescent substance abuse and dependence. Some of the treatments considered in this chapter (e.g., MST, MDFT, and a combination of FFT and cognitive-behavioral therapy) are integrative therapy models because they employ the use of multiple therapeutic models. Other family treatments (e.g., FFT and BSFT) are more narrowly focused family interventions, and adhere more closely to traditional family therapy models.

MST (Henggeler, Schoenwald, Borduin, Rowland, & Cunningham, 1998), MDFT (Liddle, 2002), and FFT (Alexander & Parsons, 1982) are three family treatments that have shown, through multiple and rigorous studies, effectiveness in treating adolescent substance abuse. BSFT (Szapocznik, Hervis, & Schwartz, 2003) also deserves mention as an evidence-based treatment, but it will be described as a brief therapy below. Evidence for each treatment will be presented within its respective section.

Multisystemic Therapy

MST (Henggeler et al., 1998) is based on the ecological theory of human development (Bronfenbrenner, 1979) and earlier family therapy approaches including structural (Minuchin, 1974) and strategic family therapy (Haley, 1976). Bronfenbrenner's ecological theory states that human beings develop in the context of multiple systems. The most basic and important of these systems is the family. Other systems include the community, school, work, and larger society in general. These systems shape the individual both directly (through interaction with the individual) and indirectly (through interaction with other systems). In addition, the individual and the systems interact with each other in a reciprocal manner; individuals shape the systems just as the systems shape individuals. Bronfenbrenner's theory is central to the practice of MST because the MST therapist acts as an advocate for and intervention specialist in the adolescent, family, and the extrafamilial systems (Schoenwald & Henggeler, 2005).

MST also is based on the tenets of structural (Minuchin, 1974) and strategic (Haley, 1976) family therapy. MST is both problem-focused and change-oriented, and suggests that desired changes can be achieved in multiple ways, which is called equifinality (Schoenwald & Henggeler, 2005). In other words, MST attempts to eliminate problems through interventions with the adolescent, family, and extrafamilial systems. Change to the MST therapist comes from influencing how adolescents, their families, and other systems mutually interact.

MST is a home-based therapy. A primary therapist, who is part of a larger treatment team, implements MST by providing therapy to the adolescent, family, and other systems in their environments (Schoenwald & Henggeler, 2005). The prescribed use of a treatment team is the most unique aspect of MST. The treatment team consists of the primary therapist, a supervisor, and other MST therapists. While the primary therapist is ultimately responsible for carrying out the treatment interventions, the treatment team helps in assessment and provides feedback on the therapist's conceptualization of the case. In the past, manuals and session-by-session guides were not used in MST because therapy continually evolved to fit what was occurring in a family and with the adolescent (Henggeler, Mihalic, Rone, Thomas, & Timmons-Mitchell, 1998); however, a treatment manual for MST is currently being completed. Assessment is constantly occurring in MST, so the treatment team monitors and makes changes to the treatment plan based on whether targeted changes are taking place. The treatment team makes it possible for an MST therapist to be available to clients 24 hours a day, 7 days a week by making a treatment team member available as a therapist in the absence of the primary therapist. The supervisor's role is to motivate the therapist to implement the MST interventions in a timely manner. The treatment team is essential to the successful implementation of MST.

MST has a well-defined analytical process known as the "Do Loop" (Swenson, Henggeler, Taylor, & Addison, 2005). The "Do Loop" is a series of steps that guide the MST treatment team in assessment and intervention. First, the therapist assesses what problems brought about the family's referral to MST. Next, the therapist assesses the goals of the key players involved in the process (e.g., adolescent, parents, school officials, coworkers, or work supervisors). Once those goals are decided upon, the treatment team formulates overarching goals for the family. The therapist then begins to determine the fit between the problems and the ecology of the youth (Swenson et al., 2005). To do so, the therapist observes the strengths of the family and the surrounding systems, and refines the assessment as information is discovered. Next, the therapist formulates short-term treatment goals that are linked to the overarching goals.

When all the goals are formulated, the therapist begins to implement interventions meant to help the family and extrafamilial systems accomplish those goals (Schoenwald & Henggeler, 2005). During this period, the therapist monitors the success of the interventions. When a barrier to success appears (whether at the family, extrafamilial, or therapeutic level), the treatment team formulates strategies to overcome those barriers. The therapist implements those strategies and reevaluates.

Another unique aspect of MST is that, at any point in the therapeutic process, MST prescribes a self-reflexive process for the therapists and treatment teams. Success and failure of treatment are evaluated by both the therapist and the treatment team. The therapist, treatment team, and supervisor monitor their own behavior in relation to the therapeutic process. The self-reflexive process is unique because many other therapies do not prescribe it as a crucial part of therapy, and because a treatment team plays an integral role in the process. While other therapies, in theory, can function without such a process, MST requires it as a part of a faithful adherence to the treatment model.

MST has been evaluated as an effective treatment for youth violence, delinquency, and substance use (Curtis, Ronan, & Borduin, 2004; Henggeler, Clingempeel, Brondino, & Pickrel, 2002; Henggeler, Melton, Brondino, Scherer, & Hanley, 1997; Henggeler, Melton, & Smith, 1992; Henggeler, Pickrel, & Brondino, 1999; Liddle, 2004; Liddle & Dakof, 1995). Henggeler et al. (1991) reported that 4% of all juvenile offenders in the MST condition had a substance-related arrest in a 4-year follow-up, compared to 15% of those in individual therapy. In a 4-year follow-up study to an earlier study published in 1999, which was a randomized clinical trial, Henggeler et al. (2002) found that adolescents in the MST condition abstained from marijuana significantly more frequently than did adolescents in the treatment-as-usual condition (55% vs 28%, respectively). In a study of dropout rates from treatment (Henggeler, Pickrel, Brondino, & Crouch, 1996), investigators found that 98% of MST families completed treatment, while only 22% of youths and families in the treatment-as-usual condition completed treatment they initiated. Treatment engagement is a prerequisite for successful treatment.

Multidimensional Family Therapy

MDFT (Liddle, 2002) is based in developmental psychology, Bronfenbrenner's (1979) ecological theory, and some tenets of family therapy. As part of its focus in developmental psychology, MDFT emphasizes the developmental appropriateness of interventions. Similarly to MST, in the treatment of adolescent substance abuse, MDFT targets the adolescent, family, and extrafamilial systems. MDFT emphasizes that adolescent substance abuse develops along various pathways that sometimes intersect (Liddle, Rodriguez, Dakof, Kanzki, & Marvel, 2005). In other words, the MDFT therapist assumes that adolescent substance abuse develops along pathways involving peer relationships, family relationships, individual psychological issues, and interactions with the educational and justice systems. MDFT targets those pathways individually and at the points where they intersect (which could be termed mesosystemic interactions). For example, MDFT may target an adolescent's peer relationships in the context of the school setting or examine how relationships with peers are affecting interactions with parents.

Despite their similarities, MST and MDFT take different approaches to the therapeutic process, which is consistent with the concept of equifinality (i.e., multiple pathways may lead to the same goal). While MST permits individual sessions it is preferred that the therapist intervene with the entire family. In addition, unlike MST, there is no prescription for a treatment team to be involved in MDFT. The therapists in MST and MDFT are self-reflexive, but MST therapists have the added advantage of a treatment team that is available to be actively involved in the therapeutic process as both observers and actors.

MDFT is a manualized treatment system (Liddle et al., 2005). MDFT is designed to tailor the treatment to the characteristics of the adolescent, family, and their involvement with extrafamilial systems. For that reason, MDFT has been modified into several formats to account for varying individual and family circumstances (Liddle, 2004). MDFT is similar to MST in its goals and some of its concepts, but MDFT takes a different approach to the process of therapy.

MDFT is implemented in stages with modules within each stage (Liddle, 2002). Initially, the therapist meets with the entire family to begin assessing family interactions, and then the therapist moves on to the first stage. The first stage is engagement. Within this stage, the MDFT therapist usually meets with the adolescent (module 1) and parents (module 2) separately for a few sessions to allow for engagement and to gain information about the unique perspectives of each individual. Some interventions take place in the engagement stage as well. After the individual sessions are complete, the therapist brings the family together (module 3) to further assess family interactions and history, as well as to begin to define the therapeutic process. The therapist also begins to shape family interactions on a smaller scale (e.g., the therapist may ask family members to use I-statements or may have family members explore one another's perspectives or emotions). Larger scale, and more stress-inducing, changes and interventions (e.g., enactments, prescribed changes to interactions outside of therapy) are accomplished in later stages. In module 4, the therapist makes contact with representatives from the extrafamilial systems that have an interest in the adolescent's well-being. The therapist assesses the needs of the extrafamilial systems in relation to the adolescent and establishes a working relationship with them. Of course, as with MST, the therapist receives the family's permission to contact those systems.

Stage 2 is the primary intervention stage (Liddle et al., 2005). Module 1 is insight-oriented, skill-oriented, and solution-focused. The therapist encourages self-examination in the adolescent, helps to improve functioning in critical areas (e.g., anger management), and focuses on solutions and alternatives for living. The therapist also collaborates with other treatment systems (e.g., psychiatrists) with which the adolescent is involved. In module 2, the therapist helps the parents to learn how to engage in self-care activities (e.g., stress-reduction, and assessing needs and desires), employs parenting training, and helps solve interparent conflict (i.e., help them work as a team). In module 3, the therapist facilitates discussion among family members to bring conflict into the open and to deal with it directly. The therapist also encourages the discussion of past hurts and emotions surrounding the problem and parental attempts to solve the problem.

In Stage 3, the therapist acknowledges changes that have been made by the family, making them overt and visible to the family (Liddle et al., 2005). MDFT emphasizes that treatment is not perfect, and that all changes, whether desirable or imperfect, are part of the family's narrative about a future that includes those changes. In this stage, the therapist also explores termination of therapy with the family.

MDFT has proven effective in reducing substance abuse in adolescent client populations (Liddle, Rowe, Dakof, Ungaro, & Henderson, 2004; Liddle et al., 2001). In a randomized clinical trial, MDFT, compared to adolescent group therapy and a multifamily educational intervention, yielded clinically significant and greater reductions in substance abuse and improved family functioning between pretreatment and posttreatment, and at 6- and 12-month follow-ups (Liddle et al., 2001). Clinically significant reductions were judged to be a reduction in substance abuse below the threshold set for entry into the study (i.e., marijuana use at least three times per week over a period of a month, or an instance of using "hard drugs"). Liddle et al. (2004) found that MDFT led to greater maintenance of treatment gains when compared to peer group treatment.

Functional Family Therapy

FFT (Alexander & Parsons, 1982) follows the same theoretical principles and therapy models as MST and BSFT (e.g., family systems theory, structural family therapy, and strategic family therapy). In addition, although this is the case with all therapeutic approaches, FFT explicitly emphasizes that the therapist is an integral part of the therapeutic system. Because of FFT's assumption that every family is different, the therapist must be creative in the treatment of the family (Sexton & Alexander, 2005). However, the need for creativity does not preclude the need for structure in the therapeutic process. The FFT therapist must be attuned to the dialectic tension between creativity and structure, and be able to balance the two (Sexton & Alexander, 2005).

FFT developed out of the earlier family therapy models of structural and strategic family therapy (Sexton & Alexander, 2005). Those two models, as with other therapies discussed in this chapter, emphasize assessing repeated patterns of interactions in families and intervening in an active and purposeful manner by targeting the problems that are most amenable to change. FFT has more recently included social constructionist and ecological theories to provide (1) an approach that is open to therapist creativity and (2) a comprehensive approach that considers the multiple systemic interactions that difficult client populations (such as substance abusing adolescents) experience (Sexton & Alexander, 2005).

To provide the structure needed for sound therapy, the creators of FFT developed a clinical model that consists of three phases: engagement/motivation, behavior change, and generalization (Sexton & Alexander, 2005). The overarching goals of the engagement phase are to reduce blaming and negativity, and to create a shared family focus on the presenting problem. Whereas other treatment models focus much more on individual behavior change in the adolescent (and sometimes the parents), FFT emphasizes that the family's interactions are central to problem development. Therefore, in the behavior change phase, change occurs through family-based interventions (Sexton & Alexander, 2005). FFT therapists work with family risk and protective factors to activate change. For example, the FFT therapist may target a particular family strength (e.g., positive regard for one another) to reduce negative affect or poor communication in interactions. The final phase, generalization, involves the therapist linking changes in the family to other areas of family functioning peripheral to the original presenting problem, with the goal of transferring treatment gains into multiple areas of family functioning. The FFT therapist also makes connections between the family and other community resources. For example, the FFT therapist may link the family with support groups or community recreation centers.

While all the therapies mentioned in this chapter are attuned to the same guiding principles of family therapy as FFT, there are notable differences among them. For example, FFT does not prescribe individual sessions with the adolescent or other family members. According to FFT, individual behavior change is best accomplished in the context of the family; therefore, the preferred tool is relational interventions. However, as with MST, individual sessions would be appropriate in FFT if the therapist deemed them necessary.

Another difference among FFT, MST, and MDFT is in the level of focus on extrafamilial systems. While FFT considers extrafamilial systems (e.g., relationships with peers, the family's support network) in the generalization phase, there is no direct consultation or intervention with those systems during the first two stages of therapy. Both MST and MDFT therapists interact directly with extrafamilial systems during the course of therapy.

According to several clinical trials, FFT has demonstrated effectiveness in reducing delinquency and substance abuse (Liddle, 2004; Waldron, 1997; Waldron, Slesnick, Brody, Turner, & Peterson, 2001). Liddle cited FFT as one of the more effective models of family therapy for adolescent drug abuse. Friedman (1989) found that FFT significantly reduced substance use and improved psychiatric and family functioning, but the effects were not significantly greater than those in the other treatment condition (i.e., parent training group). However, in a randomized clinical trial, FFT demonstrated significantly greater effectiveness in reducing heavy to minimal adolescent marijuana use at 7 months posttreatment than did cognitive-behavioral therapy (CBT) alone and group interventions (Waldron et al., 2001).

Promising Family Treatments

Certainly, treatments with strong empirical support are the best options for clinicians who wish to ensure they are utilizing the best available treatments. However, there are alternative approaches that show promise. Some treatments have not been developed fully into a treatment model or have not yet been shown to be effective, yet they show promise as viable treatment alternatives. The most promising of these is described below.

Cognitive-Behavioral Therapy and FFT (Integrative Treatment)

Integrative treatment has shown promise in recent research, but has not been insti-tutionalized in the form of a manual or developed beyond being a treatment condi-tion in clinical trials. Waldron et al. (2001) combined CBT and FFT to serve as a treatment condition in testing the effectiveness of FFT as a treatment for adolescent substance abuse. Waldron et al. also tested CBT by itself in the study. The CBT model used in the study focused on developing self-control and coping skills to help the adolescents avoid substance abuse. When combined with a family therapy model such as FFT, this rendition of CBT adds an additional skill-based component that is not always present in traditional family therapy.

When combined, FFT and CBT offered an integrative treatment that (1) identi-fies and intervenes in family interactions that maintain adolescent substance abuse and (2) initiates behavioral change in the adolescent and helps the adolescent gain skills to avoid the use of substances. Waldron et al. (2001) found that the condition that combined FFT and CBT outperformed both component treatments. The FFT/CBT combination resulted in a greater reduction in heavy to minimal marijuana usage from pretreatment to 7 months posttreatment (89.7% vs 55.6%) than did the FFT condition (86.6% vs 62.1%).

Brief Therapy Options

Another family treatment approach that has demonstrated effectiveness is BSFT (Szapocznik et al., 2003). Like the other approaches reviewed in this chapter, BSFT adheres to family systems theory, as well as structural and strategic family therapy models (Horigian et al., 2005). BSFT is different than the others in that it is a short-term therapy alternative. BSFT is intended to be completed within 12–16 sessions, with booster sessions after termination as needed (Horigian et al., 2005). BSFT sub-scribes to the same theories as FFT, but it has different emphases within its process.

BSFT has three main stages: joining, diagnosing, and restructuring (Horigian et al., 2005). During the joining phase, the therapist focuses on engaging the adoles-cent and family in therapy. The therapist attempts to form a new system with the family – the therapeutic system. The therapeutic system includes all members of the family and the therapist, with the therapist acting as both an observer and a change agent. As both an observer and a change agent, the BSFT therapist is very active. Joining is crucial to the therapist becoming a change agent because the ther-apist must gain the family's trust in order to direct change in an active way. Joining involves simultaneously attending to the individuals within the family and patterns of family interaction. Because the therapist must assess family functioning as it typically and naturally occurs during the joining phase, substantive interventions are not implemented during this stage.

At the diagnosing stage, the therapist begins to more actively assess the family. Part of the diagnosing stage involves creating enactments (Horigian et al., 2005). Enactments should fulfill two purposes: (1) create an atmosphere in which family members can interact as they normally do and (2) provide the therapist with an assessment opportunity to passively observe the family. The therapist should intervene only in early enactments to redirect the family members to interact with each other during the enactment rather than to talk to the therapist.

The therapist attends to several factors during assessment (Horigian et al., 2005). Paying attention to family hierarchy, subsystem organization, and the communication flow enable the therapist to understand how the family organizes itself around interactions. The therapist also focuses on the connections and responsiveness among family members. It is important for the therapist to assess the family's developmental stage, especially when children are in adolescence. One of the family interactional patterns most closely associated with adolescent behavior problems occurs when one or both parents do not allow for developmentally appropriate autonomy (Micucci, 1998). Finally, the therapist attends to family interactions organized around maintaining the adolescent as the identified patient. In doing so, the therapist identifies who blames the adolescent for family problems, and who contributes to the adolescent maintaining that role (Horigian et al., 2005).

The final stage before termination of treatment is restructuring (Szapocznik et al., 2003). Once the therapist has assessed the family, clinical goals are formulated and interventions are assigned to each goal. Interventions focus on reshaping present interactions. That is, therapists work to pinpoint what is happening in the therapy room and use those interactions as the basis for change (Horigian et al., 2005). Families in therapy often want to focus on the content of their past interactions ("he said/she said"), but it is the therapist's responsibility to redirect the family to process-oriented interactions in the here-and-now.

The therapist uses reframing to motivate change. When reframing, the therapist helps the family create alternative meanings behind interactions. Reframing is not meant to change individual cognitions, but to create an alternate frame of reality in which the family can successfully operate (Worden, 2003). For instance, in the context of exploring what parents term as an adolescent's "rebellion," the therapist may reframe the rebellion as an attempt by the adolescent to become more independent from the parents so that he or she can one day live without the parents' assistance. If the parents buy into the reframe, then they can set up a system in which they feel less need to control the adolescent and will be able to help develop that autonomy in more adaptive ways.

The BSFT therapist also works to change the family's boundaries to de-emphasize alliances that are maintaining maladaptive behavior in the adolescent (Horigian et al., 2005). For instance, if the adolescent has an overinvolved relationship with one parent, the therapist might assign tasks designed to increase the frequency of positive interactions with the other parent. The BSFT therapist also assigns tasks to the family to be completed outside of sessions (Horigian et al., 2005). Assigning tasks accomplishes two goals: (1) it maintains the family's effort outside of therapy sessions and (2) it helps the family continue its success following treatment. The belief is that if the family members can successfully complete tasks while outside of the therapy room, then they will continue to carry their success and new tools after treatment.

BSFT differs from the other therapies mentioned in this chapter in several ways. First, it is a brief therapy option, and is less intensive than MST and MDFT. It is a viable alternative when a therapist does not have the resources to be available to clients 24 h a day, 7 days a week (as MST requires). It is meant to be completed within a relatively brief time period. MST, MDFT, and FFT do not have a set number of sessions. BSFT also differs in that there is no prescription for intervention with extrafamilial systems.

BSFT has been shown to be effective in treating adolescent drug abuse (Santisteban et al., 2003; Szapocznik, Kurtines, Foote, Perez-Vidal, & Hervis, 1986; Szapocznik et al., 1988). Santisteban et al. (2003) found that 60% of BSFT participants reliably decreased marijuana usage, compared to 17% in the group therapy condition. Szapocznik et al. (1988) found that 93% of adolescent drug abusers in the BSFT condition were successfully engaged in treatment, which is a strong predictor of treatment success.

Family Treatments That Do Not Work

Although research on family treatments of adolescent substance abuse has not revealed specific family treatments that do not work, clinicians should be cautious about the types of family treatments they use in light of the evidence on the treatments that do work. One of the hallmarks of successful family treatments of adolescent substance abuse is that therapy is present- and problem-focused. Adolescent substance abuse is an acute problem for adolescents and their families. Although there may be an intergenerational influence on an adolescent's substance misuse, certain aspects of intergenerational and psychodynamic approaches (e.g., the use of genograms in Bowen Family Systems Therapy; Bowen, 1978) may not be as effective as present-focused techniques that concentrate on patterns of interaction in the here-and-now. MDFT allows for adolescents and family members to talk about past hurts. However, that specific aspect of the approach has not yet been shown to be either effective or ineffective.

Family Treatments for Specific Abused Substances

There are no family treatment approaches to our knowledge that are *designed* to target a specific drug. However, one of the treatments mentioned in the chapter has been demonstrated to be effective in the treatment of marijuana usage in teens. Santisteban et al. (2003) found that BSFT was more effective than adolescent group therapy in the treatment of adolescents who abused marijuana. At posttreatment,

60% of the adolescents in the BSFT condition improved (i.e., decreased use) and 15% deteriorated (i.e., increased use), while 17% of those in the group therapy condition improved and 50% deteriorated.

Parental substance abuse can also be a target of family therapy interventions with adolescent substance users. Parental substance abuse is a systemic issue that needs to be addressed when it occurs in the home of an adolescent. It is not uncommon for adolescents to abuse drugs or alcohol that they witness their parents using. It is somewhat less common, but possibly more therapeutically significant, that some parents abuse drugs *with* their children. It may be helpful for the therapist to target those specific drugs that the parents abuse, whether alone or with their children, when facilitating family therapy.

Conclusion: Treatment Recommendations

Our overarching treatment recommendation is that clinicians treating substance abusing adolescents or their families should strive to use those treatment strategies that have been shown to be empirically effective. Researchers testing the effectiveness of MST, MDFT, FFT, and BSFT have demonstrated their ability to produce both short-term and long-term reductions in substance misuse of adolescents, above and beyond the effects of other treatments popular in treatment communities (Curtis et al., 2004; Henggeler et al., 1991, 2002; Liddle et al., 2001, 2004). Many available treatment options have shown some effectiveness in treating other disorders and family problems. It is a natural tendency of treatment professionals to gravitate toward the treatment models under which they trained, and with which they have experienced some success in other contexts. However, it should be the goal of every clinician to utilize treatment approaches that are effective for the specific populations and problems with which the clinician works (e.g., adolescent substance abuse).

There are specific aspects of evidence-based family treatments that have been connected with treatment success with substance abusing adolescent populations. The following aspects of evidence-based treatments could be used as criteria for discerning effective treatment protocols from ineffective ones.

- Engagement – Researchers examining evidence-based treatments have demonstrated the effectiveness of family-based treatments in engaging adolescents and their families in treatment (Curtis et al., 2004; Liddle et al., 2001, 2005; Schoenwald & Henggeler, 2005). The engagement process is also referred to as joining (Horigian et al., 2005). Engaging adolescents and their families in treatment is important to maintaining them in treatment long enough for treatment to have a significant effect on the identified problems. Family-based treatments emphasize engaging the entire family, not just the adolescent with the identified problem.
- A present- and problem-focused approach – Evidence-based treatments emphasize the use of both present- and problem-focused approaches to therapy (Horigian et al., 2005; Schoenwald & Henggeler, 2005; Sexton & Alexander,

2005). Present-focused approaches rely on family interaction patterns that take place during and between therapy sessions for both assessment and intervention. MDFT therapists encourage clients to talk about past hurts, but they make sure that clients talk to each other about such things rather than to the therapist in order to maintain a process focus.

• A multisystemic (ecological systems) orientation – Most evidence-based treatments for adolescent substance abuse incorporate multisystemic interactions and how they are related in a reciprocal manner to the identified problem (Liddle et al., 2005; Schoenwald & Henggeler, 2005; Sexton & Alexander, 2005). Interventions with the systems surrounding the adolescent and family (e.g., work, school, legal system, and peers) produce changes in the systems, beyond the family, that maintain the adolescent's substance misuse.

Our recommendation for the treatment of substance abusing adolescents is a family-based approach that encompasses all of the above criteria. MST, MDFT, and FFT all meet these criteria. BSFT includes the first two listed, but does not explicitly focus on multisystemic processes. However, BSFT is a brief therapy option; a multisystemic orientation requires more long-term and intensive therapy. However, even with a short intervention, it might be advisable for BSFT therapists to consider multisystemic influences on the family in assessment and intervention.

A final recommendation is that clinicians should choose a therapy approach geared toward the context within which each client/family operates. MST, MDFT, and FFT have been validated with juvenile-justice populations, and are more appropriate for them. BSFT, as a brief therapy option, is more appropriate for adolescents and families who are not or are minimally involved with the legal system.

References

Alexander, J. F., & Parsons, B. V. (1982). *Functional family therapy: Principles and procedures*. Carmel, CA: Brooks & Cole.

Bowen, M. (1978). *Family therapy in clinical practice*. New York: Jason Aronson.

Bronfenbrenner, U. (1979). *The ecology of human development: Experiments by nature and design*. Cambridge, MA: Harvard University Press.

Bronfenbrenner, U. (1988). Strengthening family systems. In E. F. Zigler & M. Frank (Eds.), *The parental leave crisis: Toward a national policy* (pp. 143–160). New Haven, CT: Yale University Press.

Curtis, N. M., Ronan, K. R., & Borduin, C. M. (2004). Multisystemic treatment: A meta-analysis of outcome studies. *Journal of Family Psychology, 18*, 411–419.

Friedman, A. S. (1989). Family therapy vs. parent groups: Effects on adolescent drug abusers. *American Journal of Family Therapy, 17*, 335–347.

Haley, J. (1976). *Problem solving therapy*. San Francisco, CA: Jossey-Bass.

Henggeler, S. W., Borduin, C. M., Melton, G. B., Mann, B. J., Smith, L., Hall, J. A., et al. (1991). Effects of multisystemic therapy on drug use and abuse in serious juvenile offenders: A progress report from two outcome studies. *Family Dynamics of Addiction Quarterly, 1*, 40–51.

Henggeler, S. W., Clingempeel, W. G., Brondino, M. J., & Pickrel, S. G. (2002). Four-year follow-up of multisystemic therapy with substance-abusing and substance-dependent juvenile offenders. *Journal of the American Academy of Child and Adolescent Psychiatry, 41*, 868–874.

Henggeler, S. W., Melton, G. B., Brondino, M. J., Scherer, D. G., & Hanley, J. H. (1997).
Multisystemic therapy with violent and chronic juvenile offenders and their families: The role
of treatment fidelity in successful dissemination. *Journal of Consulting and Clinical
Psychology, 65*, 821–833.

Henggeler, S. W., Melton, G. B., & Smith, L. A. (1992). Family preservation using multisystemic
therapy: An effective alternative to incarcerating serious juvenile offenders. *Journal of
Consulting and Clinical Psychology, 60*, 953–961.

Henggeler, S. W., Mihalic, S. F., Rone, L., Thomas, C., & Timmons-Mitchell, J. (1998).
Multisystemic therapy. In D. S. Elliot (Ed.), *Blueprints for violence prevention* (6th ed., pp.
7–80). Boulder, CO: Institute of Behavioral Science.

Henggeler, S. W., Pickrel, S. G., & Brondino, M. J. (1999). Multisystemic treatment of substance-
abusing and dependent delinquents: Outcomes, treatment fidelity, and transportability. *Mental
Health Services Research, 1*, 171–184.

Henggeler, S. W., Pickrel, S. G., Brondino, M. J., & Crouch, J. L. (1996). Eliminating (almost)
treatment dropout of substance abusing or dependent delinquents through home-based multisystemic therapy. *American Journal of Psychiatry, 153*, 427–428.

Henggeler, S. W., Schoenwald, S. K., Borduin, C. M., Rowland, M. D., & Cunningham, P. B.
(1998). *Multisystemic treatment of antisocial behavior in children and adolescents.* New York:
Guilford Press.

Horigian, V. E., Suarez-Morales, L., Robbins, M. S., Zarate, M., Mayorga, C. C., Mitrani, V. B.,
et al. (2005). Brief strategic family therapy for adolescents with behavior problems. In J. L.
Lebow (Ed.), *Handbook of clinical family therapy* (pp. 73–102). Hoboken, NJ: Wiley.

Liddle, H. A. (2002). *Multidimensional family therapy for adolescent cannabis users, Cannibis
Youth Treatment (CYT) Series, Volume 5*, Rockville, MD: Center for Substance Abuse
Treatment, Substance Abuse and Mental Health Services Administration.

Liddle, H. A. (2004). Family-based therapies for adolescent alcohol and drug use: Research contributions and future research needs. *Addiction, 99*, 76–92.

Liddle, H. A., & Dakof, G. A. (1995). Efficacy of family therapy for drug abuse: Promising but
not definitive. *Journal of Marital and Family Therapy, 21*, 511–543.

Liddle, H. A., Dakof, G. A., Parker, K., Diamond, G. S., Barrett, K., & Tejeda, M. (2001).
Multidimensional family therapy for adolescent drug abuse: Results of a randomized clinical
trial. *The American Journal of Drug and Alcohol Abuse, 27*, 651–688.

Liddle, H. A., Rodriguez, R. A., Dakof, G. A., Kanzki, E., & Marvel, F. A. (2005). Multidimensional
family therapy: A science-based treatment for adolescent drug abuse. In J. L. Lebow (Ed.),
Handbook of clinical family therapy (pp. 128–163). Hoboken, NJ: Wiley.

Liddle, H. A., Rowe, C. L., Dakof, G. A., Ungaro, R. A., & Henderson, C. (2004). Early intervention for adolescent substance abuse: Pretreatment to posttreatment outcomes of a randomized
controlled trial comparing multidimensional family therapy and peer group treatment. *Journal
of Psychoactive Drugs, 36*, 2–37.

Micucci, J. A. (1998). *The adolescent in family therapy: Breaking the cycle of conflict and control.*
New York: Guilford Press.

Minuchin, S. (1974). *Families and family therapy.* Cambridge, MA: Harvard University Press.

Santisteban, D. A., Coatsworth, J. D., Perez-Vidal, A., Kurtines, W. M., Schwartz, S. J., LaPerriere,
A., et al. (2003). Efficacy of brief strategic family therapy in modifying Hispanic adolescent
behavior problems and substance use. *Journal of Family Psychology, 17*, 121–133.

Schoenwald, S. K., & Henggeler, S. W. (2005). Multisystemic therapy for adolescents with serious
externalizing problems. In J. L. Lebow (Ed.), *Handbook of clinical family therapy* (pp. 103–
127). Hoboken, NJ: Wiley.

Sexton, T. L., & Alexander, J. F. (2005). Functional family therapy for externalizing disorders in
adolescents. In J. L. Lebow (Ed.), *Handbook of clinical family therapy* (pp. 164–191).
Hoboken, NJ: Wiley.

Substance Abuse and Mental Health Services Administration (2005). *National survey on drug use
and health.* Retrieved June 16, 2007, from www.drugabusestatistics.samhsa.gov.

Swenson, C. C., Henggeler, S. W., Taylor, I. S., & Addison, O. W. (2005). *Multisystemic therapy and neighborhood partnerships: Reducing adolescent violence and substance abuse.* New York: Guilford.

Szapocznik, J., Hervis, O. E., & Schwartz, S. (2003). *Brief strategic family therapy for adolescent drug abuse* (NIDA *Therapy Manuals for Drug Addiction* Series). Rockville, MD: NIDA.

Szapocznik, J., Kurtines, W. M., Foote, F., Perez-Vidal, A., & Hervis, O. (1986). Conjoint versus one-person family therapy: Further evidence for the effectiveness of conducting family therapy through one person. *Journal of Consulting and Clinical Psychology, 54,* 395–397.

Szapocznik, J., Perez-Vidal, A., Brickman, A. L., Foote, F. H., Santisteban, D., Hervis, O., et al. (1988). Engaging adolescent drug abusers and their families in treatment: A strategic structural systems approach. *Journal of Consulting and Clinical Psychology, 56,* 552–557.

Waldron, H. (1997). Adolescent substance abuse and family therapy outcome: A review of randomized trials. In T. H. Ollendick & R. J. Prinz (Eds.), *Advances in clinical child psychology* (Vol. 19, pp. 199–234). New York: Plenum Press.

Waldron, H. B., Slesnick, N., Brody, J. L., Turner, C. W., & Peterson, T. R. (2001). Treatment outcomes for adolescent substance abuse at 4- and 7-month assessments. *Journal of Consulting and Clinical Psychology, 69,* 802–813.

Weidman, A. A. (1987). Substance-abusing adolescents in family therapy. *International Journal of Family Psychiatry, 8,* 211–219.

Worden, M. (2003). *Family therapy basics* (3rd edition). Toronto, Canada: Brooks-Cole.

Chapter 7
Residential Treatment of Adolescents with Substance Use Disorders: Evidence-Based Approaches and Best Practice Recommendations

Robert W. Plant and Peter Panzarella

Introduction

The rate of alcohol and drug abuse among adolescents and the number of youth at risk for the development of substance use disorders later in life remain a serious national health concern. Intervention and prevention in adolescence is particularly indicated considering that most long-term patterns of abuse and dependence originate in youth or young adulthood. Although most of the early efforts to address adolescent substance abuse utilized adult treatment models, more recent efforts have been based on research with adolescent populations and are informed by theories and knowledge of adolescent development.

Residential care of adolescents with substance abuse disorders represents one level of care in the continuum of treatment approaches. A residential treatment center has been defined as a 24-hr facility designed for the treatment of mental health disorders (including substance abuse) that is not licensed or designated as a hospital (Connor, Miller, Cunningham, & Melloni, 2002). Leichtman (2006) and others note that there is no consensus on the defining characteristics of residential treatment and that there is tremendous heterogeneity among programs. This makes the measurement of effectiveness extremely difficult. Although many programs have incorporated group, family, and individual therapies, the essence of residential treatment has often resided in the concept of the "milieu," a shadowy and elusive concept that is not well articulated. One often cited core aspect of the therapeutic milieu is that the most powerful therapeutic intervention is the moment-to-moment and day-to-day interactions between direct care staff and program participants. The purpose and intent of those interactions and the methods used to structure them are at the core of residential care.

It should be understood that residential treatment is a highly complex treatment intervention that encompasses all of the rules, therapies, staff interactions, structures, philosophies, etc. involved in 24-hr care, 7 days a week, typically lasting 6 months or longer. Beyond this general and overarching definition of residential care, no specific models of adolescent substance abuse residential treatment have been sufficiently articulated and/or investigated and programs are characterized by a high degree of variability and heterogeneity.

C.G. Leukefeld et al. (eds.) *Adolescent Substance Abuse*,
DOI: 10.1007/978-0-387-09732-9_7, © Springer Science + Business Media LLC 2009

There has been controversy regarding whether or not residential treatment is effective, in general, or in the treatment of adolescent substance abuse, in particular. The use of residential treatment for adolescents with behavioral, psychiatric, and substance use disorders had been growing steadily since the early 1900s, and according to Leichtman had "assumed a prominent place among mental health services for children" (Leichtman, 2006, p. 285). Connor et al. (2002) reported that the number of youth receiving this form of treatment grew steadily between 1982 (29,000 youth in care) through 1997 (117,720 youth in care). However, "by the 1990s, residential treatment had lost much of its luster" (Leichtman, 2006, p. 286). In response to system of care and other community mental health movements, residential care underwent significant scrutiny and was found lacking due to the practice of separating children from their parents, little to no involvement of family in treatment, poor aftercare planning, and a general failure to maintain treatment gains in the community postdischarge. In a special issue of the *American Journal of Orthopsychiatry*, Pumariega (2006a) concluded that there is limited evidence for the effectiveness of residential treatment. An earlier review by Curry (1991) concluded that the research on residential treatment has not been able to demonstrate the effectiveness of any particular model of residential care. Similarly, in a review of residential care provided to youth with emotional disturbance, Hoagwood and Cunningham (1992) found that 63% of youth did not improve and that what happened after treatment (e.g., family support, the availability of community resources) was the most important factor in predicting positive outcome. A major review of evidence-based treatments (Hoagwood, Burns, Kiser, Ringeisen, & Schoenwald, 2001) concluded that residential treatment for children and adolescents is a widely used but empirically unjustified service and that any gains made during treatment are seldom maintained once the adolescent returns to the community.

A further concern regarding residential treatment is the potential iatrogenic effects of placing youth with substance abuse problems in settings that may be dominated by a deviant peer culture where drug use is glorified and antisocial behavior encouraged. This issue is a particular concern in the case of placing "light" users in the same program with heavier users. In light of these challenges, the clinical management and composition of the group experiences that form the core of the milieu take on added importance (Kaminer, Blitz, Burleson, Kadden, & Rounsaville, 1998).

On the other side of the debate regarding the effectiveness of residential care, Lyons and McCulloch (2006, p. 251) warn that "it is important that residential treatment not be dismissed as an ineffective intervention because of the barriers that its complexity poses for conducting randomized clinical trials." In a position statement on residential care, the Child Welfare League of America (Child Welfare League of America, CWLA, 2005) maintains that residential treatment is an important component in the continuum of care and cites several studies of effectiveness while acknowledging the limitation of much of the research in the field.

In general, most adolescents receiving residential substance abuse treatment (RSAT) show reduction in use and associated problems in the year following treatment (Williams & Chang, 2000). According to Sealock, Gottfredson, and Gallagher (1997), substance abusing youthful offenders randomly assigned to residential vs outpatient treatment reported decreased drug use and delinquent behavior and exhibited a longer time till rearrest. Leichtman, Leichtman, Barber, and Neese (2001) reported that intensive short-term residential treatment can be an effective treatment intervention with adolescents when it includes family therapy, connection to community activities, and effective discharge planning. A meta-analysis of adjudicated delinquents in residential treatment reviewed 111 studies (Garrett, 1985) and reported that recidivism was modestly improved as were adjustment in the institution, academic performance, and psychological adjustment. The authors concluded that residential treatment does "work." Frensch and Cameron (2002) conducted a review of studies of adolescent residential treatment centers. They determined that despite the lack of a uniform treatment approach and numerous methodological limitations, some youth appear to show improvement in functioning, although that improvement tends to dissipate post discharge. Hooper and colleagues (Hooper, Murphy, Devaney, & Hultman, 2000) reported that 60% of youth receiving residential care demonstrated successful outcomes and that long-term treatments that incorporated home and school components were most successful. In a review of 18 outcomes studies conducted between 1993 and 2000, Hair (2005) concluded that residential treatment is beneficial in both the short-term and the long-term. Finally, researchers in Washington State evaluated the economic costs and benefits of adolescent RSAT (French, Salome, & Carney, 2002) and found that the benefits outweighed the costs by a factor of 4.34 to 1 for a net cost-savings of $16,418 per treatment episode.

On the basis of the preceding review, a reasonable adolescent, parent, provider, or policy maker might conclude that some but not all adolescents are likely to show some level of improvement following a period of residential treatment. However, to justify the costs, removal from the community, and disruption of family life associated with residential care, there will need to be evidence that residential care is superior to other forms of less intrusive treatment, even if only for a specific subpopulation of adolescents that abuse drugs and alcohol. The American Academy of Child and Adolescent Psychiatry (2005) practice parameter on adolescent substance abuse treatment recommends that treatment should always occur in the least restrictive environment and residential treatment should be recommended only when previous treatment efforts have failed, when there is a need for additional structure and supervision that cannot be provided in a less restrictive setting, or when there are specific goals of treatment that cannot be accomplished in community-based settings.

Given the paucity of randomized clinical trials of well-defined and adequately articulated residential models for the treatment of adolescents with drug and alcohol problems, this chapter focuses on the features of successful residential programs and the integration of evidence-based treatment approaches into the residential milieu.

Prevalence, Need for Treatment, and Population Parameters: National Prevalence and Trends in Use

According to the Substance Abuse and Mental Health Services Administration's National Household Survey on Drug Use and Health (2006), 8% of 12–17-year-olds meet diagnostic criteria for substance abuse and/or dependency for illicit drugs and alcohol. This 8% figure represents slightly more than 2 million youth who meet clinical criteria with many more at high risk for developing a substance abuse disorder. The most prevalent drug of abuse is alcohol at 5.5% of the adolescent population followed by marijuana at 3.3%. While the general prevalence of substance abuse disorders in adolescence ranges from 6.2% to 9.8%, rates are significantly higher within particular sectors of care including Juvenile Justice (62.1%), Mental Health (40.8%), Serious Emotional Disturbance (SED – 23.6%), and Child Welfare (19.2%) (Aarons, Brown, Hough, Garland, & Wood, 2001).

There is growing concern regarding the increasing rate of adolescent abuse of prescription drugs, including pain relievers. The estimated rate of abuse of prescription drugs is 1.3% of the adolescent population. Increased access to any psychoactive substance has been shown to be a factor in increased rates of abuse. Access to prescription drugs has been made easier by illicit sales over the Internet, and the wider presence of prescription drugs in the typical American medicine cabinet. Increased advertising of prescription drugs, in general, has also been implicated as a factor in the increased use of prescription drugs and, indirectly, to their tendency to be abused.

Beginning in the 1990s researchers noted a significant increase in the number of adolescent new users of marijuana. The increase has been attributed to parent and youth perception of less harm combined with easier access. More recently, the rate of new adolescent users of marijuana has begun to level off (Substance Abuse and Mental Health Services Administration, 2004). In general, the use of substances has been declining over the past 10 years. However, the use of opiates, LSD, inhalants, and steroids has increased at various times during the past 20 years (American Academy of Child and Adolescent Psychiatry, 2005).

The gender gap in the incidence and prevalence of adolescent substance abuse has closed. There are now no major differences between adolescent males and females in the numbers initiating use and/or needing treatment.

Need for Treatment

According to national surveys (N-SSAT, National Survey of Substance Abuse Treatment, 2005), 0.7% of adolescents received treatment in the past year. On average 1 in 10 adolescents in need of treatment for alcohol or drug abuse actually receives it. During 2006, marijuana and alcohol represented the most common drugs targeted for treatment in adolescent substance abuse programs accounting for 51% and 49% of all adolescent substance abuse treatment episodes, respectively.

For those adolescents reporting treatment in the past year, 20% reported they received treatment in an inpatient facility and 13% received treatment within an emergency room. The 2005 National Survey of Substance Abuse Treatment Facilities (N-SSAT, 2005) found that on March 31, 2005, there were 87,611 clients under age 18 in substance abuse treatment. Clients under age 18 have comprised 8% of all clients every year from 2000 through 2005. Eighty-four percent of those under 18 were in specialty programs designed just for adolescents with 12% being inpatient care. The survey found 42% of all substance abuse treatment facilities had adolescent specialty programs.

The age of first use is an important factor in adolescent admissions. The Treatment Episode Data Set (TEDS) shows that the average age of first use is 12.8 years for admissions of those under 18.

Population Parameters

Co-occurrence of substance use problems and psychiatric disorders is common in adolescents (Weinberg, Rahdert, Colliver, & Glantz, 1998). The most common co-occurring disorders include mood disorders (61%), conduct disorder (54%), and anxiety disorders (43%). Sixteen percent to 51% of all adolescents seeking treatment for substance abuse disorders meet criteria for a depressive disorder. Subramanian, Stitzer, Clemmey, Kolodner, and Fishman (2007) found that over 50% of adolescents in RSAT had clinically elevated scores on the Beck Depression Inventory and the presence of depression at intake was associated with increased postdischarge substance use. The data also shows that depression, victimization, and other mental health conditions are related to an earlier age of initiation and increased consequences of use at an early age. Adolescents with a major depressive episode in the past year were twice as likely to use alcohol and other drugs. Early intervention with depressed adolescents may reduce the onset of substance abuse. Youth with lower SES were also more likely to have a comorbid disorder.

Although high rates of dual diagnosis among adolescents with substance abuse problems are well documented, most children are placed in residential settings without consideration given to matching the adolescent's individual treatment needs with the particular expertise and service package of the treatment program (Weiner, Abraham, & Lyons, 2001). Boys and girls with dual diagnoses were more likely to have problems with suicidality, development, and delinquency. Those who have co-occurring mental health and psychiatric disturbance, early onset delinquency and conduct disorder, or a history of abuse have poorer outcomes. It has been noted that the most vulnerable children who are most often referred to residential care may be the least suited to benefit from it (Connor, Miller, Cunningham, & Melloni, 2002). Commenting on the rate and variability of relapse, Tomlinson, Brown, and Abrantes (2004, p. 168) noted that "heterogeneity within substance-abusing samples including co-morbid psychopathology may account for a portion of the variability in relapse rates." Those adolescents with comorbid psychiatric conditions returned to substance use more quickly and at a higher rate following discharge from short-term RSAT.

In addition to comorbid psychiatric conditions, youth receiving treatment in residential substance abuse programs are very likely to have experienced trauma in their lives and to demonstrate symptomatic responses to traumatic exposure. In one study, 71% of residential program participants reported lifetime exposure to trauma and 29% met criteria for PTSD. Trauma-exposed adolescents reported more behavioral problems and were more likely to leave treatment sooner (Jaycox, Ebener, Damesek, & Becker, 2004).

Rounds-Bryant, Kristiansen, and Hubbard (1999) reported that residential treatment was characterized by serving mostly males and overrepresented African Americans, Hispanics, and clients referred by the juvenile justice system. The findings on gender are troubling considering the newest data showing that males and females are equally susceptible to the development of substance abuse disorders. While ethnic disparities in healthcare methods and outcomes are common in general medical practice as well as specialty treatments, the findings here are similarly troubling and suggest that criteria regarding what constitutes "least restrictive care" may be unevenly applied.

In an investigation of the role of client factors in treatment retention, Edelen et al. (2007) reported that positive self-attitude, problem recognition, and having a strong social network predicted retention in care for 90 days or more. Remaining in care for 90 days or more is a known predictor of better outcome postdischarge. Those who do better in residential care also include those with better overall functioning and academic ability, lower rates of conduct problems, and the involvement of a child's family in treatment (Connor et al., 2002). Other client factors often related to successful outcome include completing treatment, low pretreatment use of substances, peer and parent social support, and nonuse of substances by the youth's familial and social network (Williams & Chang, 2000).

Researchers have found that laboratory measures of distress tolerance (e.g., cold pressor tests and stressful cognitive challenges as measures of an individual's general ability to tolerate distress) can predict early dropout from adolescent residential treatment (Daughters et al., 2005). The study authors suggest that efforts be taken to improve distress tolerance of children and youth in residential care given the significance of dropout in this level of care.

Theoretical Background and Principal Interventions

Recent advances in adolescent substance abuse treatment research and evaluation have stimulated a renaissance in the field. Between 1930 and 1997, there were 16 treatment studies with average participation rates under 50% and follow-up rates below 50–40%. Quality assurance protocols and standardized assessment were rarely used. In 1997–2005, there were 200 treatment studies with typical participation rates over 80% and follow-up rates over 85%. The use of standardized assessments, improved research methodology, and the use of quality assurance and adherence measures have contributed to more knowledge about what works, better definition of specific interventions, and a growing technology regarding implementation, replication, monitoring fidelity, and standardized assessment.

Despite these significant advancements, very little quality research has been conducted on outcomes from RSAT. In particular, few studies have adequately defined the treatment to be delivered and, as noted earlier, the complexity of the intervention makes it difficult to identify those aspects of treatment that are related to positive outcomes. However, the literature is helpful in several areas, including identification of the primary residential adolescent substance abuse treatment models and theories.

The primary approaches to adolescent RSAT include the Minnesota Model (12 steps), The Multidisciplinary Professional Model, The Seven Challenges, and the Therapeutic Community (TC).

Kaminer (1994) describes two models of adolescent residential treatment that represent opposite ends of the treatment spectrum: The Minnesota Model and the Multiisciplinary Professional Model.

The Minnesota Model, based on the 12 steps of AA, is focused on several primary treatment goals related to recognizing addiction, admitting the need for help, identification of what needs to change, making changes, and adjusting one's lifestyle to sustain changes (Kaminer, 1994). The Minnesota Model incorporates the disease concept of addiction and includes elements of social support, relationship to a "higher power," motivation for change, and the importance of lifestyle. 12-Step approaches have been adapted for adolescents and have been shown to have some effectiveness (Winters, Stinchfield, Opland, Weller, & Latimer, 2000). The limited availability of adolescent 12-step groups in community settings has been identified as a limitation of this approach. The social networking opportunities afforded by the Internet could be helpful in connecting youth with 12-step groups and like-minded peers interested in recovery. Application of the 12 steps is a common element of most adolescent residential treatment programs.

The Minnesota Model is an effective model of treatment resulting in decreased use of substances posttreatment, particularly for those who completed treatment (Winters et al., 2000). Fishman and colleagues (Fishman, Clemmey, & Hoover, 2003) describe the treatment approach of the Mountain Manor Treatment Center, an exemplary model of adolescent substance abuse treatment. They report positive results with an eclectic milieu therapy approach that incorporates elements of the 12 steps, as well as TC, motivational enhancement therapy (MET), and multisystemic approaches.

The Multidisciplinary Professional Model employs a team of professionals, often led by a physician, that provides a range of treatment modalities across several primary domains: substance use/abuse, education/vocation, social/leisure, medical, family, and legal. While this approach has been widely utilized in residential treatment programs, the approach has not been well defined, is often combined with other approaches, and there is scant quality treatment outcome research supporting its effectiveness.

The Seven Challenges is a relatively new approach to treatment of adolescent substance abuse that originated in the field and has received recent research attention. The Seven Challenges incorporates knowledge of adolescent development (Schwebel, 2004). The program has been found to be effective in multiple treatment settings (e.g., outpatient and residential or milieu-based settings) and is considered a promising practice (Dennis & Kaminer, 2006). The model is a relationship-based approach that incorporates aspects of motivational enhancement therapy, cognitive behavioral approaches, and health decision making focusing on the adolescent's particular need for autonomy, self-determination, and choice.

The TC is a well-established model of residential treatment for adults that has been adapted for the treatment of adolescents. The TC approach views addiction holistically, as the external behavioral expression of a complex combination of personal and developmental problems. Adaptations of the approach for an adolescent population include "increased emphasis on recreation, a less confrontational stance than is found in adult programs, more supervision and evaluation by staff members, assessment of psychological disorders, a greater role for family members in treatment, and more frequent use of psychotropic medication for emotional disorders" (Morral, Jaycox, Smith, Becker, & Ebener, 2003, p. 215). An evaluation without random assignment showed that the Phoenix Academy TC approach was superior to matched controls receiving treatment as usual on measures of substance use and psychological adjustment (Morral, McCaffery, & Ridgeway, 2004).

Specific Treatments by Drugs of Abuse

Regional and local differences have been documented in types of drugs of abuse including differences in rates of abuse and availability of heroin, methamphetamine, and other illicit drugs. There is growing concern about prescription drug abuse and increased interest in the specialty treatment for opiates and oxycontin. Burprenorphine, Suboxune, and Subutex are brand names for medications used in the treatment of opiate addiction. Buprenorphine is a semi-synthetic opioid that has properties of both an antagonist and a partial agonist. Recent studies on adolescents using Buprenorphine are promising.

Although effective with adults, little is known about the effectiveness of pharmacological agents such as methadone or naltrexone in the treatment of adolescent substance abuse (Weinberg et al., 1998).

Researchers have also been exploring whether the appropriate treatment of attention deficit disorder (with and without hyperactivity) with psycho-stimulants can be protective against the development of substance abuse disorders in adolescents. While some have worried that use of stimulant medication would "send the wrong message about substance use" and lead to higher levels of addiction, the evidence is that children appropriately treated with stimulant medications are at significantly lower risk for problems with drugs and alcohol (Wilens, Faraone, Biederman, & Gunawardene, 2003).

Although there are situations in which substance-specific treatments are indicated, research indicates that use of marijuana is often associated with smoking cigarettes and drinking alcohol, suggesting that generic treatments that target a variety of substances may be most effective (Rey, Martin, & Krabman, 2004).

Interventions that Work – Features of Successful Programs

Although there is tremendous variation in the approach taken to the residential treatment of adolescent substance abuse, researchers have begun to identify common key elements and features most often related to positive outcomes.

Kaminer (1994, p. 208) listed the common elements of adolescent alcohol and drug treatment programs including "individual counseling, individual therapy, self-help groups, substance abuse education, random urinalysis for psychoactive substances, breathalyzer testing, family therapy or involvement or both, relapse prevention techniques, educational or vocational counseling, legal assistance, various types of group activities or therapies, contingency contracting, medications, and pencil-and-paper assignments relating to the recovery process."

Research has consistently demonstrated a positive association between longer duration of residential treatment and positive posttreatment outcome (Latimer, Newcomb, Winters, & Stinchfield, 2000), although short length of treatment is often confounded with premature treatment termination. In one evaluation of residential treatment, treatment completers were 3–4 times more likely to show improvement than were noncompleters (Winters et al., 2000). In an investigation of the role of client factors in treatment retention, Edelen et al. (2007) reported that positive self-attitude, problem recognition, and having a strong social network predicted retention in care for 90 days or more (a known predictor of better outcome postdischarge). Hair's summary of the treatment literature emphasizes the need for programs to be "multimodal, holistic, and ecological" in order to achieve maximum effectiveness (Hair, 2005, p. 551).

Family involvement has consistently been cited as a key factor in achieving positive outcomes and posttreatment maintenance of gains (Frensch & Cameron, 2002). Despite significant evidence that family contact and involvement in treatment are positively associated with improved response to treatment, a survey of parents with children in residential care found that most programs restrict parent–child contact during initial adjustment periods to care, and treat contact as a privilege that must be earned through point or level systems (Robinson, Kruzich, Friesen, Jivanjee, & Pullman, 2005). The authors argue that policy, licensing, and accreditation standards should be written to support the value and need for early, frequent, and meaningful contact with family during residential care.

Mayes and Handley (2005) reported that improved treatment outcome in a residential treatment program for adolescents with co-occurring disorders was achieved when programs adopted a model where rules were relaxed, and a motivational approach was utilized that focused on harm reduction. Improvement included increased program retention, abstinence, and employment and reduced rates of hospitalization.

Prompted by earlier findings showing that high-quality preventive pediatric care and child day care often cost more than lower quality services, Schackman, Rojas, Gans, Falco, and Millman (2007) found that higher rates of reimbursement predicted higher quality residential care.

In a survey evaluation of 144 highly regarded adolescent substance abuse treatment programs (Brannigan, Schackman, Falco, & Millman, 2004), a panel of 22 experts identified 9 key elements of effective treatment programs. The nine features they identified included (1) proper assessment and treatment matching, (2) a comprehensive integrated treatment approach, (3) family involvement in treatment, (4) a developmentally appropriate approach, (5) engagement and retention in treatment, (6) employing qualified staff, (7) providing gender-specific and culturally competent care, (8) continuity of care, and (9) assessment of treatment outcome. According to the survey, most programs did not perform well on most of the key elements. The elements where programs scored the lowest included assessment and treatment matching, engagement and retention, gender and cultural competence, and treatment outcomes. The highest quality programs were more likely to employ multidimensional family approaches and/or utilize a TC approach. The top programs were not more likely to be accredited than others. Contrary to this finding, Lieberman and Bellonci (2007) provide argument for the value of licensing, regulation, accreditation, and internal program standards in efforts to obtain more consistently positive results with residential treatment.

Interventions that Might Work – Application of Evidence-Based Practices in Residential Settings

Given the inherent complexity and heterogeneity of residential treatment, efforts have been made to incorporate and/or integrate those evidence-based practices that have shown success in home and community settings into the residential milieu. In particular, cognitive behavioral approaches [cognitive behavioral therapy (CBT)], MET, and family-based and/or multisystemic approaches including Multiple Systemic Therapy (MST), Functional Family Therapy (FFT), Brief Strategic Family Therapy (BSFT) and Multidimensional Family Therapy (MDFT) are gradually being incorporated into residential care.

Kaminer (2001) reported that newer treatments showing promise included FFT, MET, Community Reinforcement, 12-step programs, CBT, and contingency management reinforcement. Despite the promising outcomes with these approaches, high rates of relapse remain. Kaminer (2001) recommends the use of aftercare approaches to bolster and sustain early treatment gains. The Assertive Continuing Care (ACC; Godley, Godley, Dennis, Funk, & Passetti, 2002) protocol is one such aftercare program.

CBT is a broadly utilized model of care that has been adapted for the treatment of adolescent substance abuse and other psychiatric disorders. Cognitive behavioral approaches are, as the name suggests, a combination of behavioral and cognitive therapies. These therapies view addictive behavior as shaped by a combination of environmental reinforcements, thoughts, emotions, and expectations. CBT for drug and alcohol abuse involves the identification of environmental triggers of behavioral and affective sequences, rehearsal and utilization of alternative responses to craving and/or drug-seeking behavior, identification and manipulation of new sources of reinforcement, and learning of coping skills.

In the treatment of addictions, CBT has been combined with MET, a complementary treatment approach that focuses on enhancing client motivation by facilitating movement across stages of change (Prochaska & DiClemente, 1992) from precontemplation through active and sustained change. MET is particularly focused on the role of self-determination in making behavioral change. Given the developmental significance of autonomy during adolescence, it is believed that MET is particularly suited to the treatment of this population.

MET combined with cognitive behavioral treatment (MET/CBT) has been successful in the treatment of adult substance abuse, has been adapted for adolescent development, and has been manualized (Sampl & Kadden, 2001). MET/CBT has been shown to be cost-effective. In the Cannabis Youth Treatment study (Dennis et al., 1998), a randomized-controlled trial of a 5-session version (CBT/MET5) was compared to typical outpatient treatment and a 12-session version (CBT/MET12). CBT/MET5 produced superior outcomes in comparison to typical outpatient and the 12-session version. While CBT is often informally incorporated into residential substance abuse individual and group treatment, it has not been formally evaluated in the residential setting.

French and colleagues (French et al., 2002) evaluated the economic impact of a combination of MET and CBT as well as the Family Support Network (FSN – a combination of case management, parent groups, home visits, and group support), the Assertive Community Reinforcement Approach (ACRA), and a clinic-based version of MDFT. They found that for three conditions (MET/CBT5, MET/CBT12, and MET/CBT12 plus FSN), the costs of outpatient treatment were outweighed by the short-term economic benefits.

Despite advances in the efficacy of adolescent substance abuse treatment, the majority of adolescents continue to have problems posttreatment. Most have relapses that are related to the recovery environment and other social risk factors (Dennis, Godley, & Titus, 1999). ACC and other models are being tested to extend the recovery period following discharge from residential care by ensuring that aftercare plans are being implemented and to enhance the recovery environment (Godley, Godley, Dennis, Funk, & Passetti 2002). The ACC protocol is well defined and includes case management and community reinforcement approaches. An evaluation of ACC demonstrated improvements in short-term outcome, including higher rates of abstinence from marijuana and reduced use of alcohol postdischarge (Godley et al., 2002). The goal is to consolidate the gains that have been accomplished in semi-controlled residential setting and generalize them to the family and community.

Family-based treatments have emerged as some of the most effective treatments of adolescent substance abuse and other behavioral and psychiatric disorders. Family-based treatments have been proven effective with substance use disorders, externalizing disorders, school and behavior problems associated with attention deficit/hyperactivity disorder (ADHD), and as adjuncts in the cognitive-behavioral treatment of anxiety disorders and depression (Diamond & Josephson, 2005). Family treatment can also help to improve compliance, retention, engagement, and

maintenance of treatment gains. In part, because of their focus on family relationships and social ecology, family approaches have been slow to be incorporated into
residential settings where, by design, children and youth are separated from
their families and live apart in an artificially constructed "therapeutic" social
environment.

According to some, outpatient family therapy appears to be superior to other
forms of treatment for adolescent behavior problems and substance abuse (Rowe &
Liddle, 2003; Williams & Chang, 2000). The American Academy of Child and
Adolescent Psychiatry Practice Parameter on Adolescent Substance Abuse (2005)
agrees with this assessment citing the superiority of outpatient family approaches,
including FFT, MST, BSFT, and MDFT. However, some evidence suggests that
other approaches to care may be just as effective. In an evaluation of family-based
and group treatment of substance abuse, Hall and colleagues (Hall, Smith, Williams,
& Delaney, 2005) found both approaches to be effective at reducing substance
abuse and related problems. They could not find an advantage of one approach
versus another.

Many of the family therapy approaches are based in theories of adolescent
development, developmental psychopathology, and structural and strategic family
therapy. These approaches recognize that adolescent substance abuse often involves
difficulty in regulating emotions and disturbed communication patterns within the
family. Studies have shown that family therapy is effective in engaging the youth
and family in treatment and changing the targeted behaviors associated with substance abuse and delinquency (Liddle & Dakof, 1995). In general, these programs
(FFT, MST, MDFT, and BSFT) are adaptable in terms of treatment intensity (e.g.,
from standard once a week outpatient to highly intensive interventions with high
levels of case management), subpopulations to be served (e.g., substance abuse,
juvenile justice, selected mood disorders with disturbances of conduct), and the
settings in which they are delivered (e.g., in-home, outpatient, as a component of a
therapeutic milieu).

In addition to their treatment effects, family models may also prevent substance
abuse by teaching parents how to improve their monitoring, supervision, and promotion of prosocial activities. This approach is very consistent with what is known
about the protective role of parental supervision and positive engagement and the
risk factors of negative peer influences and ease of access to alcohol and illicit
substances (Hawkins, Catalano, & Miller, 1992). These family models appreciate
the significance of the child and family's social ecology and organize their interventions to maximize protection and reduce risk. For example, it is known that families
who have dinner together are at reduced risk for a variety of antisocial and risk-
prone behaviors (Safeway Foundation, 2007). Encouraging and supporting family
dinners is a way of promoting the kind of bonding, family structure, and supervision
that can reduce delinquency and drug and alcohol abuse.

Pumariega (2006b) argues that the prolonged separation and reduced family
contact that is typical of many placement experiences contributes to problems
with reunification due to families reorganizing into new roles and modes of

relating that exclude the child in treatment. Incorporating effective family treatment models into residential care could reduce the likelihood of this occurring by increasing regular meaningful contact and maintaining the child's "place" in the family. Others have recommended modifications of policy to promote increased family contact (Leichtman, 2006). These changes include removing family contact from the list of privileges that must be earned, inviting the family into the milieu, and awarding milieu privileges based on improvements in behavior with family.

Interventions That Do Not Work

Assuming that adolescents will outgrow their substance abuse problem or that it is merely a "phase" is a highly ineffective strategy. The roots of most life-long patterns of substance abuse begin in adolescence and although many youth who experiment with drugs and alcohol do not go on to develop substance abuse disorders, early patterns of use that contribute to psychosocial dysfunction should never be ignored. In addition to simply ignoring the problem, boot camps, Scared Straight Programs, and punitive treatment approaches have been shown to be ineffective in the treatment of adolescent substance abuse and in some cases may cause harm.

Boot camps, popular in the eighties and nineties as a treatment for substance abuse and juvenile delinquency, have been found to be ineffective and potentially harmful (Mihalic, Irwin, Elliott, Fagan, & Hansen, 2001). Similarly, Scared Straight Programs are neither cost-effective nor do they prevent subsequent delinquency or reduce drug and alcohol use. Hooper et al. (2000) report that residential programs with a punitive orientation show poor outcome with 84% of youth rearrested within 3 years of discharge.

Brief Treatment Approaches

Screening and brief intervention in trauma units, emergency rooms, and primary health have been shown to be a cost-effective intervention for adults. The research on cost-effectiveness for adolescents is promising. The use of screening and brief substance abuse interventions in primary care or emergency settings is similar to the approach taken to combat hypertension through standard screening in a variety of settings. An opportunistic screen by the health professional has been recommended (McPherson & Hersch, 2000). Early detection could have a significant impact on changing high-risk behavior before it progresses and to identify the population in need of treatment. This approach shows promise in directly reducing substance use and indirectly reducing criminal behaviors.

Best Practice Recommendations

Despite the relative lack of quality research and compelling empirical evidence in favor of residential treatment, it is clear that many children and youth benefit from this level of care. The likelihood of positive outcomes can be increased by understanding the features and characteristics of the target population, borrowing from successful programs, and incorporating evidence-based practices that can be adapted to residential substance abuse programs. Even the most effective community-based practices fail to achieve positive outcomes with ~20% of the youth served and there remains a compelling need for residential treatment. The following recommendations are offered.

Treatment Recommendations

- **Screening and Assessment:** Few programs do an adequate job screening and assessing the youth who enter care. Youth should be screened for psychiatric conditions, trauma, drug and alcohol use, and health conditions often associated with drug and alcohol abuse (hepatitis, HIV-AIDS, STDs, etc.). Assessment should be comprehensive, including assessments of strengths, inclusion of collateral sources of information, measures of quantity, frequency and age of first substance use, and assessment in the following domains, Developmental History, Educational/Vocational History, Social/Interpersonal History, Family History, Medical History, Legal History, Substance Abuse History, Recreational History, Trauma History, Psychiatric History, Sexual History, Mental Status, Functional Assessment and Activities of Daily Living, Objective Measures of Functioning and Symptomolgy, Cultural/Language Assessment, Summary and Clinical Formulation, Individual and Family Strengths and Problems, DSM-IV TR Diagnosis, Recommendations & Initial Plan of Care. Programs should also utilize objective measures of key outcomes administered throughout treatment and utilized in real time to inform practice.
- **Engagement and Retention:** Programs must develop methods of actively engaging adolescents and their families in treatment and promoting treatment retention. Engagement and retention should be measured and tracked as part of quality improvement activities and programs should adopt methods, such as MET and family-based approaches, that emphasize engagement. Promotion of autonomy and active involvement of youth and families in treatment planning are also recommended to improve engagement.
- **Family Involvement:** Active involvement of families in treatment should occur whenever possible. Policies and procedures should be family friendly and active outreach is required. Specifically, family contact should not be contingent on program performance, families should be invited to participate in the milieu, and programs should consider making program privileges contingent on appropriate behavior with family. The families role in supporting the youth's treatment

should be explicitly addressed as well as family members own use or abuse of substances. Families should be encouraged (when safe and appropriate) to be involved in treatment and visit youth even when reunification is not the goal at discharge. Therapists should be trained in family- based approaches and receive appropriate supervision from a qualified supervisor. Consider adopting variations of evidence-based family approaches (e.g., MST, FFT, MDFT, and BSFT) that have proven success in community settings.

- **Cultural and Linguistic Competence:** Minorities are overrepresented in residential care and programs must deliver care in a manner that is culturally and linguistically competent. Special care should be taken in making admission decisions to avoid bias leading to disproportionate representation. Staff composition, policies and procedures, training, assessment, and treatment approaches should be evaluated in terms of cultural and linguistic competence.
- **Gender Specific:** Although the gender gap in the prevalence of substance abuse disorders has closed, girls and boys present with differing treatment needs and require gender-specific approaches.
- **Developmentally Appropriate:** RSAT should meet the developmental needs of children and youth in care and treatments designed for adults should not be applied to adolescents without appropriate modification.
- **Co-occurring Disorders:** The co-occurrence of psychiatric disorders with adolescent substance abuse is the norm. Programs must adequately screen for co-occurring disorders and maintain capacity to effectively treat them. Utilization of CBTs should be considered given the availability of effective evidence-based treatments for mood, anxiety, and traumatic stress disorders as well as substance abuse.
- **Trauma:** The majority of youth treated in RSAT have experienced trauma. Programs should screen for the presence of trauma and trauma-related symptoms, create a trauma-sensitive environment, train staff in the impact of trauma, and offer trauma treatment, either directly or through referral relationships with allied providers.
- **Strength Based:** RSAT programs should borrow a page from the system of care and family- based approaches that recognize client and family strengths and use them to support the goals of treatment.
- **Drug Screens and Breathalyzers:** Drugs screens and breathalyzers are useful as ongoing supports for sobriety.
- **Medications:** RSAT programs should consider psychiatric medication when appropriate for co-occurring psychiatric conditions but must also guard against overmedication and overuse of substances to contain behavior. Use of psychotropic medications for treatment of specific substance abuse disorders should be considered, especially Buprenorphine for the treatment of opioid dependence. Appropriate stimulant therapy of ADHD should be viewed as protective against substance abuse; however, the potential for abuse or sale to others should be attended to.
- **12-Step Approaches:** 12-step approaches have been successfully adapted for adolescents and are especially helpful in linking youth with a network of positive recovery supports. The availability of 12-step chat rooms has expanded the options for youth and is consistent with the popularity among youth of computer-assisted social networking.

- **Avoid Punitive Approaches:** Programs that are overly rule-oriented and focus on compliance rather than treatment progress do not produce positive outcomes. Beware of the deterioration of point and level systems into a punitive staff culture and do not confuse behavioral containment with treatment.
- **Harm Reduction:** A focus on harm reduction that emphasizes the primary risks associated with drug and alcohol abuse and strategies to reduce those risks is warranted.
- **Discharge Planning and Aftercare:** Discharge planning should be comprehensive and consider the educational, social, and recreational needs of the youth as well as clinical and family issues. Discharge planning should be followed up with a formal aftercare and a follow-up program with specific goals and expectations. Consider using the ACC model described above.

Organizational Recommendations

- **Multidisciplinary Staff:** The complex and diverse needs of youth entering RSAT requires a multimodal approach and multiple specialties. Staff should be prepared to provide assistance with education, vocation, legal issues, health and wellness, psychiatric needs, recreation and socialization, family, and general life skills.
- **Quality Improvement:** Internal standards should be set and monitored through a comprehensive quality improvement program. Benchmarking against past performance and other programs is highly recommended.
- **Standards of Care:** Licensing, accrediting, and other regulatory standards can improve the overall quality and consistency of care. Higher standards should be encouraged and pursued.
- **Appropriate Reimbursement:** Policymakers should be certain that rate setting methodologies take into consideration all the costs associated with delivering high-quality care. Rates should be sufficient to support the elements of care known to contribute to successful outcomes.

References

Aarons, G. A., Brown, S. A., Hough, R. L., Garland, A. F., & Wood, P. A. (2001). Prevalence of adolescent substance use disorders across five sectors of care. *Journal of the American Academy of Child and Adolescent Psychiatry, 40*(4), 419–426.

American Academy of Child and Adolescent Psychiatry. (2005). Practice parameter for the assessment and treatment of children and adolescents with substance abuse disorders. *Journal of the American Academy of Child and Adolescent Psychiatry, 44*(6), 609–621.

Brannigan, R., Schackman, B. R., Falco, M., & Millman, R. B. (2004). The quality of highly regarded adolescent substance abuse treatment programs: Results of an in-depth national survey. *Archives of Pediatric Adolescent Medicine, 158*, 904–909.

Child Welfare League of America (CWLA). (2005). *Position statement on residential services.* Washington, DC. Retrieved on January 8, 2008, from at http://www.cwla.org/programs/group-care/rgcpositionstatement.pdf

Connor, D. F., Miller, K. P., Cunningham, J. A., & Melloni, R. H. (2002). What does getting better mean? Child improvement and measure of outcome in residential treatment. *American Journal of Orthopsychiatry, 72*(1), 110–117.

Curry, J. (1991). Outcome research on residential treatment: Implications and suggested directions. *American Journal of Orthopsychiatry, 61,* 348–357.

Daughters, S. B., Lejuez, C. W., Bornovalova, M. A., Kahler, C. W., Strong, D. R., & Brown, R. A. (2005). Distress tolerance as a predictor of early treatment dropout in a residential substance abuse treatment facility. *Journal of Abnormal Psychology, 114*(4), 729–734.

Dennis, M. L., Babor, T., Diamond, G. C., Donaldson, J., Godley, S. H., Tims, F., et al . (1998). *Treatment for cannabis use disorders general research design and protocol for the Cannabis Youth Treatment (CYT) Cooperative Agreement.* Bloomington, IL: Chestnut Health Systems.

Dennis, M. L., Godley, S. H., & Titus, J. (1999). Co-occurring psychiatric problems among adolescents: Variations by treatment, level of care and gender. *TIE Communiqué, 5–8,* 16.

Dennis, M. L., & Kaminer, Y. (2006). Introduction to special issue on advances in the assessment and treatment of adolescent substance use disorders. *American Journal on Addictions, 15*(S1), 1–3.

Diamond, G., & Josephson, A. (2005). Family-based treatment research: A 10-year update. *Journal of the American Academy of Child and Adolescent Psychiatry, 44*(9), 872–887.

Edelen, M. O., Tucker, J. S., Wenzel, S. L., Paddock, S. M., Ebener, P., Dahl, J., & Mandell, W. et al. (2007). Treatment Process in the therapeutic community: Associations with retention and outcomes among adolescent residential clients. *Journal of Substance Abuse Treatment, 32*(4), 415–421.

Fishman, M., Clemmey, P., & Hoover, A. (2003). Mountain manor treatment center: Residential adolescent addictions treatment program. In S. J. Stevens & A. R. Morral (Eds.), *Adolescent substance abuse treatment in the United States: Exemplary models from a national evaluation study* (pp. 135–153). New York: The Haworth Press.

French, M. T., Roebuck, M. C., Dennis, M., Diamond, G., Godley, S., Tims, F., et al. (2002). The economic cost of outpatient marijuana treatment for adolescents: Findings from a multisite experiment. *Addiction, 97,* S84–S97.

French, M. T., Salome, H. J., & Carney, M. (2002). Using the DATCAP and ASI to estimate the costs and benefits of residential addiction treatment in the State of Washington. *Journal of Substance Abuse Treatment, 23*(1), 21–32.

Frensch, K. M., & Cameron, G. (2002). Treatment of choice or a last resort? A review of residential mental health placements for children and youth. *Child and Youth Forum, 31*(5), 307–339.

Garrett, C. J. (1985). Effects of residential treatment on adjudicated delinquents: A meta-analysis. *Journal of Research in Crime and Delinquency, 22*(4), 287–308.

Godley, M. D., Godley, S. H., Dennis, M. L., Funk, R., & Passetti, L. (2002). Preliminary outcomes from the assertive continuing care experiment for adolescents discharged from residential treatment. *Journal of Substance Abuse Treatment, 23,* 21–32.

Hair, H. J. (2005). Outcomes for children and adolescents after residential treatment: A review of research from 1993 to 2003. *Journal of Child and Family Studies, 14*(4), 551–575.

Hall, J. A., Smith, D. C., Williams, J. K., & Delaney, P. J. (2005). Comparison of family and group based treatment for adolescent substance abuse (pp. 1–47). Center for Substance Abuse Treatment. PowerPoint presentation.

Hawkins, J. D., Catalano, R. F., & Miller, J. Y. (1992). Risk and protective factors for alcohol and other drug problems in adolescence and early adulthood: Implications for substance abuse prevention. *Psychological Bulletin, 112,* 64–105.

Hoagwood, K., Burns, B., Kiser, L., Ringeisen, H., & Schoenwald, S. (2001). Evidence-based practice in child and adolescent mental health services. Psychiatric Services, 52(9), 1179–1189.

Hoagwood, K., & Cunningham, M. (1992). Outcomes of children with emotional disturbance in residential treatment for educational purposes. *Journal of Child and Family Studies, 1*(2), 129–140.

Hooper, S. R., Murphy, J., Devaney, A., & Hultman, T. (2000). Ecological outcomes of adolescents in a psycho-educational residential treatment facility. *American Journal of Orthopsychiatry, 70*(4), 491–500.

Jaycox, L. H., Ebener, R., Damesek, L., & Becker, K. (2004). Trauma exposure and retention in adolescent substance abuse treatment. *Journal of Traumatic Stress, 17*(2), 113–121.

Kaminer, Y. (1994). *Adolescent substance abuse: A comprehensive guide to theory and practice.* New York: Plenum Medical Book Company.

Kaminer, Y. (2001). Adolescent substance abuse treatment: Where do we go from here? *Psychiatric Services, 52*(2), 147–149.

Kaminer, Y., Blitz, C., Burleson, J. A., Kadden, R. M., & Rounsaville, B. J. (1998). Measuring treatment process in cognitive-behavioral and interactional group therapies for adolescent substance abusers. *Journal of Nervous and Mental Disorders, 186*, 407–413.

Latimer, W. L., Newcomb, M., Winters, K. C., & Stinchfield, R. D. (2000). Adolescent substance treatment outcome: The role of substance abuse problem severity, psychosocial, and treatment factors. *Journal of Consulting and Clinical Psychology, 68*(4), 684–696.

Liddle, H. A., & Dakof, G. A. (1995). Family-based treatment for adolescent drug abuse: State of the science. In E. Rahdert & E. Czechowics (Eds.), *Adolescent drug abuse: Clinical assessment and therapeutic interventions* (DHHS Publication No. 95–3908, NIDA Research Monograph Series 156. pp. 218–254). Rockville, MD: National Institute on Drug Abuse.

Leichtman, M. (2006). Residential treatment of children and adolescents: Past, present, and future. *American Journal of Orthopsychiatry, 76*(3), 285–294.

Leichtman, M., Leichtman, M. L., Barber, C. C., & Neese, D. T. (2001). Effectiveness of intensive short-term residential treatment with severely disturbed adolescents. *American Journal of Orthopsychiatry, 71*(2), 227–235.

Lieberman, R. E., & Bellonci, C. (2007). Ensuring the preconditions for transformation through licensing, regulation, accreditation, and standards. *American Journal of Orthopsychiatry, 77*(3), 346–347.

Lyons, J. S., & McCulloch, J. R. (2006). Monitoring and managing outcomes in residential treatment: Practice-based evidence in search of evidence-based practice. *Journal of the American Academy of Child and Adolescent Psychiatry, 45*(2), 247–251.

Mayes, J., & Handley, S. (2005). Evolving a model for integrated treatment in a residential setting for people with psychiatric and substance abuse disorders. *Psychiatric Rehabilitation Journal, 29*(1), 59–62.

McPherson, T. L., & Hersch, R. K. (2000). Brief substance use screening instruments for primary care settings: A review. *Journal of Substance Abuse Treatment, 18*(2), 193–202.

Mihalic, S., Irwin, K., Elliott, D., Fagan, A., & Hansen, D. (2001, July). Blueprints for violence prevention. *Juvenile Justice Bulletin,*: pp. 1–17.

Morral, A. R., Jaycox, L. H., Smith, W., Becker, K., & Ebener, P. (2003). An evaluation of substance abuse treatment services provided to juvenile probationers at Phoenix Academy of Los Angeles. In S. J. Stevens & A. R. Morral (Eds.), *Adolescent substance abuse treatment in the United States: Exemplary models from a national evaluation study* (pp. 213–232). Binghamton, NY: Haworth Press.

Morral, A. R., McCaffery, D. F., & Ridgeway, G. (2004). Effectiveness of community based treatment for substance-abusing adolescents: 12 month outcomes of youths entering Phoenix Academy or alternative probation dispositions. *Psychology of Addictive Behaviors, 18*(3), 257–268.

National Survey of Substance Abuse Treatment Services. (2005). *Data on substance abuse treatment facilities.* Washington, DC: Department of Health and Human Services. Retrieved January 8, 2008, from http://www.dasis.samhsa.gov/05nssats/NSSATS2k5index.htm

Prochaska, J. O., & DiClemente, C. C. (1992). Stages of change in the modification of problem behaviors. In M. Hersen, P. M. Miller, & R. Eisler (Eds.), *Progress in behavior modification* (Vol. 28, pp. 184–218). New York, NY: Wadsworth Publishing.

Pumariega, A. J. (2006a). Residential treatment for youth: Introduction and a cautionary tale. *American Journal of Orthopsychiatry, 76*(3), 281–284.

Pumariega, A. J. (2006b). Residential treatment for children and youth: Time for reconsideration and reform. *American Journal of Orthopsychiatry, 77*(3), 343–345.

Rey, J. M., Martin, A., & Krabman, P. (2004). Is the party over? cannabis and juvenile psychiatric disorder: The past 10 years. *Journal of the American Academy of Child and Adolescent Psychiatry, 43*(10), 1194–1205.

Robinson, A. D., Kruzich, J. M., Friesen, B. J., Jivanjee, P., & Pullman, M. D. (2005). Preserving family bonds: Examining parent perspectives in the light of practice standards for out-of-home treatment. *American Journal of Orthopsychiatry, 75*(4), 632–643.

Rounds-Bryant, J. L., Kristiansen, P. L., & Hubbard, R. L. (1999). Drug abuse treatment outcome study of adolescents: A comparison of client characteristics and pretreatment behaviors in three treatment modalities. *The American Journal of Drug and Alcohol Abuse, 25*(4), 573–591.

Rowe, C. L., & Liddle, H. A. (2003). Substance abuse. *Journal of Marital and Family Therapy, 29*(1), 97–120.

Safeway Foundation. (2007). The importance of family dinners IV, September 14, 2007. Retrieved by Robert W. Plant, Ph.D., from http://www.casacolumbia.org/absolutenm/articlefiles/380-Importance%20of%20Family%20Dinners%20IV.pdf

Sampl, S., & Kadden, R. (2001). A 5 Session *Motivational enhancement therapy and cognitive behavioral therapy (MET-CBT-5) for adolescent cannabis users* (DHHS Publication No. (SMA) 01-3486, Cannabis Youth Treatment (CYT) Manual Series, Vol. 1). Rockville, MD: Center for Substance Abuse Treatment, Substance Abuse and Mental Health Services Administration. Retrieved January 8, 2008, by R.W. Plant from http://www.chestnut.org/li/cyt/products/mcb5_cyt_v1.pdf

Schackman, B. R., Rojas, E. G., Gans, J., Falco, M., & Millman, R. B. (2007). Does higher cost mean better quality? Evidence from highly-regarded adolescent drug treatment programs. *Substance Abuse Treatment, Prevention, and Policy, 2*(23), 1–6.

Schwebel, R. (2004). *The seven challenges manual (39 pp.).* Tuscon, AZ: Viva Press.

Sealock, M. D., Gottfredson, D. C., & Gallagher, C. A. (1997). Drug treatment for juvenile offenders: Some good and bad news. *Journal of Research in Crime and Delinquency, 34*(2), 210–236.

Subramanian, G. A., Stitzer, M. A., Clemmey, P., Kolodner, K., & Fishman, M. J. (2007). Baseline depressive symptoms predict poor substance abuse outcome following adolescent residential treatment. *Journal of the American Academy of Child and Adolescent Psychiatry, 46*(8), 1062–1069.

Substance Abuse and Mental Health Services Administration, Office of Applied Studies. (2004). *Results from the 2003 National Survey on Drug Use and Health: National findings.* Rockville, MD: Author. Retrieved January 8, 2008, by R.W. Plant from http://oas.samhsa.gov/nhsda/2k3nsduh/2k3ResultsW.pdf

Substance Abuse and Mental Health Services Administration, Office of Applied Studies. (2006). *Results from the 2005 National Household Survey on Drug Use and Health: National findings.* Rockville, MD: Author. Retrieved from Office of Applied Studies. Retrieved January 8, 2008, by R.W. Plant from http://www.oas.samhsa.gov/nsduh/2k5nsduh/2k5Results.pdf

Tomlinson, K. L., Brown, S. A., & Abrantes, A. (2004). Psychiatric comorbidity and substance use treatment outcomes of adolescents. *Psychology of Addictive Behaviors, 18*(2), 160–169.

Weinberg, N. Z., Rahdert, E., Colliver, J. D., & Glantz, M. D. (1998). Adolescent substance abuse: A review of the past 10 years. *Journal of the American Academy of Child and Adolescent Psychiatry, 37*(3), 252–261.

Weiner, D. A., Abraham, M. E., & Lyons, J. (2001). Clinical characteristic of youths with substance use problems and implications for residential treatment. *Psychiatric Services, 52*, 793–799.

Wilens, T. E., Faraone, S. V., Biederman, J., & Gunawardene, S. (2003). Does stimulant therapy of attention-deficit/hyperactivity disorder beget later substance abuse? A meta-analytic review of the literature. *Pediatrics, 111*, 179–185.

Williams, R. J., & Chang, S. Y. (2000). A comprehensive and comparative review of adolescent substance abuse treatment outcome. *Clinical Psychology: Science and Practice, 7*(2), 138–166.

Winters, K. C., Stinchfield, R. D., Opland, E. O., Weller, C., & Latimer, W. W. (2000). The effectiveness of the Minnesota Model approach in the treatment of adolescent drug abusers. *Addiction, 95*(4), 601–612.

Chapter 8
Primary Prevention in Adolescent Substance Abuse

Martin Bloom and Thomas P. Gullotta

What Is Primary Prevention?

Helping is one of the oldest activities among humans, a necessary part of the great drama of species survival. Over time, that helping was aided by discovered or invented substances and methods that made helping more effective, less painful, and as a by-product, more hopeful that when problems occurred, something might be done to treat the problem and eventually bring the person back as a functioning member of society.

Primary prevention is a recent addition to the art and science of helping. Defined in the wicked spirit of Ambrose Bierce's (1911/1948) *Devil's Dictionary*, primary prevention involves a collective exercise in an ultimately personal activity, for which there is a mountain of literature and a molehill of recent hard research, in which large numbers of persons untrained in this specific field attempt to humanize abstract terms and old wives' tales through almost incomprehensible rituals that are voluntarily performed after forced indoctrination at the hands of loving family members or dedicated school personnel. Unfortunately, there are grains of truth in this formulation. However, in keeping with the optimistic spirit of this book, we offer a slightly different definition:

> **Primary prevention** involves actions taken by individuals or groups to **prevent** predictable problems, **protect** existing states of health and healthy functioning, and **promote** desired states of being and functioning within supportive or benign physical and socio-cultural environments.

Contemporary thought emphasizes the dynamic ecological perspective integrating preventive, protective, and promotive actions among persons and groups, and the settings in which they live (Durlak, 2003). This dynamic perspective is seen very clearly in discussions of the prevention of substance abuse in which physiological, psychological, social, and cultural factors are actively engaged for the soul of the would-be abuser.

The background for a contemporary discussion of primary prevention emerges from the mists of folklore, which represents the ever-present hope of ordinary people that problems might be anticipated and prevented, before ever needing the substances and methods of the medical arts. Remember that for thousands of years

C.G. Leukefeld et al. (eds.) *Adolescent Substance Abuse,*
DOI: 10.1007/978-0-387-09732-9_8, © Springer Science + Business Media LLC 2009

medical treatment involved bleedings, blistering, enemas, and induced vomiting. Surgery was not considered medicine and relegated to "barbers" who undertook their tasks without effective anesthesia. No wonder people avoided getting "help" that involved voluntary torture as part of the cure.

Throughout history, people self-medicated, or more to the point, self-anesthetized their problems. Indeed, wines and beers were an early concomitant of ordinary social life, and their benefits were merely extended to extreme medical situations. For some, this self-anesthetizing became a chronic condition for a wide variety of social ills and personal problems. Often, self-anesthetizing and/or self-stimulation through substances were undertaken for recreational purposes beyond ordinary social affairs in relatively healthy individuals, which is still the case today.

History as Mirror to Today

Eventually, thoughtful people began to explore possibilities of taking informed action before problems emerged, or before desired goals had been achieved, while protecting what worked well at the moment. (This triple nature of primary prevention goals is necessary to consider, even if it makes for difficulties on sentence construction.) Following Santayana's axiom that those who ignore history are likely to repeat its errors, let us review the beginnings of primary prevention, with special reference to the prevention of intemperance. In 1817, the New York Society for the Prevention of Pauperism (NYSPP) became what might be considered the first scientifically based preventive helping in the New World (Bloom & Klein, 1995–1996). This group of mainly Quaker philanthropists broke into various study groupings that dealt with a handful of topics believed to be stemming from poverty. For example, one committee collected information on juveniles in contact with the police that led, ultimately in the Haines Report (1822), to removing them from adult prisons, and attempting to restructure and reform their lives before a fixed criminal pattern had set in. (A resulting institution, the New York House of Refuge, lasted for over 100 years.)

The NYSPP purchased firewood in the summer when it was cheap so as to sell it to the poor in winter when it was expensive. (This did not work; the poor were poor in the summer as well as in the winter.) Another committee investigated the presumed evils of pawnshops. (It found few evils, just poor people giving up whatever treasures they had to survive.) The NYSPP sent around friendly visitors anticipating social workers nearly 75 years later, and tried to encourage healthful lives, frugality, and moral lives. (It learned first hand how difficult it was to make meaningful changes in impoverished lives from moral exhortations.)

But it was "intemperance" in the use of ardent spirits (whisky or gin) that was a perpetual thorn in the moral side of the NYSPP, and on which it was almost perpetually defeated in its efforts at its prevention. In its Second Annual Report (New York Society for the Prevention of Pauperism, NYSPP, 1819, p. 8), it wrote that intemperance

… consumes every virtue, dissolves every social tie, and destroys every noble family. It banishes industry, honesty and self-regard. It forms the nursery of crime and outrage … who can count the monuments of its desolation, in the dark valley of death!

The study group on intemperance discovered that there were 1,431 persons licensed to retail liquor, which it pointed out was one "tippling house" (drinking establishment) for every 17 houses then existing in the city. In the Fourth Annual Report of the NYSPP (1821, pp. 9–10), it reports its continuing efforts, without much success. However, this report did cite a natural experiment that it hoped would be a model of action for others. It seems that a Mr. James P. Allaire, proprietor of a large foundry at Corlaer's Hook, took it upon himself to oppose a common folklore of the times, that the laboring classes could not sustain themselves under the harsh working conditions without the regular use of ardent spirits. (There was apparently no thought at this time to make the working conditions less harsh.) Mr. Allaire noticed that many of his male employees were in great debt, while others were "in easy circumstances, and their children were well provided for at school." Differences in salary did not make any difference to the level of debt – but the use or nonuse of hard liquor made all the difference. So, he took it upon himself to prohibit the use of hard liquor during working hours. This drove only 1 of his 60 employees away, and over time, he observed great changes:

… those who, from excessive drinking, had become of but little worth to me, and in many instances, of less to their families, have now become able and steady; earn more money; and their families as well as themselves, have expressed, in a language not to be misunderstood, the many comforts and domestic happiness, which they enjoy in consequence.

One of their few successes regarding substance use came at the city level, when the NYSPP encouraged the mayor to prohibit drinking establishments from being open on Sundays, which had a positive effect on reducing the numbers of assault and battery cases coming before the court.[1]

However, all of its other proposals for legislation against intemperance were rejected.

Why spend valuable space in this chapter writing about this long-forgotten bit of American history? Let me point out that this fledgling prevention enterprise and its members dealt face to face with individuals and families, with institutions (such as savings banks for the poor and schools where they gave out selections of *Poor Richard's Almanac* to encourage the virtues of self-enterprise), and with city, state, and federal levels of social welfare policy. These were a full ecological plate of preventive activities, which does not include many other ideas that never came to fruition in the 8-year history of this society, such as centrally organizing charities to avoid duplication, job training programs (some existed at the time, so the NYSPP did not enter that field), and educational programs for the poor. It was, indeed, a

---

[1]This is an example of community organization leading to a systems intervention that will be described later in this chapter.

moralistic enterprise, which is to say that strong public values directed its efforts at helping the poor, both materially if necessary, but with dignity throughout, so as not to encourage dependency as then-existing alms societies tended to do.

Moreover, one of the leaders of the NYSPP was John Griscom, a self-taught chemist, educator – he used the Lancasterian system of older children teaching younger children as a way of multiplying the education of large numbers of the poor – and philanthropist. He was also a one-man Campbell Collaboration, as the American correspondent for Silliman's scientific journal regarding new developments in Europe. He traveled abroad for 1 year and wrote about his visits to public institutions and creative thinkers throughout that continent. President Thomas Jefferson said that the Griscom book gave the most satisfactory view of public institutions abroad that he had ever read (Griscom, 1859, p. 152). Thus, the NYSPP, especially through its leaders, sought the best available evidence as basis for its preventive practices, using the none-too-good available demographic information to describe the scope of problems. All of these activities were in great distinction from the do-gooding philosophy of charities of the times, and bear a strong resemblance to evidence-based practice of our own day.

What is instructive about this small piece of the history of primary prevention is the difficulty to communicate effectively what are probably reasonably good suggestions for individuals, groups, and society at large. In spite of people's good intentions to be healthy, to have happy families, and to be part of a well-functioning society, things fall apart. Individuals become substance abusers harming themselves and their families. Society in turn spends enormous sums of money for ineffective methods to control the sources of drugs, the channels by which they are distributed, and the users of those substances whose addictive powers are legendary. Those early preventers of 1817 were no less enthusiastic, imaginative, and energetic than are our contemporaries. Let us hope the intervening 175 years have given us more knowledge than they had to do the good work of primary prevention.

To be blunt, America is an alcohol-drenched society and culture, and some large-scale efforts (like prohibition) or some small-scale efforts (like Sunday closing laws) have been unsuccessful in changing people's fundamental use of alcohol and substances. This notion of an alcohol-drenched society and culture has several dimensions that recent research provides clearer understanding. Even the NYSPP recognized that alcohol was a lucrative industry. It estimated that New York drinkers paid about US $1,612,500, which should be multiplied about 100 times to get the rough equivalent contemporary dollar amount. The New York Society for the Prevention of Pauperism recognized its own terms how greed overcame positive feelings toward fellow creatures; there was a strong economic dimension in any substance problem. But alcohol and drugs also affect basic physical and mental structures of the person, particularly with young substance users. In combination of the lack of future perspective of the young and their susceptibility to social pressures and indeed cultural styles and fashions involving drinking and drugs, the problems associated with preventing abusers is greatly multiplied.

On the contrary, there are many young people who do not succumb to drugs and alcohol as problematic substances, including those whose family backgrounds might predict otherwise. The issue of such resilience has only recently hit the radar screens of social science, and explorations are being made as to what constitutes the factors that make some people less vulnerable to substance abuse (Werner & Smith, 1982, 1992).

Explanatory Models of Prevention and Substance Abuse

Our prior discussion of historic background is relevant for the general and special forms of definitions of primary prevention with regard to substance abuse. Our working definition of primary prevention involves those planned actions addressing (1) predictable problems in relatively healthy individuals and groups, (2) protecting existing states of health and healthy functioning, and (3) promoting desired future states not yet attained. This general statement has to be qualified with regard to substance use and abuse.

First, efforts have to be directed toward relatively healthy and problem-free individuals. This does not mean that people will be totally free of experiences with alcohol, cigarettes, or other substances, licit and illicit. If that were a requirement, there would be few participants in these pure primary prevention programs – about 90% of Americans drink some amount of alcohol at some times in their lives (Johnston, O'Malley, Bachman, & Schulenberg, 2007), and many of these "non-drinkers" would be too young to benefit from programs delivered long in advance of the presenting challenges. It does not mean that the families of healthy young people are free of the use of any substances, because it would be hard to find families that used neither legal medications nor recreational substances, without considering any illicit ones. Yet, the factual record is clear, that children coming from families that abuse alcohol, drugs, or other substances are themselves more likely to succumb to substance abuse. It does not mean that a society or culture has to be free of the use of alcohol or other substances, since the modern world seems wedded to medications and social/recreational substances that no amount of religious or moralistic sermonizing is going to change. So "relatively healthy and problem-free" individuals translate to mean those who, to some degree, use substances that do not interfere with their personal or social obligations.

We must also define primary prevention with reference to the substance use and abuse context. It might be better to define these terms in the sense of contextual outcomes, that people who are free of the problems associated with substance abuse will be fully involved in the nonsubstance world (of work, family, children, associations, etc.) and free of the stresses (personal and social/cultural) that would push them in the direction of using substances to resolve these stresses. These people will move about in a substance-drenched social environment, surrounded by media campaigns with beautiful sexy pictures promoting substances, and with friends and associates whose contacts are frequently bathed in alcohol and cigarette smoke. They should be able to pick and choose whether or not to participate, and to what degree, recognizing the outcome of their participation on self and others. Tea-totaling, while living on an isolated mountain top, is not the likely course that many contemporary people would take. So, we have to place any contemporary prevention effort within a context of countervailing forces and structures of great strength.

To give some semblance of a balanced presentation, we should explore what are the benefits of substances for abuse-free people in the contemporary world. What attracts people, early in their developmental history (Leukefeld et al., 2005), to late in their lives (Kastenbaum, 1988)? We know that a small amount of daily alcohol use has been related to preventing heart diseases, although grape juice could do the same thing.

This light use of alcohol may also be associated with reducing minor stresses of everyday life. Set within a family context of light drinking, norms are created for responsible actions that last into a child's own adulthood. This same light use of alcohol may be associated with "social fun" in settings where others are likewise less inhibited. Some people argue that marijuana is helpful in pain reduction, when other medications do not work (Grinspoon & Bakalar, 1993). Some substances are related to enhanced sexual stimulation that can be useful in some situations (some might say ecstatically wonderful), although they may lead to unanticipated consequences that could be deadly. And, let us face it, some use of substances occur just for the hell of it, because society, parents, teachers, and other goodie-goodie-two-shoes say we should not, which is not a bad reason in an overregulated world.

Even the second part of our working definition of primary prevention, protecting existing states of health and healthy functioning, has to be qualified in terms of preventing substance abuse. Preventers may be failing to see that people, especially young people, do not so much want to protect their current states of healthy functioning as *use* these states to attain more enjoyment in life. It may be the difference between saving assets under our mattress versus investing those assets in the stock market. Prevention is a touch conservative – except when it comes to anticipating a better future, primary prevention wins.

People in general, but especially young people, are not well tuned to anticipate and plan for a better future. The level of saving for various desired futures is terribly low displaced by current gratifications and living for today. Piaget helped us understand this cognitive limitation in children, but this theory does not extend to adults. Eat, drink, and be merry, for tomorrow we may die – yes, this is a folk wisdom that is true as far as it goes, but it fails to note that tomorrow we may live, and yet again live into the tomorrow beyond that. And then what?

Social routines provide the structures that most people live by: "I will work, have a family, have some fun, retire into relative comfort, and die before Alzheimer's gets me (after a very brief and painless illness)." There is some truth to some of these structural assumptions, but not all of them for all people. We have to plan for that future, including alternative scenarios that are less pleasant to contemplate. Primary prevention offers some planned efforts through which individuals may shape that future to the extent that it is possible to be influenced.

So, what do adolescents (let alone their parents) know of all this? Not a lot, which is both the problem for primary preventers and a possible curriculum for delivering some solutions. Theories supply the conceptual ingredients for prevention practitioners, by identifying abstract structures and forces that can be influenced to attain desired goals. Those "desired goals" are value-loaded, which is where our balanced discussions of the pros and cons of the use of substances comes into play. Some practitioners may not like this, but we have to deliver primary prevention with regard to adolescent substance use within the real world context, not within our own pipe dreams of how reality ought to be.

Let's take the social-cognitive model of Albert Bandura (1986), whose work guides many studies across a wide range of social behaviors. Briefly, Bandura argues not only against the internal unconscious forces directing people ala Freud but also against the external forces directing people ala Skinner. Rather, Bandura proposes a multidimensional model that provides clients with relevant knowledge, skills, and motivation for obtaining a desired future, along with efforts to increase the self-efficacy of those clients, that is, the belief that they can do certain specific things. It does not matter if people have the knowledge, skill, and motivation to stop using substances; they also have to believe that they can stop using substances. To help clients reach this level of self-efficacy, preventers can use two strong tools, and two more limited ones. The first strong tool is mastery; preventers can train clients to do some specific things that are concrete steps toward the ultimate goal. Mastering these stepping-stones is a powerful inducement for self-efficacy. Likewise, showing clients how others who are like themselves are performing these steps and gaining some positive reinforcement thereby leads to vicarious learning, another powerful tool. Exhortations are more limited ways of influencing clients – "You can do it, Joe!" And physiological training, like taking a deep breath before public speaking, will reduce anxiety to some degree. We will look at how this theory is used in the prevention of adolescent substance use and abuse shortly.

Another theoretical model of many names involves the identification of risks of succumbing to substance use, along with protective factors against succumbing, in combination with promotive factors or resiliency factors that lead people in positive directions (Durlak, 2003). It is not enough not to do something negative; one must also do something positive in its place (Cowen, 2000). This general probabilistic model says that the likelihood of a person becoming involved in substance use and abuse is predictable from the *risk* factors – biological, psychological, and socio-cultural – that push a person into that untoward situation such as substance abuse, reduced by the *protective* factors in the same categories that pull this person away from that untoward situation, and turned around by *promotive* factors, which move this person in some positive direction. These biological/psychological/socio-cultural factors are numerous. Werner (1993) identified over one hundred factors related to resilience that can be placed into personal, interpersonal, societal, and environmental categories, from having a pleasing personality, an optimistic view of the future, and sense of humor, to finding alternative adult role models and sources of support when one's own family was lacking (see also Antonishak & Reppucci, 2008). We'll discuss how this theory can be used in prevention programming for adolescent substance use and abuse shortly.

There are also multiple systems models that involve the family, the extended family and substitutes, the relevant local social settings like schools, and the local community as well (Albee, 1983; Bloom, 1996; D'Amico, Chinman, Stern, &

Wandersman, in press). These models are closely linked to practice, and thus use as many of the real-world forces and structures that have strong influences on individuals' choices toward or against substance use and abuse. We generalize from the Sexton, Gilman, and Johnson-Erickson (2005, pp. 112–115) list of the conceptual assumptions for this kind of model (their list is made with reference to multisystemic therapy): (1) that all important social behaviors are multidetermined; (2) that primary group caregivers and educators are important for long-term developments and changes of behavior; (3) that evidence-based practice should direct interventions, along with the clinical expertise in applying this general information to the specific client; (4) that barriers to service require as much attention as the intervention itself; and (5) evaluation is an important part of practice to progress and to assess outcomes, as well as confirm the fidelity of the program when transported to new settings. These and other principles guide programs in the prevention of substance use and abuse, which we will discuss shortly.

The Tools of Primary Prevention

Gullotta (1983, 1987, 1994) and Gullotta and Bloom (2003) have described five technologies that are used to achieve illness prevention and health promotion. These technologies appear so often and in so many of the special topic areas of primary prevention that we are inclined to call them general strategies that should be considered as beginning points, and in combination, for any future preventive effort, including the prevention of substance abuse with adolescents.

Education is the first general strategy of primary prevention. It is the most often used technology that preventionists apply to reducing risk and promoting resiliency; however, it is rarely, if ever, effective when used alone. This is because clients and consumers of primary prevention usually require some knowledge about a given topic, but simple *information* alone may not affect attitudes, and probably will not change behaviors that are a product of thoughts, feelings, and external situations. For example, adolescents probably know something about the hazards of substance use (although their knowledge is often limited, fuzzy, or both). They may state their intention to stay away from these hazards or stop using substances if they are already engaged in doing so. But major behavior changes are not usually based on such cognitive factors alone. Thus, the "Just Say NO!" campaign of the 1980s was destined to failure from the outset.

Education can be public, as in school lessons on the nature of substances and their effects on the body. Teachers, parents, and ministers often say to children, "do as I say" regarding substances, and "not as I do." Use of legal substances is limited to adults, and the transition period between childhood and adulthood is the perfect storm for conflict over the beginning use of substances. Rather, adults might be wiser to use information as *anticipatory guidance*, in which a nonuser (or beginning user) is informed about the immediate and long-term effects. The immediate (such as bad tobacco breath) may appeal to younger adolescents, but eventually the long-term effects of life-threatening harm to their bodies may be understood as a basis for action. This aspect of education slides into a third type, (self-instruction), the *development of self-control* to achieve future goals rather than immediate gratification.

The promotion of *self-competency* is the second technology. To be socially competent involves people interacting with other people over the lifetime in mutually satisfying ways. This begins when an individual is brought into a group, and the group values the membership of that individual who eventually comes to make meaningful contributions to the group. This circularity of mutual interactions where both individual and group benefit is learned throughout one's life, and draws on personal characteristics (e.g., a developing sense of self-esteem, an internal locus of control, and a growing sense of mastery over valued activities) and social conditions (e.g., the need for members to perform certain roles in relation to others and the need to survive against an indifferent world).

Prevention's third technology is *natural caregiving*. Gullotta identified three forms of this technology. First, there are *mutual self-help groups*. These are not led by helping professionals, but rather involve those drawn together by common experiences for which members are both caregivers and care receivers. Some members are further along in these experiences, and can guide others in preparing for what to expect. They are informal groupings where exchanges are common, sharing of small triumphs, and supporting those suffering large losses. Being human together generates support for all, by helping others and by being helped, in turn.

The second way of natural caregiving that can be found is in the way society has informally conferred on some people the expectation that they will lend a listening ear and helpful advice to others in times of need. These *trained indigenous caregivers* are ministers, teachers, police officers, coaches, youth leaders in scouting and 4H to name a few. They are not specifically trained in counseling or mental health services as such, yet their advice as caring adults is important as a first line of service for people in need. Indeed, for many, this caring enables the vast majority of individuals in society to cope and adapt when stressful demands are placed upon them.

The last form natural caregiving can take is found within the actions of each of us as individuals and can be described as *friendship*. The simple act of extending social support to another is a powerful agent for health that enables a person to receive empathy, constructive feedback, and another perspective on issues that may be either joyful or filled with sorrow.

The fourth technology of primary prevention goes beyond the individual to focus its attention on changing community behavior and institutions (community organization and systems intervention). In each of the examples that follow, a group of people have banded together to express their (common) concerns and to develop solutions for these concerns. They may work within the problematic system or from outside. Their own "organization" may be informal or formal, depending on the circumstances. To illustrate, Mothers Against Drunk Driving (MADD) began with one grief-stricken parent who had lost a loved one. Her effort was soon joined by others who too had seen a child or spouse die because of the irresponsible actions of a drunken driver. MADD spoke to the entertainment community. Their message was drunken behavior was not the stuff of comedy. MADD enlisted the law enforcement community as an ally to advocate for tougher legal repercussions against drunken driving. MADD lobbied legislators to pass laws that lowered blood alcohol rates to be considered for a driving under the influence (DUI) arrest. Collectively, these actions by citizens who have lost a loved one to a drunken driver have produced a major change in community attitudes and behavior. MADD is not alone in its success to correct societal injustice. The National Association for the Advancement of Colored People (NAACP) and its use of the legal system to achieve justice is a second example with Rosa Parks' refusal to sit at the back of the bus, an excellent illustration of this. Contrary to popular belief, Rosa Parks' action was not an unplanned refusal spurred by an "I'm mad as hell and not gonna take this any more attitude." On the contrary, this well-educated dignified lady acted with the NAACP's knowledge to begin a process that would eventually grow to actually changing the Constitution of the United States to ensure the civil rights of all Americans.

Other community organizational activities may not be as landmark as either of the two previous examples but are as equally effective. For a humorous example, with the increasing buildup of housing in many areas and a rise in lawsuits, most communities no longer permit dogs to run free in public parks, and heaven forbid they should ever stray onto a playing field even if their owner carries a pooper-scooper. The choice for a dog lover was to either buy a home with a sufficiently larger yard (cost prohibitive in Manhattan) or jettison the family canine. Both were unacceptable choices. The result – canine owners joining together on behalf of their pets to advocate for pet parks. Initially, the thought of a place for Fido to run and play with Lassie and Rin-Tin-Tin was laughed at, but with persistence and increasing members of the pet-owning community adding their howl to the call, pet parks are appearing across the country. The point of these three examples is that change to remedy a perceived injustice can and does happen when like-minded people set forth to do so.

But not all change is at the community level. Some changes happen, should happen, and can happen at the institutional level. In these instances one or more individuals identify dysfunctional practices within an institution and act to change that behavior. In her writing Ciporah Tadmor (2003) has provided two outstanding examples of this. In both cases, well-meaning health care professionals in a respected hospital were providing necessary medical treatments but doing so in such a way as to increase significantly the emotional distress and depression of the patients receiving treatment. In both cases the staff were ignorant of their behavior and rejecting of the need for change. Nevertheless, persistence and courageous individual behavior forced needed changes into the delivery of services with a corresponding decrease in the emotional suffering of the client population.

The fifth technology of primary prevention focuses on the *redesign of the environment*. Ecologists and Buddhists have emphasized the interrelationship of all things, so that when we consider actions relevant to adolescents with the potential for substance use or abuse we consider not only the individuals themselves, with their complex genetic history and social psychological experiences but also the primary and secondary groups that make up their social and cultural world.

These we have discussed above, and ad nauseam everywhere else. What tends to receive far less attention is the impact of the physical environment on human beings, and the effect of human activities on the physical environment.

This is an "inconvenient truth" as Al Gore (2006) has vividly described, that we are harming this necessary physical environment in ways beyond our imagination and more rapidly than most pessimists had dreamed. Greed, pride, and stupidity have combined to make a crisis situation at almost every turn. American automobile manufacturers promise to reduce harmful emissions some time by the year 2020, even though European manufacturers have arrived at these lower levels now, not a decade later. Increasing percentages of Americans are growing obese, including young children who are now becoming subject to diseases at an earlier age than their (couch potato) parents, which will be putting a severe strain on the health care system that is the "best in the world" for some people, but not for the millions of uninsured others. These and other trends are worldwide conditions, rapidly increasing demands on the physical environment, such as burning down huge areas of the Amazon rain forest to grow soybeans for the exploding population of China.

Ultimately, we have to put every primary prevention question into this perspective: How will what we propose to do for some specific population of clients affect and be affected by the physical world in which we live? For example, laws against substance use in the United States affect how land will be used abroad to grow the plants used in making illicit drugs. It will also affect how third-party nations will develop factories to make chemicals to transform these plants into hard drugs. Everywhere, from the farmers, to the chemists, to the transporters, to the drug sellers, there is little concern for the effects on the physical environment and what alternative uses of land, labor, and transport there would be.

Thus, the full circle is completed – education informs, natural caregiving unites, social competency enables, social institutions create, and the physical environment supports. All are needed to institute an effective primary prevention program.

Prevention, Evidence-Based Practice, and Substance Abuse

We live in an age of evidence-based primary prevention practice. This complex model means, at least, that there needs to be, first, theories or principles to explain the nature of clients, problems, change agents, and the meaning of change itself. Second, there has to be specific rules for planned actions. As Sexton et al. (2005, pp 111–112) suggest, the principles address questions like how does the client function? What is the nature of the problem that needs change? What knowledge and skills do change agents require? What should we look for when "change" occurs, or does not occur?

The rules for planned actions deal with questions like what actions should I take, if I do X, will Y occur? When should I take these actions? How will I know whether the actions had their desired outcome?

We would interpret the principles idea to refer to evidence-based preventive practice and the rules idea to refer to evaluation-informed preventive practice. Let's deal with evidence-based practice first. Clearly, we need evidence, which involves both the conceptual mapping of areas of human behavior in social and physical environments and the empirical studies that provide evidence on the usefulness of these conceptual mappings. Let's say we are involved in a prevention program on adolescent substance abuse. What theories or conceptual systems are available to us, so as not to reinvent the wheel? While the days of a knowledgeable John Griscom (of the NYSPP) are over, we can replicate his efforts through the use of computer retrieval systems, going initially to the Cochrane Collaboration (http://www.cochrane.org) for medical and health care–related studies, or to the Campbell Collaboration (http://www.compbellcollaborative.org) for information on social and behavioral interventions, as well as information on education, criminal justice, and social welfare. Access to scholarly information is available also through Google Scholar, as well as PsychINFO, and many other engines for searching specific terms pertinent to your client. A vast quantity of uneven material is accessible in a short period of time; it takes more time to digest the information and to translate it into terms relevant to a client situation.

With evaluation-informed practice (Bloom, Fischer, & Orme, in press), we look to an ongoing evaluation of practice to monitor how well we are approaching (or backing away from) our goals of practice, so as to make suitable changes to increase the effectiveness of specific interventions (based on evidence-based practice research and transported into the current situation). This evaluation of practice is as much a part of good practice as is incorporating evidence-based research into these programs.

Applications of These Theories/Research-Based Practices in Field Settings

A recent style of summarizing applications of theory and research is to distinguish, on one basis or another, those projects that work, that are promising, and that do not work (Gullotta & Bloom, 2003; Sexton et al., 2005). We will summarize a recent literature, recognizing that as soon as something is set to type, it is already dated.

Emshoff, Johnson, and Jacobus (2003) review prevention research on children of substance abusers and find no studies that meet their criterion of strategies that work. Rather, they describe nine projects that are promising. We'll illustrate these promising efforts with the Creating Lasting Connections (CLCs) program (Johnson et al., 1996) which the Center for Substance Abuse Prevention and the National Prevention Network selected as 1 of 16 exemplary prevention programs. This program is designed to deal with risk and resiliency factors associated with high-risk youth (among who are children of substance abusers). It focuses on increasing parent knowledge about alcohol and other drugs (education), improving family management skills (competency promotion), communication skills within the family (natural caregiving), increasing community involvement of the youth (community mobilization), and utilizing community services if needed. Research from an experimental design indicates that participants in the program (compared to a control group) improved their knowledge of substances and community services. There were some successes in increasing youth resiliency, bonding among family members, improved communications, and use of community services as needed.

Partridge and Flay (2003) address the prevention of substance abuse in childhood and find a lack of research on effectiveness, and thus present five promising programs needing further research. For example, *Preparing for the Drug Free Years (PDFY)* is a parent-education curriculum focusing on parent–child communications and improved parent–child interactions (education and natural caregiving) in children ranging from 8 years to 14 years (Kosterman et al., 1997). Long-term follow-ups of these childhood home-visitation programs also indicate decreased childhood and adolescent substance use and a range of factors mediating substance use (Olds, 1997).

Ringwalt and Paschall (2003) address adolescent substance use and abuse, focusing on a half dozen types of projects, of which we will describe one: The *Life Skills Training* program (Botvin, Baker, Dusenburg, Botvin, & Diaz, 1995; Botvin, Griffin, Diaz, & Ifill-Williams, 2001). It uses a universal classroom curriculum based on social learning theory that addresses risk and protective factors through personal and social skills training in conjunction with drug resistance skills (cf. Durlak, 2003). This is a 3-year program, with 15 lessons in the first year, 10 in the second, and 5 in the third, for middle school students. Over 20 years of research has indicated that this curriculum can reduce substance use by at least 50% of experimental students (compared to controls). And with the use of the booster sessions in the second and third years, significant effects are reported up to 6 years from the initial baseline. These findings are true of white, middle-class students, with recent indications that they apply as well to minorities (Botvin et al., 2001; Sexton et al., 2005, p. 120).

It is important to indicate programs that do not work, or do not work as well as those cited above as promising. Meta-analyses by Tobler and her colleagues are instructive: Streke, Roona, and Marshall (2003, p. 1062) use a detailed analysis of a large number of studies which lead to the following general conclusions: Family-based programs are less effective than school-based comprehensive life-skills programs (Schinke & Gilchrist, 1983). The effects on substance use are very weak, compared to findings on conduct disorder and aggression. Interactive programs are more effective than those that are noninteractive (solely dydactic), but only for some grade levels (junior, high, and above). They recommend the use of universal school programs (targeting all students in a given grade), supplemented with some family-focused interventions (especially with selective and indicated populations that are showing more signs of emerging problems than students in general). However, they conclude with a recommendation for more community-level interventions that affect social norms and environmental determinants of individual behaviors. This last remark mirrors the conclusion of the chapter in this book by D'Amico, Chinman, Stern, and Wandersman (in press): Primary prevention at the macro level needs an interactive systems framework that includes an intervention development component, which is readied for use in a prevention synthesis and translation system, followed by a prevention delivery system in which this intervention is put into place. They note that a prevention support system is needed to link the research domain with the field practice arena, in order that all these good ideas are to be utilized in practice.

Conclusion

As I look at bouncy adolescents frolicking at the local community center in my hometown, I wonder whether or what substances they are taking, here or elsewhere. It is difficult to differentiate "normal" adolescent behavior – if there is such a thing – from substance-enhanced behaviors, licit or illicit. These wonderful developing youths will all too soon be adults, taking their places in society, just as we did years ago. While their bounce may disturb the tranquility of us old folks, I, for one, am glad to see them lively and engaged with life. But I worry, as a preventer, protector, promoter, that some of what they do without a whole lot of thought or anticipation of their distant future will be to their detriment, and ultimately, of ours. Reviewing the range of individual, group, institution, and community-level interventions that work, all we can do is to advocate for these effective programs with the powers that be, and hope for the best with individual members of that bouncy tribe. The good news is that we know about many things that work to prevent predictable problems, protect existing states of healthy functioning, and promote desired goals (Gullotta & Bloom, 2003). Let 'er roll!

References

Albee, G. W. (1983). Psychopathology, prevention, and the just society. *Journal of Primary Prevention, 4*(1), 5–40.

Antonishak, J., & Reppucci, N. D. (2008). Ecological and community level influences on child development. In T.P. Gullotta & G.M. Blau (Eds.), *Handbook of childhood behavioral issues: Evidence-based approaches to prevention and treatment* (pp. 69–86). New York: Routledge.

Bandura, A. (1986). *Social foundations of thought and action: A social cognitive theory.* Englewood Cliffs, NJ: Prentice-Hall.

Bierce, A. (1911/1948). *Devil's dictionary.* Cleveland, OH: World Publishing Co.

Bloom, M. (1996). *Primary prevention practices.* Thousand Oaks, CA: Sage.

Bloom, M., Fischer, J., & Orme, J. (in press). *Evaluating practice: Guidelines for the accountable professional* (6th edition).

Bloom, M., & Klein, W. C. (1995–1996). John Griscom and primary prevention at the beginning of the 19th century. *Journal of Applied Social Science, 20*(1), 15–24.

Botvin, G. J., Baker, E., Dusenburg, L., Botvin, E. M., & Diaz, T. (1995). Long-term follow-up results of a randomized drug abuse prevention trial in a white middle-class population. *The Journal of the American Medical Association, 273*, 1106–1112.

Botvin, G. J., Griffin, K. W., Diaz, T., & Ifill-Williams, M. (2001). Drug abuse prevention among minority adolescents: One year follow-up of a school-based preventive intervention. *Prevention Science, 2*, 1–13.

Cowen, E. L. (2000). Psychological wellness: Some hopes for the future. In D. Cicchetti, J. Rappoport, I. Sandler, & R.P. Weissberg (Eds.), *The promotion of wellness in children and adolescents* (pp. 477–503). Washington, DC: CWLA Press.

D'Amico, E. J., Chinman, M., Stern, S. A., & Wandersman, A. (2008). Community prevention handbook on adolescent substance abuse prevention and treatment: Evidence-based practices. In C. Leukefeld, T.P. Gullotta, & M. Staton-Tindall (Eds.), *Handbook on adolescent substance abuse prevention and treatment: Evidence-based practice* (pp. 213–249). New York: Springer.

Durlak, J. A. (2003). Effective prevention and health promotion programming. In T.P. Gullotta & M. Bloom (Eds.), *Encyclopedia of primary prevention and health promotion* (pp. 61–69). New York: Kluwer Academic/Plenum.

Emshoff, J. G., Johnson, J., & Jacobus, L. (2003). Substances (children of substance abusers), childhood. In T.P. Gullotta & M. Bloom (Eds.), *Encyclopedia of primary prevention and health promotion* (pp. 61–69). New York: Kluwer Academic/Plenum.

Gore, A. (2006). *An inconvenient truth*. Emmaus, PA: Rodale.

Grinspoon, L., & Bakalar, J. B. (1993). *Marijauna forbidden medicine*. New Haven, CT: Yale University Press.

Griscom, J. H. (1859). *Memoir of John Griscom, LL.D., late professor of chemistry and natural philosophy; with an account of the New York High School; Society for the Prevention of Pauperism; the House of Refuge; and other institutions*. Compiled from an autobiography, and other sources. New York: Robert Carter and Brothers.

Gullotta, T. P. (1983). Prevention's developing technology. Institute at the Annual American Orthopsychiatric Meeting, Boston.

Gullotta, T. P. (1987). Prevention's technology. *Journal of Primary Prevention, 7*(4), 176–196.

Gullotta, T. P. (1994). The what, who, why, where, when, and how of primary prevention. *Journal of Primary Prevention, 15*(1), 5–14.

Gullotta, T. P., & Bloom, M. (Eds.). (2003). *Encyclopedia of primary prevention and health promotion*. New York: Kluwer Academic/Plenum.

Haines Report. (1822). *Report on the penitentiary system in the United States, prepared under a resolution of the Society of the Prevention of Pauperism, in the City of New York*. New York: M. Day.

Johnson, K., Strader, T., Bercaum, M., Bryant, D., Bucholtz, G., Collins, D., & et al. (1996). Reducing alcohol and other drug use by strengthening community, family and youth resiliency: An evaluation of the Creating Lasting Connections Program. *Journal of Adolescent Research, 11*, 36–67.

Johnston, L. D., O'Malley, P. M., Bachman, J. G., & Schulenberg, J. E. (2007). *Monitoring the future: National survey results on drug use, 1975–2006*. Bethesda, MD: National Institute on Drug Abuse.

Kastenbaum, R. (1988). In moderation: How some older people find pleasure and meaning in alcoholic beverages. *Generations, 12*(4), 68–71.

Kosterman, R., Hawkins, J. D., Spoth, R., Haggerty, K. P., & Zhu, K. (1997). Effects of a preventive parent-training intervention on observed family interactions: Proximal outcomes from preparing for the drug free years. *Journal of Community Psychology, 25*, 337–352.

Leukefeld, C. G., Smiley McDonald, H. M., Stoops, W. W., Reed, L., & Martin, C. (2005). Substance misuse and abuse. In T.P. Gullotta & G.R. Adams (Eds.), *Handbook of adolescent behavioral problems: Evidence-based approaches to prevention and treatment* (pp. 439–465). New York: Springer.

New York Society for the Prevention of Pauperism. (1819). *Second Annual Report*. New York: E. Conrad.

New York Society for the Prevention of Pauperism. (1821). *Fourth Annual Report*. New York: E. Conrad.

Olds, D. (1997). The prenatal/early infancy project: Fifteen years later. In G.W. Albee & T.P. Gullotta (Eds.), *Issues in children's and families' lives series: Primary prevention works* (Vol. 6, pp. 41–67). Thousand Oaks, CA: Sage Publications, Inc.

Partridge, T., & Flay, B. (2003). Substances, childhood. In T.P. Gullotta & M. Bloom (Eds.), *Encyclopedia of primary prevention and health promotion* (pp. 1052–1059). New York: Kluwer Academic/Plenum.

Ringwalt, C. L., & Paschall, M. J. (2003). Substances, adolescence. In T.P. Gullotta & M. Bloom (Eds.), *Encyclopedia of primary prevention and health promotion* (pp. 1065–1073). New York: Kluwer Academic/Plenum.

Schinke, S., & Gilchrist, L. (1983). Primary prevention of tobacco smoking. *Journal of School Health, 53*(7), 416–419.

Sexton, T. L., Gilman, L., & Johnson-Erickson, C. (2005). Evidence-based practices. In T.P. Gullotta & G.R. Adams (Eds.), *Handbook of adolescent behavioral problems: Evidence-based approaches to prevention and treatment* (pp. 101–128). New York: Springer.

Streke, A., Roona, M., & Marshall, D. (2003). Substances, childhood (meta-analysis). In T.P. Gullotta & M. Bloom (Eds.), *Encyclopedia of primary prevention and health promotion.*(pp. 1059–1064). New York: Kluwer Academic/Plenum.

Tadmor, C. S. (2003). Perceived personal control. In T.P. Gullotta & M. Bloom (Eds.), *Encyclopedia of primary prevention and health promotion* (pp. 812–821). New York: Kluwer Academic/Plenum.

Werner, E. E. (1993). Risk, resilience, and recovery: Perspectives from the Kauai longitudinal study. *Development and Psychopathology, 5*(4), 503–515.

Werner, E. E., & Smith, R. S. (1982). *Vulnerable but invincible: A longitudinal study of resilient children and youth.* New York: McGraw-Hill Book Company.

Werner, E. E., & Smith, R. S. (1992). *Overcoming the odds: High risk children from birth to adult-hood.* Ithaca, NY: Cornell University Press.

Chapter 9
Religious Involvement and Adolescent Substance Use

Terrence D. Hill, Amy M. Burdette, Michael L.Weiss, and Dale D. Chitwood

Religious involvement – indicated by observable feelings, beliefs, activities, and experiences in relation to spiritual, divine, or supernatural entities – is a prevalent and powerful force in the lives of American adolescents. According to national estimates, over 80% of adolescents report affiliations with religious groups (mostly Catholic and Conservative Protestant denominations), roughly 38% attend religious services at least once per week, and over 90% believe in God and Heaven (Gallup & Bezilla, 1992; Regnerus, 2007; Smith, Denton, Faris, & Regnerus, 2002). Studies show that religious involvement is associated with a wide range of favorable adolescent outcomes, including generally healthier lifestyles, greater mental and physical well-being, conformity to rules and laws, positive family relationships, and lower rates of risky sexual practices (Regnerus, 2003; Smith, 2003a; Wallace & Forman, 1998).

Given the far-reaching impact of religion in adolescence, it is not at all surprising to find that religious involvement may also promote abstinence and moderate substance use behaviors and favorable treatment outcomes. In this chapter, we provide an overview of published research on the association between religious involvement and substance use in adolescence. Although we consider the research that follows to be representative of the field, it is not intended to be exhaustive. After describing the basic association between religious involvement and substance use in adolescence, we discuss several theoretical and empirical explanations for this association. We conclude with a discussion of the strengths and limitations of prior research and several viable avenues for future research.

Basic Associations

In this section, we describe the basic association between religious involvement and substance use in adolescence. We summarize prior research on religious involvement and several substance use outcomes. These outcomes include alcohol consumption, tobacco smoking, illicit drug use, and substance use treatment.

C.G. Leukefeld et al. (eds.) *Adolescent Substance Abuse,*   171
DOI: 10.1007/978-0-387-09732-9_9, © Springer Science+Business Media LLC 2009

Alcohol Consumption

Prior research on religious involvement and substance use in adolescence has focused primarily on alcohol consumption. This body of research suggests that religious involvement is associated with lower levels of alcohol consumption in adolescence (see Benda, 1997; Benda & Corwyn, 1997; Corwyn, Benda, & Ballard, 1997; Grunbaum, Tortolero, Weller, & Gingiss, 2000; Hodge, Cardenas, & Montoya, 2001; Turner et al., 1994; Yarnold, 1998a, for exceptions). This general pattern is consistent across a range of favorable drinking outcomes, including higher lifetime abstinence rates (Amey, Albrecht, & Miller, 1996; Amoateng & Bahr, 1986; Burkett, 1977, 1980; Dunn, 2005; Jeynes, 2006; Wallace, Brown, Bachman, & Laveist, 2003), lower consumption frequencies and quantities (Amoateng & Bahr, 1986; Bahr, Maughan, Marcos, & Li, 1998; Benda, 1995; Burkett & White, 1974; Cochran, 1993; Donahue & Benson, 1995; Dunn, 2005; Hadaway, Elifson, & Petersen, 1984; Lorch & Hughes, 1985; Marsiglia, Kulis, Nieri, & Parsai, 2005; Miller, Davies, & Greenwald, 2000; Nonnemaker, McNeely, & Blum, 2003; Park, Ashton, Causey, & Moon, 1998; Park, Bauer, & Oescher, 2001; Ritt-Olson et al., 2004; Rodell & Benda, 1999; Steinman, Ferketich, & Sahr, 2006), and lower rates of heavy and binge drinking (Benda, 1995; Benda, Pope, & Kelleher, 2006; Donahue & Benson, 1995; Dunn, 2005; Jeynes, 2006; Wallace & Forman, 1998; Wallace et al., 2007). Although the majority of these studies employ cross-sectional designs, there is considerable longitudinal evidence to suggest that religious involvement is associated with favorable alcohol consumption trajectories (Foshee & Hollinger, 1996; Mason & Windle, 2001; Mason & Windle, 2002; Regnerus & Elder, 2003; Steinman & Zimmerman, 2004; Sussman, Skara, Rodriguez, & Pokhrel, 2006).

Tobacco Smoking

Surprisingly, few studies have considered the association between religious involvement and tobacco smoking in adolescence. Nevertheless, this body of research indicates that religious involvement is associated with lower rates of smoking (see Grunbaum et al., 2000, for an exception). This pattern is consistent for lifetime prevalence rates (Griesler & Kandel, 1998; Kaufman et al., 2002; Kutter & McDermott, 1997; Marsiglia et al., 2005; Wallace et al., 2003; Yarnold, 1999a) and 30-day incidence rates (Dunn, 2005; Kutter & McDermott, 1997; Marsiglia et al., 2005; Nasim, Utsey, Corona, & Belgrade, 2006; Nonnemaker et al., 2003; Ritt-Olson et al., 2004; Steinman & Zimmerman, 2004; Wallace et al., 2007). In our review of the literature, we could find only four longitudinal studies of the association between religious involvement and smoking behavior in adolescence. These studies suggest that religious involvement is associated with favorable smoking trajectories (Juon, Ensminger, & Sydnor, 2002; Nonnemaker, McNeely, & Blum, 2006; Steinman & Zimmerman, 2004; van den Bree, Whitmer, & Pickworth, 2004).

Illicit Drug Use

Numerous studies have examined the association between religious involvement and illicit drug use during adolescence. Consistent with prior research on drinking and smoking behaviors, this body of research suggests that religious involvement is associated with lower rates of illicit substance use in adolescence (see Benda, 1995; Benda & Corwyn, 1997; Burkett & Warren, 1987; Corwyn et al., 1997; Sussman et al., 2006, for exceptions). Published research on religious involvement and illicit substance use in adolescence has focused primarily on marijuana use. These studies show that religious involvement is associated with lower rates of marijuana use (Amey et al., 1996; Amoateng & Bahr, 1986; Benda, 1995; Burkett, 1977; Burkett & White, 1974; Donahue & Benson, 1995; Dunn, 2005; Hadaway et al., 1984; Hodge et al., 2001; Jessor, Chase, & Donovan, 1980; Jeynes, 2006; Kutter & McDermott, 1997; Lorch & Hughes, 1985; Marsiglia et al., 2005; McLuckie, Zahn, & Wilson, 1975; Miller et al., 2000; Nasim et al., 2006; Nonnemaker et al., 2003; Ritt-Olson et al., 2004; Rohrbaugh & Jessor, 1975; Steinman et al., 2006; Wallace & Forman, 1998; Wallace et al., 2003, 2007; Yarnold & Patterson, 1998).

Research also suggests that religious involvement is associated with other favorable substance use outcomes, including lower usage rates for stimulants (e.g., cocaine and amphetamines) (Bahr et al., 1998; Corwyn et al., 1997; Dunn, 2005; Grunbaum et al., 2000; Jeynes, 2006; Miller et al., 2000; Sussman et al., 2006; Yarnold, 1999b), depressants and opiates (e.g., barbiturates, sedatives, tranquilizers, anesthetics, ketamine, and heroin) (Bahr et al., 1998; Corwyn et al., 1997), anabolic steroids (Yarnold, 1998b), polydrug use (Lorch & Hughes, 1985), and nonspecific substance use (Amey et al., 1996; Benda, 1997; Benda & Corwyn, 2000; Benda et al., 2006; Brownfield & Sorenson, 1991; Cochran, Wood, & Arneklev, 1994; Hadaway et al., 1984; Hodge et al., 2001; Johnson, Larson, Li, & Jang, 2000; Kutter & McDermott, 1997; McLuckie et al., 1975; Nasim et al., 2006; Neumark-Sztainer et al., 1997; Wills, Gibbons, Gerrard, Murry, & Brody, 2003).

There is longitudinal evidence to suggest that religious involvement is associated with favorable usage trajectories for marijuana (Jang & Johnson, 2001; Steinman & Zimmerman, 2004; Sussman et al., 2006; but see Burkett & Warren, 1987, for an exception), stimulants (Sussman et al., 2006), and nonspecific substance use (Jang & Johnson, 2001; Regnerus & Elder, 2003; Wills, Yaeger, & Sandy, 2003; but see Sussman et al., 2006, for an exception). In our review of the literature, we could find only one study (Sussman et al., 2006) of the association between religious involvement and hallucinogenic substance use (e.g., LSD, PCP, mushrooms, and ecstasy). This study found religious involvement to be unrelated to usage trajectories for hallucinogenic substances. Although studies sometimes assess the use of inhalants (e.g., amyl nitrite, glue, and other solvents) through measurements for nonspecific substance use outcomes, we were unable to find any specific evidence for this class of substances.

Substance Use Treatment

Although prior research suggests that religious involvement is associated with lower levels of alcohol consumption and lower rates of smoking and illicit drug use, these studies do not exclude the possibility that many religious adolescents drink, smoke, and use illicit drugs. When religious youth use substances, they may require treatment to overcome problems associated with substance misuse. Research suggests that religious involvement may help adolescents to avoid the use of alcohol and drugs and, by extension, entry into substance use treatment. When religious adolescents succumb to problems associated with substance use, religious involvement may also support favorable treatment outcomes.

Very few studies have focused on religious involvement and substance use treatment outcomes. Nevertheless, research conducted in adult populations suggests that religious involvement is associated with positive substance use treatment outcomes, including greater program commitment (i.e., actively working on problems during treatment) during treatment (Atkins & Hawdon, 2007; Shields, Broome, Delany, Fletcher, & Flynn, 2007; Tonigan, Miller, & Schermer, 2002) and active and sustained 12-step involvement (e.g., attendance at 12-step meetings, reading group literature, application of steps in daily life, and communicating with sponsors and other group members) after treatment (Carrico, Gifford, & Moos, 2007; Mankowski, Humphreys, & Moos, 2001; Tonigan, 2007).

In their study of 193 patients selected from a substance use treatment center in Houston, TX, Richard, Bell, and Carlson (2002) report that increases in religious involvement (frequency of attendance at religious services) from intake to follow-up (6 months later) are associated with concurrent reductions in crack cocaine and alcohol use over the study period. Brown et al.'s (2007) study of 26 adults enrolled in intensive outpatient substance use treatment in Houston, Texas, shows greater baseline spiritual involvement (a multi-item index of beliefs and behaviors) in those maintaining complete sobriety over the 12-week study period as compared with those who relapsed. Although these studies are suggestive, it is unclear in the literature whether religious involvement is associated with treatment retention (Shields et al., 2007) or abstinence after treatment (Tonigan, 2007).

Generally speaking, there are few studies of substance use treatment outcomes in the adolescent population. Our review of the literature yielded only one study of religious involvement and substance use treatment outcomes in adolescence. In their study of 326 Mexican American adolescents selected from four substance use programs in Texas, Barrett, Simpson, and Lehman (1988) report that religious involvement (frequency of attendance at religious services) at intake is associated with fewer problem behaviors (i.e., continued drug and alcohol use, delinquency, and any legal involvement) 3 months into treatment, net of controls for adolescent characteristics measured at intake (problem behavior, motivation, family support, and peer drug use) and during the course of treatment (counselor ratings of program participation, family support, and peer drug use). Barrett and colleagues also find that religious involvement is associated with more favorable counselor ratings of program participation (i.e., attendance at counseling and related activities) and lower levels of peer substance use (separate measures for alcohol, marijuana, and inhalants) at intake and during the course of treatment.

Theoretical and Empirical Explanations

Published research has identified several promising theoretical explanations for why religious involvement might be associated with favorable substance use outcomes (Ellison & Levin, 1998; George, Ellison, & Larson, 2002; Gorsuch, 1995; Koenig, McCullough, & Larson, 2001; Levin & Chatters, 1998; Mahoney et al., 2005; Pargament, 1997; Smith, 2003a, 2003b, 2003c; Wallace & Forman, 1998; Welch, Tittle, & Grasmick, 2006). Drawing on this body of literature and relevant empirical work, this section discusses several classes of mechanisms, including religious factors, social factors, and psychological factors (see Fig. 9.1).

Religious Factors

First and foremost, religious involvement exposes adolescents to moral directives that are supported by the authority of longstanding religious traditions and sacred texts. With prolonged exposure (through religious involvement), adolescents may internalize religious messages that discourage substance use. Adolescents may then rely on these messages and directives to support life decisions in general and substance use decisions in particular.

   Numerous studies suggest that religious involvement may discourage substance use by exposing adolescents to religious doctrines that discourage the use of specific substances (Burkett, 1980; Burkett & White, 1974; Cochran, 1993; Cochran & Akers, 1989; Cochran et al., 1994; Corwyn et al., 1997; Gorsuch, 1995; Hadaway et al., 1984; Kutter & McDermott, 1997; Miller et al., 2000; Nasim et al., 2006; Steinman & Zimmerman, 2004). In Islamic writings, the Koran condemns alcohol and other intoxicating substances in unequivocal language. For example, Surah (5:90) stipulates: "Believers, strong drink and games of chance, idols, and divining arrows are abominations devised by Satan. Avoid them so that you may prosper." Islamic doctrine also denounces persons who merely brew or serve alcoholic beverages (McBride, Mutch, & Chitwood, 1996). Although more common Judeo-Christian teachings permit or even advise light to moderate alcohol use in adulthood, there are clear Biblical proscriptions against heavy alcohol consumption (e.g., Galatians 5:19–21; Luke 21:34; Proverbs 23:21–35). For instance, Proverbs (23:31–33) warns: "Do not look on the wine when it is red… At the last it bites like a serpent, and stings like a viper. Your eyes will see strange things, and your heart will utter perverse things."

   Specific religious proscriptions may help to explain why religious adolescents might avoid alcohol consumption, but they cannot account for the effects of religious

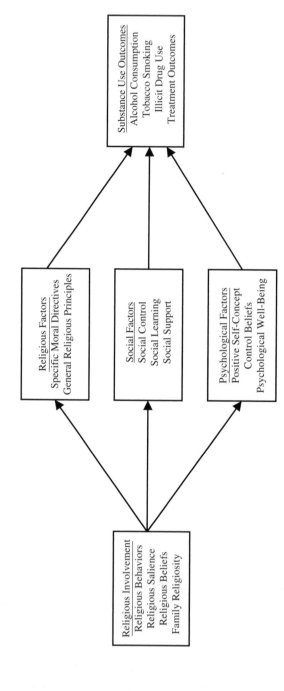

Fig. 9.1 Conceptual model relating religious involvement to adolescent substance use through religious, social, and psychological factors

involvement on other substances that are unspecified in religious scripture. Interestingly, many religious groups adhere to general religious principles that sanctify the body and promote the instrumental importance of physical health as a means to greater spiritual commitment and involvement (e.g., 1 Corinthians 3:16–17; 1 Corinthians 6:19–20). Mahoney et al. (2005) refer to sanctification as a process through which objects are infused with divine or spiritual significance. 1 Corinthians (6:19–20) provides an especially lucid example of the sanctification of the body: "...your body is the temple of the Holy Spirit who is in you...therefore glorify God in your body, and in your spirit, which are God's." Many religious groups use this passage to promote the body as a sacred object and to discourage a wide range of health-relevant behaviors, including alcohol consumption, tobacco smoking, illicit drug use, risky sexual behaviors, and even body piercing and tattooing. Not surprisingly, research suggests that adolescents who either view the body as a manifestation of God (e.g., believe that the body is the temple of God, or the body is a gift from God, or the body is an instrument of God) or perceive the body as having sacred or spiritual qualities (e.g., believe that the body is blessed, holy, or divine) are more likely to disapprove of and exhibit lower levels of alcohol consumption and illicit drug use and experimentation, but not heavy smoking (Mahoney et al., 2005).

Religious involvement might also direct adolescents to avoid substance use by encouraging deference to authority, conformity to social norms, and adherence to rules and laws (Welch et al., 2006). Indeed, numerous biblical passages counsel adherents to submit to various "authorities" and "ordinances" (e.g., Hebrews 13:17; Peter 2:13–14; Romans 13:1–7). For instance, Romans (13:1–2) advises: "Let every soul be subject to the governing authorities. For there is no authority except from God, and the authorities that exist are appointed by God. Therefore whoever resists the authority resists the ordinance of God, and those who resist will bring judgment on themselves." Welch et al. (2006) explain that religious involvement may favor conformity through fear of divine retribution, internalized moral codes and guilt avoidance, and the social context of obedient peer networks. If religious individuals are more sensitive to authority, they may, for example, be more likely to adhere to parental regulations, formal laws, and medical regimens that discourage substance use in adolescence.

Teen Challenge, one of the more widely known religiously-based substance use intervention programs, explicitly bases its treatment on conservative religious doctrine. Despite being in operation for almost 50 years, however, it is unclear whether *Teen Challenge* is more or less effective than secular programs in providing substance use treatment (Koenig et al., 2001; National Center on Addiction and Substance Abuse, 2001). Twelve-step fellowships, such as Alcoholics Anonymous (AA) and Narcotics Anonymous (NA), are sponsored by religious congregations and often meet in churches. While these programs are not explicitly religious, they are based on spiritual principles, such as a self-defined Higher Power, self-examination, prayer, and meditation (Carroll, 1993). Some researchers speculate that because 12-step and other self-help programs have such a strong spiritual component, religious individuals may be especially amenable to the values and goals of substance use treatment (Atkins & Hawdon, 2007; Carrico et al., 2007; Humphreys & Gifford, 2006; Mankowski et al., 2001). There is contradictory evidence regarding the effectiveness of twelve-step programs. Although some research finds that both AA and NA are successful in preventing future substance use (Alford, Koehler, & Leonard, 1991; Emrick, Tonigan, Montgomery, & Little, 1993), other studies find no significant differences in abstinence between those attending these fellowships and individuals in other programs or not in treatment (see Peele, 1990, for a review of this literature).

Social Factors

Religious involvement may favor lower levels of substance use through the processes of social control, social learning, and social support. As key elements of social control, behavioral monitoring and social sanctions function to reinforce specific moral directives and general religious principles that favor abstinence (Amoateng & Bahr, 1986; Benda, 1995; Brownfield & Sorenson, 1991; Burkett, 1977, 1993; Burkett & Warren, 1987; Cochran et al., 1994; Gorsuch, 1995; Hadaway et al., 1984; Kutter & McDermott, 1997; Mason & Windle, 2002; Miller et al., 2000; Nasim et al., 2006; Steinman & Zimmerman, 2004; Wills et al., 2003). Research suggests that involvement in religious institutions and communities is associated with increased behavioral monitoring (by parents, elders, and peers) of counternormative behavior (Sherkat & Wilson, 1995; Smith, 2003a, 2003b). Religious involvement is also associated with direct and indirect exposure to social sanctions (e.g., gossip, ostracism, and formal punishments) that function to elevate the costs (actual and perceived) associated with substance use, which presumably deter experimentation and use.

But does social control explain the association between religious involvement and substance use in adolescence? Research by Benda (1995) suggests that social control mediates the effect of religiosity (a multi-item index) on marijuana use, but not alcohol use. Cochran et al. (1994) report that social control mediates the effect of religious salience on illicit drug use (marijuana and nonspecific hard drug use), but not on legalized drugs (alcohol and tobacco use).

It has been suggested in the literature that religious involvement may discourage substance use by exposing adolescents to coreligionist peers and adults who espouse antisubstance use norms and, presumably, exhibit low levels of substance use and high rates of abstinence (Amoateng & Bahr, 1986; Bahr et al., 1998; Burkett & Warren, 1987; Gorsuch, 1995; Hardesty & Kirby, 1995). Through the process of "peer selection," religious adolescents are often embedded in antisubstance use networks that are defined by models of moderation and abstinence (e.g., pastors, youth leaders, and other role models). Prior investigations suggest that peer substance use is one of the strongest risk factors for substance use in adolescence (Ary, Tildesley, Hops, & Andrews, 1993; Bahr, Marcos, & Maughan, 1995; Hawkins, Catalano, & Miller, 1992; Khavari, 1993), and there is evidence to suggest that religious involvement in adolescence is associated with lower levels of peer drug use (Bahr et al., 1998; Barrett et al., 1988; Hardesty & Kirby, 1995). For example, in their study of 475 high school students selected from a Midwestern city, Hardesty and Kirby (1995) report that family religiousness (a multi-item index of family religious activities) is associated with lower peer usage of beer, distilled alcohol, marijuana, cocaine, crack, and amphetamines.

Although peer selection and social learning processes are theoretically viable explanations for the association between religious involvement and substance use in adolescence, empirical support for this theory is, to this point, mixed. In their study of 240 high school students selected from the Pacific Northwestern United States, Burkett and Warren (1987) report that religious involvement (a multi-item index of religious commitment and activities) is indirectly associated with lower levels of marijuana use over 2 years through fewer associations with marijuana-using peers. In an analysis of data collected from over 13,000 adolescents from Utah, Bahr et al. (1998) observed that peer drug use failed to mediate the effects of religious involvement on alcohol use, marijuana use, and amphetamine/sedative use.

Religious involvement may also lead to lower levels of substance use through supportive relationships with coreligionists (Carrico et al., 2007; Humphreys & Gifford, 2006). Studies show that religious involvement is associated with larger and more diverse social networks, more contact with network members, more extensive family ties, and more types of social support (Ellison & George, 1994). Larger social networks, especially those consisting of coreligionists, may discourage substance use and aid in treatment recovery through the provision of informational, emotional, and instrumental support. Informational support such as warnings concerning the health-damaging effects of substance use can be directly related to lower levels of substance use in adolescence. Emotional support may satisfy the need for intimacy and connectedness and help adolescents to manage stressful life experiences, recovery efforts, and negative emotions that sometimes lead to substance use as a means of palliative escape. Instrumental support (e.g., small favors) might also help adolescents to avoid stressful life circumstances in the first place.

Psychological Factors

Religious involvement may also discourage substance use in adolescence by promoting positive self-perceptions (e.g., self-esteem and control beliefs) and psychological well-being (e.g., lower levels of psychological distress) (Gorsuch, 1995; Regnerus & Elder, 2003; Smith, 2003a). According to Ellison (1993), active religious participants are often valued for skills and abilities that are connected with church-related activities (e.g., singing in choir and participation in religious discussion groups), respected for service to others in the community (e.g., volunteering and specific leadership roles), and admired for personal spiritual qualities (e.g., wisdom and morality). To the extent that these kinds of activities and experiences promote the self-esteem, self-confidence, and self-worth of adolescents, positive self-perceptions gained through religious involvement could discourage substance use by reducing stress, negative affect, and passive coping strategies.

Another mechanism through which religious involvement might be associated with lower levels of substance use in adolescence is by fostering self-control and generic self-regulatory capacities (Carrico et al., 2007; Foshee & Hollinger, 1996; Humphreys & Gifford, 2006; Nasim et al., 2006; Smith, 2003a). In a systematic review of empirical research, McCullough and Willoughby (in press) show that religious individuals consistently score higher than do their less religious counterparts on measures of self-control (e.g., ability to control one's impulses, appetites, and emotions). They demonstrate that self-control appears to be one of the mechanisms through which religious involvement obtains its association with substance use among adolescents. In a study of 435 African-American adolescents selected from the Southeastern United States, Nasim et al. (2006) find that the association between religious involvement and substance use (separate models for tobacco use, alcohol use, marijuana use, and nonspecific illicit substance use) is mediated by refusal efficacy (i.e., the ability to resist temptation to use substances under stressful conditions). Research by Carrico et al. (2007) suggests that religious involvement encourages continued 12-step involvement by promoting posttreatment self-regulation skills (a latent construct indicated by approach coping, self-efficacy, and process change) after discharge from substance use treatment.

Finally, religion may reduce substance use in adolescence by improving psychological well-being (Gorsuch 1995). Very few studies have considered the connection between religious involvement and mental health in adolescence. Those few studies that have suggest that religious involvement is associated with lower levels of depression among adolescents (Nooney, 2005; Sinha, Cnaan, & Gelles, 2006). Numerous other studies report that religious involvement is protective against depression and anxiety in adult populations (see Koenig et al., 2001, for a review of this research). In the *Handbook of Religion and Health*, Koenig et al. (2001) note that religious involvement is correlated with several factors that are known to benefit mental health, including greater hope and optimism, a greater sense of meaning and purpose, and greater social support. Psychological well-being gained through religious involvement might favor lower levels of substance use and abstinence by reducing negative coping behaviors (e.g., self-medication or tension reduction) and feelings of fear and hopelessness, which often inhibit efforts to design and carryout healthy lifestyles. Even though studies suggest that psychological distress is a risk factor for substance use among adolescents and young adults (Diego, Field, & Sanders, 2003; Needham, 2007; Poulin, Hand, Boudreau, & Santor, 2005), it is unclear in the literature whether religious involvement actually operates through mental health.

Strengths, Limitations, and Future Directions

This chapter described the basic association between religious involvement and substance use in adolescence and discussed several theoretical and empirical explanations for this association. Our review of the literature suggests that religious involvement is associated with lower levels of alcohol consumption, lower rates of tobacco smoking and illicit drug use, and more favorable substance use treatment outcomes. Although explanations for these associations are not well established, our review highlights several classes of mechanisms that are at least theoretically viable, including religious (specific moral directives and general religious principles), social (social control, social learning, and social support), and psychological (positive self-concept, control beliefs, and psychological well-being) factors.

Prior research on religious involvement and substance use in adolescence is characterized by several strengths, including consistent patterns across studies, comprehensive measurements of religious involvement, and sophisticated statistical techniques. The general patterns (that religious involvement is associated with lower levels of substance use and favorable treatment outcomes) are remarkably consistent across studies and disciplines, including substance use and addiction, general public health, sociology, adolescent studies, criminology, family studies, social work, religious studies, and psychology.

Comprehensive measurement of religious involvement is also characteristic of the literature. Religious involvement is widely recognized as a multidimensional phenomenon. Consistent with this perspective, the studies reviewed in this chapter employ numerous measures of religious involvement, including affiliation to proscriptive denominations, frequency of attendance at religious services and other religious activities, frequency of prayer and Bible study, belief in God and the Devil and life after death, religious salience, religious satisfaction, and spiritual experiences (e.g., Born again experiences), religious coping practices, general religiosity, and family and parental religiosity.

Most studies of religious involvement and substance use in adolescence employ sophisticated statistical techniques. These techniques include ordinary least squares regression (for modeling continuous outcomes), logistic regression analyses (for modeling binary and ordinal outcomes), structural equation modeling (for modeling observed and latent processes), and lagged endogenous dependent variable models and growth curve models (for modeling substance use trajectories).

The research reviewed in this chapter is also limited in terms of data quality, research design, and analytic strategy. Although many studies employ data collected from large, national probability samples, the bulk of this research is limited to small, regional nonprobability samples. There is solid longitudinal support for the association between religious involvement and substance use in adolescence; however, most studies are based on cross-sectional designs and, as a consequence, are unable to establish the causal order of any observed associations. There is also the potential for bias due to social desirability. For example, it is possible that some adolescents might falsely respond to questions by overestimating religious involvement and/or underestimating the frequency of substance use in order to protect their religious values and identities. Since studies generally fail to control for social desirability, reports may exaggerate the association between religious involvement and substance use in adolescence. To this point, however, there is very little empirical support for social desirability as an alternative explanation for religious influence (see Regnerus and Smith, 2005).

Although we describe the comprehensive measurement of religious involvement as a strength of prior research, the same cannot be said of the measurement of substance use outcomes. The studies reviewed in this chapter consider a wide range of substance use outcomes; however, the overwhelming majority of these studies are restricted to alcohol consumption and marijuana use. Clearly, additional research is needed to establish the effects of religious involvement on tobacco smoking (to our surprise) and other forms of illicit drug use, including stimulants, depressants and opiates, hallucinogenic substances, inhalants, and anabolic steroids. It is also important for studies to continue to examine the effects of religious involvement on adolescent substance use treatment outcomes. To this point, it is unclear in the literature whether religious involvement is associated with treatment retention and involvement or, more importantly, abstinence after treatment.

While studies tend to emphasize the main effects of religious involvement, little is known about potential indirect effects. Although several studies speculate as to why religious involvement might be associated with favorable substance use outcomes, empirical support for these explanations is sorely lacking. It is also unclear in the literature whether the effect of religious involvement on substance use outcomes varies according to theoretically relevant subgroups. Several studies consider potential subgroup variations by stratifying analyses and testing statistical interactions, but variations in data, measures, and statistical procedures have produced inconsistent patterns. Some research suggests that religious involvement is more protective for older adolescents (Jang & Johnson, 2001), girls (Benda et al., 2006; Burkett, 1993), and non-Hispanic whites (Amey et al., 1996; Wallace et al., 2003), while other studies show no variations by age (Benda & Corwyn, 2000), sex (Bahr et al., 1998; Dunn, 2005), or race/ethnicity (Park et al., 1998; Marsiglia et al., 2005). If religious involvement is associated with lower levels of alcohol consumption, lower rates of tobacco smoking and illicit drug use, and more favorable substance use treatment outcomes, how might we explain these associations? Under which conditions is religious involvement more or less protective? If we are going to advance our understanding of the association between religious involvement and substance use in adolescence, future research will need to answer these questions.

We would like to end by encouraging future research to move beyond basic associations and elaboration models (see Fig. 9.2). Adolescent religious involvement could serve as a moderator (Model A). For example, studies show that religious involvement may buffer adolescents from risk factors for substance use, including adverse neighborhood conditions (Jang & Johnson, 2001) and stressful life events (Wills et al., 2003). Foshee and Hollinger (1996) speculate that religious involvement could also protect against psychological distress as a motivation for substance use in adolescence. Adolescent religious involvement might also operate as a mediator. For example, adolescent religious involvement could mediate (through processes of socialization and social learning) the association between parental religious involvement and adolescent substance use outcomes (Model B). Research by Burkett (1993) suggests that parental religious involvement is associated with lower levels of alcohol consumption through adolescent religious commitment. Finally, if religious involvement is associated with lower levels of

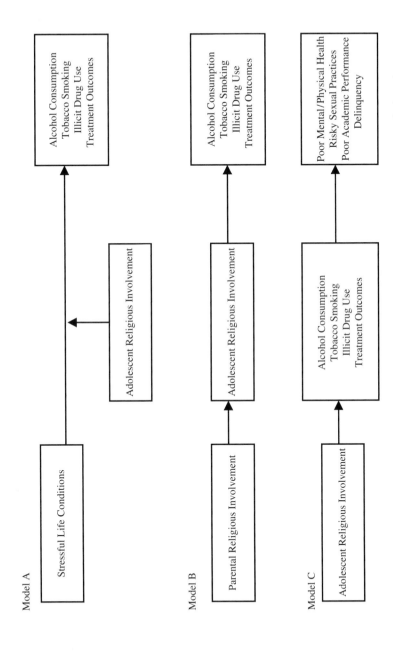

Fig. 9.2 Alternative conceptual models of the protective effects of religious involvement on adolescent substance use and other adverse outcomes

substance use, it is important for future research to consider logical extensions of this general pattern (Model C). Substance use is associated with a wide range of adverse adolescent outcomes, including poor mental and physical health, risky sexual practices, poor academic performance, and delinquency (National Institute on Drug Abuse, 2007). It is conceivable that adolescent religious involvement could protect against these kinds of adverse outcomes by promoting abstinence and moderate substance use behaviors and favorable treatment outcomes in adolescence.

References

Alford, G. S., Koehler, R. A., & Leonard, J. (1991). Alcoholics anonymous-narcotics anonymous model inpatient treatment of chemically dependent adolescents: A 2-year outcome study. *Journal of Studies on Alcohol, 52*, 118–126.

Amey, C. H., Albrecht, S. L., & Miller, M. K. (1996). Racial differences in adolescent drug use: The impact of religion. *Substance Use & Misuse, 31*, 1311–1332.

Amoateng, A. Y., & Bahr, S. J. (1986). Religion, family, and adolescent drug-use. *Sociological Perspectives, 29*, 53–76.

Ary, D. V., Tildesley, E., Hops, H., & Andrews, J. A. (1993). The influence of parent, sibling, and peer modeling and attitudes on adolescent use of alcohol. *International Journal of the Addictions, 28*, 853–880.

Atkins, R.G., & Hawdon, J.E. (2007). Religiosity and participation in mutual-aid support groups for addiction. *Journal of Substance Abuse Treatment, 33*, 321–331.

Bahr, S. J., Marcos, A. C., & Maughan, S. L. (1995). Family, educational and peer influences on the alcohol use of female and male adolescents. *Journal of Studies on Alcohol, 56*, 457–469.

Bahr, S. J., Maughan, S. L., Marcos, A. C., & Li, B. (1998). Family, religiosity, and the risk of adolescent drug use. *Journal of Marriage and the Family, 60*, 979–992.

Barrett, M., Simpson, D., & Lehman, W. (1988). Behavioral changes of adolescents in drug abuse intervention programs. *Journal for the Scientific Study of Religion, 44*, 461–473.

Benda, B. B. (1995). The effect of religion on adolescent delinquency revisited. *Journal of Research in Crime and Delinquency, 32*, 446–466.

Benda, B. B. (1997). An examination of a reciprocal relationship between religiosity and different forms of delinquency within a theoretical model. *Journal of Research in Crime and Delinquency, 34*, 163–186.

Benda, B. B., & Corwyn, R. F. (1997). A test of a model with reciprocal effects between religiosity and various forms of delinquency using 2-stage least squares regression. *Journal of Social Service Research, 22*, 27–52.

Benda, B. B., & Corwyn, R. F. (2000). A theoretical model of religiosity and drug use with reciprocal relationships: A test using structural equation modeling. *Journal of Social Service Research, 26*, 43–67.

Benda, B. B., Pope, S. K., & Kelleher, K. J. (2006). Church attendance or religiousness: Their relationship to adolescents' use of alcohol, other drugs, & delinquency. *Alcoholism Treatment Quarterly, 24*, 75–87.

Brown, A., Pavlik, V., Shegog, R., Whitney, S., Friedman, L., Romero, C., et al. (2007). Association of spirituality and sobriety during a behavioral spirituality intervention for twelve step (TS) recovery. *The American Journal of Drug and Alcohol Abuse, 33*, 611–617.

Brownfield, D., & Sorenson, A. M. (1991). Religion and drug-use among adolescents: A social support conceptualization and interpretation. *Deviant Behavior, 12*, 259–276.

Burkett, S. R. (1977). Religion, parental influence, and adolescent alcohol and marihuana use. *Journal of Drug Issues, 7*, 263–273.

Burkett, S. R. (1980). Religiosity, beliefs, normative standards and adolescent drinking. *Journal of Studies on Alcohol, 41*, 662–671.

Burkett, S. R. (1993). Perceived parents religiosity, friends drinking, and hellfire: A panel study of adolescent drinking. *Review of Religious Research, 35*, 134–154.

Burkett, S. R., & Warren, B. O. (1987). Religiosity, peer associations, and adolescent marijuana use: A panel study of underlying causal structures. *Criminology, 25*, 109–131.

Burkett, S. R., & White, M. (1974). Hellfire and delinquency: Another look. *Journal for the Scientific Study of Religion, 13*, 455–462.

Carrico, A., Gifford, E., & Moos, R. (2007). Spirituality/religiosity promotes acceptance-based responding and 12-step involvement. *Drug and Alcohol Dependence, 89*, 66–73.

Carroll, S. (1993). Spirituality and purpose in life in alcoholism recovery. *Journal of Studies on Alcohol, 54*, 297–301.

Cochran, J. K. (1993). The variable effects of religiosity and denomination on adolescent self-reported alcohol-use by beverage type. *Journal of Drug Issues, 23*, 479–491.

Cochran, J. K., & Akers, R. L. (1989). Beyond hellfire: An exploration of the variable effects of religiosity on adolescent marijuana and alcohol-use. *Journal of Research in Crime and Delinquency, 26*, 198–225.

Cochran, J. K., Wood, P. B., & Arneklev, B. J. (1994). Is the religiosity-delinquency relationship spurious? A test of arousal and social-control theories. *Journal of Research in Crime and Delinquency, 31*, 92–123.

Corwyn, R. F., Benda, B. B., & Ballard, K. (1997). Do the same theoretical factors explain alcohol and other drug use among adolescents? *Alcoholism Treatment Quarterly, 15*, 47–62.

Diego, M., Field, T., & Sanders, C. (2003). Academic performance, popularity, and depression predict adolescent substance use. *Adolescence, 38*, 35–42.

Donahue, M. J., & Benson, P. L. (1995). Religion and well-being of adolescents. *Journal of Social Issues, 51*, 145–160.

Dunn, M. S. (2005). The relationship between religiosity, employment, and political beliefs on substance use among high school seniors. *Journal of Alcohol and Drug Education, 49*, 73–88.

Ellison, C. G. (1993). Religious involvement and self-perception among Black Americans. *Social Forces, 71*, 1027–1055.

Ellison, C. G., & George, L. (1994). Religious involvement, social ties, and social support in a southeastern community. *Journal for the Scientific Study of Religion, 33*, 46–61.

Ellison, C., & Levin, J. (1998). The religion-health connection: Evidence, theory, and future directions. *Health Education & Behavior, 25*, 700–720.

Emrick, C. D., Tonigan, J. S., Montgomery, H., & Little, L. (1993). Alcoholics Anonymous: What is currently known? In B.S. McGrady & W.R. Miller (Eds.), *Research on Alcoholics anonymous: Opportunities and alternatives* (pp. 41–76). New Brunswick, NJ: Rutgers Center of Alcohol Studies.

Foshee, V. A., & Hollinger, B. R. (1996). Maternal religiosity, adolescent social bonding, and adolescent alcohol use. *Journal of Early Adolescence, 16*, 451–468.

Gallup, G. H., Jr., & Bezilla, R. (1992). *The religious life of young Americans.* Princeton, NJ: The George H. Gallup International Institute.

George, L., Ellison, C., & Larson, D. (2002). Explaining the relationships between religious involvement and health. *Psychological Inquiry, 13*, 190–200.

Gorsuch, R. (1995). Religious aspects of substance abuse and recovery. *Journal of Social Issues, 51*, 65–83.

Griesler, P. C., & Kandel, D. B. (1998). Ethnic differences in correlates of adolescent cigarette smoking. *Journal of Adolescent Health, 23*, 167–180.

Grunbaum, J. A., Tortolero, S., Weller, N., & Gingiss, P. (2000). Cultural, social, and intrapersonal factors associated with substance use among alternative high school students. *Addictive Behaviors, 25*, 145–151.

Hadaway, C. K., Elifson, K. W., & Petersen, D. M. (1984). Religious involvement and drug-use among urban adolescents. *Journal for the Scientific Study of Religion, 23*, 109–128.

Hardesty, P. H., & Kirby, K. M. (1995). Relation between family religiousness and drug-use within adolescent peer groups. *Journal of Social Behavior and Personality, 10,* 421–430.

Hawkins, J. D., Catalano, R. F., & Miller, J. Y. (1992). Risk and protective factors for alcohol and other drug problems in adolescence and early adulthood: Implications for substance abuse prevention. *Psychological Bulletin, 112,* 64–105.

Hodge, D. R., Cardenas, P., & Montoya, H. (2001). Substance use: Spirituality and religious participation as protective factors among rural youths. *Social Work Research, 25,* 153–161.

Humphreys, K., & Gifford, E. (2006). Religion, spirituality, and the troublesome use of substances. In W. Miller and K. Carroll (Eds.), *Rethinking substance abuse: What science shows and what we should do about it* (pp. 257–274). New York: Guilford Press.

Jessor, R., Chase, J. A., & Donovan, J. E. (1980). Psychosocial correlates of marijuana use and problem drinking in a national sample of adolescents. *American Journal of Public Health, 70,* 604–613.

Jang, S. J., & Johnson, B. R. (2001). Neighborhood disorder, individual religiosity, and adolescent use of illicit drugs: A test of multilevel hypotheses. *Criminology, 39,* 109–144.

Jeynes, W. H. (2006). Adolescent religious commitment and their consumption of marijuana, cocaine, and alcohol. *Journal of Health and Social Policy, 21,* 1–20.

Johnson, B. R., Larson, D. B., Li, S. D., & Jang, S. J. (2000). Escaping from the crime of inner cities: Church attendance and religious salience among disadvantaged youth. *Justice Quarterly, 17,* 377–391.

Juon, H. S., Ensminger, M. E., & Sydnor, K. D. (2002). A longitudinal study of developmental trajectories to young adult cigarette smoking. *Drug and Alcohol Dependence, 66,* 303–314.

Kaufman, N. J., Castrucci, B. C., Mowery, P. D., Gerlach, K. K., Emont, S., & Orleans, C. T. (2002). Predictors of change on the smoking uptake continuum among adolescents. *Archives of Pediatrics & Adolescent Medicine, 156,* 581–587.

Khavari, K. A. (1993). Interpersonal influences in college students' initial use of alcohol and drugs: The role of friends, self, parents, doctors, and dealers. *The International Journal of the Addictions, 28,* 377–388.

Koenig, H. G., McCullough, M. E., & Larson, D. B. (2001). *Handbook of religion and health.* New York: Oxford University Press.

Kutter, C. J., & McDermott, D. S. (1997). The role of the church in adolescent drug education. *Journal of Drug Education, 27,* 293–305.

Levin, J., & Chatters, L. (1998). Research on religion and mental health: An overview of empirical findings and theoretical issues. In W. Koenig (Ed.), *Handbook of religion and mental health* (pp. 33–50). San Diego, CA: Academic Press.

Lorch, B. R., & Hughes, R. H. (1985). Religion and youth substance use. *Journal of Religion & Health, 24,* 197–208.

Mahoney, A., Carels, R. A., Pargament, K. I., Wachholtz, A., Leeper, L. E., Kaplar, M., et al. (2005). The sanctification of the body and behavioral health patterns of college students. *The International Journal of the Psychology of Religion, 15,* 221–238.

Mankowski, E., Humphreys, K., & Moos, R. (2001). Individual and contextual predictors of involvement in twelve-step self-help groups after substance abuse treatment. *American Journal of Community Psychology, 29,* 537–563.

Marsiglia, F. F., Kulis, S., Nieri, T., & Parsai, M. (2005). God forbid! Substance use among religious and nonreligious youth. *American Journal of Orthopsychiatry, 75,* 585–598.

Mason, W. A., & Windle, M. (2001). Family, religious, school and peer influences on adolescent alcohol use: A longitudinal study. *Journal of Studies on Alcohol, 62,* 44–53.

Mason, W. A., & Windle, M. (2002). A longitudinal study of the effects of religiosity on adolescent alcohol use and alcohol-related problems. *Journal of Adolescent Research, 17,* 346–363.

McBride, D. C., Mutch, P. M., & Chitwood, D. D. (1996). Religious belief and the initiation and prevention of drug use among youth. In J. Inciardi, L. Metsch, & C.B. McCoy (Eds.), *Intervening with drug-involved youth: Prevention, treatment, and research* (pp. 110–130). Newbury Park, CA: Sage Publications.

McCullough, M., & Willoughby, B. (in press). Religion, self-regulation, and self-control: Associations, explanations, and implications. *Psychological Bulletin*.

McLuckie, B. F., Zahn, M., & Wilson, R. A. (1975). Religious correlates of teenage drug use. *Journal of Drug Issues, 5*, 129–139.

Miller, L., Davies, M., & Greenwald, S. (2000). Religiosity and substance use and abuse among adolescents in the national comorbidity survey. *Journal of the American Academy of Child and Adolescent Psychiatry, 39*, 1190–1197.

Nasim, A., Utsey, S. O., Corona, R., & Belgrade, F. Z. (2006). Religiosity, refusal efficacy, and substance use among African-American adolescents and young adults. *Journal of Ethnicity in Substance Abuse, 5*, 29–49.

National Center on Addiction and Substance Abuse. (2001). *So Help Me God: Substance Abuse, Religion and Spirituality*. New York: The National Center on Addiction and Substance Abuse (CASA) at Columbia University.

National Institute on Drug Abuse. (2007). Drugs, brains, and behavior: The science of addiction. *National Institutes of Health*, NIH Pub No. 07-5605.

Needham, B. L. (2007). Gender differences in trajectories of depressive symptomatology and substance use during the transition from adolescence to young adulthood. *Social Science & Medicine, 65*, 1166–1179.

Neumark-Sztainer, D., Story, M., French, S. A., & Resnick, M. D. (1997). Psychosocial correlates of health compromising behaviors among adolescents. *Health Education Research, 12*, 37–52.

Nonnemaker, J. M., McNeely, C. A., & Blum, R. W. (2003). Public and private domains of religiosity and adolescent health risk behaviors: Evidence from the National Longitudinal Study of Adolescent Health. *Social Science and Medicine, 57*, 2049–2054.

Nonnemaker, J., McNeely, C. A., & Blum, R. W. (2006). Public and private domains of religiosity and adolescent smoking transitions. *Social Science & Medicine, 62*, 3084–3095.

Nooney, J. G. (2005). Religion, stress, and mental health in adolescence: Findings from Add Health. *Review of Religious Research, 46*, 341–354.

Pargament, K. I. (1997). *The psychology of religion and coping: Theory, research, and practice*. New York: The Guilford Press.

Park, H., Ashton, L., Causey, T., & Moon, S. S. (1998). The impact of religious proscriptiveness on alcohol use among high school students. *Journal of Alcohol and Drug Education, 44*, 34–46.

Park, H., Bauer, S., & Oescher, J. (2001). Religiousness as a predictor of alcohol use in high school students. *Journal of Drug Education, 31*, 289–303.

Peele, S. (1990). Research issues in assessing addiction treatment efficacy: How cost effective are Alcoholics Anonymous and private treatment centers? *Drug and Alcohol Dependence, 25*, 179–182.

Poulin, C., Hand, D., Boudreau, B., & Santor, D. (2005). Gender differences in the association between substance use and elevated depressive symptoms in a general adolescent population. *Addiction, 100*, 525–535.

Regnerus, M. (2003). Religion and positive adolescent outcomes. *Review of Religious Research, 44*, 394–413.

Regnerus, M. (2007). *Forbidden fruit? Sex and religion in American adolescence*. New York: Oxford University Press.

Regnerus, M., & Elder, G. (2003). Religion and vulnerability among low-risk adolescents. *Social Science Research, 32*, 633–658.

Regnerus, M., & Smith, C. (2005). Selection effects in studies of religious influence. *Review of Religious Research, 47*, 23–50.

Richard, A., Bell, D., & Carlson, J. (2002). Individual religiosity, moral community, and drug user treatment. *Journal for the Scientific Study of Religion, 39*, 240–246.

Ritt-Olson, A., Milam, J., Unger, J. B., Trinidad, D., Teran, L., Dent, C. W., et al. (2004). The protective influence of spirituality and "health-as-a-value" against monthly substance use among adolescents varying in risk. *Journal of Adolescent Health, 34*, 192–199.

Rodell, D. E., & Benda, B. B. (1999). Alcohol and crime among religious youth. *Alcoholism Treatment Quarterly, 17*, 53–66.

Rohrbaugh, J., & Jessor, R. (1975). Religiosity in youth: Personal control against deviant-behavior. *Journal of Personality, 43*, 136–155.

Sherkat, D. E., & Wilson, J. (1995). Preferences, constraints, and choices in religious markets: An examination of religious switching and apostasy. *Social Forces, 73*, 993–1026.

Shields, J., Broome, K., Delany, P., Fletcher, B., & Flynn, P. (2007). Religion and substance abuse treatment: Individual and program effects. *Journal for the Scientific Study of Religion, 46*, 355–371.

Sinha, J. W., Cnaan, R. A., & Gelles, R. J. (2006). Adolescent risk behaviors and religion: Findings from a national study. *Journal of Adolescence, 30*, 231–249.

Smith, C. (2003a). Theorizing religious effects among American adolescents. *Journal for the Scientific Study of Religion, 42*, 17–30.

Smith, C. (2003b). Religious participation and network closure among American adolescents. *Journal for the Scientific Study of Religion, 42*, 259–267.

Smith, C. (2003c). Religious participation and parental moral expectations and supervision of American youth. *Reviews of Religious Research, 44*, 414–424.

Smith, C., Denton, M. L., Faris, R., & Regnerus, M. (2002). Mapping American adolescent religious participation. *Journal for the Scientific Study of Religion, 41*, 597–612.

Steinman, K. J., Ferketich, A. K., & Sahr, T. (2006). The dose-response relationship of adolescent religious activity and substance use: Variation across demographic groups. *Health Education & Behavior*. July 21, 2006 (Epub ahead of print, doi:10.1177/1090198105284839).

Steinman, K. J., & Zimmerman, M. A. (2004). Religious activity and risk behavior among African American adolescents: Concurrent and developmental effects. *American Journal of Community Psychology, 33*(3–4), 151–161.

Sussman, S., Skara, S., Rodriguez, Y., & Pokhrel, P. (2006). Non drug use- and drug use-specific spirituality as one-year predictors of drug use among high-risk youth. *Substance Use and Misuse, 41*, 1801–1816.

Tonigan, J. (2007). Spirituality and alcoholics anonymous. *Southern Medical Journal, 100*, 437–440.

Tonigan, J., Miller, W., & Schermer, C. (2002). Atheists, agnostics, and alcoholics anonymous. *Journal of Studies on Alcohol, 63*, 534–541.

Turner, N. H., Ramirez, G. Y., Higginbotham, J. C., Markides, K., Wygant, A. C., & Black, S. (1994). Triethnic alcohol-use and religion, family, and gender. *Journal of Religion & Health, 33*, 341–352.

van den Bree, M. B. M., Whitmer, M. D., & Pickworth, W. B. (2004). Predictors of smoking development in a population-based sample of adolescents: A prospective study. *Journal of Adolescent Health, 35*, 172–181.

Wallace, J. M., Brown, T. N., Bachman, J. G., & Laveist, T. A. (2003). The influence of race and religion on abstinence from alcohol, cigarettes and marijuana among adolescents. *Journal of Studies on Alcohol, 64*, 843–848.

Wallace, J. M., & Forman, T. A. (1998). Religion's role in promoting health and reducing risk among American youth. *Health Education & Behavior, 25*(6), 721–741.

Wallace, J. M., Yamaguchi, R., Bachman, J. G., O'Malley, P. M., Schulenberg, J.E., & Johnston, L. D. (2007). Religiosity and adolescent substance use: The role of individual and contextual influences. *Social Problems, 54*, 308–327.

Welch, M., Tittle, C., & Grasmick, H. (2006). Christian religiosity, self-control and social conformity. *Social Forces, 84*, 1605–1623.

Wills, T. A., Gibbons, F. X., Gerrard, M., Murry, V. M., & Brody, G. H. (2003). Family communication and religiosity related to substance use and sexual behavior in early adolescence: A test for pathways through self-control and prototype perceptions. *Psychology of Addictive Behaviors, 17*, 312–323.

Wills, T. A., Yaeger, A. M., & Sandy, J. M. (2003). Buffering effect of religiosity for adolescent substance use. *Psychology of Addictive Behaviors, 17*, 24–31.

Yarnold, B. M. (1998a). The use of alcohol by Miami's adolescent public school students 1992: Peers, risk-taking, and availability as central forces. *Journal of Drug Education*, *28*, 211–233.

Yarnold, B. M. (1998b). Steroid use among Miami's public school students, 1992: Alternative subcultures: Religion and music versus peers and the "body cult". *Psychological Reports*, *82*, 19–24.

Yarnold, B. M. (1999a). Cigarette use among Miami's public school students, 1992: Fathers versus peers, availability, and family drug/alcohol problems. *Journal of Social Service Research*, *24*, 103–130.

Yarnold, B. M. (1999b). Cocaine use among Miami's public school students, 1992: Religion versus peers and availability. *Journal of Health & Social Policy*, *11*, 69–84.

Yarnold, B. M., & Patterson, V. (1998). Marijuana use among Miami's adolescents, 1992. *Journal of Health & Social Policy*, *10*, 65–79.

Chapter 10
School Prevention[1]

Zili Sloboda

Introduction

Substance abuse prevention is shaped by national and local policies directed at controlling the use of both licit and illicit substances; general understanding about the etiology of initiating substance use and of the characteristics of substance abusers; and beliefs about the "treatability/curability" of addiction. In the United States substance abuse prevention is aimed at delaying the initiation of alcohol and tobacco use to the legal age of 21 and reducing or eliminating the use of illicit substances including the misuse of prescription drugs.

Until the establishment of the National Institute on Drug Abuse (NIDA) in 1974, existing prevention efforts were generally ineffective. Among the advances in shaping more effective prevention programming was the extensive epidemiologic research base that was developed and sustained by NIDA. This work provided information regarding the origins and pathways of substance use that has been summarized by Hawkins, Catalano, and Miller (1992) (See Table 10.1). Other important influences on the direction prevention research was to take through the 1980s and 1990s were theoretically derived behavioral models such as the Social Learning Theory and the Theory of Reasoned Action that specify those attitudes, perceptions and beliefs, and behaviors leading to substance use and other problem behaviors that become the target of prevention interventions (Coie et al., 1993). Other theories of social control have also played important roles in the development of environmental or policy interventions particularly for the use of tobacco and alcohol (Ashe, Jernigan, Kline, & Galaz, 2003; Holder, 2000, 2001; Liang, Chaloupka, Nichter, & Clayton, 2003; Luke, Stamatakis, & Brownson, 2000; Ross & Chaloupka, 2003). These theories have helped explain substance use and how best to prevent such use (Flay & Petraitis, 2003).

Until the late 1980s and early 1990s, substance abuse interventions used a public health framework to define both the targets of the interventions and the mechanisms that were applied in the interventions. However, the application of this framework

---

[1] Parts of this chapter are adapted from Sloboda (2004).

C.G. Leukefeld et al. (eds.) *Adolescent Substance Abuse,*
DOI: 10.1007/978-0-387-09732-9_10, © Springer Science+Business Media LLC 2009

Table 10.1 Risk and protective factors (Hawkins et al., 1992)

Risk factors	Protective factors
• Personal – Early Childhood	• Personal – Early Childhood
– Family history of substance use or mental illness	– Warm attachment to mother
– Poor attachment to mother	– Psychological stability of mother
– Poor family management	– Good family management
– Family conflict	– Good temperament; emotional stability
– Physiological predisposition (genetic or biochemical)	– Low sensation seeking and high harm avoidance
– Peer rejection	– Good parental modeling
• Personal – Later Childhood/Adolescence	• Personal - Later Childhood/Adolescence
– Early antisocial behavior with aggression	– Academic achievement
– Academic failure	– Good peer relationships
– Low commitment to school	– Involvement in prosocial activities
– Positive attitudes toward substance use	– Rewarding family structure
– Alienation or rebelliousness	– Parental monitoring
– Association with drug using peers	– Quality parental involvement with child's activities
– Early use of drugs	– Clear parental rules regarding the use of tobacco, alcohol, or other drugs
	– Strong school bonding
	– Strong bonding with prosocial peers
• Environmental	• Environmental
– Economic and social deprivation	– Limited accessibility to alcohol, tobacco, and drugs
– Availability of substances	– Limited exposure to ads promoting use of tobacco and alcohol
– Low neighborhood attachment/community disorganization	– Parental education/employment
– Difficult transitions and mobility	– Clear antisubstance use norms in community
– Community norms favorable to substance use	

that consisted of three levels of intervention: primary, secondary, and tertiary, reflecting the disease status of the individual, group, or population being addressed, did not satisfactorily meet the needs of those designing programs for substance abuse or mental health problems. Gordon (1983) suggested moving to a more empirically based approach, one that weighs the risk to an individual of getting a disease against the costs associated by participating in an intervention. This new model was adapted as "the mental health intervention spectrum" by the Institute of Medicine Committee on Prevention of Mental Disorders and published in the Committee's report, Reducing Risks for Mental Disorders (Mrazek & Haggerty, 1994). Three levels of prevention were defined: universal, selective, and indicated, each addressing the varying degrees of risk found in the targeted population.

Universal programs are designed to address general populations while selective programs target those segments of the population that present greater than normal risk to develop a disorder and indicated programs focus on those subgroups that exhibit signs or symptoms of developing a disorder. This nomenclature is currently in use among substance abuse prevention researchers and practitioners.

Incidence and Prevalence

There are two major sources of information on the incidence and prevalence of substance use among adolescents from the United States: the National Survey on Drug Use and Health (NSDUH; formerly the National Household Survey on Drug Abuse) conducted by the Substance Abuse and Mental Health Services Administration (SAMHSA) and the Monitoring the Future Study (MTF) conducted by the University of Michigan with support from a grant from the NIDA. Until 2005, the NSDUH collected data for selected persons aged 12 and older residing in a representative national sample of households. A new coordinated design was developed for the period beginning in 2005 through 2009 that would provide state-level estimates. Eight states have samples large enough to directly produce state estimates (California, Florida, Illinois, Michigan, New York, Ohio, Pennsylvania, and Texas). Smaller sample sizes are used to produce estimates using small area estimation techniques for the remaining 42 states. Data are collected by trained interviewers using computer-assisted interviewing (CAI) methods for most questions whereby interviewers read questions from a computer screen and enter the responses on the computer and audio computer-assisted self-interviewing (ACASI) methods. For more sensitive questions, particularly those related to substance use, the ACASI allows the respondents to read the questions on the computer screen and enter their own responses on the computer.

The MTF collects data for students in grades 8, 10, and 12 who attend a national representative sample of private and public schools. Data on substance use is collected through self-administered surveys completed in the classroom. The survey was initiated in 1975 with 12th graders and was expanded to include 8th and 10th graders in 1991.

Both surveys ask about substance use for three time periods: lifetime use (ever used at least once in lifetime), annual use (used at least once in the past 12 months), and current use (used at least once in the past 30 days). For some substances, respondents are queried about daily use.

Since the data collection methodology changed for the NSDUH in 2002, a continuous analysis of prior substance use trends is not possible. SAMHSA recommends that trends be viewed for the years prior to 2001 and then from 2002 and beyond. The most recent report from the NSDUH estimates that 19.7 million (8.1%) US residents aged 12 and older used an illicit drug at least once in the 30-day period prior to survey (current use). Marijuana accounted for 74.2% of this use; 54.5% used only marijuana and 19.6% used it in combination with other illicit drugs. The misuse of psychotherapeutics was the next major category of use with an estimated 2.6% of respondents reporting current use followed by cocaine (1.0%) and hallucinogens (0.4%). Estimates for current illicit drug use are highest for those aged 18–20 (22.3%) followed by those 21–25 (18.7%) and those 16–17 (17.0%). There were no statistically significant differences in these percentages since 2002.

The average age of initiation of illicit drug use has been between 15 and 17 since national surveys were established. For this reason, the NSDUH includes an over-sample of youth aged 12–17 years. In 2005, it was estimated that 9.9% or over 2.5 million youth had used one or more illicit drugs in the 30 days prior to survey (current use). The distribution of use of specific drugs for this age group is: marijuana, 6.8%; psychotherapeutics including pain relievers, tranquilizers, stimulants, and sedatives, 3.3%; inhalants, 1.2%; hallucinogens, 0.8%; and, cocaine, 0.6%. These rates increase by age so that the overall rate of current illicit drug use is 3.8% for those aged 12–13, 8.9% for those aged 14–15, and 17% for those aged 16–17.

The MTF focuses primarily on 8th-, 10th-, and 12th-grade youth. Like the NSDUH, the MTF conducts its surveys on an annual basis. With the change in the method of data collection in the NSDUH, the estimates of illicit drug use rates have become more comparable to those from the MTF. In the 2005 report, the equivalent rates for illicit drug use overall for 8th (13–14 years old) and 10th (15–16 years old) graders are 8.5% and 17.3%, respectively. For 12th (17–18 years old) graders, the rate is 23.1%, comparable to the 22.3% reported by the NSDUH for those 18–20 years of age.

The use of alcohol and tobacco, the licit drugs, for adolescents is of concern to prevention specialists for three major reasons. First, these substances are considered harmful to children and adolescents (Brook, Balka, Ning, Whiteman, & Finch, 2006; Georgiades & Boyle, 2007). In addition, in many jurisdictions, including school property, possession of tobacco and alcohol products by persons under the age of 18 is an offense subject to fines and other penalties (e.g., suspension, education, or community service). Finally, longitudinal studies of adolescents have found that those who use tobacco and alcohol are at higher risk to using marijuana so that tobacco and alcohol for children and adolescents are considered "gateway" drugs (Kandel, 1975).

As tobacco and alcohol are not controlled substances and considered legal for use by those over proscribed ages of 18 and 21, they are more widely used in the general population. Estimated rates of tobacco use have shown a response to the growing concern about the health effects from first-hand and secondary smoke. For instance, just for the NSDUH period 2002 through 2005 the percentage of persons aged 12 and older who smoked at least one cigarette within the 30 days prior to survey decreased significantly from 26.0% to 24.9%. For adolescents aged 12–17, there was a greater drop from 13.0% to 10.8%. In the MTF survey, for 8th and 10th graders similar decreases are noted. For 8th and 10th graders, the peak year for cigarette use was 1996 when it was estimated that 21.0% and 30.4%, respectively, had smoked at least one cigarette in the 30 days prior to survey compared to 9.3% and 14.9% in 2005. For 12th graders, for whom there is data from 1975 to the present, the peak year for cigarette use was 1976 when the estimate was 38.8% compared to 23.2% in 2005.

Prevention in Schools

The school is an appropriate setting for prevention strategies for several reasons. The most obvious is that the school is where children in the United States spend a great proportion of their time. In addition, the school remains a major socialization institution to reinforce societal values, norms, and acceptable behaviors. Furthermore, the school is a protective environment for children (Schaps & Solomon, 2003) where they should feel safe.

In order to learn the nature and extent of school-based activities that are provided to address a number of problem behaviors such as substance use, violence, accidents, and risky sexual behaviors, Gottfredson and Gottfredson (2001) conducted a survey of principals of a national probability sample of 848 public, private, and catholic schools. They found that the typical school offered a large range of such activities, from 0 to 66 within individual schools, with an average of 14 activities per school. These activities included rules and policies; information on topics such as substance use, health, mental health, and violence; and curriculum instruction. However, as the authors point out, the effectiveness of most of these activities in reducing or eliminating problem behaviors has not been demonstrated.

The process of translating effective prevention approaches to these problem behaviors, and specifically, substance abuse, however, did not begin until the mid 1990s. Concern about moving the findings from prevention research from the research setting to the community prompted the NIDA-sponsored first National Conference of Drug Abuse Prevention Research: *Putting Research to Work for the Community* in 1996. The conference was designed to foster a dialogue between researchers and practitioners. One of the major outcomes of that conference was a booklet, *Preventing Drug Use among Children and Adolescents: A Research-Based Guide* (Sloboda & David, 1997). As Bukoski writes, "This publication clearly established the beginning of the evidence-based drug abuse prevention movement that has emerged across the country …" (Bukoski, 2003, p. 6). The guide was written to translate research for community-based practitioners including findings regarding the origins and pathways to drug use and abuse and planning prevention interventions. One part of the guide examined the consistent elements of effective prevention programming drawn from NIDA-funded research (Table 10.2). These elements or principles set the stage for a number of other events that promoted evidence-based prevention programming. Since the publication of the guide, the United States Department of Education (DOE) Safe and Drug-Free Schools and Communities Act (SDFSCA) and the Center for Substance Abuse Prevention of the SAMHSA have created review processes through which programs are added to lists of effective and exemplary programs. Most of these interventions are school-based, representing the history of the field that has been more school-centered, particularly when addressing illicit drug issues.

Prior to this time, the SDFSCA program had come under scrutiny and criticism as to how it funded over $6 billion for school-based programming to improve school safety (Sherman, 2000). In response to such pressure and after NIDA's publication of the guide in 1997, the SDFSCA staff issued the *Principles of*

Table 10.2 Principles of prevention (Sloboda & David, 1997)

- Prevention programs should enhance protective factors and reverse or reduce risk factors.
- Prevention programs should address all forms of drug abuse, alone or in combination, including the underage use of legal drugs (e.g., tobacco or alcohol); the use of illegal drugs (e.g., marijuana or heroin); and the inappropriate use of legally obtained substances (e.g., inhalants), prescription medications, or over-the-counter drugs.
- Family-based prevention programs should enhance family bonding and relationships and include parenting skills; practice in developing, discussing, and enforcing family policies on substance abuse; and training in drug education and information.
- Prevention programs can be designed to intervene as early as preschool to address risk factors for drug abuse, such as aggressive behavior, poor social skills, and academic difficulties.
- Prevention programs for elementary school children should target improving academic and social-emotional learning to address risk factors for drug abuse, such as early aggression, academic failure, and school dropout.
- Prevention programs for middle or junior high and high school students should increase academic and social competence.
- Prevention programs aimed at general populations at key transition points, such as the transition to middle school, can produce beneficial effects even among high-risk families and children. Such interventions do not single out risk populations and, therefore, reduce labeling and promote bonding to school and community.
- Community prevention programs that combine two or more effective programs, such as family-based and school-based programs, can be more effective than a single program alone.
- Community prevention programs reaching populations in multiple settings – for example, schools, clubs, faith-based organizations, and the media – are most effective when they present consistent, community-wide messages in each setting.
- When communities adapt programs to match their needs, community norms, or differing cultural requirements, they should retain core elements of the original research-based intervention.
- Prevention programs should be long-term with repeated interventions (i.e., booster programs) to reinforce the original prevention goals. Research shows that the benefits from middle school prevention programs diminish without follow-up programs in high school.
- Prevention programs should include teacher training on good classroom management practices, such as rewarding appropriate student behavior. Such techniques help to foster students' positive behavior, achievement, academic motivation, and school bonding.
- Prevention programs are most effective when they employ interactive techniques, such as peer discussion groups and parent role-playing, that allow for active involvement in learning about drug abuse and reinforcing skills.
- Research-based prevention programs can be cost-effective. Similar to earlier research, recent research shows that for each dollar invested in prevention, a savings of up to $10 in treatment for alcohol or other substance abuse can be seen.

Prevention in 1998. The Principles require local school districts and other recipients of SDFSCA funds to develop programs that are based on (1) an assessment of the incidence of violence and illegal drug use, (2) analysis of data regarding risk factors, (3) established set of performance measures to ensure a safe and drug-free environment, and (4) sound research that demonstrates the program is effective (either selected from SDFSCA and SAMHSA lists or with other documentation of effectiveness). In addition, school districts are expected to evaluate the extent to which these programs meet established performance measures (U.S. Department of Education, 1998).

Over the next few years, a number of national studies had been conducted to determine the extent to which school districts know about the SDFSCA principles and carry them out and the extent to which school districts implement evidence-based prevention programming (Ennett et al., 2003; Hallfors & Godette, 2002; Ringwalt et al., 2002). In general, these studies found that most school districts did know about the principles but few delivered evidence-based interventions. For instance, Ringwalt and colleagues (2002) found that only 26.8% of schools used at least one of the ten listed effective curricula. Public schools were more likely to use effective curricula (34.6%) compared to private schools (12.6%). Furthermore, even though schools may use evidence-based curricula, the programs may not be delivered as designed. Ennett et al. (2003) found that 62.25% of substance use prevention staff in middle schools taught effective research-based content and 17.44% used effective instructional strategies. Far fewer, 14.23%, used both effective content and instructional strategies.

It is clear that some schools do implement prevention programs effectively. Payne and associates (Payne, Gottfredson, & Gottfredson, 2006) found that implementation quality was associated with both school and program factors. Those that were found to have high-quality implementation engaged in local (within schools) program selection, integrated prevention programming into school operations, had principal support, had the organizational capacity (capacity for program development, teacher–principal communication, amenability to implementation, and no obstacles to implementation), and had the means for standardization (e.g., use of an instructor's manual). Many of these findings are supported by other studies (Ringwalt, Ennett, Vincus, Rohrbach, & Simons-Rudolph, 2004; Rohrbach, Ringwalt, Ennett, & Vincus, 2005; Wenter et al., 2002).

Given the widespread availability of the Drug Abuse Resistance Education (DARE) program, reported by Hallfors and Godette (2002) in 80% of school districts, the history of DARE curricula evaluations warrants special mention here. It is important to separate DARE as a delivery system for prevention programming from the curricula that DARE officer-instructors deliver. The delivery system consists of a network of law enforcement agencies throughout the United States and over 50 countries worldwide. There is no other drug abuse delivery system with such a widespread appeal. This network is organized within a hierarchical framework from communities to states/provincial to national levels (Merrill, Pinsky, Killeya-Jones, Sloboda, & Dilascio, 2006). The DARE-officer instructors can deliver one or more of four curricula: (1) kindergarten through 4th grade, (2) 5th grade, (3) 7th grade or middle school, and (4) 9th grade or high school. The content of these curricula has been developed and periodically revised by educators to reflect available curriculum and prevention research at the time. Although DARE-America (the umbrella organization) recommends that all curricula be delivered within a school district, the availability of instructors and funding dictate which actually are provided. Information from school districts indicates that the vast majority deliver the curricula only for elementary school students (Hallfors & Godette, 2002). For this reason most of the evaluations of DARE programming that were conducted to date included only the elementary or 5th-grade curriculum. Most of these evaluations showed short-term effects that dissipated over time (Clayton, Cattarello, & Johnstone, 1996; Dukes, Stein, & Ullman, 1997; Ennett et al., 1994; Lynam et al., 1999; Norton, Bieler, Ennett, & Zarkin, 1996; Rosenbaum & Hanson, 1998). These results suggest that prevention programming targeting elementary school children must be supported by other curricula or boosters in middle and high school when students are most at risk for initiating substance use.

Specific School-Based Preventive Interventions

Although one of the NIDA principles of prevention, Principle 2 [Prevention programs should address all forms of drug abuse, alone or in combination, including the underage use of legal drugs (e.g., tobacco or alcohol); the use of illegal drugs (e.g., marijuana or heroin); and the inappropriate use of legally obtained substances (e.g., inhalants), prescription medications, or over-the-counter drugs)], encourages targeting multiple substances, not all interventions are designed to address more than one substance nor do all interventions have a consistent impact on more than one substance. A review of the National Registry of Evidence-Based Prevention Programs and Practices indicates that of the 23 school-based programs listed, two addressed only tobacco and four, alcohol (http://www.nrepp.samhsa.gov/index.htm).

Flay (2007) discusses the long-term impact of effective school-based prevention programs on tobacco use. He limited his review to programs that have 15 or more sessions, and that had both short- and long-term effects. Only three school-based programs and four school-plus-community programs met these criteria. The school-based programs that met these criteria included the Tobacco and Alcohol Prevention Project (Hansen, Malotte, & Fielding, 1988), Life Skills Training (LST), and Project SHOUT (Students Helping Others Understand Tobacco) (Elder et al., 1993). Two of the school-plus-community programs were part of a number of interventions that focused on preventing heart disease and include the North Karalia Project (Vartianien, Pallonen, McAlister, Koskela, & Puska, 1983) and the Minnesota Class of 89 (Perry, Kelder, & Siller, 1989). The other two programs, the Midwestern Prevention Project that included a school component, Project STAR (Students Taught Awareness and Resistance) (Pentz et al., 1989), and the Vermont Mass Media Project (Worden et al., 1988), added structured mass media programs with messages that supported those delivered in the classroom.

He then created another grouping of programs that consisted of those programs that had large effects and were large enough to suggest medium- and long-term impact. In this grouping are four school-based programs and one school-plus-community program. The school-based programs included the Adolescent Alcohol Prevention Trial that targeted alcohol but produced effects on cigarette smoking (Hansen & Graham, 1991; Taylor, Graham, Cumsille & Hansen, 2000), Towards No Tobacco (Sussman et al., 1993), Know Your Body (Walter & Wynder, 1989), and the Good Behavior Game (Furr-Holden, Ialongo, Anthony, Petras, & Kellam, 2004).

The only school-plus-community program that was in this grouping of programs was Project SixTeen (Biglan, Ary, Smolkowski, Duncan, & Black, 2000). This program included several community interventions: media advocacy, youth antitobacco activities, materials for families on tobacco use, and reducing youth access to tobacco products.

In the summary of his meta-analyses of the findings from these studies, Flay concludes that interactive social influences or social competence smoking prevention programs that provide at least 15 lessons offered in upper elementary or middle school and into high school produced the best medium-term results when students were in high school. The added community dimension increased the expected effect size. It should be noted that only two of these programs had been on the NREPP list and in the case of the Midwestern Prevention Project, only Project STAR is listed.

The National Research Council of the Institute of Medicine convened a committee on Developing a Strategy to Reduce and Prevent Underage Drinking and produced a report, *Reducing Underage Drinking: A Collective Responsibility* (Bonnie & O'Connell, 2004). In this report, school-based approaches to impact youth alcohol use were reviewed. Although overall effects of these approaches are modest, several programs have been found to be effective in reducing use, particularly among those who had not initiated drinking. Those interventions that establish nonuse norms, critically address alcohol advertising, and utilize interactive teaching methods have shown promising results across a range of students (Perry, Kelder, Murry, & Klepp, 1992). The report summarizes intervention components that appear to be essential in effective programs designed to reduce alcohol use (pp. 195–198). These include (1) having a multicomponent and integrated focus to create systemwide changes integrating interventions in schools and in the community like programs such as Project Northland (Perry et al., 1996); (2) providing sufficient dose and follow-up using multiyear programs or boosters; (3) establishing norms that support nonuse of alcohol; (4) training parents on parental monitoring and supervision, particularly around alcohol access; (5) creating programs that are interactive involving active participation of students; (6) implementing programs with fidelity; (7) focusing heavily on youth access to alcohol; (8) ensuring that nonuse norms and restricted access to alcohol are institutionalized; (9) avoiding focusing on information only and on congregating youth at high risk; and (10) providing interventions that support social and emotional skill development.

Designing Prevention Programs

What "works" in prevention remains an unanswered issue. The field of prevention science is young with research having some success only within the last 20 years. How to determine success and understanding what makes an intervention successful remain questions without definitive answers. The focus of NIDA's first prevention conference in 1996 was to create a forum for discussions between researchers and practitioners, but it also afforded an opportunity to put forward the findings from epidemiologic and prevention research that had implications for community planning and implementation of prevention interventions. The Research Guide (Sloboda & David, 1997) was designed to summarize this research so it would have meaning for the practitioner and program planner. As such it was formatted into three major sections. The first section presented the principles of prevention, an attempt to extract consistent findings from the research on effective interventions. The second section emphasized the link between risk and protective factors and substance use and the ways in which interventions could be used to reduce risk and enhance protection. This section also outlined ways in which planners could choose interventions to address their community needs or could assess ongoing prevention programming and activities within their schools and communities. The final section presented précis of interventions that showed effective outcomes at least 1 year postintervention based on NIDA-funded research.

Meta-analyses of programs to prevention substance use date to the late 1980s with perhaps Rundall and Bruvold (1988) and Bangert-Drowns (1988) being in the lead. These analyses were followed by a series conducted by Tobler, Lessard, Marshall, Ochshorn, and Roona (1999; Tobler, 1986, 1992, 2000). The objective of these analyses was to determine elements common to programs with positive outcomes. These meta-analyses used data from large numbers of studies. Other researchers conducted more qualitative analyses comparing the components of effective programs against each other (Dusenbury & Falco, 1995; Gottfredson & Wilson, 2003). Both of these approaches have identified the same elements: addressing normative beliefs held by adolescents regarding the prevalence of substance use by their peers; reinforcing perceived negative consequences of substance use, especially as related to adolescence; and providing life skills such as communication, decision making, and resistance and opportunities to practice these skills around real-life situations. In addition, these studies find that active engagement of students in the education process provides the necessary structure for students to internalize what they are learning. Recent studies of programs found effective in earlier years suggest that other factors may be at work to effectively impact substance using behaviors (Longshore, Ellickson, McCaffrey, & St. Clair, 2007; St. Pierre, Osgood, Mincemoyer, Kaltreider, & Kauth, 2005) or those factors found successful among adolescents of the 1980s and 1990s may not achieve the same outcomes for adolescents of the twenty-first century. Thus, the next section should be viewed within the context of the periods in which the interventions were designed and assessed.

Applying Research to Practice in Schools

There are three aspects of the school environment that lend themselves specifically to substance use prevention intervention: (1) school culture, that is, norms, beliefs, and expectancies, and school bonding, that is, connecting the individual to the school experience and community; (2) school policy or social control, the most common approach establishing disciplinary policies and procedures; and (3) class-room curriculum or packaged programs.

School Culture and School Bonding

The literature that describes the risk and protective factors associated with the initiation of substance use not only indicates the determinants that increase the vulnerability of children and adolescents to substance use but also suggests an individual–environmental interaction (Tarter et al., 1999). Prevention programs that address this interaction intend to make the school environment more attractive to students to help students develop more prosocial attitudes and affiliations and to engage in more prosocial behaviors. The intent is to increase self-efficacy and school bonding and decrease the likelihood that students will use alcohol, tobacco, or other drugs.

The common elements of strategies to create a positive normative environment for children include the following:

- Creating antisubstance/nonsubstance using settings.
- Dispelling misconceptions regarding expectancies (positive experiences) associated with the use of tobacco, alcohol, and other drugs.
- Establishing comprehensive programs that involve students, school administrators, and, when appropriate, parents/caregivers.

An example of a program designed to change school culture is the Child Development Project (CDP) (now termed Caring School Community Program) designed by Eric Schaps of the Developmental Studies Center. This program targets children when they are 5–12 years old. It is designed to promote school bonding, to enhance students' interpersonal skills and commitment to positive values, and to develop both a classroom and schoolwide atmosphere of caring (safety, respect, and helpfulness). The long-term outcomes are the reduction or elimination of the use of alcohol, tobacco, and marijuana and involvement in violent behaviors and other risky behaviors. The three program components consist of (1) intensive classroom activities that focus on cooperative learning, a literature-based reading and language arts curriculum, and developmental discipline; (2) schoolwide activities designed to involve teachers, parents, students, and extended family members in building a caring school community; and (3) family activities that are designed to bring classroom experiences into the home, promoting communication between students and their families. The program was evaluated in the 1990s using a quasi-experimental design with six demonstration and six comparison schools and their ~5,500 students from school districts. Assessments were made at baseline and then each year for 3 years. The findings showed statistically significant lower rates of alcohol and marijuana use and marginally lower involvement in delinquent behaviors for students who attended schools that implemented the CDP program as it was designed (Battistich, Schaps, Watson, Solomon, & Lewis, 2000).

Although programs to impact school culture also increase school bonding, there are a number of programs that focus primarily on school bonding per se. Common elements or principles of school bonding programs include the following:

- Focusing on early years; that is, preschool to middle school.
- Enhancing competency in reading and math.
- Providing interpersonal skills to enable students to relate positively with peers and adults.
- Involving parents in communication and parenting skills and in school activities.

There are several effective programs that emphasize school bonding. Among these are the Skills, Opportunities and Recognition (SOAR) program (Hawkins, Catalano, Kosterman, Abbott, & Hill, 1999), Incredible Years (Webster-Stratton, Reid, & Hammond, 2001), and Early Risers Skills for Success (August, Lee, Bloomquist, Realmuto, & Hektner, 2003).

The SOAR program developed at the University of Washington by the Social Development Research Group emphasizes positive personal development and academic success. This goal is achieved by providing opportunities for active involvement of elementary school aged-children in their family and in school with consistent positive recognition for their positive attitudes and behavior. The program has components for students, teachers, and parents. The student component is designed to develop acceptable social skills both in school and at home. The teacher component focuses on improving classroom management and instruction methods to increase academic skills and behavior. The parent component emphasizes developmentally appropriate parenting skills. Using a nonrandomized design with follow-up 6 years after the intervention, three treatment conditions were created: (1) full intervention group in which interventions occurred from grades 1 through 6; (2) late intervention group with interventions delivered in only grades 5 and 6; and (3) control group with no special intervention. Five hundred and ninety-eight students with parental consent were followed through age 18. It was found that students in the full implementation program had statistically significant improvements in their attachment to school and in their academic performance and had significantly lower rates of heavy drinking and violent behavior (Hawkins et al., 1999).

School Policy

Research examining school policies related to substance use within the school building have received relatively meager attention over the past two decades. School policies are especially appealing to address substance use as large numbers of the target population can be affected and the associated costs appear to be minimal. Pentz (2003) suggests there are four types of formal regulations found in schools: (1) those that focus on the production or distribution of substances and those that regulate price and the conditions of use; (2) those that control the "flow of information" regarding substance use such as warning labels; (3) those that directly regulate consumption (e.g., use of prescriptions and monitoring use by physicians); and (4) those that declare use as illegal (e.g., minimum drinking age, sanctions against possession of illicit drugs.)

Common elements or principles of effective school policy approaches to impact substance use include the following:

- Reducing or eliminating access to and availability of tobacco, alcohol, or other drugs.
- Addressing infractions of policies with positive sanctions by providing counseling or treatment and special services to the students rather than punishing them through suspension or expulsion.
- Policies should not disrupt normal school functioning.
- Policies should address the full range of drug-using behaviors from initiation to progression to abuse and dependence and relapse.
- Policies should have a small number of focused goals.
- Policies should specify the substances that are targeted.
- Policies should reflect and be reflected in other community prevention efforts.
- The student body, faculty, and students should be involved in developing the policy.
- Policies should provide positive reinforcement for policy compliance.
- Policies should provide systematic training for policy administrators and educate the target population about participation in policy aims.

Direct interventions mentioned by Pentz (2003) with specific relevance for youth consist of drug testing in schools and athletic events. Other environmental policies such as roadside testing for alcohol use; lower blood alcohol content (BAC) laws; higher minimum drinking laws; and drug and alcohol possession checks at school and public events can involve the school and other community organizations through direct involvement of school administrators in designing these policies or incorporating discussion of the legal consequences of alcohol use by minors in the school curriculum or special assemblies. Of these approaches, road-side checks and testing, lower BAC, higher minimum drinking age laws, and identification checks for the purchase of tobacco have been evaluated and found to be effective in decreasing alcohol-related accidents and tobacco purchases by youth (Forster, Wolfson, Murray, Wagenaar, & Claxton, 1997; Hingson et al., 1996; Hingson, Heeren, & Winter, 2000; Holder, 1993; Wolfson et al., 1996). It must be pointed out that in-school policies for youth are effective only when the sanctions are supportive and positive. These sanctions must be developed a priori and should be implemented expeditiously.

Other types of effective policies that extend beyond the school building but that can involve the school focus on the vendor controlling availability and access by youth. These include removal of cigarette vending machines, alerting parents about laws against serving alcohol to minors, local alcohol server and tobacco sales staff training to ensure understanding of sale restrictions to minors and the need to "card" customers, "sting" operations to determine that these deterrents are implemented, and follow through on penalties for sales of alcohol and tobacco to underage youth. (Altman, Rasenick-Douss, Foster, & Tye, 1991; Forster et al., 1997; Forster & Wolfson, 1998).

Just a note here on a recent movement in schools to randomly test students in school for drugs. In 1995, the Unites States Supreme Court upheld a school's right to conduct random drug tests of student athletes without any suspicion of use of drugs, and in 2002, the Supreme Court carried this decision further by upholding school districts' rights to extend testing to students participating in other extracurricular activities (Yamaguchi, Johnston, & O'Malley, 2003). Support for the rulings was based on observations that when drug testing was administered, drug use in the schools decreased. Goldberg and his group (2003, 2007) have conducted two studies on the impact of drug testing on high school athletes, the Student Athlete Testing Using Random Notification. In the first study, although the researchers found that drug testing did result in decreased reported use of drugs, they caution against the use of this approach until a larger, randomized longitudinal study is conducted (Goldberg et al., 2003). The larger study was completed and the findings, based on self-report, indicate no differences between control and experimental students on past month drug use (Goldberg et al., 2007). The researchers conclude that drug testing is not an effective deterrent to drug use and actually may increase the risk for future substance use.

Classroom Curriculum

Probably the most frequently occurring prevention approach is the use of a classroom curriculum that focuses on the prevention of substance use. A survey of Safe and Drug Free Schools Coordinators in a sample of 81 school districts in 11 states conducted in 1999 indicated that 80% delivered a prevention curriculum to their students. Of these 80%, 26% include elementary, middle, and high school programs, 42% reported that their districts focus primarily on the elementary school level (generally kindergarten through 5th or 6th grade), 26% on the middle school level (generally 6th or 7th grades to 8th grade), and 6% on the high school level (generally 9th through 12th grades) (Hallfors, Sporer, Pankratz, & Godette, 2000). As such, many types of classroom curricula have been developed and evaluated over the past 25 years.

Several researchers have conducted meta-analyses of the data from studies of both universal and indicated programs (Gottfredson & Wilson, 2003; Tobler, 1986, 1992; Tobler et al., 1999) while others conducted program content analyses and surveys of prevention researchers (Dusenbury & Falco, 1995; Sloboda & David, 1997) to determine common elements of effective interventions. There have been consistent findings across all of these approaches.

Common elements of universal/indicated curriculum include the following:

- Dispelling misconceptions regarding the normative nature and expectancies of substance use (i.e., the prevalence and positive/negative effects of use).
- Impacting perceptions of risks associated with substance use for children and adolescents (i.e., emphasizing the effects students will experience now not when they are adults).

- Providing and practicing what are called life skills that include making decisions, especially about initiating or continuing substance use; communicating these decisions; and resistance skills to refuse the use of tobacco, alcohol, and illicit drugs using authentic scenarios.
- Providing interventions and boosters over multiple years into middle and high school when students are most at risk.

Effective universal and indicated curricula-style interventions have been developed. Most available school curriculum-based programs would be considered universal as they target general populations that include students at different levels of risk for initiating the use of alcohol, tobacco, or other drugs. There are a number of indicated programs that target students who are considered at higher risk to initiate the use of these substances because they are not doing well in school and are experiencing high numbers of absences, suspensions, or expulsions. There are few that could be considered selective programs, that is, that address students who may have initiated low levels of substance use or are expressing other problem behaviors.

There are several examples of effective universal curricula available. These include LST (Botvin, Baker, Dusenbury, Tortu, & Botvin, 1995), Project ALERT (Ellickson, Bell, & McGuigan, 1993), and Project STAR (Pentz et al., 1989). LST developed at Cornell University by Botvin and his group has been one of the most cited effective universal curricula in the United States. LST is a program that enhances competencies of the participants. It consists of a 24-session elementary school program delivered over 3 years (3rd or 4th to 6th grades) and/or a 30-session middle school also to be delivered over 3 years (6th or 7th to 8th grades). The three major aims of the program are to provide students with skills that enable them to challenge common misconceptions regarding the use of tobacco, alcohol, and other drugs and to learn the skills needed to resist pressures to engage in the use of these substances, personal self-management skills that help them set and keep personal goals and to make well-thought out decisions, and other social skills to communicate effectively and clearly with their peers and adults. LST has been evaluated with a number of diverse populations with consistently good results. For instance, in one evaluation study in which 56 public schools were randomized to an experimental or control condition, 3,597 participating students were followed to the 12th grade. The study found that 44% fewer students exposed to a program of 15 lessons in the 7th grade, 10 booster lessons in the 8th grade, and 5 booster lessons in the 9th grade used drugs and 66% fewer used a combination of tobacco, alcohol, and marijuana (Botvin et al., 1995). In other studies conducted by this same group of researchers, it was found that even without the boosters in the 8th and 9th grades there had been a reduction of between 56% and 67% in the number of students becoming smokers who were nonsmokers at baseline without the two additional years of booster lessons. When the 2 years of booster lessons are added, the percentage of nonuse of tobacco increased to 87% (Botvin & Griffin, 2003).

Similar results were achieved with the other programs. One caveat is that these studies were conducted when substance use rates were higher than they are currently and when fewer schools were providing prevention programs including those schools that might be assigned to a control condition.

Interventions That Do Not Work

The substance abuse prevention field has had a mixed history. The lack of consistency over time is related to the failure of theory to support interventions and the failure of having sound statistical methodology available to enable researchers to control for the challenges associated with prospective studies such as missing data and having longitudinal measures that change across the study period because of the natural development of adolescents (Botvin & Griffin, 2003).

In her 2000 article, Tobler summarized what does and does not work in interventions. She found the following content and delivery features that do not work.

- Content
    - Failure to include short-term consequences
    - Failure to address perceptions of peer drug use
    - Failure to address media influences on prodrug attitudes
    - Addressing only ethical/moral decision making
    - Teaching values
    - Failure to provide interpersonal skills, particularly drug refusal skills
    - Having only an intrapersonal focus
    - Focusing only on self-esteem building
- Delivery
    - Passive participation primary delivery strategy
    - Didactic or lectures only
    - Having teacher-centered class discussions
    - Having unstructured dialogue sessions
    - Depending primarily on effective classroom management techniques without a drug program

Recommendations for School-Based Prevention and Health Promotion

This chapter offers the following guidance to school administrators considering the implementation of substance abuse prevention programming in their schools. Probably the most important recommendation is for the administrators to recognize that substance use is not the sole problem of the school. Findings from prevention research studies show that school-based programming is more effective when supported by community and/or family components (Flay, 2007). There are a number of other issues that need to be thought about when selecting school-based substance abuse prevention interventions. Botvin and Griffin (2003) mention some key issues: timing of the interventions, delivery by peers and/or adults, use of interactive teaching approaches, targeting multiple substances, targeting minority groups, durability of interventions, and implementation fidelity.

- There is agreement in the prevention field that prevention is a process that takes place across the lifespan. The factors related to increasing the risks for initiating substance use occur across developmental stages suggesting that interventions should take place at key developmental points including infancy, early childhood, childhood, preadolescence, and adolescence. Early interventions with identified vulnerable children may be most effective in the long term. Yet the expected outcomes from interventions for each developmental stage are not clear.
- Several studies and meta-analyses (Tobler, 1986, 1992; Tobler et al., 1999) suggest that interventions delivered by same age or slightly older peer leaders are more effective than when delivered by adults. On the other hand, as Botvin and Griffin (2003) point out peer leaders alone may not have the maturity to manage a classroom or to engage students in small group or open discussion, particularly when the program heavily emphasizes skills building. Their suggestion is to use peer leaders in supportive roles such as assisting with program activities with adults taking the lead in delivery.
- The meta-analyses also found that prevention programs that engage students in the learning process had better outcomes than those programs that used primarily didactic presentations. Recent reanalyses of Tobler's data (Robert Wood Johnson Foundation, 2007) suggest that interactive programs are more effective for middle school rather than high school students.
- The sequencing of substance use suggests that the risk for using marijuana is increased if a young adolescent has used alcohol or tobacco, particularly if this use was initiated in childhood or early adolescence. Therefore, prevention programs should address multiple substances. The social tolerance is unequal for each of these substances and some programs may be less effective for one or more of these substances (Werch & Owen, 2002).
- The issue of adaptation versus implementation fidelity is one of the great challenges to the prevention field. Implementation fidelity addresses the degree to which the curriculum content and delivery style consistently and completely match that of the original tested program. Often, a program taken from a research setting to the "real world" will undergo changes to meet the needs of the school or of the instructor. Understanding the curriculum design and key elements of the program is important. Sound training helps instructors comprehend why program design is essential and provides a basis for a commitment to prevention. The establishment of a monitoring system to assess program implementation and providing ongoing technical assistance would ensure fidelity of implementation.
- Finally, school administrators should be mindful of the fact that the field of drug abuse prevention is relatively new. The knowledge that is accumulating from prevention researchers changes as intervention strategies and statistical methodologies become more sophisticated. In addition, the research that serves to guide prevention intervention development, that is, epidemiology and behavioral science, is also evolving, and, finally, our children's cultural worlds and influences are ever changing. What programs may be effective for adolescents today may not be as effective for their younger siblings when they enter their teen years. Such changes suggest constant attention to updating prevention messages and strategies.

References

Altman, D. G., Rasenick-Douss, L., Foster, V., & Tye, J. B. (1991). Sustained effects of an educational program to reduce sales of cigarettes to minors. *American Journal of Public Health, 81,* 891–893.

Ashe, M., Jernigan, D., Kline, R., & Galaz, R. (2003). Land use planning and the control of alcohol, tobacco, firearms, and fast food restaurants. *American Journal of Public Health, 93*(9), 1404–1408.

August, G. J., Lee, S. S., Bloomquist, M. L., Realmuto, G. M., & Hektner, J. M. (2003). Dissemination of an evidence-based prevention innovation for aggressive children living in culturally diverse, urban neighborhoods: The Early Risers effectiveness study. *Prevention Science, 4*(4), 271–286.

Bangert-Drowns, R. L. (1988). The effects of school-based substance abuse education: A meta-analysis. *Journal of Drug Education, 18*(3), 243–264.

Battistich, V., Schaps, E., Watson, M., Solomon, D., & Lewis, C. (2000). Effects of the Child Development Project on students' drug use and other problem behaviors. *The Journal of Primary Prevention, 21*(1), 75–99.

Biglan, A., Ary, D. A., Smolkowski, K., Duncan, T., & Black, C. (2000). A randomized controlled trial of a community intervention to prevent adolescent tobacco use. *Tobacco Control, 9,* 21–32.

Bonnie, R. J., & O'Connell, M. E. (Eds.). (2004). *Reducing underage drinking: A collective responsibility.* Washington, DC: The National Academies Press.

Botvin, G. J., Baker, E., Dusenbury, L., Tortu, S., & Botvin, E. M. (1995). Long-term follow-up results of a randomized drug abuse prevention trial in a White middle-class population. *Journal of the American Medical Association, 273*(14), 1106–1112.

Botvin, G. J., & Griffin, K. W. (2003). Drug abuse prevention curricula in schools. In Z. Sloboda & W. J. Bukoski (Eds.), *Handbook of drug abuse prevention: Theory, science, and practice* (pp. 45–74). New York: Kluwer Academic/Plenum Publishers.

Brook, J. S., Balka, E. B., Ning, Y., Whiteman, M., & Finch, S. J. (2006). Smoking involvement during adolescence among African American and Puerto Ricans: Risk to psychological and physical well-being in young adulthood. *Psychological Reports, 99*(2), 421–438.

Bukoski, W. J. (2003). The emerging science of drug abuse prevention. In Z. Sloboda & W. J. Bukoski (Eds.), *Handbook of drug abuse prevention: Theory, science, and practice* (pp. 3–26). New York: Kluwer Academic/Plenum Publishers.

Clayton, R. R., Cattarello, A. M., & Johnstone, B. M. (1996). The effectiveness of Drug Abuse Resistance Education (Project D.A.R.E.): 5-year follow-up results. *Preventive Medicine, 25*(3), 307–318.

Coie, J. D., Watt, N. F., West, S. G., Hawkins, J. D., Asarnow, J. R., Markman, H. J. et al. (1993). The science of prevention: A conceptual framework and some directions for a national research program. *American Psychologist, 48*(10), 1013–1022.

Dukes, R., Stein, J. A., & Ullman, J. B. (1997). Long-term impact of Drug Abuse Resistance Education (D.A.R.E.): Results of a 6-year follow-up. *Evaluation Review, 21*(4), 483–500.

Dusenbury, L., & Falco, M. (1995). Eleven components of effective drug abuse prevention curricula. *Journal of School Health, 65*(10), 420–425.

Elder, J. P., Wildey, M., de Moor, C., Sallis, J. F., Jr., Eckhardt, L., Edwards, C. et al. (1993). The long-term prevention of tobacco use among junior high school students: Classroom and telephone interventions. *American Journal of Public Health, 83*(9), 1204–1205.

Ellickson, P. L., Bell, R. M., & McGuigan, K. (1993). Preventing adolescent drug use: Long term results of a junior high program. *American Journal of Public Health, 83,* 856–861.

Ennett, S. T., Ringwalt, C. L., Thorne, J., Rohrbach, L. A., Vincus, A., & Simons-Rudolph, A. et al. (2003). A comparison of current practice in school-based substance use prevention programs with meta-analysis findings. *Prevention Science, 4*(1), 1–14.

Ennett, S. T., Rosenbaum, D. P., Flewelling, R. L., Bieler, G. S., Ringwalt, C. L., & Bailey, S. L. (1994). Long-term evaluation of Drug Abuse Resistance Education. *Addictive Behaviors*, *19*(2), 113–125.

Flay, B. R. (2007). The long-term promise of effective school-based smoking prevention programs. In R. J. Bonnie, K. Stratton, & R. B. Wallace (Eds.), *Ending the tobacco problem: A blueprint for the nation*. Washington, DC: The National Academies Press, Appendix D-1-D-29.

Flay, B. R., & Petraitis, J. (2003). Bridging the gap between substance use prevention theory and practice. In Z. Sloboda and W. J. Bukoski (Eds.), *Handbook of drug abuse prevention: Theory, science, and practice* (pp. 289–306). New York: Kluwer Academic/Plenum Publishers.

Forster, J. L., & Wolfson, M. (1998). Youth access to tobacco: Policies and politics. *Annual Review of Public Health*, *19*, 203–2335.

Forster, J. L., Wolfson, M., Murray, D. M., Wagenaar, A. C., & Claxton, A. J. (1997). Perceived and measured availability of tobacco to youths in 14 Minnesota communities: The TPOP Study. Tobacco Policy Options for Prevention. *American Journal of Preventive Medicine*, *13*(3), 167–174.

Furr-Holden, C. D., Ialongo, N. S., Anthony, J. C., Petras, H., & Kellam, S. G. (2004). Developmentally inspired drug prevention: Middle school outcomes in a school-based randomized prevention trial. *Drug and Alcohol Dependence*, *73*(2), 149–158.

Georgiades, K., & Boyle, M. H. (2007). Adolescent tobacco and cannabis use: Young adult outcomes from the Ontario Child Health Study. *Journal of Child Psychology and Psychiatry*, *48*(7), 724–731.

Goldberg, L., Elliot, D. L., MacKinnon, D. P., Moe, E., Kuehl, K. S., Nohre, L., et al. (2003). Drug testing athletes to prevent substance abuse: background and pilot sutdy results of the SATURN (Student Athlete Testing Using Random Notification) study. *Journal of Adolescent Health*, *32*(1), 16–25.

Goldberg, L., Elliot, D. L., MacKinnon, D. P., Moe, E. L., Kuehl, K. S., Yoon, M., et al. (2007). Outcomes of a prospective trial of student-athlete drug testing: The Student Athlete Testing Using Random Notification (SATURN) study. *Journal of Adolescent Health*, *41*(5), 421–429.

Gordon, R. (1983). An operational classification of disease prevention. *Public Health Reports*, *98*, 107–109.

Gottfredson, D. C., & Wilson, D. B. (2003). Characteristics of effective school-based substance abuse prevention. *Prevention Science*, *4*(1), 27–38.

Gottfredson, G. D., & Gottfredson, D. C. (2001). What schools do to prevent problem behavior and promote safe environments. *Journal of Educational and Psychological Consultation*, *12*(4), 313–344.

Hallfors, D., & Godette, D. (2002). Will the "principles of effectiveness" improve prevention practice? Early findings from a diffusion study. *Health Education Research*, *17*(4), 461–470.

Hallfors, D., Sporer, A., Pankratz, M., & Godette, D. (2000). *Drug Free Schools Survey: Report of Results*. Unpublished report, University of North Carolina, Chapel Hill.

Hansen, W. B., & Graham, J. W. (1991). Preventing alcohol, marijuana, and cigarette use among adolescents: Peer pressure resistance training versus establishing conservative norms. *Preventive Medicine*, *20*(3), 414–430.

Hansen, W. B., Malotte, C. K., & Fielding, J. E. (1988). Evaluation of a tobacco and alcohol abuse prevention curriculum for adolescents. *Health Education Quarterly*, *15*(1), 93–114.

Hawkins, J. D., Catalano, R. F., Kosterman, R., Abbott, R., & Hill, K. G. (1999). Preventing adolescent health-risk behaviors by strengthening protection during childhood. *Archives of Pediatric and Adolescent Medicine*, *153*, 226–234.

Hawkins, J. D., Catalano, R. F., & Miller, J. Y. (1992). Risk and protective factors for alcohol and other drug problems in adolescence and early adulthood: Implications for substance abuse prevention. *Psychological Bulletin*, *112*(1), 64–105.

Hingson, R., Heeren, T., & Winter, M. (2000). Effects of recent 0.08% legal blood alcohol limits on fatal crash involvement. *Injury Prevention*, *6*(2), 109–114.

Hingson, R., McGovern, T., Howland, J., Heeren, T., Winter, M., & Zakocs, R. (1996). Reducing alcohol-impaired driving in Massachusetts: The Saving Lives Program. *American Journal of Public Health, 86*(6), 791–797.

Holder, H. D. (1993). Prevention of alcohol-related accidents in the community. *Addiction, 88*(7), 1003–1012.

Holder, H. D. (2000). Community prevention of alcohol problems. *Addictive Behaviors, 25*(6), 843–859.

Holder, H. D. (2001). Prevention of alcohol problems in the 21st century: Challenges and opportunities. *American Journal on Addictions, 10*(1), 1–15.

Kandel, D. B. (1975). Stages in adolescent involvement in drug use. *Science, 190*, 912–914.

Liang, L., Chaloupka, F., Nichter, M., & Clayton, R. (2003). Prices, policies and youth smoking. *Addiction, 98*(Suppl. 1), 105–122.

Longshore, D., Ellickson, P. L., McCaffrey, D. F., & St. Clair, P. A. (2007). School-based drug prevention among at-risk adolescents: Effects of ALERT plus. *Health Education and Behavior, 34*(4), 651–668.

Luke, D. A., Stamatakis, K. A., & Brownson, R. C. (2000). State youth-access tobacco control policies and youth smoking behavior in the United States. *American Journal of Preventive Medicine, 19*(3), 180–187.

Lynam, D. R., Milich, R., Zimmerman, R., Novak, S. P., Logan, & T. K., Martin, C., et al. (1999). Project D.A.R.E.: No effects at 10-year follow-up. *Journal of Consulting and Clinical Psychology, 67*(4), 590–593.

Merrill, J. C., Pinsky, I., Killeya-Jones, L. A., Sloboda, Z., & Dilascio, T. (2006). Substance abuse prevention infrastructure: A survey-based study of the organizational structure and function of the D.A.R.E. program. *Substance Abuse Treatment, Prevention, and Policy, 1*, 25–38.

Mrazek, P. J., & Haggerty, R. J. (1994). *Reducing risks for mental disorders.* Washington, DC: National Academy Press.

Norton, E. C., Bieler, G. S., Ennett, S. T., & Zarkin, G. A. (1996). Analysis of prevention program effectiveness with clustered data using generalized estimating equations. *Journal of Consulting and Clinical Psychology, 64*(5), 919–926.

Payne, A. A., Gottfredson, D. C., & Gottfredson, G. D. (2006). School predictors of the intensity of implementation of school-based prevention programs: Results from a national study. *Prevention Science, 7*(2), 225–237.

Pentz, M. A. (2003). Anti-drug-abuse policies as prevention strategies. In Z. Sloboda & W. J. Bukoski (Eds.), *Handbook of drug abuse prevention: Theory, science, and practice* (pp. 217–244). New York: Kluwer Academic/Plenum Publishers.

Pentz, M. A., Dwyer, J. H., MacKinnon, D. P., Flay, B. R., Hansen, W. B., Wang, E. Y., Johnson C.A, et al. (1989). A multi-community trial for primary prevention of adolescent drug abuse: Effects on drug use prevalence. *Journal of the American Medical Association, 261*, 3259–3266.

Perry, C. L., Kelder, S. H., Murry, D. M., & Klepp, K. I. (1992). Communitywide smoking prevention: Long-term outcomes of the Minnesota Heart Health Program and the Class of 1989 Study. *American Journal of Public Health, 82*(9), 1210–1216.

Perry, C. L., Kelder, S. H., & Siller, C. (1989). Community-wide strategies for cardiovascular health: The Minnesota heart health program for youth program. *Health Education Research, 4*, 87–101.

Perry, C. L., Williams, C. L., Veblen-Mortenson, S., Toomey, T. L., Komro, K. A., Anstine, P.S., et al. (1996). Project Northland: Outcomes of a communitywide alcohol use prevention program during early adolescence. *American Journal of Public Health, 86*(7), 923–925.

Ringwalt, C.L., Ennett, S.T., Vincus, A.A., Rohrbach, L.A., & Simons-Rudolph, A. (2004). Who's calling the shots? Decision-makers and the adoption of effective school-based substance use prevention curricula. *Journal of Drug Education, 34*(1), 19–31.

Ringwalt, C. L., Ennett, S. T., Vincus, A. A., Thorne, J., Rohrbach, L. A., & Simons-Rudolph, A. (2002). The prevalence of effective substance use prevention curricula in U.S. middle schools. *Prevention Science, 3*(4), 257–265.

Robert Wood Johnson Foundation (2007). *Researchers look at which school-based drug educa-tion programs are most effective*. Retrieved from http://www.rwjf.org/reports/grr/040928.htm. Retrieved October 22, 2007.

Rohrbach, L. A., Ringwalt, C. L., Ennett, S. T., & Vincus, A. A. (2005). Factors associated with adoption of evidence-based substance use prevention curricula in U.S. school districts. *Health Education Research, 20*(5), 514–526.

Rosenbaum, D. P., & Hanson, G. S. (1998). Assessing the effects of school-based drug education: A six-year multilevel analysis of Project D.A.R.E. *Journal of Research in Crime and Delinquency, 35*(4), 381–412.

Ross, H., & Chaloupka, F. J. (2003). The effect of cigarette prices on youth smoking. *Health Economics, 12*(3), 217–230.

Rundall, T. G., & Bruvold, W. H. (1988). A meta-analysis of school-based smoking and alcohol use prevention programs. *Health Education Quarterly, 15*(3), 317–334.

Schaps, E., & Solomon, D. (2003). The role of the school's social environment in preventing student drug use. *The Journal of Primary Prevention, 23*(3), 299–328.

Sherman, L. W. (2000). The safe and drug-free schools program. In D. Ravitch (Ed.), *Brookings papers on education policy* (pp. 125–156). Washington, DC: Brookings Institution Press.

Sloboda, Z. (2004). *Programas de prevencao ao uso de drogas em escolas dos EUA* [School-based drug abuse prevention programs in the United States]. In I. Pinsky & M. A. Bessa, (Eds.), *Adolescencia e Drogas* (Adolescence and Drugs) (pp. 106-121). Sao Paulo, Brazil: Editora Contexto.

Sloboda, Z., & David, S. L. (1997). *Preventing drug abuse among children and adolescents: A research-based guide*. NIH Publication No. 97–4212.

St. Pierre, T. L., Osgood, D. W., Mincemoyer, C. C., Kaltreider, D. L., & Kauth, T. J. (2005). Results of an independent evaluation of Project ALERT delivered in schools by cooperative extension. *Prevention Science, 6*(4), 305–317.

Sussman, S., Dent, C. W., Stacy, A. W., Sun, P., Craig, S., Simon, T. R., et al. (1993). Project Towards No Tobacco Use: 1-year behavior outcomes. *American Journal of Public Health, 83*(9), 1245–1250.

Tarter, R., Vanyukov, M., Giancola, P., Dawes, M., Blackson, T., Mezzich, A., et al. (1999). Etiology of early age onset substance use disorder: A maturational perspective. *Development and Psychopathology, 11*(4), 657–683.

Taylor, B. J., Graham, J. W., Cumsille, P., & Hansen, W. B. (2000). Modeling prevention program effects on growth in substance use: Analysis of five years of data from the Adolescent Alcohol Prevention Trial. *Prevention Science, 1*(4), 183–197.

Tobler, N. S. (1986). Meta-analysis of 143 adolescent drug prevention programs: Quantitative outcome results of program participants compared to a control or comparison group. *Journal of Drug Issues, 16*(4), 537–567.

Tobler, N. S. (1992). Drug prevention programs can work: Research findings. *Journal of Addictive Diseases, 11*(3), 1–28.

Tobler, N. S. (2000). Lessons learned. *The Journal of Primary Prevention, 20*(4), 261–274.

Tobler, N. S., Lessard, T., Marshall, D., Ochshorn, P., & Roona, M. (1999). Effectiveness of school-based drug prevention programs for marijuana use. *School Psychology International, 20*(1), 105–137.

U.S. Department of Education (1998). Notice of final principles of effectiveness. *Federal Register, 63*(104), 29902–29906.

Vartianien, E., Pallonen, U., McAlister, A., Koskela, K., & Puska, P. (1983). Effect of two years of educational intervention on adolescent smoking (the North Karalia Youth Project). *Bulletin of the World Health Organization, 61*(3), 529–532.

Walter, H., & Wynder, E. L. (1989). The development, implementation, evaluation, and future directions of a chronic disease prevention program for childern: The "Know Your Body" stud-ies. *Preventive Medicine, 18*(1), 59–71.

Webster-Stratton, C., Reid, J., & Hammond, M. (2001). Preventing conduct problems, promoting social competence: A parent and teacher training partnership in Head Start. *Journal of Clinical Child Psychology, 30*, 282–302.

Wenter, D. L., Ennett, S. T., Ribisl, K. M., Vincus, A. A., Rohrbach, L., Ringwalt, C. L., Jones, S.M. et al. (2002). Comprehensiveness of substance use prevention programs in U.S. middle schools. *Journal of Adolescent Health, 30*(6), 455–462.

Werch, C. E., & Owen, D. M. (2002). Iagtrogenic effects of alcohol and drug programs. *Journal of Studies of Alcohol, 63*(5), 581–590.

Wolfson, M., Toomey, T. L., Forster, J. L., Wagenaar, A. C., McGovern, P. G., & Perry, C. L. (1996). Characteristics, policies and practices of alcohol outlets and sale to underage persons. *Journal of Studies on Alcohol, 57*(6), 670–674.

Worden, J. K., Flynn, B. S., Geller, B. M., Chen, M., Shelton, L. G., Secker-Walker, R. H., et al. (1988). Development of a smoking prevention mass media program using diagnostic and formative research. *Preventive Medicine, 17*(5), 531–558.

Yamaguchi, R., Johnston, L. D., & O'Malley, P. M. (2003). Relationship between student illicit drug use and school drug-testing policies. *Journal of School Health, 3*(4), 159–164.

Chapter 11
Community Prevention Handbook on Adolescent Substance Abuse Prevention and Treatment: Evidence-Based Practices

Elizabeth J. D'Amico, Matthew Chinman, Stefanie A. Stern, and Abraham Wandersman

Introduction

The current chapter focuses on community prevention for adolescent substance abuse. First, we provide an overview of the different types of prevention programs and environmental strategies available for youth and discuss the prevalence of alcohol and drug use and consequences among this population. The chapter then focuses on factors that may contribute to both initiation and escalation of alcohol and drug use. We then discuss theories that ground community interventions and describe specific community-based prevention efforts that have been implemented across the United States. We also discuss the outcomes from these prevention efforts. We conclude by providing recommendations.

What is Community Prevention for Adolescent Substance Abuse?

In the field of prevention, drug and alcohol programs are typically classified as *universal*, designed for the general population; *selective*, designed for subgroups at risk for substance use, such as youth who have parents who abuse substances or who are already experimenting with substances themselves; or *indicated*, designed for youth who have been treated but are at high risk for relapse (Institute of Medicine, IOM, 1994; National Institute on Drug Abuse, 1997). Universal or primary prevention-oriented activities remain the most frequently used approach with young people.

Adolescence is a time when many biological, social, and cognitive changes take place, which may be associated with initiation and maintenance of alcohol and drug use (Lanza & Collins, 2002; Tarter, 2002; Tschann et al., 1994). Prevention programming content for youth must address these developmental changes in order to be effective (D'Amico & Stern, 2008). Community-based interventions are one effective way to address these many changes as they typically target multiple factors (e.g., individual, community, and peer) at once. When discussing community-based interventions, the word "community" can have different meanings. Ultimately, all

C.G. Leukefeld et al. (eds.) *Adolescent Substance Abuse,*
DOI: 10.1007/978-0-387-09732-9_11, © Springer Science+Business Media LLC 2009

types of interventions aimed at preventing youth substance abuse typically take place in a community. In other words, programs delivered in schools could still be considered to take place in the community. Thus, for this chapter, a clearer operationalization of community based is needed. In this chapter, we focus on interventions that are *delivered by whole communities* that *target whole communities* as community based. Interventions that fall into this category include (a) substance abuse prevention programs that use multiple components to target multiple sectors of the community and (b) those that are designed to prevent underage drinking through environmental prevention strategies.

What is the Estimated Number of Adolescents Using/Misusing Substances Yearly?

It is well known that alcohol and other drug use increases during adolescence (D'Amico, Ellickson, Wagner et al., 2005; Johnston, O'Malley, Bachman, & Schulenberg, 2007) and is often associated with a host of problems, including school drop out (Muthén & Muthén, 2000), delinquency (Bui, Ellickson, & Bell, 2000), psychological distress (Hansell & White, 1991), and accidents or injury (Hingson, Heeren, Jamanka, & Howland, 2000). Surveys conducted in middle school settings indicate substantial increases in alcohol and marijuana use as youth transition from 6th to 8th grade (D'Amico, Ellickson, Wagner et al., 2005; Ellickson & Hays, 1992; Simons-Morton & Haynie, 2003). Similar increases in alcohol and drug use are seen as youth enter the high school setting such that by 12th grade, 20% of seniors report using marijuana in the past 30 days, 11% report using illicit drugs other than marijuana, and 48% report drinking alcohol, with 29% reporting an episode of heavy drinking (e.g., five or more drinks in a row) in the last 2 weeks (Johnston et al., 2007).

More recently, underage drinking has become especially concerning. Almost half of high school seniors in the United States report drinking in the last 30 days and these youth are starting to drink earlier than before and to drink more than adults when they do drink (Institute of Medicine, 2004; Johnston, O'Malley, Bachman, & Schulenberg, 2006a, 2006b; Substance Abuse and Mental Health Services Administration, SAMHSA, 2006). As a result, underage drinking is a leading contributor to death from injuries for people under age 21. Annually, about 5,000 minors die from alcohol-related injuries, with about 38% of these injuries involving motor vehicle crashes (Centers for Disease Control and Prevention, 2004b; Hingson & Kenkel, 2004; Levy, Miller, & Cox, 1999; National Highway Traffic Safety Administration, 2003; Smith, Branas, & Miller, 1999). Frequent drinking is also associated with marijuana and cocaine use (Dupre, Miller, Gold, & Rospenda, 1995; Wagner & Anthony, 2002), having unprotected sex (Brook, Brook, Pahl, & Montoya, 2002; Cooper, Peirce, & Huselid, 1994; Millstein, Moscicki, & Broering, 1994), and earning poor grades in school (Grunbaum et al., 2004). All of these factors contribute to underage drinking costing the United States about $53 billion annually (Institute of Medicine, 2004).

Furthermore, alcohol and drug use during adolescence can adversely affect functioning across several different areas. For example, the adolescent brain is still developing (Sowell, Thompson, Holmes, Jernigan, & Toga, 1999) and alcohol and drug use may disrupt this maturation process and impair brain function over the long term (Chambers, Taylor, & Potenza, 2003; Tapert, Caldwell, & Burke, 2004–2005). Work by Tapert and colleagues found that adolescents who reported using alcohol and marijuana at high levels for an extended period of time exhibited modest but significant neurocognitive deficits by late adolescence (Brown, Tapert, Granholm, & Delis, 2000; Schweinsburg et al., 2005; Tapert & Brown, 2000; Tapert, Brown, Myers, & Granholm, 1999). Heavy drinking during this time period can affect memory function and may also impair the growth and integrity of certain brain structures (De Bellis et al., 2000; Tapert et al., 2004–2005).

Substance use during this period may also affect interpersonal, occupational, and educational functioning (Brown, D'Amico, McCarthy, & Tapert, 2001; Ellickson, Bui, Bell, & McGuigan, 1998). For example, early initiation of marijuana and frequent use during this time period is associated with lower grades, dropping out of school, lower life satisfaction, and earning less money in young adulthood (Brook, Balka, & Whiteman, 1999; Ellickson, Martino, & Collins, 2004). A recent study examined developmental trajectories of smoking, binge drinking, and marijuana from age 13 to age 23 and assessed how these patterns related to several psychosocial and behavioral outcomes in young adulthood at age 23. There were two groups at high risk for poorer outcomes (e.g., more substance use problems and poorer physical health) at age 23 compared to abstainers: those who were using at relatively high levels by age 13 and those who started at low levels of use at age 13, but steadily increased their use over time (Tucker, Ellickson, Orlando, Martino, & Klein, 2005). Following a cohort of youth at ages 15–16, 24–25, 28–29, and 34–35, Kandel and Chen found that adolescents who both initiated marijuana use early and engaged in heavy use were more likely to meet criteria for alcohol dependence at ages 34–35, report higher rates of illicit drug use and marijuana-related problems, and have had a psychiatric problem compared with teens who reported early-onset light use, mid-onset heavy use, and late-onset light use (Kandel & Chen, 2000). Thus, early initiation and frequent alcohol and drug use during this important developmental time can have significant ramifications on the adolescent's future potential as an adult.

Pathways into Drug Misuse

Longitudinal data from the general population indicate that adolescents who drink typically begin experimenting with beer or wine, followed by hard liquor or cigarettes. For most adolescents, the risk period for the first full drink of alcohol begins at age 11 and peaks between age 16 and 18. The risk period for onset of regular alcohol use begins around age 14 and peaks at age 19 (DeWit, Offord, & Wong, 1997). If other drug use occurs, marijuana use tends to follow alcohol use, which is then followed by other illicit drug use (Kandel & Faust, 1975; Kandel, Yamaguchi, & Chen, 1992). Initiation of marijuana use typically peaks at age 15 (Gfroerer, Wu, & Penne, 2002; Labouvie & White, 2002), with risk of initiation continuing throughout adolescence (Kosterman, Hawkins, Guo, & Catalano, 2000) and leveling off at age 22 (DeWit et al., 1997). Many high school-aged teens who use alcohol and drugs report enough problems from use to meet diagnostic criteria for a substance abuse disorder (13.8% and 22.7% in grades 9th and 12th) (Dukes, Marinex, & Stein, 1997); and many of these youth may go on to have a substance abuse or dependence disorder in late young adulthood (D'Amico, Ellickson, Collins, Martino, & Klein, 2005).

Some experimentation with alcohol and/or drugs is considered to be normal during adolescence (Chassin & DeLucia, 1996; Guilamo-Ramos, Turrisi, Jaccard, & Gonzalez, 2004; Hurrelmann, 1990), and popularity among youth is associated with minor levels of substance use and delinquency (Allen, Porter, McFarland, McElhaney, & Marsh, 2005). There is substantial evidence, however, that abstaining youth have better health outcomes and fewer alcohol and drug problems in young adulthood than do youth who experiment with substances during this time (Tucker et al., 2005). For example, youth who begin drinking before the age of 14 are more likely to become alcohol dependent compared with those who begin drinking at age 20 or older (Grant, 1998; Hingson, Heeren, & Winter, 2006). As approximately one quarter of high school students (28%) report that they have consumed alcohol before 13 years of age (Centers for Disease Control and Prevention, 2004a), this suggests that many youth may be at risk for developing future alcohol-related problems.

Theories that Ground Community Interventions

There are different theories that attempt to explain adolescent alcohol and drug use (e.g., Petraitis, Flay, & Miller, 1995). For example, biological factors have been implicated in the use of alcohol by youth, such as increased tolerance to the negative effects and sensitivity to the positive effects of alcohol (Johnston, O'Malley, & Bachman, 2003; Spear, 2000; Spear & Varlinskaya, 2005). Other biological factors include inherent personality traits such as hyperactivity, aggression, depression, withdrawal, anxiety (Zucker, Wong, Puttler, & Fitzgerald, 2003), rebelliousness (Brook, Whiteman, Finch, & Cohen, 1995), difficulty avoiding harm or harmful situations (Jones & Heaven, 1998), disinhibition (Colder & Chassin, 1997; Colder & O'Connor, 2002; Moss & Kirisci, 1995), and having first-degree relatives who are alcoholics (Donovan, 2004; Russell, 1990). Despite the relationship to underage drinking, these factors are difficult to change through intervention.

There is also a great deal of empirical evidence which emphasizes the influence that role models can have on adolescents' alcohol and drug use. It is well known that peer influence increases substantially during adolescence (Simons-Morton et al., 1999). Beliefs about peer use of substances can impact both initiation of alcohol and marijuana use and escalation of substance use (D'Amico & McCarthy, 2006). Recent research has indicated that peers may play a more important role than parents in contributing to initiation and escalation of substance use during early adolescence (Beal, Ausiello, & Perrin, 2001; Crawford & Novak, 2002; Petraitis, Flay, Miller, Torpy, & Greiner, 1998; Windle, 2000). Cross-sectional studies have found that peer social influence is the only measure independently associated with abstinence from alcohol and marijuana use (Beal et al., 2001). In addition, modeling of use by best friends and perceived prevalence of use among same-aged peers are more strongly related to initiation and experimentation of alcohol than parental modeling of use (Jackson, 1997). Longitudinal work has supported these cross-sectional findings and shown that peer alcohol use is more strongly related to adolescent alcohol use than is parental alcohol use (Windle, 2000; Zhang, Welte, & Wieczorek, 1997). Thus, many prevention programs incorporate a discussion of peer alcohol and drug use in their programming content and provide normative feedback aimed at changing adolescents' perceptions about peer substance use (e.g., Brown, Anderson, Schulte, Sintov, & Frissell, 2005; D'Amico & Fromme, 2002; Hansen & Graham, 1991).

Although the effect of family may be diminished during this time period, it is still an important influence on youth involvement in risk behaviors (Baumrind, 1987; Kandel, 1996). For example, parental behaviors, such as monitoring and disapproval of heavy drinking, are significantly negatively associated with adolescent drinking, even after controlling for the impact of peer influence (Wood, Read, Mitchell, & Brand, 2004). In addition, parental involvement in their child's activities is negatively related to adolescent drinking (Simons-Morton & Chen, 2005). Parents are also able to impact their teens' substance use indirectly. For example, Simons-Morton, Abroms, Haynie, and Chen (2004) found that parental involvement, monitoring, and expectations were protective against smoking behavior by limiting the number of the adolescent's peers who smoked cigarettes.

Parental modeling of alcohol and drug use is also strongly related to whether or not adolescents choose to use substances (Johnson & Johnson, 2001; Li, Pentz, & Chou, 2002). For example, nonusing parents have a protective effect on peer influence to use alcohol and drugs (Li et al., 2002). In contrast, parental drinking is strongly associated with adolescent drinking (Chassin, Pillow, Curran, Molina, & Barrera, 1993; Rose, Kaprio, Winter, Koskenvuo, & Viken, 1999), and youth who report that their parents use marijuana are twice as likely to smoke cigarettes, drink alcohol, and use marijuana (Li et al., 2002). Of note, siblings are also an important influence on adolescent alcohol and drug use. Studies have consistently shown that perception of sibling alcohol and drug use is associated with drinking behavior and positive beliefs about drugs (Ary, Tildesley, Hops, & Andrews, 1993; D'Amico & Fromme, 1997; Windle, 2000). Thus, the impact of family behavior may also be incorporated into prevention programming content for this age group.

Cognitive factors, especially alcohol outcome expectancies, have also been strongly and consistently linked to adolescent alcohol, cigarette, and marijuana use in both cross-sectional and longitudinal research (Aarons, Brown, Stice, & Coe, 2001; Aas, Leigh, Anderssen, & Jakobsen, 1998; Fromme & D'Amico, 2000;

Jones, Corbin, & Fromme, 1999; Leigh & Stacy, 2004; Wahl, Turner, Mermelstein, & Flay, 2005). Specifically, positive alcohol and drug outcome expectancies, or the positive beliefs that one holds about alcohol and drugs, are typically associated with both increased drinking (Smith, Goldman, Greenbaum, & Christiansen, 1995) and drug use (Aarons et al., 2001; Ames, Sussman, & Dent, 1999). In contrast, negative expectancies are typically linked with less alcohol (Jones & McMahon, 1993) and drug use (Aarons et al., 2001; Galen & Henderson, 1999).

Programs targeting social influence that provide normative feedback, teach skills, and discuss beliefs about alcohol and drug use have been effective in decreasing subsequent alcohol and drug use among youth (Borsari & Carey, 2005; D'Amico & Edelen, 2007; Ellickson, McCaffrey, Ghosh-Dastidar, & Longshore, 2003; Griffin, Botvin, Nichols, & Doyle, 2003; Larimer et al., 2001). However, effects of individual-focused programs may fade when youths live in proalcohol environments (Moskowitz, 1989) in which factors such as the cost of alcohol and the amount of underage drinking enforcement remain unchanged (Holder, 2000).

Underage drinking researchers (e.g., Hingson & Howland, 2002; Holder, 1998; Wagenaar & Perry, 1994), along with the National Institute on Alcoholism and Alcohol Abuse (2002) and the Institute of Medicine (2004), suggest that changing the environment in which drinking occurs can be one of the most effective means to reduce underage drinking because it targets whole communities. Examples of environmental factors include media portrayals of alcohol, market forces that stimulate the demand for alcohol, and the policies that regulate the use of alcohol. Public policy is important because it directly influences the degree of social controls, or the extent to which youth perceive penalties associated with alcohol use as severe and certain (Ross, 1992). Public policy also influences the physical (e.g., amount and proximity), legal (degree to which laws regulate purchase and use), and economic (e.g., cost vs. income) availability of alcohol to youth (Wagenaar & Farrell, 1988). In the environmental approach, reducing alcohol-related problems is NOT done through the education of select youth and/or the treatment of problem drinkers. Instead, efforts are directed toward affecting policymakers in positions to implement various legal and financial restrictions that affect an entire community (Holder, 2000). Such supply-oriented approaches may provide advantages over demand approaches in that they do not require the identification or even the active cooperation of at-risk individuals.

Table 11.1 highlights risk and protective factors associated with alcohol and drug use during adolescence. This chapter focuses on the community level risk and protective factors, the interventions that are used in communities to target these risk factors, and the theories that ground community-based interventions.

What Types of Preventive/Promotive Interventions are Presently Used in Communities?

As we stated above, we consider two types of community interventions: substance abuse prevention programs that use multiple components and environmental alcohol prevention strategies. Although considered separately, both these strategies tend to

Table 11.1 Risk and protective factors for alcohol and drug use

Domain	Risk factors	Protective factors
Individual	• Biological and psychological dispositions • Positive beliefs about AOD use • Early initiation of AOD use • Negative relationships with adults • Risk-taking propensity/impulsivity	• Opportunities for prosocial involvement • Rewards/recognition for prosocial involvement • Healthy beliefs and clear standards for behavior • Positive sense of self • Negative beliefs about AOD • Positive relationships with adults
Peer	• Association with peers who use or value AOD • Association with peers who reject mainstream activities and pursuits • Susceptibility to negative peer pressure • Easily influenced by peers	• Association with peers who are involved in school, recreation, service, religion, or other organized activities • Resistance to negative peer pressure • Not easily influenced by peers
Family	• Family history of AOD use • Family management problems • Family conflict • Parental beliefs about AOD	• Bonding (positive attachments) • Healthy beliefs and clear standards for behavior • High parental expectations • A sense of basic trust • Positive family dynamics
School	• Academic failure beginning in elementary school • Low commitment to school	• Opportunities for prosocial involvement • Rewards/recognition for prosocial involvement • Healthy beliefs and clear standards for behavior • Caring and support from teachers and staff • Positive instructional climate
Community	• Availability of AOD • Community laws, norms favorable toward AOD • Extreme economic and social deprivation • Transition and mobility • Low neighborhood attachment and community disorganization	• Opportunities for participation as active members of the community • Decreasing AOD accessibility • Cultural norms that set high expectations for youth • Social networks and support systems within the community
Society	• Impoverishment • Unemployment and underemployment • Discrimination • Pro-AOD-use messages in the media	• Media literacy (resistance to pro-use messages) • Decreased accessibility • Increased pricing through taxation • Raised purchasing age and enforcement • Stricter driving-under-the-influence laws

Adapted from Substance Abuse and Mental Health Services Administration (2001) and Chinman, Imm, and Wandersman (2004)
AOD = alcohol and other drug

combine individual and environmental elements focused on creating positive change and promoting well-being across multiple settings in the community (Wandersman & Florin, 2003). These types of comprehensive programs are important because they have been found to be more effective and produce longer-lasting effects than programs that target only a single domain, such as school-based programs (Flynn et al., 1997; Spoth, Redmond, Trudeau, & Shin, 2002).

Multicomponent Programs

Multicomponent programs target the behavior of interest using multiple interventions in multiple settings (Nation et al., 2003). As such, these programs tend to address multiple protective and risk factors at once: individual, peer, family, school, community, and society. The components used are typically designed to complement one another over time. For example, policy change efforts are designed to have effects on all other sectors. Media advocacy efforts can support policy change and serve to cue peers and families to make use of school- and family-based services and make healthier choices (Pentz, 2003). Comprehensive programs tend to yield larger- and longer-lasting effects than other programs. This may be because multicomponent community programs are better able to simultaneously address the different influences on youth drug use (peer, family, school, and societal norms) and provide longer-lasting program exposure (Pentz et al., 1989; Sagrestano & Paikoff, 1997) than single-component programs.

The National Institute on Drug Abuse (NIDA) published its "Red Book" that presents a series of "prevention principles" (National Institute on Drug Abuse, 2003). These principles are essentially propositions about effective prevention that are based on years of research. NIDA published this book to serve as a guide to communities implementing prevention programs. While the Red Book's 16 principles address many issues regarding prevention, three principles specifically talk about the benefit of using programs with multiple components whenever possible:

- "Community prevention programs that combine two or more effective programs, such as family-based and school-based programs, can be more effective than a single program alone" (Battistich, Solomon, Watson, & Schaps, 1997, p. 11).
- "Community prevention programs reaching populations in multiple settings—for example, schools, clubs, faith-based organizations, and the media—are most effective when they present consistent, community-wide messages in each setting" (Chou et al., 1998, p. 11).
- "Prevention programs should be long-term with repeated interventions (i.e., booster programs) to reinforce the original prevention goals. Research shows that the benefits from middle school prevention programs diminish without follow up programs in high school" (Scheier, Botvin, Diaz, & Griffin, 1999, p. 11).

While clearly advantageous, Kumpfer and colleagues (Kumpfer, Whiteside, & Wandersman, 1997) point out that community interventions can also be more costly to implement in terms of both funds and personnel time.

Environmental Alcohol Prevention Strategies

There are a variety of environmental alcohol prevention (EAP) strategies that are aimed at preventing underage drinking; however, not all of these strategies are evidence based. The report *Reducing Underage Drinking: A Collective Responsibility* by the National Research Council and the Institute of Medicine (2004) states that ten strategies have been sufficiently tested to be considered evidence based, for example, restrictions on "happy hour" drinking and providing sobriety and traffic safety checkpoints (see Table 11.2). These strategies were also endorsed by the *Blueprint for the States: Policies to Improve the Ways States Organize and Deliver Alcohol and Drug Prevention and Treatment* (Join Together, 2006), a report of findings and recommendations of the national policy panel convened by Join Together, which is a nonprofit provider of information, strategic planning assistance, and leadership development to advance effective alcohol and drug policy, prevention, and treatment.

Although IOM states that these strategies have sufficient evidence, it also recommends that (a) communities mobilize around underage drinking prevention and (b) use a comprehensive approach that includes multiple EAP strategies. We address both of these issues in the following two sections. Finally, the IOM and Join Together both recommend that these ten strategies should be continuously evaluated so that these can be continually improved.

Community Mobilization as a Platform for Alcohol Prevention

Given the environment's impact on youth drinking, it is believed that it takes an entire community to enact effective and meaningful change in underage drinking (Holder, 2000). Community coalitions are one vehicle that can be used to implement community-based programs (Zakocs & Edwards, 2006). Coalitions can be used to assess problems facing their community, develop a plan to address the needs identified, implement strategies to address the problems, and evaluate these strategies (Butterfoss & Kegler, 2002). Although coalitions are often viewed as an intervention themselves, they are actually a delivery vehicle or catalyst for many types of interventions. We therefore describe coalitions in the current chapter, but we do not evaluate the many different community coalitions that exist and that may implement community-based strategies focused on alcohol prevention as this list is too extensive and diverse.

Coalitions are defined as "inter-organizational, cooperative, and synergistic working alliances" of individuals and/or organizations (Butterfoss, Goodman, & Wandersman, 1993, p. 316). Community coalitions tend to concentrate on community planning, increasing public participation, and changing public policy. These coalitions can play an important coordinating role, "bringing together community institutions and residents to develop comprehensive, integrated approaches" (Join Together, 1999, p. 12). Mobilizing at the community level requires a variety of

Table 11.2 Evidence based strategies for preventing underage drinking

Strategy	Definition	Evidence
Increase alcohol taxes	Raise taxes on alcohol, for example, by pegging it to inflation	• Higher alcohol taxes lead to: – reductions in the levels and frequency of drinking and heavy drinking among youth (Coate & Grossman, 1988) – lower traffic crash fatality rates (Ruhm, 1996) – reduced incidence of some types of crime (Cook & Moore, 1993) • Five states with the lowest beer tax have double the percentage of 18–20-year-old binge drinkers compared to the five with the highest tax (Imm et al., 2007)
Alcohol compliance checks	Law enforcement officials supervise undercover youth who attempt to purchase alcohol, penalizing establishments for successful attempts	• Checks reduced number of outlets selling to minors: – in Concord, NH: from 28% to 10% (Centers for Disease Control and Prevention, 2004b) – in Denver, CO: from 60% to 26% (Drug Strategies, 1999)
Responsible beverage service (RBS) programs	Require training for servers and merchants on responsible serving practices (e.g., not serving obviously intoxicated patrons)	• RBS implementation leads to: – an 11.5% reduction in sales to underage youth, and a decrease in sales to intoxicated patrons, compared to establishments that did not receive the training (Alcohol Epidemiology Program, 2000) – 23% fewer single-vehicle nighttime crashes in Oregon (Holder & Wagenaar, 1994)
Restrictions on "happy hour" drink discounts	Restrict the use of happy hour or other discounted pricing schemes	• Alcohol pricing strongly related to consumption (Chaloupka, Grossman, & Saffer, 2002), especially among minors (Chaloupka et al., 2002; Grossman & Chaloupka, 1998) • Lower drink prices found to be related to binge drinking alcohol (Wechsler et al., 2003)
Limit alcohol at sports and community events	Limit or ban alcohol consumption at sporting or other public events	• Banning alcohol at football games led to a reduction of arrests, ejections, and student referrals to judicial affairs (Bormann & Stone, 2001) • US cities with more restrictions on alcohol consumption in public places had less alcohol-related traffic fatalities (Cohen, Mason, & Scribner, 2002)
Limit the density of alcohol outlets	Density is the number of alcohol merchants available to a particular population or in a particular area	• Higher alcohol outlet density is associated with drinking and driving and riding with drinking drivers, especially for youth (Treno & Lee, 2002) • US cities with higher densities had more alcohol-related traffic fatalities (Cohen et al., 2002) • Density is strongly related to binge drinking (Weitzman, Folkman, Folkman, & Wechsler, 2003)

(continued)

Table 11.2 (continued)

Strategy	Definition	Evidence
Sobriety and traffic safety checkpoints	Law enforcement stops drivers to determine if they are driving under the influence of alcohol or drugs	• Three literature reviews on checkpoint studies found: – reductions in alcohol-related fatalities ranged from 8% to 71% (Peek-Asa, 1999) – reductions in alcohol-related fatal crashes of 22% (Shults et al., 2001) and 20% (Fell, Ferguson, Williams, & Fields, 2001)
Graduated driver's license (GDLs) laws	Requiring youth to progress through stages of driving privileges starting with a highly supervised permit to a supervised license with restrictions and then to a full-privileged driver's license	• Passing GDLs have led to reductions in crashes among young drivers in: – California: 17–28% (Cooper, Gillen, & Atkins, 2004; Rice, Peek-Asa, & Kraus, 2004) – Michigan: 19% (Shope & Molnar, 2004); and – Utah: 16% (Hyde, Cook, Knight, & Olson, 2005)
Keg registration laws	Require kegs of beer to be tagged with an ID number and information to be recorded about the purchaser	• US cities with a keg registration law had fewer alcohol-related traffic fatalities (Cohen et al., 2002)
Social host laws	Holds noncommercial servers of alcohol (e.g., parents) liable when they provide alcohol to a minor or drunk individual who later causes injury or death to another	• Social host liability laws have been found to: – lower the probability of binge drinking and drinking and driving among all drinkers (Stout, Sloan, Liang, & Davies, 2000) – decrease adult alcohol-related traffic deaths across all states for the years 1984–1995 (Whetten-Goldstein, Sloan, Stout, & Liang, 2000)

activities, including the development of a diverse membership, ongoing mobilization to promote true collaboration, and systematic processes to strengthen community resources and infrastructures. Media advocacy, in which coalitions "work directly with local news outlets (radio, television, newspapers, and magazines) to increase local attention to a specific public health problem and solutions" (Holder & Treno, 1997, p. S190), is a common way coalitions work to support their EAP strategies and build momentum to change policy. In short, environmental strategies require collaboration across diverse members of a community. Butterfoss et al. (1993) suggest that coalitions are ideal for large-scale community change because they can provide an avenue for recruiting participants from diverse constituencies, help mobilize more resources than any single organization can achieve alone, minimize duplication of efforts, maximize the power of individuals and groups by increasing the "critical mass," and develop widespread public support. A recent literature review conducted by Zakocs and Edwards (2006) found that six factors were associated with indicators of effectiveness in five or more studies, including formalization of rules and procedures, leadership style, member participation, membership diversity, agency collaboration, and group cohesion.

Descriptions of community preventive interventions

In this section, we describe several community-based interventions. These programs use various combinations of the multicomponent and EAP strategies described earlier and many of the programs have been shown to improve various alcohol-related outcomes (see Table 11.3).

Saving Lives Program

The Saving Lives Program (SLP) (Hingson et al., 1996) organized community task forces in six midsize towns in Massachusetts to reduce driving after drinking and improve traffic safety. Intervention communities received a full-time municipal-based coordinator charged with convening the task forces, which consisted of private citizens and representatives from different city departments (e.g., school, police, health, and recreation). The communities, not state or federal agencies, developed most of the program initiatives. The task forces oversaw various interventions including media advocacy campaigns, business information programs, speeding and drunk driving awareness days, speed watch telephone hotlines, high school peer-led education, alcohol-free prom nights, college prevention programs, enhanced police enforcement, responsible server training, alcohol outlet surveillance, and keg registration. For funding, each community received ~$1 per town inhabitant per year.

Project Northland

Project Northland is a multilevel, multiyear program that targeted 6th to 12th graders from 1991 to 1998 in 24 school districts in northeastern Minnesota (Komro, Perry, Veblen-Mortenson, & Williams, 1994; Perry et al., 2000; Perry et al., 2002; Perry et al., 1996). Phase I occurred from 1991 to 1994 when the cohort was in 6th to 8th grade and consisted of 3 years of social-behavioral curricula in the classroom, parent involvement programs, peer leadership opportunities, and community task forces. During 1994–1996, the cohort was in 9th and 10th grade and there was an interim phase in which 9th graders received a brief five-session classroom program. This program focused on pressures to drink and drive or riding with a drunk driver, the influence of alcohol advertising, and how to deal with that influence. No programming was conducted in 10th grade. During phase II from 1996 to 1998 when the cohort was in 11th and 12th grade, a six-session classroom curriculum

Table 11.3 Community-based program trials and outcomes

Study name	Study type	Population	No. of communities	Major outcomes
Saving Lives Program (Hingson et al., 1996)	Media campaigns, business information programs, speeding and drunk driving awareness days, telephone hotlines, police training, high school peer-led education, students against drunk driving chapters, college prevention programs, alcohol-free prom nights, beer keg registration, and increased surveillance for liquor stores	Massachusetts communities varying in population size and geographic location within the state	N = 6	At 9-year follow-up, compared with the rest of Massachusetts (the control group), program cities had a decline in fatal crashes (25%), fatal crashes involving alcohol (42%), visible injuries per 100 crashes (5%), proportion of vehicles observed speeding (50%), proportion of teenagers who drove after drinking (50%), and number of fatal crashes involving drivers 15–25 years of age (39%). Among teenagers, the proportion who believed the license of a person caught drinking and driving could be suspended before trials increased (from 61% to 76%) while it did not change statewide.

# of fatal crashes

	Intervention	Control	p-value
1984	M = 178	M = 3030	p = .02
1993	M = 120	M = 2707	

# of alcohol-involved fatal crashes

	Intervention	Control	p-value
1984	M = 69	M = 1162	p = .01
1993	M = 36	M = 1039	

Note: A log scale was used to compare percentage changes between the intervention area and control area

(continued)

Table 11.3 (continued)

Study name	Study type	No. of communities	Major outcomes
Project Northland (Perry et al., 1996)	Classroom behavioral curricula (grades 6–8), parent involvement programs, and community task forces (e.g., government officials, law enforcement, health professionals, school personnel, youth workers, clergy, parents, and adolescents)	$N = 24$	At 3-year follow-up, students in intervention districts had statistically significant lower scores on likelihood of drinking, onset of alcohol use, and prevalence of alcohol use (shown) than did students who did not participate in Project Northland. Students in the intervention showed lower scores on prevalence of cigarette and marijuana use.

% past month alcohol use for all students

	Intervention	Control	p-value
1991	M = 6.9	M = 3.9	
1994	M = 23.6	M = 29.2	$p < .05$

% cigarette use for all students

	Intervention	Control	p-value
1991	M = 6.9	M = 4.7	
1994	M = 24.8	M = 30.7	ns

% marijuana use for all students

	Intervention	Control	p-value
1991	M = 0.7	M = 0.4	
1994	M = 7.4	M = 8.6	ns

The project was more successful with those students who were non-users at baseline compared with those who had already initiated use.

Project Northland (Perry et al., 2002)

Follow-up of 1996 study cohort: Classroom curricula (grades 11–12), parent education, print media campaigns, youth development, and community organizing via peer action and community action teams

School districts and adjacent rural Minnesota communities

$N = 24$

During the interim phase (grades 9 and 10) alcohol use rates increased among students in the intervention schools. During grades 11 and 12, there was a reduced tendency to use alcohol, binge drink, and ability to obtain alcohol.

Changes in past month alcohol use

	Intervention	Control	p-value
1996	M=1.96 (0.07)	M=1.83 (0.07)	p=.08
Growth rate	0.13	0.20	p=.07

Changes in binge drink (5+ drinks)

	Intervention	Control	p-value
1996	M=1.60 (0.06)	M=1.45 (0.05)	p=.02
Growth rate	0.09	0.18	p=.02

Mean success rates for ability to obtain alcohol, all outlets (analyzed at community level)

	Intervention	Control	p-value
1991	M=42.3	M=47.9	p=.57
1998	M=13.6	M=25.4	p=.05

(continued)

Table 11.3 (continued)

Study name	Study type	Population	No. of communities	Major outcomes
Communities Mobilizing for Change on Alcohol (Wagenaar et al., 2000)	Community mobilizing via local public officials, enforcement agencies, alcohol merchants, media, schools, and other community institutions to change community policies and practices	Socially and geographically diverse communities in Minnesota and Wisconsin (average population = 20,000)	$N = 15$	Several trends emerged at 3-year follow-up. Alcohol merchants in the intervention community increased ID checks and reduced alcohol sales to minors. Eighteen-to 20-year-olds reduced their likelihood of trying to buy alcohol and fewer 18- to 20-year-olds in the intervention community reported 30-day drinking.

% alcohol merchants ID checks at on-sale establishments

	Intervention	Control	p-value
1992	60.2	49.1	p=.06
1995	78.1	56.5	

% 18-20 year olds trying to buy alcohol

	Intervention	Control	p-value
1992	10.4	10.9	p=.06
1995	7.5	10.7	

% 18-20 year olds trying to buy alcohol

	Intervention	Control	p-value
1992	56.3	55.7	p=.07
1995	59.5	62.5	

Community Trials Intervention to Reduce High-Risk Drinking (Grube, 1997)

Enforcement of underage alcohol sales laws; responsible beverage service training for off-sale clerks, managers, and owners; and media advocacy designed for awareness of enforcement and increased public support for intervention activities

Intervention and comparison communities in northern California, southern California, and South Carolina (population @ 100,000 ea)

$N = 6$

At 10-month follow-up, more citations were given to beverage outlets in the intervention communities. Of 148 outlets, 22 citations were given during the 10 months of the intervention versus 4 during the previous non-intervention year.
Sales of alcohol to minors were significantly reduced after the intervention. Intervention communities had fewer sales of alcohol to minors compared to the control communities at posttest.

% outlets selling alcohol to underage buyers, all communities combined

	Intervention	Control	p-value
1995	45	47	p< .0001
1996	16	35	

(continued)

Table 11.3 (continued)

Study name	Study type	Population	No. of communities	Major outcomes
Community Trials Intervention to Reduce High-Risk Drinking (Holder et al., 2000)	Enforcement of underage alcohol sales laws; responsible beverage service training for off-sale clerks; managers, and owners; and media advocacy designed for awareness of enforcement and increased public support for intervention activities	Intervention and comparison communities in northern California, southern California, and South Carolina (population @ 100,000 ea)	N = 6	At 5-year follow-up, traffic data for the intervention communities showed a decline in nighttime injury crashes (10%), crashes in which the driver had been drinking (6%), and assault injuries observed in emergency departments (43%). Population surveys showed a decline in alcohol consumption per drinking occasion and driving after drinking versus the comparison communities (p-values and control group means were not reported in study).

Self-reported # of drinks of alcohol consumed per drinking occasion

	Intervention
1992	M = 1.37
1996	M = 1.29

Self-reported rate of driving after too much to drink, # times per 6-month period

	Intervention
1992	M = 0.43
1996	M = 0.22

Self-reported driving when over the legal limit, # times per 6-month period

	Intervention
1992	M = 0.77
1996	M = 0.38

| Project SixTeen (Biglan et al., 2000) | Classroom curricula addressing tobacco use (grades 6–9), mass media programming, youth community activities, family communications training, and merchant education to restrict sales to minors | 7th- and 9th-grade students in small Oregon communities | N = 8 | The figures provided only covariate adjusted prevalence rates; thus it was not possible to estimate the numeric value and to provide data for this study. Results indicated that smoking did not increase as significantly among youth in the communities that received the community intervention compared to the school-based intervention. Use of smokeless tobacco among boys decreased for the community intervention but not for the school-based intervention. Weekly alcohol use increased significantly over 5 years for those who participated in the school-based intervention compared to the community intervention which did not see an increase. |
| Midwestern Prevention Project (locally called Project STAR or I-STAR) (Pentz et al., 1989) | Classroom curricula (grades 6–7), mass media programming, parent program, community organization, and health policy change | Middle school students in Kansas City, MO & KS | N = 15 (42 schools) | At 1-year follow-up, results showed decreases in cigarette, alcohol, and marijuana use for the intervention group relative to the delayed intervention condition. Prevalence rates for each substance increased over the 1-year period across all groups; however, the net increase in drug use among intervention schools was half that of delayed intervention schools. |

Prevalence rates, 1-year follow up

	Intervention	Intervention-delayed
Cigarettes	17%	24%
Alcohol	11%	16%
Marijuana	7%	10%

(continued)

Table 11.3 (continued)

Study name	Study type	Population	No. of communities	Major outcomes
Midwestern Prevention Project (locally called Project STAR or I-STAR) (Chou et al., 1998)	Classroom curricula (grades 6–7), mass media programming, parent program, community organization, and health policy change	Middle school students in Indianapolis, IN	12 school districts (57 schools)	Across all follow-up points (up to 3.5 years) baseline users decreased their use of cigarettes, alcohol, and marijuana in the program relative to the control group. Odds ratios for decreasing use among baseline users in the program relative to the control group, at all four follow-ups with repeated measures

	Odds ratio	p-value
Baseline cigarette users	1.53	P <.05
Baseline alcohol users	1.54	P <.005
Baseline marijuana users	3.96	P <.05

Note: Odds ratios were repeated and were adjusted for ethnicity, socioeconomic status, gender, school type (public or private), grade, and time trend was implemented in 11th grade which focused on the social and legal responsibilities concerning alcohol use. In addition, parents received behavioral tips through postcards, print media campaigns occurred, peer action teams were created at each high school to develop and promote alcohol-free activities, and community action teams were formed to help reduce commercial and social access to alcohol among minors (Komro et al., 1994; Perry et al., 2000, 2002).

Communities Mobilizing for Change on Alcohol

Communities Mobilizing for Change on Alcohol (CMCA) is a community-based program designed to reduce youth access to alcohol by changing community policies and practices. CMCA involved 15 communities, with seven communities randomly assigned to receive the intervention and eight communities serving as control communities (Wagenaar et al., 1999; Wagenaar, Murray, Wolfson, Forster, & Finnegan, 1994). During the first phase of the intervention period, meetings were conducted with leaders and citizens to help build personal and political relationships, gain an understanding of individuals' commitments, and identify individuals for recruitment into the core leadership group. During phase II, a local core leadership group and a larger base of active citizens were developed. Baseline surveys were conducted in 1992 and each survey was repeated 3 years later in 1995 (Wagenaar et al., 1999). Data were collected through self-administered surveys of 9th and 12th graders at baseline and a follow-up of the 9th graders 3 years later, telephone surveys of youth aged 18–20, telephone surveys of alcohol retailers, alcohol purchase attempts, content analysis of media coverage of alcohol issues, archival data, such as arrest and crash indicators, and process records (Wagenaar et al., 1994, 1999). The program collaborated with local public officials, enforcement agencies, alcohol merchants, the media, schools, and other community institutions that influence the environment.

Community Trials Intervention to Reduce High-Risk Drinking

The Community Trials Intervention to Reduce High-Risk Drinking (RHRD) is a community-based program that targeted all ages and implemented five broad prevention activities. These activities comprised (1) community mobilization (e.g., increase community awareness; increase community support for prevention approaches); (2) responsible beverage service (e.g., reduce the likelihood of customer intoxication at licensed establishments); (3) focus on drinking and driving (e.g., increase community support for enforcement of driving while intoxicated laws and increase enforcement efficiency); (4) focus on underage drinking (e.g., enforcement of underage alcohol sales and media advocacy to bring attention to issue of underage drinking); and (5) alcohol access (e.g., increasing restrictions on access to alcohol) (Holder et al., 1997). The project took place over 5 years from 1992 to 1996 in three intervention communities. The intervention and comparison communities were not randomized, but they were matched on the basis of similar local geographic area characteristics, industrial/agricultural bases, and minority compositions (Holder et al., 1997). Outcomes were assessed by conducting 120 general population telephone surveys of randomly selected individuals per month for 66 months, examining traffic data on motor vehicle crashes, and conducting emergency department surveys in one intervention and one control site (Holder et al., 2000).

Project SixTeen

Project SixTeen involved a randomized controlled trial to assess whether a comprehensive community wide prevention effort was more effective than a school-based program in reducing tobacco use among youth (Biglan, Ary, Smolkowski, Duncan, & Black, 2000). Eight pairs of Oregon communities were randomly assigned to receive each program and effects were assessed by analyzing five annual surveys of 7th- and 9th-grade students. The school-based program, Project Programs to Advance Teen Health (PATH), consisted of nine levels of instruction, with four levels developed for use with 6th to 9th grade, which included materials and videos that complemented the health program. Five levels were developed for use with 10th through 12th grade and were designed to address issues related to tobacco in Health, Social Studies, Biology, and English classes. The PATH curriculum was presented in five sessions over a 1-week period.

The community intervention was conducted by a paid community coordinator and youth and adult volunteers from the community. It included a media advocacy component, which was designed to publicize the tobacco problem and included newspaper articles and presentations to local civic groups. There was also a youth anti-tobacco component, which was designed to help coordinators and youth develop anti-tobacco activities to engage young people. A family communication component incorporated activities to help parents communicate with their children that they did not want them to use tobacco. The ACCESS component focused on decreasing the proportion of stores selling tobacco to minors.

Midwestern Prevention Project

The Midwestern Prevention Project (MPP) targeted avoidance and reduction of cigarette, alcohol, and marijuana use among youth in middle/junior high school (Chou et al., 1998; Pentz et al., 1989). MPP implemented five components: (1) mass media coverage, promotional videotapes, and commercials about each program component; (2) a school-based program that included homework sessions that involved parents; (3) a parent organization program; (4) a community organization program; and (5) drug use policy change. The purpose of MPP was to reduce the prevalence of cigarettes, alcohol, and marijuana among adolescents, using the school-based program to help build skills to support resistance of drug use via interactive role-play and other interactive sessions. The other program components, for example, mass media programming and parent involvement in homework, were to aid this effort. Intervention components were introduced into 15 communities in the Kansas City metropolitan area over a 6-year period (1984–1990) with randomized intervention and delayed intervention groups. A second study was implemented in Indianapolis, IN, in 12 school districts in Marjon County, IN (1987 – 1991) and also used a randomized experimental design. Annual assessments were conducted of youth in the schools assigned to both the immediate and delayed intervention groups (Pentz et al., 1990).

Community Preventive Interventions: Findings from the Evaluations

Many of the community-based interventions we have discussed occurred across different cities/settings and also assessed many different outcomes, such as underage drinking, alcohol sales, or traffic fatalities due to alcohol. Thus, one large trial may have been implemented only once, but in 20 cities. It may have shown success on some variables (e.g., traffic fatalities due to alcohol) but not others (e.g., heavy drinking among high school youth). We describe findings below for the interventions we described above, of which most included one trial, but occurred across multiple communities and cities (see Table 11.3).

Saving Lives Program

The SLP evaluation utilized a quasi-experimental design (Hingson et al., 1996). The six program communities selected for funding were compared with the rest of the state of Massachusetts and also with five other cities that also prepared high-quality proposals but were not funded. Comparisons were made using data from five pre-program years compared to the five program years. SLP examined fatal and injury crash monitoring, direct observation of safety belt use and speeding, conducted telephone surveys, and monitored traffic citations. In SLP cities, fatal crashes that involved alcohol declined from 69 crashes to 36 crashes during the program years, which is equivalent to a 42% decline. In addition, in SLP cities, the number of fatally injured drivers with positive blood alcohol levels declined by 47% compared to the rest of the state. Safety belt use increased and the proportion of vehicles observed traveling at ten or more miles over the speed limit declined in the SLP cities compared to the state. Finally, SLP communities experience a statistically significant decline in self-reported driving after drinking among 16- to 19-year-olds compared to the rest of the state. When compared to the five other cities that were not funded, SLP cities had fewer fatal crashes and fewer alcohol-related fatal crashes.

Project Northland

For Project Northland, students in the intervention and control school districts were surveyed at baseline in 1991 and followed up each spring from 1992 to 1998. Results from phase I indicated that youth in the intervention schools were less likely to increase their tendency to drink in the past month and to binge drink than youth in the control schools. Past week alcohol use was not significantly different between the Project Northland and control schools. Intervention were also less likely to increase their perceptions of peer influence to use alcohol and their perceived access to alcohol. There were no significant differences in rates of alcohol purchases at the end of phase I.

During the interim phase, when little programming occurred, many of these positive effects were reversed. Adolescents in the intervention schools increased their tendency to use alcohol, past month alcohol use, past week alcohol use, and binge drinking. They also increased their perceptions of peer use during this time and decreased their self-efficacy to refuse alcohol.

Phase II results indicated that the intervention was again successful in reducing adolescents' tendency to use alcohol and to binge drink. No differences were found on perceptions of peer use, perceived access to alcohol, or self-efficacy to refuse alcohol. Phase II results also indicated a large reduction in underage alcohol purchases in the intervention communities.

The lack of intervention when youth were in 9th and 10th grade was associated with increases in alcohol use. Despite this negative impact, when the additional intervention activities were implemented 2 years after this hiatus, alcohol use among this cohort decreased again. Overall, these results highlight the importance of continuing prevention programming throughout the period of adolescence (Perry et al., 2002).

Communities Mobilizing for Change on Alcohol

Overall, many of the results from the CMCA trial were not statistically significant at the $p < .05$ level; however, reductions were seen in the accessibility to alcohol, which is clinically important. For example, in the intervention communities, for alcohol purchase attempts, both on-sale (e.g., bars and restaurants) and off-sale (e.g., liquor and convenience stores) establishments which sold alcohol were more likely to check ID and less likely to sell to underage buyers. However, the intervention did not affect reports from alcohol retailers about checking ID for customers; that is, there was no increase in reports of checking IDs among merchants in the intervention communities. Telephone surveys of 18- to 20-year-olds indicated a 25% decrease in the number of youth attempting to buy alcoholic beverages ($p = .06$). In contrast to this favorable result, high school seniors reported an increase of 30% in the proportion who tried to buy alcoholic beverages. In terms of drinking behavior, the proportion of 18- to 20-year olds who reported drinking alcohol in the past 30 days decreased by 7%, although this change was not statistically significant

($p = .07$). There was also no statistically significant effect of the intervention on the high school seniors who were 9th graders when the project began (Wagenaar et al., 2000). Overall, the CMCA did report some positive changes in the community, although the majority of the effects did not reach statistical significance. Thus, replication of this intervention is needed to determine whether this type of programming can significantly reduce access to alcohol and subsequent drinking among youth.

Community Trials Intervention to Reduce High-Risk Drinking

Findings from the RHRD indicated that people in the intervention communities reported less heavy drinking. In addition, there were declines in night time crashes (from 8 p.m. to 4 a.m.), driving after drinking crashes, and assault injuries observed in the emergency departments in the intervention communities when compared to the control sites (Holder et al., 2000). The RHRD intervention did not report any measurement or outcomes for youth substance use; thus the program is promising, but its effectiveness among youth has not been established.

Project SixTeen

Project SixTeen outcomes focused on cigarette and alcohol use. For smoking prevalence, both groups increased prevalence over time; however, smoking prevalence did not increase as significantly among youth in the communities that received the community intervention compared to the school-based intervention (Biglan et al., 2000). Results also indicated that prevalence of smokeless tobacco use in the past month among boys decreased for the community intervention but not for the school-based intervention. For alcohol use, 9th graders who participated in the school-based intervention increased their weekly alcohol use significantly over the 5 years whereas youth who participated in cities that received the community intervention did not increase their weekly alcohol use during this time (Biglan et al., 2000). Overall, the intervention mainly influenced smoking prevalence – it did not decrease prevalence, but did slow the increase in smoking prevalence during this time period. Findings from this study were not strong and results were not consistent for smoking and alcohol behavior. Further evaluation of these two interventions is necessary before substantive conclusions can be made about their potential efficacy in reducing smoking and drinking behavior.

Midwestern Prevention Project

The MPP involved two cohorts of youth. For the Kansas City cohort, at the 1-year follow-up, the intervention schools had reduced rates of increase for cigarettes, alcohol, and marijuana compared to the control schools (Pentz et al., 1989). For the

Indiana cohort, results indicated that across all four follow-up time points (up to 3.5 years), baseline substance users consistently demonstrated lower levels of cigarettes and alcohol use (Chou et al., 1998). Both studies showed slower growth or decreased use of all substances among baseline users, which suggests that this type of program can affect both initiation and escalation of use. Results have also indicated that after 3 years, compared to school-based or other single channel programs, the MPP found greater and more sustained effects on daily cigarette use, monthly drunkenness, and heavy marijuana use (Pentz, 1998).

Brief Interventions in Community-Based Prevention

No brief interventions were identified.

Recommendations for Community-Based Prevention and Health Promotion

Prevention for alcohol and drug use among youth has benefited from important advances over the past two decades. Most of the research studies discussed above were successful at curbing increases in substance use, with some finding more consistent effects across substance use than did others.

An important point outside of the research results, however, is that communities often face difficulties in implementing these strategies with quality and achieving outcomes demonstrated by prevention researchers. This gap between research and practice (e.g., Green, 2001; Wandersman & Florin, 2003) is often the result of limited resources in real-world settings. For example, the typical settings in which these strategies are delivered often lack resources (i.e., tools or funding) or capacity (i.e., knowledge, attitudes, and skills) to adapt and implement strategies that have been developed in resource-intense research settings. Common ways to bridge this gap, such as information dissemination, fail to change practice or outcomes at the local level in part because they do not sufficiently build capacity or use community stakeholder input to address adoption and implementation barriers.

In a recent review, Durlak and DuPre (2008) identified 23 different factors that were important to implementation. These factors cut across five different categories including community-level factors (e.g., politics and funding), provider characteristics (e.g., perceived need for innovation and self-efficacy), characteristics of the innovation (e.g., compatibility and adaptability), organizational capacity (e.g., positive work climate and norms regarding change), and factors related to the prevention support system (e.g., training and technical assistance).

What can help communities implement these programs and strategies effectively is to receive support in their prevention work from a "Prevention Support System." Wandersman and colleagues (Wandersman et al., 2008) describe an interactive systems framework for disseminating and implementing preventive innovations. In this framework, researchers develop interventions which are readied for use in a "Prevention Synthesis and Translation System" and then communities put them into practice in a "Prevention Delivery System." A "Prevention Support System" plays the key role of linking these two systems, facilitating the process of translation within the synthesis and translation system and implementation within the prevention delivery system in order to improve outcomes. One example of a prevention support system that has been specifically applied to the types of strategies described above is Getting To Outcomes™ (GTO™). GTO was developed to address the gap between prevention research and practice by building capacity (self-efficacy, attitudes, and behaviors) at the individual and program levels for effective prevention practices (e.g., choosing evidence-based practices and planning, implementing, evaluating, and sustaining those practices). The GTO model provides communities a manual that offers guidance and tools, training, and on-site technical assistance (Imm et al., 2007). GTO therefore helps organizations build upon their current capacity level to put preventive interventions into place (Chinman et al., 2008). It is in this vein that we offer the following reccomendations:

- Communities need more support to implement the programs described above. This involves providing the knowledge and skills needed to conduct the steps required, such as needs assessment, setting priorities, and program delivery. This also involves helping communities obtain buy-in from stakeholders, such as the local police force, liquor stores, and schools.
- Communities need more support to ensure that programs are implemented with fidelity. The concept of fidelity is relatively clear in school-based programs where most program developers have created tools that communities can use to monitor their level of fidelity, so it can be improved over time. However, with many multicomponent underage drinking programs, some components may be very complicated and do not easily lend themselves to tracking fidelity. For example, what does it mean to have fidelity with the component of "community mobilization," which is one of the key components of the Community Trials Intervention program? How are environmental strategies such as limiting "happy hour" discounts to be monitored to ensure that establishments in the community are implementing these strategies in the same way? As a result, communities face challenges trying to replicate these multicomponent programs. For these kinds of activities, it may be helpful to contact program developers for guidance or establish a network of communities all using the same approaches so that the lessons learned can be easily shared (e.g., "practice collaboratives," Wilson, Berwick, & Cleary, 2003). In addition, manuals such as GTO can offer tools to assist communities with planning, implementation, and self-evaluation to improve the quality of implementation (Chinman et al., 2008).
- In addition to getting assistance with fidelity, implementation of these programs should include continuous quality improvement (CQI) strategies. This involves, in a cyclical fashion, systematically tracking performance, making small

improvements, assessing the impact of those improvements, then introducing another improvement, etc. This strategy is very common in medical settings like hospitals; however, CQI is not typically utilized in community-based prevention and it should be utilized much more frequently.

- To complement the CQI process, all programs need assistance with conducting their own program evaluations. Evidence indicates that programs that evaluate themselves get better outcomes regardless of their program (Durlak & DuPre, 2008).

In sum, there are several community-based interventions – as defined above – that have been shown to help communities prevent alcohol and drug use. Communities face challenges putting these strategies into place with the same level of quality as researcher/program developers. A prevention support system, such as the GTO system, has the potential to improve communities' abilities to plan, implement, and self-evaluate these strategies, increasing the likelihood of achieving positive outcomes.

Acknowledgment We thank Michael Woodward for his invaluable assistance in the preparation of this chapter.

References

Aarons, G., Brown, S. A., Stice, E., & Coe, M. (2001). Psychometric evaluation of the marijuana and stimulant effect expectancy questionnaire for youth. *Addictive Behaviors, 26*, 219–236.

Aas, H. N., Leigh, B. C., Anderssen, N., & Jakobsen, R. (1998). Two-year longitudinal study of alcohol expectancies and drinking among Norwegian adolescents. *Addiction, 93*(3), 373–384.

Alcohol Epidemiology Program. (2000). *Alcohol compliance checks: A procedures manual for enforcing alcohol age-of-sale laws.* Minneapolis, MN: University of Minnesota.

Allen, J. P., Porter, M. R., McFarland, F. C., McElhaney, K. B., & Marsh, P. (2005). The two faces of adolescents' success with peers: Adolescent popularity, social adaptation, and deviant behavior. *Child Development, 76*, 747–760.

Ames, S., Sussman, S., & Dent, C. W. (1999). Pro-drug-use myths and competing constructs in the prediction of substance use among youth at continuation schools: A one-year prospective study. *Personality & Individual Differences, 26*, 987–1003.

Ary, D. V., Tildesley, E., Hops, H., & Andrews, J. (1993). The influence of parent, sibling, and peer modeling and attitudes on adolescent use of alcohol. *The International Journal of the Addictions, 28*, 853–880.

Battistich, V., Solomon, D., Watson, M., & Schaps, E. (1997). Caring school communities. *Educational Psychologist, 32*(3), 137–151.

Baumrind, D. (1987). A developmental perspective on adolescent risk taking in contemporary America. *New Directions for Child Development, 37*, 93–125.

Beal, A. C., Ausiello, J., & Perrin, J. M. (2001). Social influences on health risk behaviors among minority middle school students. *Journal of Adolescent Health, 28*, 474–480.

Biglan, A., Ary, D. V., Smolkowski, K., Duncan, T., & Black, C. (2000). A randomised controlled trial of a community intervention to prevent adolescent tobacco use. *Tobacco Control, 9*(1), 24–32.

Bormann, C. A., & Stone, M. H. (2001). The effects of eliminating alcohol in a college stadium: The Folsom Field beer ban. *Journal of American College Health, 50*(2), 81–88.

Borsari, B., & Carey, K. B. (2005). Two brief alcohol interventions for mandated college students. *Psychology of Addictive Behaviors, 19*(3), 296–302.

Brook, D. W., Brook, J. S., Pahl, T., & Montoya, I. (2002). The longitudinal relationship between drug use and risky sexual behaviors among Colombian adolescents. *Archives of Pediatric Adolescent Medicine, 156*(11), 1101–1107.

Brook, J. S., Balka, E. B., & Whiteman, M. (1999). The risks for late adolescence of early adolescent marijuana use. *American Journal of Public Health, 89*, 1549–1554.

Brook, J. S., Whiteman, M., Finch, S., & Cohen, P. (1995). Aggression, intrapsychic distress, and drug use: Antecedent and intervening processes. *Journal of the American Academy of Child and Adolescent Psychiatry, 34*(8), 1076–1084.

Brown, S. A., Anderson, K., Schulte, M. T., Sintov, N. D., & Frissell, K. C. (2005). Facilitating youth self-change through school-based intervention. *Addictive Behaviors, 30*, 1797–1810.

Brown, S. A., D'Amico, E. J., McCarthy, D. M., & Tapert, S. F. (2001). Four year outcomes from adolescent alcohol and drug treatment. *Journal of Studies on Alcohol, 62*, 381–388.

Brown, S. A., Tapert, S. F., Granholm, E., & Delis, D. C. (2000). Neurocognitive functioning of adolescents: Effects of protracted alcohol use. *Alcoholism: Clinical and Experimental Research, 24*, 164–171.

Bui, K. V. T., Ellickson, P. L., & Bell, R. M. (2000). Cross-lagged relationships among adolescent problem drug use, delinquent behavior, and emotional distress. *Journal of Drug Issues, 30*(2), 283–303.

Butterfoss, F. D., Goodman, R. M., & Wandersman, A. (1993). Community coalitions for prevention and health promotion. *Health Education Research, 8*(3), 315.

Butterfoss, F. D., & Kegler, M. C. (2002). Toward a comprehensive understanding of community coalitions. In R. DiClemente, R.A. Crosby, & M.C. Kegler (Eds.), *Emerging theories in health promotion practice and research* (pp. 157–193). San Francisco, CA: Jossey-Bass.

Centers for Disease Control and Prevention. (2004a). CDC surveillance summaries (Vol. MMWR 53, pp. SS-2).

Centers for Disease Control and Prevention. (2004b). WebBased injury statistics query and reporting system (WISQARS). Retrieved electronically on June 6, 2007, from http://www.cdc.gov/ncipc/wisqars/default.htm.

Chaloupka, F. J., Grossman, M., & Saffer, H. (2002). The effects of price on alcohol consumption and alcohol-related problems. *Alcohol Research & Health, 26*(1), 22–34.

Chambers, R.A., Taylor, J. R., & Potenza, M. N. (2003). Developmental neurocircuitry of motivation in adolescence: A critical period of addiction vulnerability. *American Journal of Psychiatry, 160*, 1041–1052.

Chassin, L., & DeLucia, C. (1996). Drinking during adolescence. *Alcohol Health & Research, 20*, 175–180.

Chassin, L., Pillow, D. R., Curran, P. J., Molina, B. S. G., & Barrera, M. (1993). Relation of parental alcoholism to early adolescent substance use: A test of three mediating mechanisms. *Journal of Abnormal Psychology, 102*, 3–19.

Chinman, M., Hunter, S., Ebener, P., Paddock, S. M., Stillman, L., Imm, P., et al. (2008). The getting to outcomes demonstration and evaluation: An illustration of the prevention support system. *American Journal of Community Psychology, 41,* 206–224.

Chinman, M., Imm, P., & Wandersman, A. (2004). *Getting to outcomes 2004: Promoting accountability through methods and tools for planning, implementation, and evaluation* (No. TR-TR101). Santa Monica, CA: RAND Corporation. Available at http://www.rand.org/publications/TR/TR1.1/

Chou, C. P., Montgomery, S., Pentz, M. A., Rohrbach, L. A., Johnson, C. A., Flay, B. R., et al. (1998). Effects of a community-based prevention program on decreasing drug use in high-risk adolescents. *American Journal of Public Health, 88*(6), 944–948.

Coate, D., & Grossman, M. (1988). Effects of alcoholic beverage prices and legal drinking ages on youth alcohol use. *Journal of Law and Economics, 31*, 145–171.

Cohen, D. A., Mason, K., & Scribner, R. (2002). The population consumption model, alcohol control practices, and alcohol-related traffic fatalities. *Preventive Medicine, 34*(2), 187–197.

Colder, C. R., & Chassin, L. (1997). Affectivity and impulsivity: Temperament risk for adolescent alcohol involvement. *Psychology of Addictive Behaviors, 11*, 83–97.

Colder, C. R., & O'Connor, R. (2002). Attention biases and disinhibited behavior as predictors of alcohol use and enhancement reasons for drinking. *Psychology of Addictive Behaviors, 16*, 325–332. PMID: 12503905.

Cook, P. J., & Moore, M. J. (1993). Drinking and schooling. *Journal of Health Economics, 12*(4), 411–429.

Cooper, D., Gillen, D., & Atkins, F. (2004). *Impacts of California's graduated licensing law of 1998*. Berkeley, CA: University of California Institute of Transportation Studies.

Cooper, M. L., Peirce, R. S., & Huselid, R. F. (1994). Substance use and sexual risk taking among black adolescents and white adolescents. *Health Psychology, 13*(3), 251–262.

Crawford, L. A., & Novak, K. B. (2002). Parental and peer influences on adolescent drinking: The relative impact of attachment and opportunity. *Journal of Child & Adolescent Substance Abuse, 12*, 1–26.

D'Amico, E. J., & Edelen, M. (2007). Pilot test of Project CHOICE: A voluntary after school intervention for middle school youth. *Psychology of Addictive Behaviors, 21*(4), 592–598.

D'Amico, E. J., Ellickson, P. L., Collins, R. L., Martino, S. C., & Klein, D. J. (2005). Processes linking adolescent problems to substance use problems in late young adulthood. *Journal of Studies on Alcohol, 66*, 766–775.

D'Amico, E. J., Ellickson, P. L., Wagner, E. F., Turrisi, R., Fromme, K., Ghosh-Dastidar, B., et al. (2005). Developmental considerations for substance use interventions from middle school through college. *Alcoholism: Clinical and Experimental Research, 29*, 474–483.

D'Amico, E. J., & Fromme, K. (1997). Health risk behaviors of adolescent and young adult siblings. *Health Psychology, 16*(5), 426–432.

D'Amico, E. J., & Fromme, K. (2002). Brief prevention for adolescent risk-taking behavior. *Addiction, 97*, 563–574.

D'Amico, E. J., & McCarthy, D. M. (2006). Escalation and initiation of younger adolescents' substance use: The impact of perceived peer use. *Journal of Adolescent Health, 39*, 481–487.

D'Amico, E. J., & Stern, S. A. (2008). Preventing alcohol and drug use. In J.A. Trafton & W.T. Gordon (Eds.), *Best practices in the behavioral management of health from preconception to adolescence* (Vol. 3, pp. 341–401). Los Altos, CA: Institute for Disease Management.

De Bellis, M. D., Clark, D. B., Beers, S. R., Soloff, P. H., Hall, J. H., Kersch, A., et al. (2000). Hippocampal volume in adolescent-onset alcohol use disorders. *American Journal of Psychiatry, 157*, 737–744.

DeWit, D. J., Offord, D. R., & Wong, M. (1997). Patterns of onset and cessation of drug use over the early part of the life course. *Health Education & Behavior, 24*, 746–758.

Donovan, J. E. (2004). Adolescent alcohol initiation: A review of psychosocial risk factors. *Journal of Adolescent Health, 35*, 529, e527–518. PMID: 15581536.

Drug Strategies. (1999). *Keeping score on alcohol. Drug strategies*. Retrieved electronically on June 6, 2007, from http://www.drugstrategies.org/keepingscore1999/Score99.pdf.

Dukes, R. L., Marinex, R. O., & Stein, J. A. (1997). Precursors and consequences of gang membership and delinquency. *Youth and Society, 29*, 139–165.

Dupre, D., Miller, N., Gold, M., & Rospenda, K. (1995). Initiation and progression of alcohol, marijuana, and cocaine use among adolescent abusers. *The American Journal on Addictions, 4*(1), 43–48.

Durlak, J. A., & DuPre, E. P. (2008). Implementation matters: A review of research on the influence of implementation on program outcomes and the factors that affect implementation. *American Journal of Community Psychology, 41*, 327–350.

Ellickson, P. L., Bui, K., Bell, R., & McGuigan, K. A. (1998). Does early drug use increase the risk of dropping out of high school? *Journal of Drug Issues, 28*, 357–380.

Ellickson, P. L., & Hays, R. D. (1992). On becoming involved with drugs: Modeling adolescent drug use over time. *Health Psychology, 11*(6), 377–385.

Ellickson, P. L., Martino, S. C., & Collins, R. L. (2004). Marijuana use from adolescence to young adulthood: Multiple developmental trajectories and their associated outcomes. *Health Psychology, 23*, 299–307.

Ellickson, P. L., McCaffrey, D. F., Ghosh-Dastidar, B., & Longshore, D. L. (2003). New inroads in preventing adolescent drug use: Results from a large-scale trial of project ALERT in middle schools. *American Journal of Public Health*, *93*, 1830–1836.

Fell, J. C., Ferguson, S. A., Williams, A. F., & Fields, M. (2001). Why aren't sobriety checkpoints widely adopted as an enforcement strategy in the United States? *Proceedings for the Association for the Advancement of Automotive Medicine*, *45*, 425–428.

Flynn, B. S., Worden, J. K., Secker-Walker, R. H., Pirie, P. L., Badger, G. J., & Carpenter, J. H. (1997). Long-term responses of higher and lower risk youths to smoking prevention interventions. *Preventive Medicine*, *26*(3), 389–394.

Fromme, K., & D'Amico, E. J. (2000). Measuring adolescent alcohol outcome expectancies. *Psychology of Addictive Behaviors*, *14*, 206–212.

Galen, L. W., & Henderson, M. J. (1999). Validation of cocaine and marijuana effect expectancies in a treatment setting. *Addictive Behaviors*, *24*, 719–724.

Gfroerer, J. C., Wu, L. -T., & Penne, M. A. (2002). *Initiation of marijuana use: Trends, patterns, and implications* (No. Analytic Series: A-17, DHHS Publication No. SMA 02-3711). Rockville, MD: Substance Abuse and Mental Health Services Administration, Office of Applied Studies.

Grant, B. F. (1998). The impact of family history of alcoholism on the relationship between age of onset of alcohol use and DSM-IV alcohol dependence. *Alcohol Health & Research World*, *22*, 144–147.

Green, L. W. (2001). From research to "best practices" in other settings and populations. *American Journal of Health Behavior*, *25*(3), 165–178.

Griffin, K. W., Botvin, G. J., Nichols, T. R., & Doyle, M. M. (2003). Effectiveness of a universal drug abuse prevention approach for youth at high risk for substance use initiation. *Preventive Medicine*, *36*(1), 1–7.

Grossman, M., & Chaloupka, F. J. (1998). The demand for cocaine by young adults: A rational addiction approach. *Journal of Health Economics*, *17*(4), 427–474.

Grube, J. W. (1997). Preventing sales of alcohol to minors: Results from a community trial. *Addiction*, *92*(Suppl. 2), S251.

Grunbaum, J. A., Kann, L., Kinchen, S., Ross, J., Hawkins, J., Lowry, R., et al. (2004). Youth risk behavior surveillance – United States, 2003. *Morbidity and Mortality Weekly Report Surveillance Summary*, *53*(2), 1–96.

Guilamo-Ramos, V., Turrisi, R., Jaccard, J., & Gonzalez, B. (2004). Progressing from light experimentation to heavy episodic drinking in early and middle adolescence. *Journal of Studies on Alcohol*, *65*, 494–500.

Hansell, S., & White, H. R. (1991). Adolescent drug use, psychological distress, and physical symptoms. *Journal of Health and Social Behavior*, *32*, 288–301.

Hansen, W. B., & Graham, J. W. (1991). Preventing alcohol, marijuana, and cigarette use among adolescents: Peer pressure resistance training versus establishing conservative norms. *Preventive Medicine*, *20*, 414–430.

Hingson, R., & Kenkel, D. (2004). Social health and economic consequences of underage drinking. In R.J. Bonnie & M.E. O'Connell, National Research Council and Institute of Medicine, (Eds.), *Reducing underage drinking: A collective responsibility* (pp. 351–382). Washington, DC: National Academies Press.

Hingson, R., McGovern, T., Howland, J., Heeren, T., Winter, M., & Zakocs, R. (1996). Reducing alcohol-impaired driving in Massachusetts: The saving lives program. *American Journal of Public Health*, *86*(6), 791–797.

Hingson, R. W., Heeren, T., Jamanka, A., & Howland, J. (2000). Age of drinking onset and unintentional injury involvement after drinking. *Journal of the American Medical Association*, *284*, 1527–1533.

Hingson, R. W., Heeren, T., & Winter, M. R. (2006). Age at drinking onset and alcohol dependence. *Archives Pediatric Adolescent Medicine*, *160*, 739–746.

Hingson, R. W., & Howland, J. (2002). Comprehensive community interventions to promote health: Implications for college-age drinking problems. *Journal of Studies on Alcohol*, (Suppl. 14), 226–240.

Holder, H. (2000). Community prevention of alcohol problems. *Addictive Behaviors, 25*(6), 843–859.

Holder, H., & Treno, J. (1997). Media advocacy in community prevention: News as a means to advance policy change. *Addiction, 92*(Suppl. 2), S189–S199.

Holder, H. D. (1998). Planning for alcohol-problem prevention through complex systems modeling: Results from SimCom. *Substance Use & Misuse, 33*(3), 669–692.

Holder, H. D., Gruenewald, P. J., Ponicki, W. R., Treno, A. J., Grube, J. W., Saltz, R. F., et al. (2000). Effect of community-based interventions on high-risk drinking and alcohol-related injuries. *Journal of the American Medical Association, 284*, 2341–2347.

Holder, H. D., Saltz, R. F., Grube, J. W., Voas, R. B., Gruenewald, P. J., & Treno, A. J. (1997). A community prevention trial to reduce alcohol-involved accidental injury and death: Overview. *Addiction, 92*, S155–S171.

Holder, H. D., & Wagenaar, A. C. (1994). Mandated server training and reduced alcohol-involved traffic crashes: A time series analysis of the Oregon experience. *Accident Analysis and Prevention, 26*(1), 89–97.

Hurrelmann, K. (1990). Health promotion for adolescents: Preventive and corrective strategies against problem behavior. *Journal of Adolescence, 13*(3), 231–250.

Hyde, L. K., Cook, L. J., Knight, S., & Olson, L. M. (2005). Graduated driver licensing in Utah: Is it effective? *Annals of Emergency Medicine, 45*(2), 147–154.

Imm, P., Chinman, M., Wandersman, A., Rosenbloom, D., Guckenburg, S., & Leis, R. (2007). *Preventing underage drinking: Using getting to outcomes with the SAMHSA strategic prevention framework to achieve results* (No. TR-403-SAMHSA). Santa Monica, CA: RAND Corporation.

Institute of Medicine. (1994). *Reducing risks for mental disorders: Frontiers for preventive intervention research*. Washington, DC: Academy Press.

Institute of Medicine. (2004). *Reducing underage drinking: A collective responsibility*. Washington, DC: The National Academies Press.

Jackson, C. (1997). Initial and experimental stages of tobacco and alcohol use during late childhood: Relation to peer, parent, and personal risk factors. *Addictive Behaviors, 22*(5), 685–698.

Johnson, P. B., & Johnson, H. L. (2001). Reaffirming the power of parental influence on adolescent smoking and drinking decisions. *Adolescent & Family Health, 2*, 37–43.

Johnston, L. D., O'Malley, P. M., & Bachman, J. G. (2003). *Monitoring the future national survey results on drug use, 1975–2002* (Vol. 1: Secondary school students). Bethesda, MD: National Institute on Drug Abuse.

Johnston, L. D., O'Malley, P. M., Bachman, J. G., & Schulenberg, J. E. (2006a). *Monitoring the future national survey results on drug use, 1975–2005* (Vol. 1: Secondary school students). Bethesda, MD: National Institute on Drug Abuse.

Johnston, L. D., O'Malley, P. M., Bachman, J. G., & Schulenberg, J. E. (2006b). Teen drug use continues down in 2006, particularly among older teens; but use of prescription-type drugs remains high. Retrieved electronically on June 6, 2007, from http://www.monitoringthefuture.org/pressreleases/06drugpr_complete.pdf.

Johnston, L. D., O'Malley, P. M., Bachman, J. G., & Schulenberg, J. E. (2007). *Monitoring the future national survey results on drug use, 1975–2006* (Vol. 1: Secondary school students). Bethesda, MD: National Institute on Drug Abuse.

Join Together. (1999). *Promising strategies: Results of the fourth national survey on community efforts to reduce substance abuse and gun violence*. Boston: Boston University School of Public Health.

Join Together. (2006). *Blueprint for the states: Policies to improve the ways states organize and deliver alcohol and drug prevention and treatment*. Boston: Boston University School of Public Health.

Jones, B., Corbin, W., & Fromme, K. (1999). Half full or half empty, the glass still does not satisfactorily quench the thirst for knowledge on alcohol expectancies as a mechanism of change. *Addiction, 16*, 57–72.

Jones, B. T., & McMahon, J. (1993). Alcohol motivations as outcome expectancies. In W.R. Miller & N. Heather (Eds.), *Treating addictive behaviors* (pp. 75–91). New York: Plenum Press.

Jones, S. P., & Heaven, P. C. (1998). Psychosocial correlates of adolescent drug-taking behaviour. *Journal of Adolescence, 21*, 127–134. PMID: 9585491.

Kandel, D., & Faust, R. (1975). Sequence and stages in patterns of adolescent drug use. *Archives of General Psychiatry, 32*, 923–932.

Kandel, D. B. (1996). The parental and peer contexts of adolescent deviance: An algebra of interpersonal influence. *Journal of Drug Issues, 26*, 289–315.

Kandel, D. B., & Chen, K. (2000). Types of marijuana users by longitudinal course. *Journal of Studies on Alcohol, 61*, 367–378.

Kandel, D. B., Yamaguchi, K., & Chen, K. (1992). Stages of progression in drug involvement from adolescence to adulthood: Further evidence for the gateway theory. *Journal of Studies on Alcohol, 53*, 447–457.

Komro, K. A., Perry, C. L., Veblen-Mortenson, S., & Williams, C. L. (1994). Peer participation in Project Northland: A community-wide alcohol use prevention project. *The Journal of School Health, 64*, 318–322.

Kosterman, R., Hawkins, J. D., Guo, J., & Catalano, R. F. (2000). The dynamics of alcohol and marijuana initiation: Patterns and predictors of first use in adolescence. *American Journal of Public Health, 90*, 360–366.

Kumpfer, K., Whiteside, H., & Wandersman, A. (1997). *Community readiness for drug abuse prevention: Issues, tips and tools.* Rockville, MD: National Institute of Drug Abuse.

Labouvie, E., & White, H. R. (2002). Drug sequences, age of onset, and use trajectories as predictors of drug abuse/dependence in young adulthood. In D.B. Kandel (Ed.), *Stages and pathways of drug involvement: Examining the gateway hypothesis* (pp. 19–41). Cambridge, UK: Cambridge University Press.

Lanza, S. T., & Collins, L. M. (2002). Pubertal timing and the onset of substance use in females during early adolescence. *Prevention Science 3*, 69–82.

Larimer, M. E., Turner, A. P., Anderson, B. K., Fader, J. S., Kilmer, J. R., Palmer, R. S., et al. (2001). Evaluating a brief alcohol intervention with fraternities. *Journal of Studies on Alcohol, 62*, 370–380.

Leigh, B. C., & Stacy, A. W. (2004). Alcohol expectancies and drinking in different age groups. *Addiction, 99*, 215–227.

Levy, D. T., Miller, T. R., & Cox, K. C. (1999). *Costs of underage drinking.* Washington, DC: Department of Justice, Office of Justice Programs, Office of Juvenile Justice and Delinquency Prevention.

Li, C., Pentz, M. A., & Chou, C. -P. (2002). Parental substance use as a modifier of adolescent substance use risk. *Addiction, 97*, 1537–1550.

Millstein, S. G., Moscicki, A. B., & Broering, J. M. (1994). Female adolescents at high, moderate, and low risk of exposure to HIV: Differences in knowledge, beliefs, and behavior. *Journal of Adolescent Health, 15*, 133–141.

Moskowitz, J. M. (1989). The primary prevention of alcohol problems: A critical review of the research literature. *Journal of Studies on Alcohol, 50*(1), 54–88.

Moss, H. B., & Kirisci, L. (1995). Aggressivity in adolescent alcohol abusers: Relationship with conduct disorder. *Alcoholism: Clinical and Experimental Research, 19*, 642–646. PMID: 7573787.

Muthén, B. O., & Muthén, L. K. (2000). The development of heavy drinking and alcohol-related problems from ages 18 to 37 in a US national sample. *Journal of Studies on Alcohol, 61*, 290–300.

Nation, M., Crusto, C., Wandersman, A., Kumpfer, K. L., Seybolt, D., Morrissey-Kane, E., et al. (2003). What works in prevention: Principles of effective prevention programs. *American Psychologist, 58*(6–7), 449–456.

National Highway Traffic Safety Administration. (2003). *Traffic safety facts 2002, state alcohol estimates.* Washington, DC: National Highway Traffic Safety Administration.

National Institute on Alcoholism and Alcohol Abuse. (2002). *A call to action: Changing the culture of drinking at US colleges*. Rockville, MD: National Institute on Alcoholism and Alcohol Abuse Task Force of the National Advisory Council.

National Institute on Drug Abuse. (1997). *Drug abuse prevention for at risk groups*. Rockville, MD: DHHS, National Institutes of Health, National Institute on Drug Abuse, Office of Science Policy and Communications.

National Institute on Drug Abuse. (2003). *Preventing drug use among children and adolescents* (Vol. 04-4212, B). Bethesda, MD: NIH.

Peek-Asa, C. (1999). The effect of random alcohol screening in reducing motor vehicle crash injuries. *American Journal of Preventive Medicine, 16*(1), 57–67.

Pentz, M. A. (1998). *Preventing drug abuse through the community: Multicomponent programs that make a difference* (NIDA Publication No. 98-4293). Rockville, MD: National Institute on Drug Abuse.

Pentz, M. A. (2003). Evidence-based prevention: Characteristics, impact, and future direction. *Journal of Psychoactive Drugs, 35*(Suppl. 1), 143–152.

Pentz, M. A., Dwyer, J. H., MacKinnon, D. P., Flay, B. R., Hansen, W. B., Wang, E. Y., et al. (1989). A multicommunity trial for primary prevention of adolescent drug abuse: Effects on drug use prevalence. *Journal of the American Medical Association, 261*(22), 3259–3266.

Pentz, M. A., Trebow, E. A., Hansen, W. B., MacKinnon, D. P., Dwyer, J. H., Flay, B. R. et al. (1990). Effects of program implementation on adolescent drug use behavior: The midwestern prevention project (MPP). *Evaluation Review, 14*(3), 264–289.

Perry, C. L., Williams, C. L., Komro, K. A., Veblen-Mortenson, S., Forster, J. L., Bernstein-Lachter, R., et al. (2000). Project Northland high school interventions: Community action to reduce adolescent alcohol use. *Health Education and Behavior, 27*, 29–49.

Perry, C. L., Williams, C. L., Komro, K. A., Veblen-Mortenson, S., Stigler, M. H., Munson, K. A., et al. (2002). Project Northland: Long-term outcomes of community action to reduce adolescent alcohol use. *Health Education Research, 17*, 117–132.

Perry, C. L., Williams, C. L., Veblen-Mortenson, S., Toomey, T. L., Komro, K. A., Anstine, P. S., et al. (1996). Project Northland: Outcomes of community-wide alcohol use prevention program during early adolescence. *American Journal of Public Health, 7*, 956–965.

Petraitis, J., Flay, B. R., & Miller, T. Q. (1995). Reviewing theories of adolescent substance use: Organizing pieces in the puzzle. *Psychological Bulletin, 117*(1), 67–86.

Petraitis, J., Flay, B. R., Miller, T. Q., Torpy, E. J., & Greiner, B. (1998). Illicit substance use among adolescents: A matrix of prospective predictors. *Substance Use & Misuse, 33*, 2561–2604.

Rice, T. M., Peek-Asa, C., & Kraus, J. F. (2004). Effects of the California graduated driver licensing program. *Journal of Safety Research, 35*(4), 375–381.

Rose, R. J., Kaprio, J., Winter, T., Koskenvuo, M., & Viken, R. J. (1999). Familial and socioregional environmental effects on abstinence from alcohol at age sixteen. *Journal of Studies on Alcohol Supplement, 13*, 63–74.

Ross, H. (1992). *Confronting drunk driving: Social policy for saving lives*. New Haven, CT: Yale University Press.

Ruhm, C. J. (1996). Alcohol policies and highway vehicle fatalities. *Journal of Health Economics, 15*(4), 435–454.

Russell, M. (1990). Prevalence of alcoholism among children of alcoholics. In M. Windle & J.S. Searles (Eds.), *Children of alcoholics: Critical perspectives* (pp. 9–38). New York: Guilford.

Sagrestano, L., & Paikoff, R. L. (1997). Preventing high risk sexual behavior, sexually transmitted diseases, and pregnancy among adolescents. In R. Weissberg, T.P. Gullotta, R.L. Hampton, B.A. Ryan & G.R. Adams (Eds.), *Enhancing children's wellness* (pp. 76–104). Newbury Park, CA: Sage.

Scheier, L. M., Botvin, G. J., Diaz, T., & Griffin, K. W. (1999). Social skills, competence, and drug refusal efficacy as predictors of adolescent alcohol use. *Journal of Drug Education, 29*(3), 251–278.

Schweinsburg, A. D., Schweinsburg, B. C., Cheung, E. H., Brown, G. G., Brown, S. A., & Tapert, S.F. (2005). fMRI response to spatial working memory in adolescents with comorbid marijuana and alcohol use disorders. *Drug and Alcohol Dependence*, *79*, 201–210.

Shope, J. T., & Molnar, L. J. (2004). Michigan's graduated driver licensing program: Evaluation of the first four years. *Journal of Safety Research*, *35*(3), 337–344.

Shults, R. A., Elder, R. W., Sleet, D. A., Nichols, J. L., Alao, M. O., Carande-Kulis, V., et al. (2001). Reviews of evidence regarding interventions to reduce alcohol-impaired driving. *American Journal of Preventive Medicine*, *21*(Suppl. 4), 66–88.

Simons-Morton, B., Abroms, L., Haynie, D. L., & Chen, R. (2004). Latent growth curve analyses of peer and parent influences on smoking progression among early adolescents. *Health Psychology*, *23*, 612–621.

Simons-Morton, B., & Chen, R. (2005). Latent growth curve analyses of parent influences on drinking progression among early adolescents. *Journal of Studies on Alcohol*, *66*, 5–13.

Simons-Morton, B., Haynie, D. L., Crump, A. D., Saylor, K. E., Eitel, P., & Yu, K. (1999). Expectancies and other psychosocial factors associated with alcohol use among early adolescent boys and girls. *Addictive Behaviors*, *24*(2), 229–238.

Simons-Morton, B. G., & Haynie, D. L. (2003). Psychosocial predictors of increased smoking stage among sixth graders. *American Journal of Health Behavior*, *27*, 592–602.

Smith, G. S., Branas, C. C., & Miller, T. R. (1999). Fatal nontraffic injuries involving alcohol: A meta-analysis. *Annals of Emergency Medicine*, *33*(6), 659–668.

Smith, G. T., Goldman, M. S., Greenbaum, P. E., & Christiansen, B. A. (1995). Expectancy for social facilitation from drinking: The divergent paths of high-expectancy and low-expectancy adolescents. *Journal of Abnormal Psychology*, *104*, 32–40.

Sowell, E. R., Thompson, P. M., Holmes, C. J., Jernigan, T. L., & Toga, A. W. (1999). In vivo evidence for post-adolescent brain maturation in frontal and striatal regions. *Nature Neuroscience*, *2*, 859–861.

Spear, L. P. (2000). The adolescent brain and age-related behavioral manifestations. *Neuroscience & Biobehavioral Reviews*, *24*, 417–463.

Spear, L. P., & Varlinskaya, E. I. (2005). Adolescence. Alcohol sensitivity, tolerance, and intake. In *Recent developments in alcoholism: Alcohol problems in adolescents and young adults: Epidemiology, neurobiology, prevention, treatment* (Vol. 17, pp. 143–159). New York: Springer.

Spoth, R. L., Redmond, C., Trudeau, L., & Shin, C. (2002). Longitudinal substance initiation outcomes for a universal preventive intervention combining family and school programs. *Psychology of Addictive Behaviors*, *16*(2), 129–134.

Stout, E. M., Sloan, F. A., Liang, L., & Davies, H. H. (2000). Reducing harmful alcohol-related behaviors: Effective regulatory methods. *Journal of Studies on Alcohol*, *61*(3), 402–412.

Substance Abuse and Mental Health Services Administration (SAMHSA). (2001). *Science-based substance abuse prevention: A guide* (DHHS Publication No. SMA d-3505). Rockville, MD: US DHHS.

Substance Abuse and Mental Health Services Administration (SAMHSA). (2006). *National survey on drug use and health, 2005*. Rockville, MD: US DHHS.

Tapert, S. F., & Brown, S. A. (2000). Substance dependence, family history of alcohol dependence and neuropsychological functioning in adolescence. *Addiction*, *95*(7), 1043–1053.

Tapert, S. F., Brown, S. A., Myers, M. G., & Granholm, E. (1999). The role of neurocognitive abilities with adolescent relapse to alcohol and drug use. *Journal of Studies on Alcohol*, *4*, 500–508.

Tapert, S. F., Caldwell, L., & Burke, M. A. (2004–2005). Alcohol and the adolescent brain – Human studies. *Alcohol Research & Health*, *28*, 205–212.

Tarter, R. E. (2002). Etiology of adolescent substance abuse: A developmental perspective. *American Journal on Addictions*, *11*(3), 171–191.

Treno, A. J., & Lee, J. P. (2002). Approaching alcohol problems through local environmental interventions. *Alcohol Research & Health*, *26*(1), 35–40.

Tschann, J. M., Adler, N. E., Irwin, C. E., Jr., Millstein, S. G., Turner, R. A., & Kegeles, S. M. (1994). Initiation of substance use in early adolescence: The roles of pubertal timing and emotional distress. *Health Psychology*, *13*, 326–333.

Tucker, J. S., Ellickson, P. L., Orlando, M., Martino, S. C., & Klein, D. J. (2005). Substance use trajectories from early adolescence to emerging adulthood: A comparison of smoking, binge drinking, and marijuana use. *Journal of Drug Issues*, *35*, 307–332.

Wagenaar, A. C., & Farrell, S. (1988). Alcohol beverage control policies: Their role in preventing alcohol impaired driving. In *Office of the surgeon general, surgeon general's workshop on drunk driving: Background papers* (pp. 1–14). Rockville, MD: Office of the Surgeon General.

Wagenaar, A. C., Gehan, J. P., Jones-Webb, R., Toomey, T. L., Forster, J. L., Wolfson, M., et al. (1999). Communities mobilizing for change on alcohol: Lessons and results from a 15-community randomized trial. *Journal of Community Psychology*, *27*, 315–326.

Wagenaar, A. C., Murray, D. M., Gehan, J. P., Wolfson, M., Forster, J. L., Toomey, T. L., et al. (2000). Communities mobilizing for change on alcohol: Outcomes from a randomized community trial. *Journal of Studies on Alcohol*, *61*, 85–94.

Wagenaar, A. C., Murray, D. M., Wolfson, M., Forster, J. L., & Finnegan, J. R. (1994). Communities mobilizing for change on alcohol: Design of a randomized community trial. *Journal of Consulting Psychology*, *22*(CSAP Special Issue), 79–101.

Wagenaar, A. C., & Perry, C. L. (1994). Community strategies for the reduction of youth drinking: Theory and application. *Journal of Research on Adolescence*, *4*(2), 319–345.

Wagner, F. A., & Anthony, J. C. (2002). Into the world of illegal drug use: Exposure opportunity and other mechanisms linking the use of alcohol, tobacco, marijuana, and cocaine. *American Journal of Epidemiology*, *155*(10), 918–925.

Wahl, S. K., Turner, L. R., Mermelstein, R. J., & Flay, B. R. (2005). Adolescents' smoking expectancies: Psychometric properties and prediction of behavior change. *Nicotine & Tobacco Research*, *7*, 613–623.

Wandersman, A., Duffy, J., Flaspohler, P., Noonan, R., Lubell, K., Stillman, L., et al. (2008). Bridging the gap between prevention research and practice: The interactive systems framework for dissemination and implementation. *American Journal of Community Psychology*, *41*, 171–181.

Wandersman, A., & Florin, P. (2003). Community interventions and effective prevention. *American Psychologist*, *58*, 441–448.

Wechsler, H., Nelson, T. F., Lee, J. E., Seibring, M., Lewis, C., & Keeling, R. P. (2003). Perception and reality: A national evaluation of social norms marketing interventions to reduce college students' heavy alcohol use. *Quarterly Journal of Studies on Alcohol*, *64*(4), 484–494.

Weitzman, E. R., Folkman, A., Folkman, M. P., & Wechsler, H. (2003). The relationship of alcohol outlet density to heavy and frequent drinking and drinking-related problems among college students at eight universities. *Health Place*, *9*(1), 1–6.

Whetten-Goldstein, K., Sloan, F. A., Stout, E., & Liang, L. (2000). Civil liability, criminal law, and other policies and alcohol-related motor vehicle fatalities in the United States: 1984–1995. *Accident Analysis and Prevention*, *32*(6), 12.

Wilson, T., Berwick, D. M., & Cleary, P. D. (2003). Performance improvement – What do collaborative improvement projects do? Experience from seven countries. *Joint Commission Journal on Quality and Safety*, *29*(2), 85–93.

Windle, M. (2000). Parental, sibling, and peer influences on adolescent substance use and alcohol problems. *Applied Developmental Science Special Issue: Familial and Peer Influences on Adolescent Substance Use*, *4*, 98–110.

Wood, M. D., Read, J. P., Mitchell, R. E., & Brand, N. H. (2004). Do parents still matter? Parent and peer influences on alcohol involvement among recent high school graduates. *Psychology of Addictive Behaviors*, *18*, 19–30.

Zakocs, R. C., & Edwards, E. M. (2006). What explains community coalition effectiveness? *American Journal of Preventive Medicine*, *30*, 351–361.

Zhang, L., Welte, J. W., & Wieczorek, W. F. (1997). Peer and parental influences on male adolescent drinking. *Substance Use and Misuse*, *32*(14), 2121–2136.

Zucker, R. A., Wong, M. A., Puttler, L. I., & Fitzgerald, H. E. (2003). Resilience and vulnerability among sons of alcoholics: Relationships to developmental outcomes between early childhood and adolescence. In S.S. Luthar (Ed.), *Resilience and vulnerability: Adaptation in the context of childhood adversities* (pp. 76–103). New York: Cambridge University Press.

Epilogue: The Status of Knowledge Development and the Unknown

Michele Staton-Tindall, Thomas P. Gullotta, William Walton Stoops, and Carl G. Leukefeld

From the conceptualization of this volume through the writing process to this final chapter, the editors have had a remarkable learning experience. In our journey we uncovered the recipe for brewing Chicha, discovered the reasons why tobacco is so addictive that half of the smokers continue their destructive habit despite loosing a lung to cancer, understand the value of some therapeutic techniques, and the harm that other interventions can have. In this epilogue, we revisit some of our discoveries and share with the reader our understanding of a field that is moving from an art in which the personal magnetism of the healer blowing smoke is being replaced by a science in which such enemas are no longer seen as powerful medicine.

Evidence-Based Practice

Recent interest in evidence-based practice can be traced to the publication of *Effectiveness and Efficiency: Random Reflections on Health Services* by the Scottish epidemiologist Archie Cochrane (1972/1999). His pioneering efforts led to the establishment of a medical research database that has grown into an international collaboration directed at identifying medical practices that actually work. Cochrane's interest began with the recognition that much of medical practice was rooted in oral tradition. That is, clinical reports based on personal experience were the means by which knowledge was transferred from one healer to the other. Thus, Joseph Lister's positive experience in treating the deadly illness "Milk Fever,"[1] which afflicted new mothers, with washing one's hands before examining the new mom, was shared with his colleagues. Now, depending on the persuasiveness of the healer and the reported experiences of other doctors, a new treatment, *if it did not*

---

[1] In Lister's time (1860s) the high fever some women experienced shortly after the birth of their child was attributed to the start of lactation. No one thought that the filthy hands of the attending physician examining the new mother's mother's bruised and damaged birth area was in any way related to the infection "Milk Fever."

disturb the existing social reality, gradually became a part of medical practice. In Joseph Lister's case, this was initially not to be. He was ridiculed for his ludicrous beliefs that cleanliness mattered and the practice of examining new mothers with soiled hands continued much to the dismay of orphans who lost their mothers to infectious "Milk Fever." Therein rested the problem of oral tradition. If the new information challenged an existing cherished belief, say, for example, Hippocrates four humors (black bile, yellow bile, phlegm, and blood which Galen repopularized and whose medical theories dominated medical treatment for centuries), then the information was rejected and existing treatments derived from humoral theory, namely, bloodletting, purging (vomiting), blistering, and enemas, to balance the humors and return the patient to health continued. From this example, realize that the conceptualization of an issue, which is imaging how something behaves, is more important then how it actually operates!

This paradigm shift in physical medicine from thinking something works to evidence that it actually works extends today into the treatment and prevention of behavioral disorders to include science-based interventions, technology transfer, and the novel idea that practitioners should be helpful.

The Institute of Medicine (IOM, 2001) defined evidence-based practice as "the integration of best research evidence with clinical practice and patient values" (IOM, 2001, p. 47). This definition not only recognizes that clinical observations give rise to suspicions (hypothesizes) that can then be tested but also goes further to embrace the critical role the client has in this process because (and this is not attended to enough) it is the client's life!

Impressions

Treatment

The talented group of authors brought together for this project accomplished their assignment of providing readers with the current state of knowledge on the bio-psycho-social-environmental dimensions of adolescent substance abuse and evidence-based practices for its treatment and prevention. From their work, we saw that substance misuse led to several negative health and social consequences for adolescents. Further, these researchers and practitioners identified a number of social factors contributing to adolescent misuse including family environment and family relationships, peer associations, religious involvement, and school and community settings.

In these chapters, we discovered the current state of knowledge about evidence-based practices that "work" for adolescents across different treatment modalities. One intriguing observation from our reading was that while some therapeutic approaches are considered "evidence-based" for outpatient or family therapy, they have not been "proven" in another setting (residential for example). Clearly, much work remains to be done. The following table summarizes our understanding of suitable evidence-based practices in different therapeutic settings for adolescent substance users:

Intervention	Goal	Use
Cognitive Behavioral Therapy (CBT)	Improves the patient's cognitive (i.e., attitudes, values) and behavioral skills for changing his/her problematic drug use.	Individual, Outpatient
Behavioral Therapy	Emphasizes overcoming skill deficits and strengthening the patient's ability to cope with high-risk situations.	Individual, Outpatient
Brief Intervention	Involves a small number of sessions, which capitalize on the readiness of individuals to change their behavior (i.e., Motivational Enhancement Therapy, MET).	Individual, Outpatient
Node-Link Mapping	Incorporates visual representations of the range of difficulties, issues, and their potential solutions.	Individual, Outpatient
Relapse Prevention Therapy (RPT)	Identifies and changes problematic behavior through examining positive and negative consequences of continued drug use.	Individual, Outpatient
Trauma-Focused Cognitive Behavioral Therapy (TF-CBT)	Adapts CBT for use among children who have been exposed to such traumatic experiences as physical abuse.	Individual, Outpatient
Multidimensional Treatment Foster Care (MTFC)	Involves a behavioral intervention for delinquent youths and youths in need of out-of-home placement.	Individual, Outpatient
Multisystemic Therapy (MST)	Reduces drug use problems through interventions with the adolescent, family, and extrafamilial systems.	Family-based
Multidimensional Family Therapy (MDFT)	Focuses on reducing drug use by tailoring treatment to the characteristics of the adolescent, family, and their involvement with extrafamilial systems.	Family-based
Functional Family Therapy (FFT)	Emphasizes that the family's interactions are central to problem development and change occurs through family-based interventions.	Family-based

Evidence-based practices for residential treatment among adolescent substance users are less defined and supported by the clinical and empirical literature. Although there is tremendous variation in the approach taken to the residential treatment of adolescent substance abuse, researchers have begun to identify common key elements and features related to positive outcomes. From the Plant and Panzarella chapter in this volume, we offer these observations:

1. Treatment retention – Adolescents who remain longer in residential substance abuse treatment have demonstrated more positive treatment outcomes.

2. Family involvement – Working with the family as a unit and including the family members in residential treatment interventions has been associated with positive outcomes.
3. Therapeutic milieu – Developing a therapeutic environment that is a good fit for adolescents that includes a motivational approach focused on harm reduction has been associated with positive outcomes.

Building on these key components of success in residential treatment, a number of interventions that have demonstrated effectiveness in home and community settings are being modified and integrated into residential modalities. In particular, Cognitive behavioral approaches (CBT), Motivational Enhancement Therapy (MET), and family-based and/or multisystemic approaches including Multiple Systemic Therapy (MST), Functional Family Therapy (FFT), Brief Strategic Family Therapy (BSFT), and Multidimensional Family Therapy (MDFT) are being incorporated into residential care. The current state of research and knowledge is developing in this area to understand whether these approaches should be considered promising for adolescents in residential substance abuse treatment.

In addition to spotlighting practices that worked, we asked authors to identify practices that were not effective in treating adolescent substance misusers. Authors identified individual or group (Supportive) therapy, and interactional therapy because there is a lack of skill-building to enable adolescents to handle high-risk situations. In addition, group therapy has been associated with negative outcomes for adolescents. The primary reason group therapy is ineffectual is that participants associate with deviant peers in the context of the group environment encouraging their dysfunctional behavior. With regard to residential programs, intervention with negative outcomes included boot camps, Scared Straight Programs, and treatment approaches that incorporated punishment as a consequence for noncompliance.

Prevention

In addition to a focus on evidence-based interventions for adolescent substance use, this volume examined approaches to prevent substance misuse. With roots in the Quaker tradition of helping individuals with social problems that were largely believed to be tied to poverty, a number of successful prevention efforts have been launched over the last 200 years to address substance abuse. The reality is that alcohol and drug abuse remain significant social problems which have largely been unchanged by large-scale (Prohibition) or small-scale (state laws) policy changes. Nonetheless, the call for continued evidence-based prevention interventions remains and this volume offers several promising avenues to achieve that end.

Bloom in this volume states that primary prevention involves planned actions focusing on (1) predictable problems in relatively healthy individuals and groups, (2) protecting existing states of health and healthy functioning, and (3) promoting desired future states not yet attained. One of the most important venues for substance abuse prevention interventions is the school. The need for school-based prevention and evidence-based practices is important because of the harmful effects of substance use for adolescents, the fact that possession of tobacco and alcohol products by persons under the age of 18 is illegal, and research which suggests that use of tobacco and alcohol may increase risk for later, more extensive drug use. School-based prevention interventions have been shown to be effective, due in large part because adolescents spend a significant amount of time in school, schools provide an environment conducive to enforcing social norms, and schools are a safe place for adolescents and children. In addition to school-based prevention interventions, interventions that are delivered by whole communities that target whole communities have also demonstrated effectiveness for adolescent substance abuse.

Whether evidence-based prevention interventions are delivered in schools or in the community, the use of technology is critical to the development, implementation, and dissemination of prevention practices for adolescent substance users. Bloom described five technologies to consider as fundamental elements of any adolescent substance abuse prevention effort: education, promotion of self-competency, connections with natural caregivers, impacting change at the community organization and systems level, and redesigning the social environment.

Final Thoughts

We end this book on two hopeful notes and a challenge for graduate programs. Encouragingly, the psychological bloodletting, purging, blistering, and enemas of yesteryear have been replaced with more successful interventions. Still, too many youth do not respond to current treatments and too many return to dysfunctional behaviors too quickly. We do not seek a utopia in which self-destructive behavior does not exist. We are too old for that dream. Rather, we seek a society that acknowledges the pathway it has paved for bio-psycho-social-environmentally vulnerable youth to walk and to better attend to environmental controls to limit the number of those who fall prey to the misuse of legal and illegal substances. We are encouraged by the progress that those who seek to promote resiliency and prevent substance misuse in schools and other settings have made, but these remain baby steps and more remains to be done particularly with harm risk reduction and distribution of consumption models. Further, the first generation of evidence-based models in treatment and prevention are just that – first generation. Improvements to these approaches and the development of still more robust actions that can withstand the inevitable tinkering that occurs in the field must be encouraged. We urge those who would fund these new developments to invest their dollars in a variety of approaches that are both interdisciplinary and multifactorial. If we have learned anything from the field of prevention, it is that single technology approaches are of limited, if any, value.

Toward that end, we have challenged graduate programs to reengineer the process by which doctoral degrees are conferred (Gullotta & Blau, 2008). Presently, the system is built around a course of study and the undertaking of a dissertation of marginal value that will reside forlorn in some neglected corner of cyberspace. Imagine instead a school, ideally many schools in an international collaboration, embarking on a behavioral research database developing, testing, refining, and disseminating practices that work. We have no shortage of theories (psychoanalytic, behavioral, humanistic, transpersonal) offering a multitude of approaches for helping those in need. Are the adherents of logotherapy, gestalt, analysis, behaviorism, theosophy, and a thousand other interventions blowing worthless smoke over and into those seeking their help? Are new "Dare," carding, and traffic stop points effective prevention efforts? Granted, there are beginning databases collecting information. But these are potentially flawed efforts packed with programs that have been well funded by the maintainers of the database. Recall our earlier observation about social reality. Change in practice occurred if it did not disturb the existing pattern of social beliefs. The creation, maintenance, and entry into a database maintained by Gallen would value the humors, by Freud would favor the Oedipal complex, or by behavioral analysts would omit feelings. Transpersonal approaches would find no place in their databases, and yet in the new North America where both Canada and the US are in the midst of ethnic and cultural transformation theosophical approaches matter. This could be a time of psychological renaissance across schools of higher learning and the field identifying *effective* approaches to maintain existing health, foster new health abilities, prevent distress, and successfully treat illness when it develops. We know there is no magic silver bullet to achieve this. We suspect this behavioral formulary will be as large as it is for pharmacology. Still, it needs to be undertaken and now is the time.

References

Cochrane, A. (1972/1999). *Effectiveness and efficiency: Random reflections on health services.* London, UK: Royal Society of Medicine.

Gullotta, T. P., & Blau, G. M. (2008). Epilogue. In T. P. Gullotta & G. M. Blau (Eds.), *Handbook of childhood behavioral issues: Evidence-based approaches to prevention and treatment* (pp. 399–401). NY: Routledge.

Institute of Medicine (IOM). (2001). *Crossing the quality chasm: A new health system for the 21st century.* Washington, DC: National Academy Press.

About the Editors

Thomas P. Gullotta is C.E.O. of Child and Family Agency and a member of the psychology and education departments at Eastern Connecticut State University. He is the senior author of the 4th edition of *The Adolescent Experience*, coeditor of *The Encyclopedia of Primary Prevention and Health Promotion*, and editor emeritus of the *Journal of Primary Prevention*. He is the senior book series editor for *Issues in Children's and Families' Lives*. Tom holds editorial appointments on the *Journal of Early Adolescence*, *The Journal of Adolescent Research* and the *Journal of Educational and Psychological Consultation*. He has published extensively on adolescents and primary prevention. Tom was honored in 1999 by the Society for Community Research and Action, Division 27 of the American Psychological Association, with its distinguished Contributions to Practice in Community Psychology Award.

Dr. Carl G. Leukefeld is Professor and Chair of the Department of Behavioral Science and Director of the Center on Drug and Alcohol Research. Dr. Leukefeld has published over 200 articles, chapters, books, and monographs. He has served on the NIH Community-Level Health Promotion Study Section and the NIH/NIDA Health Services Initial Review Group as well as a reviewer and consulting editor for seven journals. His research interests include treatment outcomes, HIV, criminal justice, health services, and rural populations.

Michele Staton-Tindall, Ph.D., M.S.W., is currently Assistant Professor in the College of Social Work and a faculty associate of the Center on Drug and Alcohol Research and the Center on the Study of Violence Against Children. She is the principal investigator on the state-funded Criminal Justice Kentucky Treatment Outcome Study (CJ-KTOS) which evaluates prison and jail-based substance abuse treatment program. She is a coinvestigator for a NIDA-funded project investigating interventions for substance-involved offenders.

About the Authors

Shanna Babalonis, M.A., is a doctoral candidate in the Behavioral Neuroscience and Psychopharmacology Division of the Experimental Psychology Ph.D. Program in the Psychology Department at the University of Kentucky. Specific research interests include hormonal modulation of drug effects as it relates to women's vulnerability to drug abuse; laboratory measures of impulsivity and their relation to drug use and abuse; behavioral economics and mathematical models of behavior; and individual differences in vulnerability to drug abuse.

Martin Bloom is addicted to primary prevention in any of its forms. He persists in doing professional research and writing even though he has retired years ago, indicating a slow learning curve. He continues to take art classes at several universities, as well as doing art at home, hoping to make something of himself one of these days. If you wish to purchase his fine art collages at exorbitant prices, contact him at martin.bloom@uconn.edu.

Andria M. Botzet, M.A., has worked in the Center for Adolescent Substance Abuse Research at the University of Minnesota for over 10 years, conducting assessments and interventions on youth with drug and gambling addictions. She received her B.A. and M.A. in Counseling Psychology from the University of Minnesota. Ms. Botzet has also published several research articles on addictions, and has been involved with multiple community organizations in roles that include providing counseling services to runaway youth and serving as a board member on a human sexuality committee.

Amy M. Burdette is a postdoctoral fellow in the Carolina Population Center at the University of North Carolina – Chapel Hill. She received her Ph.D. in Sociology at the University of Texas at Austin. Her primary research interests include religious involvement, physical and mental health, family life, and adolescent development.

Mr. Shaun I. Calix earned his M.S. in Marriage and Family Therapy at the University of Southern Mississippi in 2005. During that program, he completed two internships in substance abuse and addiction treatment (one in primary treatment and one in secondary treatment). After graduating, he worked as a substance abuse therapist for Region 8 Mental Health Services in Mississippi. He is currently in the Ph.D. program in Human Development and Family Studies at the University of Missouri, Columbia.

Dr. Matthew Chinman is a behavioral scientist at the RAND Corporation where his recent focus has been to develop strategies to enhance the prevention capacity of community-based practitioners. As such, he codeveloped the Getting To Outcomes (GTO) model and led the development of the RAND Report, *Getting to Outcomes 2004: Promoting Accountability through Methods and Tools for Planning, Implementation, and Evaluation*, which is a step-by-step guide to planning, implementing, and evaluating prevention programs.

Dale D. Chitwood, Ph.D., is Professor of Medical Sociology in the Departments of Sociology, Epidemiology & Public Health, and Psychiatry & Behavioral Sciences at the University of Miami where he is an Associate Director of the Comprehensive Drug Research Center and Director of the Social Epidemiology Research Group. His substantive research interests include the epidemiology of drug misuse and HIV/AIDS, health services, religiosity, and the transition to drug injection.

Elizabeth J. D'Amico is a behavioral scientist at RAND and a licensed clinical psychologist who is recognized for her developmentally focused prevention research with youth. She has over 14 years of experience in conducting research on the underlying mechanisms of adolescent risk-taking behavior and in the development of innovative psychosocial interventions for adolescents and young adults. She has recently developed a voluntary intervention for middle school youth, a brief motivational intervention for substance-abusing youth in a primary care setting, and a motivational intervention to reduce drug use, HIV risk behaviors, and violence and victimization among impoverished teens and women who reside in homeless shelters.

Richard Dembo, Ph.D., is Professor of Criminology at the University of South Florida. He has published in the areas of criminology, substance use, mental health, and program evaluation. He has extensive experience working with troubled youths in a variety of settings and in applying research technology to social problems.

Michael L. Dennis is the GAIN Coordinating Center Director and Senior Research Psychologist at Chestnut Health Systems in Bloomington, IL. He is the lead developer of the Global Appraisal of Individual Needs (GAIN), was the coordinating center principal investigator of the Cannabis Youth Treatment (CYT) experiments, Chair of the Society for Adolescent Substance Abuse Treatment Effectiveness, and received the 2006 Research to Evidenced-Based Practice Award from the Joint Meeting on Adolescent Treatment Effectiveness (JMATE).

Tamara Fahnhorst received her master's degree in Maternal and Child Public Health from the University of Minnesota in 2000. Since 1988, she has worked in the Department of Psychiatry at the University of Minnesota on numerous preventive and early intervention initiatives for children and adolescents who are at risk for drug abuse. Ms. Fahnhorst is involved in both administrative and therapeutic capacities including implementation of individual and group interventions for children and their parents.

Mark A. Fine is a Professor in the Department of Human Development and Family Studies at the University of Missouri – Columbia. He was editor of *Family Relations* from 1993 to 1996 and was editor of the *Journal of Social and Personal Relationships* from 1999 to 2004. His research interests lie in the areas of family transitions, such as divorce and remarriage; early intervention program evaluation; social cognition, and relationship stability. He was coeditor, along with David Demo and Katherine Allen, of the *Handbook of Family Diversity*, published in 2000 by Oxford University Press. He recently coauthored, along with John Harvey, *Children of Divorce: Stories of Hope and Loss,* published in 2004 by Erlbaum; coedited, with John Harvey, *The Handbook of Divorce and Relationship Dissolution,* published in 2005 by Erlbaum; and coedited, with Jean Ispa and Kathy Thornburg, *Keepin' On: The Everyday Struggles of Young Families in Poverty*, published in 2006 by Brookes Publishing Company. He has published almost 200 peer-reviewed journal articles, book chapters, and books. In 2000, he was selected as a Fellow of the National Council on Family Relations.

Terrence D. Hill is an Assistant Professor of Sociology at the University of Miami. He received his Ph.D. in Sociology at the University of Texas at Austin. His research focuses on the social distribution of health and health-relevant behaviors, with special emphasis on the effects of religious involvement, neighborhood conditions, socioeconomic status, and social relationships. His recent publications appear in the *American Journal of Public Health*, *Journal of Health & Social Behavior*, and *Preventive Medicine*.

Melissa L. Ives is a Research Associate at Chestnut Health Systems in Bloomington, IL. She received her MSW in Community Organization/Social Planning from the Boston College and has been the lead developer of the code used to manage and analyze data received by the GAIN Coordinating Center.

Alessandra N. Kazura, M.D., is Assistant Professor, Department of Psychiatry and Human Behavior, Brown Medical School. She is board certified in pediatrics, psychiatry, and child and adolescent psychiatry. Her research interests include neurobehavioral mechanisms of adolescent tobacco use and substance use prevention in health care settings. Dr. Kazura has received research funding from NIH and private foundations. She serves on the American Academy of Child and Adolescent Psychiatry Task Force on Strategic Planning in Substance Abuse Education & Research.

Thomas H. Kelly, Ph.D., is Robert Straus Professor and Vice-Chair of the Department of Behavioral in the College of Medicine, University of Kentucky (joint appointments in Psychiatry and Psychology). He is a clinical behavioral pharmacologist with interests in the experimental analysis of drug–behavior interactions and individual differences in drug abuse vulnerability and serves as Scientific Director for the Center for Drug Abuse Research Translation and a faculty-affiliate of the Center for Drug Abuse Research.

Rachel Koskey, B.A., is a Research Assistant in the Department of Psychiatry, University of Minnesota, and an undergraduate at University of St. Thomas (St. Paul, MN).

Karen M. Lommel, D.O., is an Assistant Professor of Psychiatry and Pediatrics. She completed her residency training in the Triple Board Program (Pediatrics, Adult Psychiatry, and Child Psychiatry) at the University of Kentucky College of Medicine. She has worked in the inpatient child and adolescent psychiatry setting and is currently the Director of Pediatric Psychiatry Consultation Liaison Services in the Kentucky Children's Hospital. In these roles she has been involved in training medical students, residents, and child psychiatry fellows. Her research interests include sensation-seeking behavior in early adolescents and chronic pain and fibromyalgia in an adolescent psychiatric population.

Catherine A. Martin, M.D., is Professor and Vice Chair for Research and E.A. Edwards Professor in the Department of Psychiatry. She completed her medical and psychiatry and child psychiatry training at the University of Kentucky College of Medicine. Particular research and clinical interests include the relationship of impulsivity and inattention to nicotine use; development of pharmacological strategies that impact on impulsivity, inattention, and nicotine use; pubertal changes and drug abuse liability; and individual differences in drug effects of drugs of abuse. She is also involved in the training of clinical researchers locally and nationally.

Randolph D. Muck is the Lead Public Health Advisor/Team Leader for adolescent treatment programs at the Center for Substance Abuse Treatment, Substance Abuse and Mental Health Services Administration, US Department of Health and Human Services. He is responsible for the development, implementation, and evaluation of national programs for the treatment of adolescent substance use disorders. His current programmatic responsibilities include over one-hundred grantee sites focusing on implementation of evidence-based and promising practices for youth and their families.

Peter Panzarella, M.A., M.S., LADC, LPC, has over 30 years of experience in the field of addiction and mental health services. He is a licensed alcohol and drug counselor and also a licensed professional counselor. He has written and received a numerous federal grants. He has two master's degrees, a master's in Arts in Community/Clinical Psychology from Lesley University and master's in Science in Public Administration from State University of New York College at Buffalo. He has bachelor's degree in Psychology from the State University of New College at Buffalo. In 2007 he was awarded the National Leadership award from the National Center on Substance Abuse and Child Welfare and the Government Facilitator award from the Joint Meeting on Adolescent Treatment Effectiveness.

Robert W. Plant, Ph.D., is the Director of Children's Behavioral Health Programs and Services for the Connecticut Department of Children and Families. Dr. Plant earned his Ph.D. from the University of Rochester and completed his clinical training at Yale University Medical School where he is currently a clinical instructor at the Yale Child Study Center. His professional interests include motivation, autonomy, program development, and the wide scale implementation of evidence-based practice.

Jessica M. Ramos received her B.A. degree in Psychology from Eastern Connecticut State University. She is a Research Assistant at Child and Family

Agency of Southeastern Connecticut. Jessica has assisted in the editorial process of books on primary prevention, prevention and treatment of behavioral problems in childhood and adolescents, Asperger's Syndrome, promotion of prosocial behavior, and interpersonal violence in the African-American community. She is involved in agency research and reviews cases for quality assurance.

Zili Sloboda, Sc.D., is Senior Research Associate at the Institute for Health and Social Policy, The University of Akron. Prior to coming to the university in 1999, she was the Director of the Division of Epidemiology and Prevention Research, National Institute on Drug Abuse. She has published in the areas of drug abuse epidemiology and prevention. Her recent books are *Handbook of Drug Abuse Prevention: Theory, Science and Practice* (2003) and *Epidemiology of Drug Abuse* (2006).

Stefanie A. Stern is a Health Research Assistant at RAND where she has helped develop research interventions in primary care and educational settings. Stefanie manages the day-to-day implementation and evaluation of a brief motivational intervention for substance-abusing youth in a free primary care clinic. Stefanie has an M.A. in Higher Education and Organizational Change from UCLA.

Dr. Randy Stinchfield, Ph.D., L.P., is the Associate Director, Center for Adolescent Substance Abuse Research, Department of Psychiatry, University of Minnesota Medical School. He received his Ph.D. in Clinical Psychology from Brigham Young University in 1988 and completed an internship in Clinical Psychology at the Minneapolis VA Medical Center. Dr. Stinchfield conducts assessment and treatment research in the areas of alcohol and drug abuse and gambling. Dr. Stinchfield has conducted both clinical studies and survey research on adult and youth alcohol and drug abuse and gambling. He has published this research in a number of journal articles and book chapters. Dr. Stinchfield serves on the editorial board of *Psychology of Addictive Behaviors and Journal of Gambling Studies* and is an ad hoc editorial reviewer for the *Journal of Consulting and Clinical Psychology* and the *American Journal of Psychiatry*.

Dr. William Walton Stoops earned his bachelor's degree in Psychology from Davidson College in Davidson, NC, and his master's degree and Ph.D. in Psychology from the University of Kentucky in Lexington, KY. His primary research interests relate to examining the behavioral and pharmacological determinants of the abuse potential of stimulant and opioid drugs using drug discrimination and drug self-administration procedures in humans and determining prevalence and correlates of methamphetamine use in Kentucky.

Abraham Wandersman, Ph.D., is a Professor of Psychology at the University of South Carolina-Columbia. Dr. Wandersman performs research and program evaluation on citizen participation in community organizations and coalitions and on interagency collaboration. He is a coeditor of two books on empowerment evaluation, and a coauthor of *Getting to Outcomes*. In 1998, he received the Myrdal Award for Evaluation Practice from the American Evaluation Association. In 2000, he was elected President of the Society for Community Research and Action (SCRA). In 2005, he was awarded the Distinguished Theory and Research Contributions Award by SCRA.

Michael L. Weiss, M.A., is a doctoral student in the Department of Sociology and a Research Assistant in the Sociology Research Center at the University of Miami. His research interests include the use and misuse of drugs and alcohol, sociological and criminological theories, adolescent behavior, HIV/AIDS, religiosity, and suicide.

Michelle K. White is the Assistant Director of the GAIN Coordinating Center and a Research Scientist at Chestnut Health Systems in Bloomington, IL. She received her Ph.D. in Sociology from the University of Illinois under a National Research Service Award (NRSA) from the National Institute on Drug Abuse (NIDA) and is particularly interested in using screening and briefing intervention in child welfare and juvenile justice settings to reduce health disparities.

Ken C. Winters, Ph.D., is the Director of the Center for Adolescent Substance Abuse Research, a Professor in the Department of Psychiatry at the University of Minnesota, and a Senior Scientist with the Treatment Research Institute, Philadelphia, PA. He received his B.A. from the University of Minnesota and a Ph.D. in Psychology (Clinical) from the State University of New York at Stony Brook. His primary research interests are the assessment and treatment of adolescent drug abuse. Dr. Winters has published numerous research articles in this area, and has received several research grants from the National Institute of Health and various foundations. He is an Associate Editor for the *Psychology of Addictive Behaviors*, and is on the Editorial Boards of the *Journal of Child and Adolescent Substance Abuse*, *Journal of Gambling Studies*, and *Journal of Substance Abuse Treatment*. He was also the lead editor for two *Treatment Improvement Protocol Series* (# 31 and # 32) published by the Center for Substance Abuse Treatment (SAMHSA) that focused on adolescent drug abuse assessment and treatment. He is a consultant to many organizations, including the Hazelden Foundation, National Institute on Drug Abuse, Center for Substance Abuse Treatment, World Health Organization, and the Mentor Foundation (an international drug abuse prevention organization).

Index

INDEX

Note: Page numbers in italics refer to figures and tables.

international currency conflicts,
14–16
low inflation, politics of, 16–17
Economic liberalization, 8, 13
Economic migration, 42–43
EDC (European Defence Community),
232
Edelman, Benjamin, 303
Egypt
Islamist insurgency, 173, 193
labor remittances, 56, 186
media environment, 81, 183, 189
Einstein, Albert, 56
El Salvador, 56
EMEAP (Executives' Meeting of East
Asia-Pacific Central Banks), 266
EMU (European Monetary Union), 16
English East India Company, 132n16
Entertainment industry, 23–24
Epstein, Rachel, 25, 114, 188, 212, 277,
278, 280–281, *325*, 327, 329, 331
Equatorial Guinea, 117, 120, 137n74,
137n78
Eritrea, *44*, 56, 219
ESA (European Space Agency), 87
ETA (Euskadi Ta Askatasuna), 63
Ethiopia, 218–219
EU. *See* European Union
Euro, 15, 16
European Aeronautic, Defence and
Space Company (EADS), 239
European Aerospace Defence Company
(EADC), 240–241
European Defence Community (EDC),
232
European Monetary Union (EMU), 16
European security
defense industry consolidation,
238–242
defense industry integration,
231–232, 232–233, 235–237, 252
intelligence gathering capacity,
254n17
military capability, 234, 243–244,
253n8
personnel emphasis, 243, 253n8
political authority, reconstitution of,
248–251
European security, globalization threats,
233–234, 242–248

marginalization, 243–244, 252
weapons proliferation, 244–248, 252
European Space Agency (ESA), 87
European Union (EU), 164n5
border control, 49
ICTs, 86, 87
migration, 39, *61*, 67n24
Muslim communities, 186
radio-frequency identification tags,
96
U.S. hegemony, threat to, 15, 16,
165n10
European Union Code of Conduct, 250
EUROPOL, 236–237
Euskadi Ta Askatasuna (ETA), 63
Executive Outcomes (private security
company), 107, 129
Executives' Meeting of East Asia-Pacific
Central Banks (EMEAP), 266
Exxon (energy company), 137n74

F

Failing states, 146, 154–157, 168n60, 330
Fairbanks, Charles, Jr., 205, 219
Falklands War, 247
Falun Gong, 294, 302
FARC (Fuerzas Armadas
Revolucionarias de Colombia),
117
FBI (Federal Bureau of Investigation), 92
Feldstein, Martin, 16
Financial globalization. *See* Economic
exchange
Forced migration, 41–42
Fordham, Ben, 138n83
France, 26n6
arms market, 246–247, 250, 256n50
defense industry, 240–241, 242,
249–250
force market, historical use of, 109,
110
migration, *40, 41, 61*
national identity, 51, 53, 70n73
NATO and, 236
nuclear proliferation, 247
Frasure, Bob, 118
Free Iraq Forces, 57
Freeman, Gary, 46
FSX (combat aircraft), 277–278, 290n82

Hussein, King of Jordan, 176
Hypermedia environment, 6–7, 17–20,
    328. *See also* ICTs; Information
    flows
Hyperterrorist organizations, 152–157,
    167n36, 167n41, 168n47. *See also*
    Al Qaeda; Terrorist organizations

I

ICTs (information and communication
    technologies), 75–98, 306. *See
    also* Hypermedia environment;
    Information flows; Internet
  China, 20, 78, 81, 82, 83, 86–87,
    294–295, 301–305
  EU, 86, 87
  Middle East, 179, 183–184
  military balance of power and, 77–78,
    84–88
  nonstate actors, 78–79, 88–93
  Pakistan, 87
  regime survival, 77, 80–84
  Russia, 86
  state capacity and autonomy, 79,
    93–97
  terrorist organizations, use of, 155,
    330
  U.S., 86–87, 92
Identity communities, transnational,
    51–52
IDPs (internally displaced persons), 41
IEPG (Independent European
    Programme Group), 255n27
IETF (Internet Engineering Task Force),
    91
Illegal arms trafficking, 214–215,
    216–217
Illegal migration, 45, 49
  organized crime networks, 48, 58–59,
    60–62, *61*
IMF (International Monetary Fund)
  Asian Financial Crisis and, 13–14,
    267–268
  economic tool of U.S., 14, 267, 300
  structural adjustment programs,
    failure of, 177
Imhausen-Chemie (weapons
    manufacturer), 247

Immigration and Naturalization Service
    (U.S.), 48, 63
IMU (Islamic Movement of Uzbekistan),
    220
Independent European Programme
    Group (IEPG), 255n27
Independent International Commission
    on Kosovo, 59
India, 17, 245
  migration, *40, 41, 61*
Indonesia, 17, 19, 267, 268, 286n30, 300
Information flows, 3, *10*, 17–20, 323,
    325. *See also* Hypermedia
    environment; ICTs
  international conflict and, 3,
    333–334, *334*
  state capacity and autonomy, 18–20,
    76, 332
  state control of, 80–81, 82–84,
    293–294, 301–305, 314–315
Information revolution, 75–76
Information technology. *See* Hypermedia
    environment; ICTs; Internet
Information warfare (IW), 311–312, 313
Infosphere, 89
INGOs (international non-governmental
    organizations)
  institutional malformation,
    contributions to, 126–127
  PSCs, contracting of, 108
Innis, Harold, 93–94
Institute for Information Industry
    (Taiwan), 307
Institutional malformation, 124–127
INS (U.S.), 48, 63
Interdependence sovereignty, 69n50
Internally displaced persons (IDPs), 41
Internal migration, 40–41
International conflict. *See* Conflict,
    international
International Crisis Group, 210, *212*, 215
International currency conflicts, 14–16
International migration, 35–66
  defined, 37
  determinants, 39
  economic *vs.* political, 42–45
  legal *vs.* illegal, 45
  motives for, 35–36
  permanent *vs.* temporary, 45–46
  voluntary *vs.* forced, 41–42